DEFINING MANAGEMENT

Defining Management charts the expansion of management as an idea and practice from a time when it was limited to churches and households to its current ubiquity, focusing in particular on the role of business schools, consultants, and business media in this process.

How did an entire industry develop around business schools, consultants, and business media which are now widely considered *the* authorities regarding best management practice? This book shows how these actors, on their own and in interaction:

- became taken-for-granted and gained such definitional power over management and managers;
- expanded across the globe from often modest and not always respected origins; and
- impacted, and continue to impact businesses and increasingly, the broader economic and social context.

Building on extant as well as new research, the book is unique in bringing together issues and actors that have been examined elsewhere separately.

Any student or professional of management interested in the evolution of their field or the rise of business schools, consultants, and business media will find this book both novel and thought-provoking.

Lars Engwall is Professor Emeritus of Business Studies at Uppsala University, Sweden. He has published widely on institutional change and the diffusion of management ideas, in particular the role of management education and of the media.

Matthias Kipping is Professor of Policy and Richard E. Waugh Chair in Business History at the Schulich School of Business, York University, Canada. He has published many articles and co-edited two books on the management consulting business.

Behlül Üsdiken is Professor of Management and Organization at Sabancı University, Turkey. His work on business education and organizational research has appeared in various journals, including the *Journal of Management Studies*, as well as in edited collections.

DEFINING MANAGEMENT

Business Schools, Consultants, Media

Lars Engwall, Matthias Kipping and Behlül Üsdiken

NEW YORK AND LONDON

First published 2016
by Routledge
711 Third Avenue, New York, NY 10017

and by Routledge
2 Park Square, Milton Park, Abingdon, Oxon OX14 4RN

Routledge is an imprint of the Taylor & Francis Group, an informa business

© 2016 Taylor & Francis

The right of Lars Engwall, Matthias Kipping & Behlül Üsdiken to be identified
as authors of this work has been asserted by them in accordance with sections
77 and 78 of the Copyright, Designs and Patents Act 1988.

All rights reserved. No part of this book may be reprinted or reproduced or
utilized in any form or by any electronic, mechanical, or other means, now
known or hereafter invented, including photocopying and recording, or in any
information storage or retrieval system, without permission in writing from the
publishers.

Trademark notice: Product or corporate names may be trademarks or registered
trademarks, and are used only for identification and explanation without intent
to infringe.

British Library Cataloguing in Publication Data
A catalogue record for this book is available from the British Library

Library of Congress Cataloging in Publication Data
Names: Engwall, Lars, author. | Kipping, Matthias, author. | Üsdiken, Behlül,
author.
   Title: Defining management/Lars Engwall, Matthias Kipping, and Behlül
Üsdiken.
   Description: New York, NY : Routledge, 2016.
   Identifiers: LCCN 2016000874| ISBN 9780415727877 (hbk) | ISBN
9780415727884 (pbk) | ISBN 9781315851921 (ebk)
   Subjects: LCSH: Management–History. | Management–Study and teaching–
History. | Business education–History.
   Classification: LCC HD31 .E6457 2016 | DDC 658–dc23
LC record available at http://lccn.loc.gov/2016000874

ISBN: 978-0-415-72787-7 (hbk)
ISBN: 978-0-415-72788-4 (pbk)
ISBN: 978-1-315-85192-1 (ebk)

Typeset in Bembo
by Taylor & Francis Books

CONTENTS

List of Illustrations	*xi*
Acknowledgments	*xiv*

1 Introduction: The Rise of Management   1

2 Background: Views on the Development of Management   9

Management as Practice 9
    The Origins of Management and Managers 10
    Further Expansion and Transformation 12
    Changing Backgrounds of Managers 13
Management as Innovation 14
    Early Origins of Management Ideas 14
    Moving beyond the Shopfloor 16
    The Dominant Narrative and its Critics 17
Management as Fashion 18

3 Approach: Three "Fields" in Historical, Comparative, and Integrative Perspective   24

Business Schools, Consultants, and Media as
  Organizational Fields 24
    Defining Organizational Fields 24
    Characteristics of Fields: Structures and Logics 27
    Relations and Interactions between Fields 28
A Historical, Comparative, and Integrative Perspective 29

vi   Contents

The Development of the Three Fields 29
Cross-national Comparisons and Linkages 30
Interactions among the Fields and with Practice 33

PART I
Diverse Origins   39

4   The Emergence of Schools of Commerce   41

Organizing Higher Commercial Education 41
United States: Inclusion into Universities 42
Europe: Left on the Outside 44
Pioneering Initiatives and Early Expansion 45
United States: Failed and Successful Foundations 45
Europe: Multiple Moves and Influences 48
International Circulation of Models 53

5   Accountants and Efficiency Engineers as Early Consultants   59

Situating the Origins of Consulting: A Variety of Views 59
Accountants as Invisible Frontrunners 61
Scientific Management and the "Efficiency Experts" 64
The United States as the Seedbed 64
Consulting Emergent: Many Individuals and
One Firm 67
Spreading the Gospel – and the Business 70

6   Modest Beginnings for Business Publishing   75

Frontrunners in Business and Management Publishing 75
The Origin of Four Significant Publishing Houses 75
The Four Publishing Houses in Context 77
*The Business Press: Specialized Challengers to the
Established Newspapers 80*
Four Significant Entrants 80
The Entrants in Context 81
Academic Journals: Early Steps Towards Institutionalization 82
Points of Departure 82
Five American Frontrunners 83
The Five Frontrunners in Context 85

Contents **vii**

PART II
In Search of Directions   **91**

7 Establishing a Place for Business Education   93

The Struggle for Recognition as a Professional School in the
United States 93
    Changing Nomenclature, Continuing Diversity 93
    Claims toward "Profession" and "Science" 95
    Expansion, Increasing Stratification, First Critiques 98
Diverging Developments in Europe and Elsewhere 101
    Turning into a "Science" and a Faculty in Germany 101
    Fragile Developments in France and the
    United Kingdom 103
    Diverse Influences, Different Outcomes in Other Parts of
    the World 104

8 Old Certainties and New Departures in Consulting   110

Scientific Management: Still on a Mission, Now
Also Internationally 110
    Expanding Taylorist Ideology and Practice 110
    Waning Efforts in Japan, China, and Russia 113
    Building an Alternative: Germany's
    Cooperative Logic 114
Efficiency as a Growing Business 115
    US Consulting Engineers at Home and Abroad 115
    Paling Them All: Charles E. Bedaux and His Firm 117
    Moving Abroad and Engendering Local Firms 119
The "Others": Ongoing Trends and New Developments 121
    Still in the Shadows: Accounting and
    HR Consulting 121
    What the Future Would Bring: A Professional Vision for
    the Field 123

9 Broadening Audiences for Business Publications   129

Publishers: New Actors and Increasing Numbers of
Management Books 129
    Wiley, Harper, Macmillan, and McGraw-Hill 129
    Other Early Entrants: The Ronald Press and
    University Presses 132

viii Contents

Four Additional Publishers 133
The Emergence of General Management Books 134
*Expansion of the Business Press: Higher Circulation and
New Titles 136*
*Academic Journals: New Initiatives from Universities and
Professional Associations 137*
Four Interwar Entrants 137
Impact and Orientation of the Nine *FT*45 Journals 140
The *FT*45 Journals in Context 141

PART III
Post-World War II Expansion   **147**

10 Making Business Education Scientific   149

Post-war Transformation in the United States 149
*The New Look "Business School" and the MBA in the
United States 153*
American-style Business Education Moves Abroad 155
The Post-war US Offensive 155
The Stand-alone Schools 156
Penetration into the University 160
The University-based Graduate Business School and
the MBA 161
*Growth in Business Education Outside the United States and
its Limitations 162*

11 The Assertion of Management Consulting   168

Consulting Engineers: Mixed Fortunes 168
United States: Out With the Old, In With the New 169
European Consulting Engineers Dominating Europe 172
The Triumph of Science ... eh, Professionalism 174
Science on the Rise – For a While 174
A Triumphant Professional Model 177
International Expansion and Replication 182
"The Accountants Are Coming!" 184

12 Growth and Diversification of Management Publishing   191

*Publishers: Expansion, New Establishments,
and Restructuration 191*

Wiley, Harper, Macmillan, and McGraw-Hill 191
Other Already Established Publishers 194
Entrants and Restructuration 196
The Business Press: Circulation Figures Taking Off 198
Academic Journals: New Titles and the Move to
Publishing Firms 200
New Foundations: Expansion and Specialization 201
Significant Papers Published by the Entrants 204
Further Additions to the Field 205

PART IV
Markets Reign 213

13 The Business School and the MBA Become "Global" 215

US Business Schools: A Transforming and Spreading Model 215
Becoming More Market-driven at Home 215
Accreditation: A US Institution Expanding – and
Replicated – Internationally 217
Media Rankings: Defining and
Measuring Reputation 222
Globalizing the "Business School" and the "MBA" 223
Expansion in Europe: Still in Different Ways and to
Varying Degrees 224
Expansion in Asia and Latin America:
Governments Intervene 226
New Areas of Expansion 227
Internationalization 228

14 Consulting as Global Big Business 234

The End of Engineering? Kind of… 234
IT and its Beneficiaries: Established Actors and Newcomers 236
The Accountants: Forward to the Past? 236
From the Margins to the Center of the
Field: IT Firms 241
The Marginal and Ephemeral: Inside Out and
"Fast Five" 244
Strategy and Organization Consulting: Melting Ice Cubes? 246

x Contents

15 Mergers and Mass Markets in Media 255

Publishers: Concentration among Multinational
Multimedia Companies 255
    Wiley, Harper, Macmillan, and McGraw-Hill:
     Considerable Changes 255
    Further Restructuration of the Field 258
The Business Press: Changing Ownerships in
Booming Markets 263
Academic Journals: Scholars and Publishers in Interaction 265
    Another Dozen *FT*45 Journals 265
    Significant Papers and Author Origins 268
    Further Growth in Journals 271
Looking Ahead 273

16 Conclusions: Commoditizing Management? 280

Processes: The Trajectories of the Three Fields 280
    From Survival to Legitimacy and Authority 280
    Toward a Single US-dominated Global Model? 284
    From Missionary Zeal to Market-orientation 287
Outcomes: Turning "Management" into a Global Commodity 290
Final Considerations: Better Ways? 294

Index 297

LIST OF ILLUSTRATIONS

Figures

1.1 The Occurrence of "M/management" in Google Books 1800–2000 2
1.2 Cover of *Beeton's Book of Household Management* 3
5.1 Arthur Young family tree 62
6.1 A model of the organizing of scientific disciplines 82
12.1 Estimates of the cumulated number of titles from Wiley, Harper, Macmillan and McGraw-Hill including "management" in the period 1946–80 192

Tables

4.1 Schools (and Faculties) of Commerce Established in Europe, 1819–1919 49
6.1 Foundations of Four Early Publishers in Management 76
6.2 Year of Foundation for Early University Presses 79
6.3 Four Economically Oriented Publications Founded in the Early Period 80
6.4 Academic Journals on the *FT*45 List Founded in the Early Period 83
8.1 The International Expansion of the Bedaux Consulting Firm during the 1930s 119
8.2 Booz: Changing Names and Identity? 123

xii List of Illustrations

9.1   A Selection of Management Publications Published in the
      Interwar Period   130
9.2   Academic Journals on the *FT*45 Founded in the
      Interwar Period   138
9.3   The Most Cited Papers in July 2014 from the Interwar
      Period in the Nine *FT*45 Journals   141
10.1 Examples of Post–World War II Schools and Institutes
      Established with US Technical Assistance or Inspired by US
      Models, 1945–1969   157
11.1 Top 20 Consulting Firms in the US by Billings, 1968   170
11.2 The Expansion of US Management Consultants to
      Europe, 1960s   183
11.3 Top 20 Consulting Firms in the US by Revenue, 1982   186
12.1 The Most Cited Papers in July 2014 from the Post-war
      Period in the Nine *FT*45 Journals Founded before 1946   200
12.2 Journals among the *FT*45 Founded in the Post-war Period   202
12.3 The Most Cited Papers from the Post-war Period in July
      2014 in the 11 *FT*45 Journals Founded between
      1946 and 1965   204
12.4 The Most Cited Papers from the Post-war Period in July
      2014 in the 13 *FT*45 Journals Founded between
      1966 and 1980   206
13.1 Universities, Faculties and Schools of Business Accredited by
      the End of 2006 and 2014   220
14.1 Arthur Andersen, Revenue Shares and Growth, 1984–1987   238
14.2 Two Estimates of the Largest Global Consulting Firms
      in 2013   241
15.1 The Largest Publishers Involved in Management Publishing
      in 2013   262
15.2 Journals among the *FT*45 Founded since 1980   265
15.3 Two-year Impact Factors, 2013 and Years of Foundation for
      the *FT*45 Journals   267
15.4 The 15 Top Papers in the *FT*45 Journals in the Recent
      Period According to Google Scholar in December 2014   269

Boxes

4.1   Wharton School of Finance and Economy: The First
      Three Decades   46
4.2   Harvard Graduate School of Business Administration: The
      First Decade   48

4.3	The German *Handelshochschulen*	52
5.1	Frederick Winslow Taylor: The Grandfather of Management Consulting	66
5.2	Lillian Gilbreth: First Lady of Management	69
6.1	Cambridge University Press and Oxford University Press	78
6.2	Eugen Schmalenbach: Nestor of German Business Economics	86
7.1	Dean Donham and the "Case Method" at HBS	97
7.2	The German *Betriebswirtschaftslehre* (BWL)	102
8.1	Lyndall Fownes Urwick (1891–1983): Prolific Propagator of Management	112
8.2	Charles E. Bedaux: Self-made Man, Socialite, and Nazi Agent?	118
9.1	Peter F. Drucker: Philosopher of Management	135
9.2	The *Harvard Business Review*	139
10.1	Showcase of the "New Look": The GSIA at the Carnegie Institute of Technology	151
10.2	An American School in Fontainebleau: INSEAD	159
11.1	Remaking Management Consulting in the Image of the Legal Profession	180
12.1	Philip Kotler: Global Marketing Man	195
12.2	Pearson: From Construction and Engineering toward Media Conglomerate	199
13.1	AACSB: From American Association to Global Accreditation	218
14.1	McKinsey is Everywhere	251
15.1	Elsevier: Science, Prestige – and Profits	259
15.2	Thomson Reuters: From Fleet Street to Web of Science	261

ACKNOWLEDGMENTS

This book has benefitted from multiple supports for which we are very grateful. Sponsorship for our earlier work on this topic was received from the European Commission (TSER Contract SOE1-CT97-1072) and the Swedish Research Council (324-2009-6717). Trips for various meetings to develop and coordinate our thinking received funding from the Marcus and Amalia Wallenberg Foundation, the Royal Society of Sciences at Uppsala as well as our own institutions, Uppsala University, the Schulich School of Business and Sabanci University. Many of these meetings were kindly hosted by Lars and his wife Gunnel at their home in Stockholm. We would also like to express our gratitude to our editor, Sharon Golan, and her assistant, Erin Arata, for their patience and encouragement as we kept postponing the delivery deadline. Last not least, our families exhibited great patience and understanding for our frequent physical and mental absences. As customary, the responsibility for the final outcome of all these efforts remains solely ours.

1

INTRODUCTION

The Rise of Management

Today, the term "management" is everywhere, describing, as the corresponding entry in *Merriam-Webster's Dictionary* (9 September 2015) suggests, "the act or art of managing: the conducting or supervising of something (as a business)." That "as a business" is put into parenthesis and uses the comparator "as" is significant: It shows that the term is no longer confined to the "administration of business concerns or public undertakings; persons engaged in this," as the earlier entry in *The Concise Oxford Dictionary* noted (Fowler, Fowler, and Thompson 1995). Over the past decades, the application of management as a term and as a practice has decisively moved beyond business, and even public administration, to all kinds of organizations, including hospitals, universities, and museums, and even entered into everyday life – a development that some authors have referred to, usually critically, as "managerialism" (e.g., Enteman 1993; Fitzsimons 1999; Locke and Spender 2011). It has also spread internationally with the word "manager" now used in many languages concurrent with or in place of native terms to denote people with responsibility for others – an early example being the German publication *Manager Magazin*, founded in 1971, addressed at people traditionally referred to as *leitende Angestellte* or *Führungskräfte*, literally translated as leading employees or leadership forces, respectively.

But even in English, the term itself did not come into more widespread use until after World War II, as suggested by Figure 1.1, which is based on a limited sample, i.e. Google Books, yet indicative of a broader trend.

Such a restrictive earlier use is actually not surprising given the origins of the word, which can be traced back to the mid-sixteenth-century Italian word *maneggiare*, which in turn is based on the Latin word for hand, *manus*, and, in this early context, referred particularly to the handling of horses (*Oxford Dictionaries* and *Online Etymology Dictionary*, 19 July 2015). In the eighteenth and nineteenth

2 Introduction

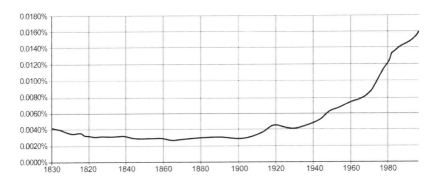

FIGURE 1.1 The Occurrence of "M/management" in Google Books 1800–2000

centuries, "management" was used for small units, namely churches and households. For instance, a humoristic book on *The Church Rambler; or, Sermon Taster* included "a pleasant account of the humours, management and principles of the Great Pontif Machiavel" (Wildair 1724). Another of many more examples is the title of a sermon about "the duty of a Christian church to manage their affairs with charity" (Balch 1735). The nineteenth century saw the first "management" bestseller: *Beeton's Book of Household Management* by Isabella Beeton (see Figure 1.2). First published in 1861, the book had 1,112 pages and 2,751 numbered entries, most of them recipes but also descriptions of the duties of the various household staff. The book sold two million copies already by 1868 and is still in print (Stark 2001; Russell 2010).

The activity referred to today as management was described at the time in other terms, which can for instance be found in an eight-volume book on *Modern Business Practice* published in 1912, which did not discuss management in the text but, in its glossary of commercial terms, contained a somewhat circular definition of a "manager" as "a person appointed by a company to manage its business, or by a proprietor to manage an office or shop or department, or other undertaking" (Raffety 1912: Vol. 8, 206).

How management spread from such a rather narrow use and became so ubiquitous is therefore a phenomenon that deserves attention by all those involved in practicing or studying it. And, while it has received some attention both in more popular and more academic literatures, quite a few authors have used the term rather indiscriminately without historicizing it – for instance by tracing "basic management techniques" back to ancient Sumer in 3000 BC (Pindur, Rogers, and Kim 1995; see also Witzel 2001). As Chapter 2 will discuss in more detail, most histories of management have either examined how its practice has evolved with the corresponding (business) organizations – with summary accounts to be found in business history textbooks (e.g. Chandler, McCraw, and Tedlow 1996; Blackford 2008; Amatori and Colli 2011); or how certain individuals,

FIGURE 1.2 Cover of *Beeton's Book of Household Management*

4 Introduction

characterized usually as "innovators," developed new, meaning: better ideas of how to manage – a progressive story told in books on the history of management thought (e.g. Wren and Bedeian 2009; Witzel 2012).

More recent literature, also discussed in Chapter 2, has drawn attention to a different set of actors, in particular business schools, management consultants, and business publications. This literature points to another phenomenon worthy of attention, namely the fact that these sets of actors are today widely considered what could be called "authorities" on management by defining what is "world-class" or "best practice" – a fact also highlighted by a study of "cited experts" in the above mentioned *Manager Magazin* between 1980 and 1996. While there was a declining trend for managers as experts, down from around 60 to just over 30 percent, consultants and academics more than doubled their joint share, respectively from under 15 percent to over 30 percent, with the remainder made up by other practitioners (Faust 2002: 158–160).

When looked at in detail, this kind of authority or definitional power is quite stunning: Take the story of a British top manager, told by himself in the aptly titled documentary *Masters of the Universe* (Films of Record 1999: Part 1), of how he bought Michael Hammer and James Champy's (1993) book *Reengineering the Corporation* at the train station on his way home from London, read it *twice* over the weekend – ignoring his wife, and, when returning on Monday morning, bought all the available copies at that same book store, took them to the office and distributed them to his managers, telling them: "This is what we're doing. Read it, we are going to work to this thing." And he was clearly not the only manager finding the book appealing, since it remained on the *New York Times* non-fiction best-seller list for a staggering 41 weeks. It also warranted Hammer's inclusion on *Time* magazine's 1996 list of "America's 25 Most Influential People" (Hevesi 2008).

Interviewed for the same documentary Hammer himself pointed to an even wider use of his ideas by expressing regret to not have negotiated a commission on all the fees management consultants generated from latching on to the reengineering concept, which he estimated to be "well in the billions of dollars." A vice president of Capgemini, a large consulting firm, indirectly confirmed this approach – referred to by an academic study as "hitchhiking on a hype" (Benders, van den Berg, and van Bijsterveld 1998) – stating that they always tried to spot "the next wave." Some of these firms apparently not only looked for new ideas but also tried to boost them by buying thousands of copies of their books themselves in order to drive up their rank on best-seller lists (Micklethwait and Wooldridge 1996: 23–24). The representative of another of the large global consulting firms, Andersen Consulting, now Accenture, also stated that annually his firm received three million applications from want-to-be consultants worldwide – sounding very surprised himself: "When I heard the number, I fell off my chair." Perhaps most stunning, these actors have even succeeded in penetrating the Vatican, where a recent observer noted the presence of "a group of M.B.A.

types speaking English" and pointed to the reliance "on major companies from the capitalist world: McKinsey, Deloitte Consulting, EY (formerly Ernst & Young)" for the management of its finances (Stille 2015) – with Pope Francis himself turned into a kind of rockstar by the global media.

Again, this is even more surprising when going back in time. Take another interview from the historical part of the documentary mentioned above: an engineer, who was hired in the early 1930s by Bedaux, then the largest global consulting firm – employing just over 200 efficiency engineers in offices in the US, the UK, France, Italy, and Germany (Kreis 1992: 157; Kipping 1999: 197–198). The number sounds ridiculously low today – even when taken relative to the size of the corporate economy. More surprising, even if probably told jokingly, is that, rather than admitting to joining a consulting firm, he preferred telling his mother that he was hired as a pianist at the local brothel (Films of Record 1999: Part 1). Or take famed Stanford sociologist Thorstein Veblen, who in 1918 compared departments of business to departments of athletics and categorically stated that neither of them should have a place in "the corporation of learning" (Veblen 1918: 209–210). University presidents must be glad not to have listened to him, since business schools nowadays tend to be the most popular – and richest – parts of many academic institutions.

How did this change? When did it become not only acceptable but *desirable* to be a business graduate or to join a consulting firm, and since when did executives look at business books sold at train stations and airports to tell them what to do? In other words, when and how did what today are called business schools, management consultants, and business media become taken-for-granted and gain such definitional power over management? This book will trace this process from the origins of these actors to their authoritative role today. As such it will also contribute to the story of the expansion of management itself, since both developed largely in parallel. *Defining Management*, the title of this book, in that sense has a double meaning: On the one hand, it refers to the current ability of these actors to define what "good" management is. On the other hand, it points to the role these authorities have had in the process of management becoming ubiquitous. To examine this process of authority building, the book takes a perspective that is historical, comparative, and integrative by:

Looking at developments over time, since it does not take the authority or even legitimacy of these three sets of actors as a given, but shows how they were constructed gradually since the late nineteenth century. The historical narrative is subdivided into four parts, with the two World Wars and the 1980s, when most of the globe was opened to capitalism, providing important transitional and transformational periods with respect to all three authorities.

Comparing their trajectories in different countries/regions, since these authorities did not develop in the same way around the world, but saw the emergence of a variety of models and patterns, which were also transmitted across national boundaries. This helps identify those models that eventually became dominant

6 Introduction

and to understand how they developed. Tracing these developments in some detail also contributes to understanding the depth at which these models took hold outside their own countries.

Integrating the narratives for all three sets of actors, building on the so far isolated literatures for each of them, supplementing them with original evidence, when necessary. This allows not only to identify parallels in their respective developments, but also to look at their interrelationships, ranging between competition and cooperation, as well as the permeability of their boundaries, namely regarding individual actors moving across two or more of the authorities.

Defining Management can be read in conjunction with the histories of business and/or those of management thought mentioned above. The book can also be read on its own, because it summarizes these literatures in Chapter 2 and, throughout the remainder, also links back to the broader economic, social, and ideological contexts, in which these authorities evolve. Chapter 3 presents the approach taken in the book, illustrated with selected examples.

The core of the book, Chapters 4 through 15 subdivided into Parts I to IV, traces the rise of the authorities and the concurrent expansion of management. This core is structured in a way that allows what could be called modular reading. The four parts reflect, as mentioned above, a periodization based on broader developments from the late nineteenth through the twenty-first century. Each part contains three chapters respectively addressing business schools, management consultants, and business media. It is therefore possible to proceed in an integrated fashion by reading about all three authorities in one period and then move on to the next. Alternatively, one can read all the chapters for one of the authorities through all periods and then do the same for the other two. In turn, each chapter is subdivided into sections based on the main structuring features of each of the authorities: For business schools, these sections compare the developments in the United States to those elsewhere, mainly Europe; for management consultants, they distinguish their origins, namely in engineering, accounting – later including IT, and "professionalism" – mainly grounded in a mimicry of law firms; for business media, they examine, respectively, the development of book publishers, the business press, and academic journals.

Finally, Chapter 16 provides answers – some more tentative than others – to the fundamental questions raised in this introductory chapter, summarizing how business schools, management consultants, and business media gradually came to be taken for granted and to define management.

References

Amatori, F. and Colli, A. (2011) *Business History: Complexities and Comparisons*, London: Routledge.

Balch, W. (1735) *The Duty of a Christian Church to Manage their Affairs with Charity. A sermon preached October 4, 1732*, Boston, MA. www.worldcat.org/title/duty-of-a-christian-church-to-manage-their-affairs-with-charity-a-sermon-preached-october-4-1732-at-the-gathering-of-the-second-church-of-christ-in-rowley/oclc/55825342 (accessed 31 December 2015).

Beeton, I. (1861) *Beeton's Book of Household Management*, London: Beeton Publishing.

Benders, J., van den Berg, R.-J. and van Bijsterveld, M. (1998) "Hitch-hiking on a hype: Dutch consultants engineering re-engineering," *Journal of Organizational Change Management*, 11(3): 201–215.

Blackford, M. G. (2008) *The Rise of Modern Business: Great Britain, the United States, Germany, Japan, and China*, Chapel Hill, NC: University of North Carolina Press.

Chandler, A. D., Jr, McCraw, T. K., and Tedlow, R. S. (1996) *Management: Past and Present. A casebook on the history of American business*, Cincinnati, OH: South-Western College Publishing.

Enteman, W. F. (1993) *Managerialism: The emergence of a new ideology*, Madison, WI: University of Wisconsin Press.

Faust, M. (2002) "Consultancies as actors in knowledge arenas: Evidence from Germany," in M. Kipping and L. Engwall (eds), *Management Consulting*, Oxford: Oxford University Press, pp. 146–163.

Films of Record (1999) *Masters of the Universe*, a 3-part documentary on management consultants, screened on Channel 4 (UK), London.

Fitzsimons, P. (1999) "Managerialism and education," in M. Peters, T. Besley, A. Gibbons, B. Žarnić and P. Ghiraldelli (eds), *The Encyclopaedia of Educational Philosophy and Theory*. http://eepat.net/doku.php?id=managerialism_and_education (accessed 9 September 2015).

Fowler, H. W., Fowler, F. G., and Thompson, D. (eds) (1995) *The Concise Oxford Dictionary of Current English*, 9th edn, Oxford: Clarendon Press.

Hammer, M. and Champy, J. (1993) *Reengineering the Corporation: A manifesto for business revolution*, New York: Harper Business.

Hevesi, D. (2008) "Michael Hammer, business writer, dies at 60," *New York Times*, 4 September.

Kipping, M. (1999) "American management consulting companies in Western Europe, 1920 to 1990: Products, reputation and relationships," *Business History Review*, 73(2): 190–220.

Kreis, S. (1992) "The diffusion of scientific management: The Bedaux Company in America and Britain, 1926–1945," in D. Nelson (ed.), *A Mental Revolution: Scientific Management Since Taylor*, Columbus, OH: Ohio State University Press, pp. 156–174.

Locke, R. R. and Spender, J.-C. (2011) *Confronting Managerialism: How the business elite and their schools threw our lives out of balance*, London: Zed Books.

Merriam-Webster's Dictionary. www.merriam-webster.com/dictionary/management (accessed 9 September 2015).

Micklethwait, J. and Wooldridge, A. (1996) *The Witch Doctors: What the management gurus are saying, why it matters and how to make sense of it*, London: Heinemann.

Online Etymology Dictionary. www.etymonline.com/index.php?term=manage (accessed 19 July 2015).

Oxford Dictionaries. http://oxforddictionaries.com/definition/english/manage (accessed 19 July 2015).

Pindur, W., Rogers, S. E., and Kim, P. S. (1995) "The history of management: A global perspective," *Journal of Management History*, 1(1): 59–77.

Raffety, F. W. (ed.) (1912) *Modern Business Practice*, 8 vols., London: The Gresham Publishing Company.

Russell, P. (2010) "Mrs Beeton, the first domestic goddess," *Financial Times*, 3 December. www.ft.com/cms/s/2/be9d91a6-fcd8-11df-ae2d-00144feab49a.html#axzz3lHVRsWK3 (accessed 9 September 2015).

8 Introduction

Stark, M. (2001) "Domesticity for Victorian dummies," *January Magazine*, July. www.janua rymagazine.com/cookbook/mrsbeeton.html (accessed 9 September 2015).

Stille, A. (2015) "Holy orders: A determined Pope Francis moves to reform a recalcitrant Curia," *The New Yorker*, 14 September. www.newyorker.com/magazine/2015/09/14/holy-orders-letter-from-the-vatican-alexander-stille (accessed 19 September 2015).

Veblen, T. (1918) *The Higher Learning in America: A memorandum on the conduct of universities by business men*, New York: B. W. Huebsch.

Wren, D. A. and Bedeian, A. G. (2009) *The Evolution of Management Thought*, 6th edn, Hoboken, NJ: Wiley.

Wildair, H. (1724) *The Church Rambler; or, Sermon Taster: Being a merry and diverting description of the nature and character of those who straggle from church to church to hear sermons*, 2nd edn, London. www.worldcat.org/title/church-rambler-or-sermon-taster-being-a-merry-and-diverting-description-of-the-nature-and-character-of-those-who-straggle-from-church-to-church-to-hear-sermons-with-a-pleasant-account-of-the-humours-management-and-principles-of-the-great-pontif-machiavel-his-scarfians-pickld-herrings-and-other-fashionable-broachers-of-religion-and-politicks-the-whole-made-publick-for-the-imrovement-of-the-wits-of-the-age-in-a-letter-from-one-great-man-to-another/oclc/508079784 (accessed 31 December 2015).

Witzel, M. (2001) *Builders and Dreamers: The making and meaning of management*, London: FT Prentice Hall.

Witzel, M. (2012) *A History of Management Thought*, London: Routledge.

2

BACKGROUND

Views on the Development of Management

This chapter summarizes the extant – and quite extensive – literature that has examined the expansion of management. It shows that most authors have taken a long-term view, even if the periods being considered vary relatively widely and the degrees of historical sensitivity even more so. The chapter subdivides the relevant literature into three main strands, looking, respectively, at management as (i) a practice, relating to changes in (business) organizations and the emergence of a distinctive occupational as well as social group; (ii) a series of innovative and, for most, increasingly sophisticated ideas; and, more recently, (iii) a succession of management fashions, promoted by various actors. The chapter will briefly present each of these strands, critically summarizing their main insights and discussing how the historical, comparative, and integrative examination of the management authorities in this book draws on these insights while complementing and extending them.

Management as Practice

The first of the three strands of investigation and writing mentioned above looks at the emergence and expansion of management as a result of changes in organizations, in particular business organizations, and how these created a new occupational group, collectively referred to as "managers." This group, as some of this literature has also shown, became, on the one hand, increasingly differentiated and stratified internally, while, on the other, gaining more recognition, legitimacy, and influence not only in their own organizations but also within society at large. When it comes to the role of business schools, consultants, and the media in defining management, the key question with respect to this literature is how these three authorities both benefitted from these changes and how they contributed to them. Put more concretely, for business schools this means finding

10 Background

out how they have come to determine who should belong to this group of managers, and how that selection process – and the education they provide – has helped their graduates to elevate their status within organizations against other occupational groups and within society against elites based on other selection mechanisms including "birth." For consultants, this includes examining their role in spreading and legitimizing organizational structures and practices that required more management and managers and/or gave them more power. For the business media, finally, the task is to find out how they were involved in these processes: directly, by promoting new practices and supporting managers as a group – or not, and indirectly, by propping up the legitimacy of both business schools and consultants.

The Origins of Management and Managers

In the literature on management as a practice, some have located its origins in ancient times, namely by trying to identify parallels for current organizational arrangements, activities and roles in religious institutions and public administration (e.g., Pindur, Rogers, and Kim 1995). Others have pointed to the government-operated, large-scale arsenals and manufactures of the pre-industrial period. The Venice Arsenal is among the most analyzed in this respect; during its heydays in the sixteenth century, it employed 16,000 people and held up to 100 ships in different stages of production, repair or maintenance, using what many consider "modern" management and accounting methods (e.g., Zan 2004). It even employed Galileo Galilei as a "consultant," though mainly on technical questions even if he apparently also advised on production processes (Valleriani 2010: Chapter 4). However, for this and other early organizations little is known about those who actually managed the various processes and the many workers employed.

Some authors link *The Genesis of Modern Management* to the so-called first industrial revolution, originating in late eighteenth and early nineteenth-century Britain and spreading quickly to the European continent and the other side of the Atlantic. An example is Pollard's (1965) eponymous book, where he introduced a distinction between entrepreneurs, who decided which business to be in, and managers who worked systematically towards realizing the goals set by the former, leading, in his view, to the development of "a theory and practice of 'management', as distinct from ad-hoc and unrelated decision-making" (Pollard 1965: 6; see also his Chapter 7). Others, more influentially, have pointed to the second industrial revolution since the late nineteenth century, which saw the emergence of much larger-scale organizations, initially in the US and then elsewhere. Among the first to identify the consequential rise of a new group of actors were Berle and Means (1932), who highlighted the growing separation between an increasingly dispersed ownership in the American corporation and the control exercised over the latter by hired managers, whose interests they saw as "different from and often radically opposed to those of ownership" (p. 114) – foreshadowing what was later called "agency theory" (e.g., Jensen and Meckling 1976). While Berle and Means (1932) focused on publicly quoted corporations, Burnham (1941), from a Marxist point of view, went even further, arguing that this new group of "managers" had come to "drive for social dominance, for power and privilege, for the position of ruling class" (p. 71) regardless of who owned the means of production: a private individual, dispersed shareholders, or the state.

But while these authors examined what they saw as the consequences of the rise of managers as a distinct group or class, it was Alfred Chandler, who examined their historical origins. He highlighted in particular the importance of the railroads as "pioneers in modern corporate management," because they developed many of the organizational features and practices later applied in other large-scale organizations. Moreover, they served as a kind of training ground for those running them, most of whom – not surprisingly – had an engineering background (Chandler 1965). In his view, the construction of the railroad network also became part of the conditions that fostered the emergence and expansion of large corporations – and those who ran them. Based on a study of the largest US companies, he suggested that the quest to serve growing urban markets and the introduction of scale-intensive technologies with high fixed costs in the late nineteenth century required an increasing replacement of Adam Smith's "invisible hand" of the market with the "visible hand" of managers, who ensured a steady flow from raw material inputs through production to marketing and distribution (Chandler 1977; see further John 1997).

These early organizations, which Chandler labelled unitary or U-form, also saw a differentiation of managers in terms of their hierarchical levels and their functions within the organization, including purchasing, production, and sales. While Chandler, in the tradition of Berle and Means, had linked these developments with a separation of ownership and control (see esp. Chandler 1990), managerial hierarchies were created even in countries where many large corporations remained in the hands of private owners: the UK, France, and Germany (Cassis 1997), and Japan (Fruin 1992). Going further, Hannah (2007) has argued that, even in the case of the US, managerialization cannot necessarily be equated with a move towards dispersed ownership in the form of publicly quoted companies.

Others have moved beyond these firm-centric and efficiency-driven accounts, where the rise of management was seen to have resulted from the organizational imperatives of growing markets and scale-intensive technologies. Thus, based on the analysis of several engineering magazines, Shenhav (2000) has linked the origins of management to the struggle of engineers to expand their own power – and emerging professional jurisdiction – by introducing rational, standardized, and systematic practices and ideologies into the early corporate organizations in the US. But while showing how dominant discourses evolved during this period, he says little about why many of those promoting systematic and scientific management worked as external consultants (e.g., Nelson 1995); nor does he address the growing role played since the beginning of the twentieth century by those educated in

12 Background

what were then called schools of commerce (e.g., Engwall and Zamagni 1998). Zunz (1990) looks outside these organizations in an even broader way by investigating how the emerging group of white-collar workers and middle managers transformed American middle-class culture in the image of the corporations that employed them. At the same time, he remains firm-centric by examining corporate cultures in a number of selected organizations, including Ford and DuPont, without looking, for instance, in more detail at the educational origins of their managers.

Further Expansion and Transformation

Management as a practice and as an occupational as well as social group saw additional and significant growth during the first half of the twentieth century both in the US and elsewhere. It was once again Chandler (1962), who studied this process in some detail based on summary statistics for the largest 100 US corporations combined with in-depth case studies for DuPont, General Motors, Standard Oil of New Jersey, and Sears Roebuck. He showed how these four companies independently pioneered a decentralized "product-division structure" as a way to deal with the increased complexity and the "administrative overload" of managers, resulting from the diversification of their product offerings and/or geographic expansion. This new organization, which Chandler called multidivisional or M-form, was marked by a separation between a corporate center and several operating divisions based on different products or geographic markets. The latter were autonomous in their decision-making but accountable to the corporate center, which made strategic decisions about the businesses the company should pursue, allocated resources to each of the divisions, and monitored their performance through an elaborate planning and budgeting process (Chandler 1962).

The introduction of the M-form signified both a qualitative and a quantitative transformation in the process of managerialization. Qualitative, because it incorporated entrepreneurial decisions into the organizational hierarchy, by letting the corporate center decide which business(es) the company should be in (Penrose 1959; Chandler 1962). In quantitative terms, the related introduction of new levels of organization – not only through the creation of the divisions but also within these – significantly swelled the ranks of managers and also contributed to further specialization among them. This had already been recognized by Peter Drucker (1946) who, in his case study of General Motors, pointed to the important role of decentralization and the related delegation of authority for "developing and training leaders capable of decisions and assuming responsibility" (p. 128). Chandler's view – shared by Williamson (e.g., 1985) and others – that saw the creation of the M-form as a way to increase efficiency has been questioned more recently by Freeland (2001). In another in-depth case study of General Motors, he pointed to middle managers themselves as significant actors, engaged in a continuous struggle with top managers with the aim to increase their power as well as their numbers. Whatever their conceptual approach, all of these authors have said little about the role played in these developments by the three authorities examined in this book. The exception is Chandler (1962: 394), who briefly noted the role of consulting firms in the subsequent dissemination of the M-form – a topic explored in more detail by the literature on the history of management consulting (e.g., Kipping 1999; McKenna 2006).

In the US, the M-form – and the increased number of managers that came with it – expanded more widely after World War II, with some variation across different industrial sectors (Chandler 1962: Chapter 7; Rumelt 1974; Fligstein 1985). During the post-war period it also caught on quickly in Europe (Franko 1974). While some authors pointed out indigenous origins (see, e.g., for two large German corporations, Feldenkirchen 1987 and Fear 2005), most highlighted the role of the US example and the influence of American consulting firms, in particular McKinsey, in the adoption process – albeit without much detail (Channon 1973; Dyas and Thanheiser 1976). As more recent survey studies have shown, the M-form has now become the dominant type of organization in core as well as peripheral European countries (Whittington and Mayer 2000; Binda 2013). Since the mid-1960s, it has also been introduced in many North American, European, and even Japanese banks – with a significant involvement by consulting firms, once again mainly McKinsey (Kipping and Westerhuis 2014).

Changing Backgrounds of Managers

With the few noted exceptions, much of the literature has used a rather amorphous notion of management or managers, saying little about their changing educational background for instance. But there are separate studies that specifically focus on this background. What they show, simplistically put, is a significant increase of managers holding business degrees. In the German case, for instance, an earlier dominance of engineering degrees was gradually overcome by those with a *Diplom-Kaufmann* – the degree awarded to students of business economics (BWL). In France, university graduates remain less important than those from the so-called *grandes écoles*, higher-level elite education institutions, but among the latter those focusing on business gradually gained ground against those in engineering (for both, see Joly 2005). Similar results are reported for Sweden (Engwall, Gunnarsson, and Wallerstedt 1996). What these specific studies have not done, however, is to discuss how the educational institutions delivering these degrees rose to such prominence turning into a quasi-obligatory passage to a position in management. And neither have they looked, more generally, at possible parallels between the expansion of management or the emergence and transformation of the managerial "class" on the one hand, and the development of business schools, consultants or the business media, on the other.

There are a few studies that take a somewhat more integrated approach – albeit confined to developments in the US. Here, changes in organizational structures and practices and the expansion of management are more contextualized and

14 Background

linked to the composition of management as an occupational group. Probably the best example is the work by Fligstein (1990, 2001) about the origins of corporations in the US since the late nineteenth century and their subsequent transformations. He suggests, in particular, that exogenous changes, namely anti-trust regulation and the effects of wars or crises allowed new groups of owners and managers to offer an alternative "conception of control" – shared cognitive and practical frameworks regarding the corporation's internal and external relationships – that remained dominant for a certain period. What matters most in the context of this book is that, in Fligstein's view, these periods were associated with different educational backgrounds of managers. Thus, in the earlier periods most managers were owners; then, during the manufacturing conception of control, engineers came to dominate, followed, in response to expanding markets, by CEOs with backgrounds in marketing and, as corporations themselves developed into quasi-markets, by those with finance backgrounds.

Another attempt to provide a broader account of the evolution of management in the US is Khurana (2007). While couched in terms of a history of the American business school, his book tells the story of management in the US more broadly, namely with respect to its quest for legitimacy and an ultimately failed attempt at professionalization (see also Augier and March 2011). A similar account for a European country can be found in Engwall (2009) regarding the origins and rise of business education in Sweden. But while these accounts are trying to link broader developments in the economic, political, and social context with changes in managerial background, they still have numerous limitations, namely their focus on single countries, in particular the US. And neither do they investigate the parallels between the rise of business schools and the expansion of management consultants and the business media.

Management as Innovation

The second approach to the expansion of management is a literature that is widely known as the history of management thought. Probably the earliest example of this literature is the three-volume set by Urwick and Brech (1945, 1946, 1948) on *The Making of Scientific Management*. Since then, work that can be considered under this broad umbrella has been characterized by two main foci: the historical evolution of specific management ideas and/or the particular individuals who are believed to have been major contributors, variously referred to as "pioneers" (Urwick and Brech 1945), "great organizers" (Dale 1960), "philosophers" (George 1968), and "innovators" (Wren and Greenwood 1998).

Early Origins of Management Ideas

In a marked parallel with some historical accounts of management practice, those looking at the history of management thought often seek its roots in ancient civilizations with references to legal codes, government hierarchies, military administration, and rules for the conduct of business (e.g., Witzel 2012). Similarly, the production and accounting methods employed at the Venetian Arsenal figure prominently in these accounts (e.g., George 1968). The formal statement of double-entry bookkeeping by Pacioli (1494) has also been noted as an important and lasting innovation and so has Machiavelli's (1532) famous *Il principe* or *The Prince* with respect to sources of leadership and power. But, like in the examinations of management practice, the widespread consensus links the pioneering ideas on management with the two industrial revolutions, originating, respectively, in late eighteenth-century Britain and the late nineteenth-century US. Most authors would situate the major turning point in management thinking in the latter context with the movement that came to be known as "scientific management" and was symbolized by the aspirations, principles, and methods of the American engineer Frederick W. Taylor. His pioneering role has received innumerable treatments both as part of comprehensive histories of management thought and on its own (see, e.g., Nelson 1980; Kanigel 1997).

Nevertheless, management historians have also identified individual entrepreneurs, amateur scientists, and engineers from the UK and the US, who predated Taylor – some, like Robert Owen, paying particular attention to the management of workers (Wren 1972). Urwick and Brech (1945), for example, singled out 13 "pioneers," who include, in addition to Taylor, a predecessor, Charles Babbage, as well as Taylor's followers such as Henry L. Gantt and Frank B. Gilbreth in the US or Henry Le Châtelier in Europe. Their list of pioneers is significant in other respects. First of all, it includes a practitioner, Walther Rathenau, chairman of the German electro-technical company AEG, who was eclipsed, however, in subsequent accounts by others, namely Henry Ford. Second, they drew attention to the pioneering role of governments, often forgotten today, by examining "The President's Committee on Administrative Management" – the president being Franklin D. Roosevelt and the committee members Louis Brownlow, Charles Merriam, and Luther Gulick. Third, as significant as those included in the list were those absent from it, in particular Harrington Emerson and Charles E. Bedaux, who played a much more significant role in spreading scientific management globally (Wright and Kipping 2012), but did so through commercially driven consulting activities.

Equally remarkable and very surprising from today's perspective is the inclusion of *The Hawthorne Investigations* as volume III in a book series dedicated to *The Making of Scientific Management*. Most subsequent writers would see the studies carried out at the Hawthorne plant of the Western Electric Company in the latter part of the 1920s and the early 1930s as the start of a radically different approach, usually referred to as "human relations." The ideas of its proponents, and in particular Elton Mayo, were seen as an antithesis of scientific management due to the emphasis that was placed on the effects of social influences, informal relations, supervisory styles, and individual attitudes on worker behavior. This is apparent for instance

16 Background

from *The History of Management Thought* by George (1968) published two decades after Urwick and Brech's volumes. He provided a similar, albeit longer list and identified what he called the "philosophers of management" – writers who, in his view, brought into management thinking the question of values, ethics, and humanity. The distinction between scientific management and human relations became even starker in subsequent writings – partially as the result of Braverman's (1974) highly influential view about the role of Taylorism in de-humanizing the labor process. It is only very recently that the apparent "deification" of Mayo and human relations – and the corresponding vilification of scientific management has been questioned and partially revised (see, e.g., Bruce and Nyland 2011).

What should be noted here is that this distinction also reflects a view, prevalent in most of this literature, that these new, innovative ideas progressively improve both the understanding of management as an object of study and its actual practice.

Moving beyond the Shopfloor

George (1968) not only reflects the still widely held view about the juxtaposition between scientific management and human relations, he was also among the first to draw attention to those, who looked beyond the shop floor towards the organization and the management of the business enterprise as a whole. He namely pointed to pioneering publications involving three practitioners during the 1930s, i.e. James D. Mooney (Mooney and Reiley 1931), Lyndall F. Urwick (Gulick and Urwick 1937) and Chester Barnard (1938). Urwick, together with Luther H. Gulick, also introduced Henri Fayol, the French "pioneer" of general management to an English-speaking audience. They were followed since the 1940s, most notably perhaps, by Peter Drucker, who focused on the purposes and the tasks of management, arguing that it was neither an art nor a science but a practice (Wren and Greenwood 1998).

In the late 1940s and the 1950s, this reorientation toward the entire business enterprise was also picked up by US academics, who began publishing textbooks based on a Fayolian management process or functions approach (Wren 1972). The generation of ideas about management was thus shifting from individuals to schools of business, accentuated by the turn toward "scientism" in the 1950s and the 1960s (Augier and March 2011). The outcome was a range of new ideas and approaches, some of which extended the earlier human relations and management process literatures, while others involved drawing upon social sciences or quantitative methods in the study of organizations and management. The resulting diversity generated controversy and an early concern with integration, leading some to describe the state of the management literature as a "jungle" (Koontz 1961) or a "maze" (George 1968).

It was in this context that US business school academics began to more systematically classify and periodize the various approaches to management. Scott

(1961) was the first to develop such an evolutionary frame. Based not on the management literature at large but what he referred to as "organization theory," he distinguished among what he labelled "classical," "neo-classical," and "modern" theories of organization. For him, the classical doctrine originated from scientific management but was better represented by Mooney and Reiley (1931), mentioned above, whereas the neo-classical was an offshoot of human relations. In his view, modern organization theory constituted the most advanced stage, based, as it was, on the emergent scientism in US business schools and the systems approach. More recently, Guillén (1994) provided a similar but somewhat broader approach, looking beyond organization theory at the development and application of three "models of management" – understood both as ideologies and techniques: scientific management, human relations, and what he calls "structural analysis," which is traced to Fayol, Drucker, Dale, and Chandler. He compared their trajectories in four different countries, the US, the UK, Germany, and Spain – an important contribution, given the almost exclusive focus on the US by most others.

The Dominant Narrative and its Critics

The still most widely used interpretation of management writing and thinking in evolutionary terms was provided by Wren (1972) whose book is running up to six editions (now Wren and Bedeian 2009). An abbreviated version of Wren's account of the history of management thought has become the standard in introductory chapters of mainly US-based textbooks on management, organization theory, and design (e.g., Robbins and Coulter 2014; Daft 2016). Wren and Bedeian (2009) argue – with a broader international outlook in the earlier stages, but then focusing more on the US – that management thinking was shaped by changes in the economic, social, political, and technological context. Their periodization is also threefold, made up of "scientific management," "social man," and the "modern" era. The latter entails the scienticized extensions of earlier thinking, such as the turn from human relations to organizational behavior and to what came to be labelled management science, which relied on mathematical formulations and quantitative analyses. Differently from Scott (1961) however, they locate later stages of the Fayolian management process approach within the modern era – albeit tracing its origins to earlier periods as they also do for scientific management and human relations. Most important perhaps in this respect is Wren's (1972) inclusion, for the first time, of the German scholar Max Weber within the scientific management era together with Fayol.

Only recently have similar books as well as alternative readings of the history of management thought begun to appear – mainly from non-US authors (e.g., Witzel 2012; Witzel and Warner 2013). Both in the later editions of Wren's book and in other recent books (e.g., Witzel 2012), the history of management thought practically ends with the 1980s with only some general references to current concerns like ethics, business and society, the digital age and globalization.

18 Background

According to Witzel (2012: 172 and 197), this is justified by the growing specialization within management as an academic discipline, induced by the turn to scientism that began in US business schools, and the consequent distancing of the literature from offering practical guidance to managers. Given the post-World War II accent on theory-based specialized research, a novel orientation in this kind of literature are personal accounts of the development of major theories currently in vogue (see, e.g., Smith and Hitt 2005).

The unidirectional, progressive history of management thought as told by Wren (1972) and Wren and Bedeian (2009) has been criticized on at least two grounds: first, the extent to which the pattern described for the US is actually universal – questioned for instance by Guillén (1994) based on the variations he observed across the four countries studied (see above); second, whether even in the US the development of management thinking has followed the widely accepted linear and upward trajectory – with Barley and Kunda (1992) instead suggesting a cyclical pattern oscillating between what they labelled "normative," i.e., people-oriented, and "rational," i.e., technique-oriented forms of control, adopted in response to long-term business cycles in the US economy. A third, more recent critique has pinpointed the highly individualized nature of all these accounts, i.e. their focus on "heroic' thinkers and practitioners, or "management intellectuals" as Guillén (1994) has called them. Instead, this literature looks at these and other related actors as part of a larger integrated whole.

Management as Fashion

The third strand of the literature examining the development of management is significantly different from the accounts of changes in management practice and from the history of management thought – and arose in large part in opposition to these. It namely rejects assumptions that the ideas that were adopted were necessarily more efficient and automatically benefitted their adopters (Abrahamson 1991). It consequently questions the progressive view of the development of management, characterizing it instead as a quick succession of passing "fashions," even "fads" given the speed of obsolescence. Empirically, the fast rise and equally fast if not faster fall of these fashions/fads is usually demonstrated through bibliometric citation analysis (e.g., Abrahamson and Fairchild 1999).

Even more importantly in the context of this book, this literature points to the agentic nature of these developments, where a set of actors promoted these fashions usually out of a commercial interest. These actors were referred to, alternatively, as the "management-fashion-setting community" (Abrahamson 1996), "management knowledge industry" (Micklethwait and Wooldridge 1996), "management arena" (Faust 2002) or "carriers of management knowledge" (Sahlin-Andersson and Engwall 2002). They have tended to include management authors and consultants, business schools as well as the business media, and were attributed a significant degree of authority in deciding what the "best" or most "up-to-date" management ideas are. There was also some discussion about the mechanism behind their apparent success. For instance, looking at management thinkers from Fayol and Taylor onwards, Huczynski (1993) conceptualized them as "gurus," drawing attention to the discursive nature of their activity and the need for them to engender a certain belief among their followers. Focusing on consultants, Ernst and Kieser (2002) suggested that they used the inherent fears of managers of being left behind by competing organizations to make them "addicted" to the successive waves of fashions. Others pointed to the "collusion" between these consultants and different groups within organizations intent on increasing their legitimacy and budget allocations. In the case of "knowledge management" for example, this included human resources departments vying for higher training budgets or IT wanting to install a better infrastructure (Scarbrough 2003).

These sets of actors were seen more often than not to act jointly or at least in symbiosis – another departure from the heroic management "innovator" or "philosopher." This is probably most evident from the Enron case (see, e.g., McLean and Elkind 2003), where, as is well known, Andersen provided both audit and advisory services – ultimately leading to its downfall. Less known but equally significant, is the fact that the CEO, Jeff Skilling, was a former partner of McKinsey, which also consulted Enron. In addition, another McKinsey partner, Richard Foster, attended Enron board meetings and celebrated the company in a book (Foster and Kaplan 2001) as did other McKinsey consultants (Michaels, Handfield-Jones, and Axelrod 2001). Business papers and magazines also covered Enron and its executives on their front pages, portraying them in a positive light. And so did the Harvard Business School in several teaching cases – quickly removed once the scandal erupted and the company went bankrupt in December 2001. Attention was also drawn to less visible actors, namely the editors at the book publishing houses, who were seen to play a significant role in helping management gurus identify ideas that would sell (Clark and Greatbatch 2002).

These studies and the all-powerful roles they attribute to the various actors on their own and collectively have not remained without their critics. Thus, some authors have pointed to the limitations of using a bibliometric approach as a proxy for the rapid succession of new management fashions. This, so the suggestion by Clark (2004) for instance, tells us as much or even more about how the business media, from which the data are drawn, work rather than demonstrating the actual adoption of these ideas. Others (e.g., Fincham 1999) have criticized how the prevalent explanations have portrayed managers as "gullible victims" of these actors. As Sturdy (1997) points out, consultants tend to be equally, if not more "insecure" given the project-based nature of their activity, where the continuity of business is never assured beyond a few months, if that.

Compared to the other two strands of the literature discussed above, this approach is clearly more integrative, looking at sets of actors and their interaction with each other as well as practising managers – even if the latter are often somewhat caricatured. At the same time, it is much less, if at all, historical, since it

20 Background

focuses only on the most recent period since the 1980s, and neither is it comparative, because all the actors and their fashions are unquestioningly seen as universal. While this might be an accurate reflection of this particular phase in the development of management, marked by the global commercialization, even commoditization of management ideas, the questions of how these sets of actors acquired their prominence and authority and how this process might have varied from one country to the next remain unanswered. These questions will be addressed in the present book based on an historical, comparative, and integrative approach outlined in the next chapter.

References

Abrahamson, E. (1991) "Managerial fads and fashions: The diffusion and rejection of innovations," *Academy of Management Review*, 16(3): 586–612.

Abrahamson, E. (1996) "Management fashion," *Academy of Management Review*, 21(1): 254–285.

Abrahamson, E. and Fairchild, G. (1999) "Management fashion: Lifecycles, triggers, and collective processes," *Administrative Science Quarterly*, 44(4): 708–740.

Augier, M., and March, J. G. (2011) *The Roots, Rituals, and Rhetorics of Change: North American business schools after the Second World War*, Stanford, CA: Stanford University Press.

Barley, S. R. and Kunda, G. (1992) "Design and devotion: Surges of rational and normative ideologies of control in managerial discourse," *Administrative Science Quarterly*, 37(3): 363–399.

Barnard, C. I. (1938) *The Functions of the Executive*, Cambridge, MA: Harvard University Press.

Berle, A. A. and Means, G. C. (1932) *The Modern Corporation and Private Property*, New York: Macmillan.

Binda, V. (2013) *Dynamics of Big Business: Structure, strategy, and impact in Italy and Spain*, New York: Routledge.

Braverman, H. (1974) *Labor and Monopoly Capital: The degradation of work in the twentieth century*, New York: Monthly Review Press.

Bruce, K. and Nyland. C. (2011) "Elton Mayo and the deification of human relations," *Organization Studies*, 32(3): 383–405.

Burnham, J. (1941) *Managerial Revolution: What is happening in the world*, New York: John Day.

Cassis, Y. (1997) *Big Business: The European experience in the twentieth century*, Oxford: Oxford University Press.

Chandler, A. D., Jr (1962) *Strategy and Structure: Chapters in the history of the industrial enterprise*, Cambridge, MA: MIT Press.

Chandler, A. D., Jr (1965) "The railroads: Pioneers in modern corporate management," *Business History Review*, 39(1): 16–40.

Chandler, A. D., Jr (1977) *The Visible Hand: The managerial revolution in American business*, Cambridge, MA: Belknap Press.

Chandler, A. D., Jr (1990) *Scale and Scope: The dynamics of industrial capitalism*, Cambridge, MA: Belknap Press.

Channon, D. F. (1973) *The Strategy and Structure of British Enterprise*, London: Macmillan.

Clark, T. (2004) "The fashion of management fashion: A surge too far?" *Organization*, 11(2): 297–306.

Clark, T. and Greatbatch, D. (2002) "Collaborative relationships in the creation and fashioning of management ideas: Gurus, editors, and managers," in M. Kipping, and L. Engwall (eds), *Management Consulting*, Oxford: Oxford University Press, pp. 129–145.

Daft, R. L. (2016) *Organization Theory and Design*, 12th edn, Boston, MA: Cengage Learning.

Dale, E. (1960) *The Great Organizers*, New York: McGraw-Hill.

Drucker, P. F. (1946) *Concept of the Corporation*, New York: John Day.

Dyas, G. P. and Thanheiser, H. T. (1976) *The Emerging European Enterprise: Strategy and structure in French and German industry*, London: Macmillan.

Engwall, L. (2009) *Mercury Meets Minerva: Business studies and higher education – the Swedish case*, 2nd edn, Stockholm: EFI, The Economic Research Institute.

Engwall, L., Gunnarsson, E., and Wallerstedt, E. (1996) "Mercury's messengers: Swedish business graduates in practice," in R. P. Amdam (ed.), *Management Education and Competitiveness*, London: Routledge, pp. 194–211.

Engwall, L. and Zamagni, V. (eds) (1998) *Management Education in Historical Perspective*, Manchester: Manchester University Press.

Ernst, B. and Kieser, A. (2002) "In search of explanations for the consulting explosion," in K. Sahlin-Andersson and L. Engwall (eds), *The Expansion of Management Knowledge*, Stanford, CA: Stanford University Press, pp. 47–73.

Faust, M. (2002) "Consultancies as actors in knowledge arenas: Evidence from Germany," in M. Kipping and L. Engwall (eds), *Management Consulting*, Oxford: Oxford University Press, pp. 146–163.

Fear, J. R. (2005) *Organizing Control: August Thyssen and the construction of German corporate management*, Cambridge, MA: Harvard University Press.

Feldenkirchen, W. (1987) "Big business in interwar Germany: Organizational innovation at Vereinigte Stahlwerke, IG Farben, and Siemens," *Business History Review*, 61(3): 417–451.

Fincham, R. (1999) "The consultant-client relationship: Critical perspectives on the management of organizational change," *Journal of Management Studies*, 36(3): 335–351.

Fligstein, N. (1985) "The spread of the multidivisional form among large firms, 1919–1979," *American Sociological Review*, 50(3): 377–391.

Fligstein, N. (1990) *The Transformation of Corporate Control*, Cambridge, MA: Harvard University Press.

Fligstein, N. (2001) *The Architecture of Markets: An economic sociology of twenty-first-century capitalist societies*, Princeton, NJ: Princeton University Press.

Foster, R. and Kaplan, S. (2001) *Creative Destruction: From "built to last" to "built to perform"*, London: FT Prentice Hall.

Franko, L. G. (1974) "The move toward a multidivisional structure in European organizations," *Administrative Science Quarterly*, 19(4): 493–506.

Freeland, R. F. (2001) *The Struggle for Control of the Modern Corporation: Organizational change at General Motors, 1924–1970*, Cambridge: Cambridge University Press.

Fruin, W. M. (1992) *The Japanese Enterprise System: Competitive strategies and cooperative structures*, Oxford: Clarendon.

George, C. S., Jr (1968) *The History of Management Thought*, Englewood Cliffs, NJ: Prentice-Hall.

Guillén, M. F. (1994) *Models of Management: Work, authority and organization in a comparative perspective*, Chicago, IL: University of Chicago Press.

Gulick, L. and Urwick, L. (eds) (1937) *Papers on the Science of Administration*, New York: Columbia University.

Hannah, L. (2007) "The 'divorce' of ownership from control from 1900 onwards: Re-calibrating imagined global trends," *Business History*, 49(4): 404–438.

Huczynski, A. A. (1993) *Management Gurus: What makes them and how to become one*, London: Routledge.

22 Background

Jensen, M. and Meckling, W. H. (1976) "Theory of the firm: Managerial behavior, agency costs and ownership structure," *Journal of Financial Economics*, 3(4): 305–360.

John, R. R. (1997) "Elaborations, revisions, dissents: Alfred D. Chandler, Jr.'s, 'The Visible Hand' after twenty years," *Business History Review*, 71(2): 151–200.

Joly, H. (2005) *Formation des élites en France et en Allemagne*, Cergy Pontoise: CIRAC.

Kanigel, R. (1997) *The One Best Way: Frederick Winslow Taylor and the enigma of efficiency*, New York: Viking.

Khurana, R. (2007) *From Higher Aims to Hired Hands: The social transformation of American business schools and the unfulfilled promise of management as a profession*, Princeton, NJ: Princeton University Press.

Kipping, M. (1999) "American management consulting companies in Western Europe, 1920 to 1990: Products, reputation, and relationships," *Business History Review*, 73(2): 190–220.

Kipping, M. and Westerhuis, G. (2014) "The managerialization of banking: From blueprint to reality," *Management & Organizational History*, 9(4): 374–393.

Koontz, H. (1961) "The management theory jungle," *Journal of the Academy of Management*, 4(3): 174–188.

Machiavelli, N. (1532) *Il principe*, Florence: Antonio Blado d'Asola.

McKenna, C. D. (2006) *The World's Newest Profession: Management consulting in the twentieth century*, New York: Cambridge University Press.

McLean, B. and Elkind, P. (2003) *The Smartest Guys in the Room: The amazing rise and scandalous fall of Enron*, New York: Portfolio/Penguin.

Michaels, E., Handfield-Jones, H., and Axelrod, B. (2001) *The War for Talent*, Boston, MA: Harvard Business School Press.

Micklethwait, J. and Wooldridge, A. (1996) *The Witch Doctors: What the management gurus are saying, why it matters and how to make sense of it*, London: Heinemann.

Mooney, J. D. and Reiley, A. C. (1931) *Onward Industry!*, New York: Harper & Brothers.

Nelson, D. (1980) *Frederick W. Taylor and the Rise of Scientific Management*, Madison, WI: University of Wisconsin Press.

Nelson, D. (1995) "Industrial engineering and the industrial enterprise," in N. R. Lamoreaux and D. M. G. Raff (eds), *Coordination and Information: Historical perspectives on the organization of enterprise*, Chicago, IL: University of Chicago Press, pp. 35–50.

Pacioli, Luca (1494) *Somma de arithmetica, geometria, proportioni, & proportionalita*, Venice: Paganinus de Paganinis.

Penrose, E. T. (1959) *The Theory of the Growth of the Firm*, Oxford: Basil Blackwell.

Pindur, W., Rogers, S. E., and Kim, P. S. (1995) "The history of management: A global perspective," *Journal of Management History*, 1(1): 59–77.

Pollard, S. (1965) *The Genesis of Modern Management: A study of the industrial revolution in Great Britain*, Cambridge, MA: Harvard University Press.

Robbins, S. P. and Coulter, M. (2014) *Management*, 12th edn, Upper Saddle River, NJ: Prentice Hall.

Rumelt, R. P. (1974) *Strategy, Structure, and Economic Performance*, Boston, MA: Harvard Business School Press.

Sahlin-Andersson, K. and Engwall, L. (eds) (2002) *The Expansion of Management Knowledge: Carriers, flows and sources*, Stanford, CA: Stanford University Press.

Scarbrough, H. (2003) "The role of intermediary groups in shaping management fashion: The case of knowledge management," *International Studies of Management & Organization*, 32(4): 87–103.

Scott, W. G. (1961) "Organization theory: An overview and an appraisal," *Journal of the Academy of Management*, 4(1): 7–26.

Shenhav, Y. (2000) *Manufacturing Rationality: The engineering foundations of the managerial revolution*, New York: Oxford University Press.

Smith, K. G. and Hitt, M. A. (eds) (2005) *Great Minds in Management: The process of theory development*, Oxford: Oxford University Press.

Sturdy, A. (1997) "The consultancy process: An insecure business?" *Journal of Management Studies*, 34(3): 389–413.

Urwick, L. and Brech, E. F. L. (1945, 1946, 1948) *The Making of Scientific Management*, vols. I–III, London: Management Publications Trust.

Valleriani, M. (2010) *Galileo Engineer*, Dordrecht: Springer.

Whittington, R. and Mayer, M. (2000) *The European Corporation: Strategy, structure, and social science*, Oxford: Oxford University Press.

Williamson, O. E. (1985) *The Economic Institutions of Capitalism: Firms, markets, relational contracting*, New York: Free Press.

Witzel, M. (2012) *A History of Management Thought*, London: Routledge.

Witzel, M. and Warner, M. (eds) (2013) *The Oxford Handbook of Management Theorists*, Oxford: Oxford University Press.

Wren, D. A. (1972) *The Evolution of Management Thought*, New York: Ronald Press.

Wren, D. A. and Bedeian, A. G. (2009) *The Evolution of Management Thought*, 6th edn, Hoboken, NJ: Wiley.

Wren, D. A. and Greenwood, R. G. (1998) *Management Innovators: The people and ideas that have shaped modern business*, Oxford: Oxford University Press.

Wright, C. and Kipping, M. (2012) "The engineering origins of management consulting and their long shadow," in M. Kipping and T. Clark (eds), *The Oxford Handbook of Management Consulting*, Oxford: Oxford University Press, pp. 29–49.

Zan, L. (2004) "Accounting and management discourse in proto-industrial settings: The Venice Arsenal in the turn of the 16th century," *Accounting and Business Research*, 34(2): 145–175.

Zunz, O. (1990) *Making America Corporate, 1870–1920*, Chicago, IL: University of Chicago Press.

3

APPROACH

Three "Fields" in Historical, Comparative, and Integrative Perspective

This chapter explains the approach used in the remainder of this book to show how business schools, management consultants, and business media have become institutionalized and acquired legitimacy and authority over management. The chapter first introduces the notion of organizational fields, which is used subsequently to discuss the three authorities, highlighting in particular the characteristics of fields, namely in terms of structures and logics, and their relations and interactions. It then introduces the more specific perspective taken, which involved tracing the historical development of these sets of actors from their early origins to their current forms, comparing the three fields across countries and examining their interrelationships with each other as well as with management practice. While drawing on a broader literature, the chapter uses selected examples from all three authorities to illustrate the conceptual frameworks and the historical, comparative, and integrative approach applied in this book.

Business Schools, Consultants, and Media as Organizational Fields

Defining Organizational Fields

The attention to "organizational fields" has been a distinguishing feature of the so-called institutional perspective on organizations. Among a variety of definitions, Scott (2008: 434) characterizes fields as "a set of interdependent populations of organizations participating in the same cultural and social sub-system." Based on this definition, business schools, management consultants, and business media can be approached as fields that have emerged within respective national contexts. In the case of the business media though, there has not been a single overarching field until more recently, but three separate, albeit interrelated and partially overlapping ones, i.e., publishers of business books, the business press and academic journals in business and management. In addition, the three overarching sets of actors can be conceived as interconnected fields that also interact with management practice.

Fields arise from the increasing interactions of organizations engaged in emergent or newly defined common lines of activity or, in some cases, as a result of state initiative (Fligstein and McAdam 2012). The former is exemplified by the emergence of the field of "higher commercial education" in the US between the late 1890s and the mid-1920s including the founding of the now prominent AACSB or American Association of Collegiate Schools of Business as it was called at the time (Marshall 1928). A recent example of field creation through state action would be the formation of business education in the People's Republic of China beginning in the early 1990s (see, e.g., Goodall, Warner, and Lang 2004).

The emphasis in Scott's (2008) definition that fields constitute a "cultural and social system" links to a key aspect of the so-called institutional perspective in management research, namely its attempt to go beyond a purely efficiency-based rationale for the existence of particular organizational forms and practices, pointing instead to the importance of widely accepted beliefs, values and norms (see, e.g., Greenwood et al. 2008). Thus, fields, first and foremost, delineate the "institutional environment" in which organizations operate. Institutions, as Scott (2014: 57) puts it, "are multifaceted, durable social structures, made up of symbolic elements, social activities, and material resources." Common beliefs, accreditations by professional associations or state regulations and laws are examples of such institutions. The institutional environment can be viewed, on the one hand, as associated with "ideas and symbols" that constitute "models" which turn into "cultural prescriptions" for field participants. On the other hand, institutions or institutional environments can also be – and have been – conceived as a "framework of (primarily state) agencies and policies" (Greenwood et al. 2008: 12). In the case of business schools in the US, for example, a widely held belief and a strong norm has been that the so-called undergraduate degree should incorporate a "liberalizing" component, meaning that the first two years should be made up of courses in languages, literature, humanities, science, and mathematics (see, e.g., Marshall 1928; Khurana 2007). By contrast, such a "cultural prescription" did not exist in Europe. However, given much greater state involvement in European countries, a highly salient element in the institutional environments of schools or university faculties of business has been the regulatory frameworks governing higher education (e.g., Clark 1995).

In early stages of formation, fields are likely to be characterized by diversity in organizational practices and actions as well as by struggles and contestation. Order becomes established through a process of "structuration" which arises as organizations become more aware of one another, as the flow of information and interactions among them increase and as positions, roles, and behaviors of constituent organizations and patterns of domination become established (DiMaggio and Powell 1983: 148). A key element at play in this process is the quest for legitimacy, which Suchman (1995: 574) defines as "a generalized perception or assumption that the actions of an entity are desirable, proper or appropriate within some socially constructed system of norms, values, beliefs and definitions."

Possessing characteristics and engaging in actions viewed as legitimate enables access to valued resources and enhances survival chances. To acquire legitimacy, organizations incorporate structures, practices, or labels from the institutional environment, which explains for instance the continuing use of the notion of "partnership" among management consulting firms, even if most of them are incorporated and many even publicly quoted. As more organizations within an emerging field do the same, they tend to become increasingly similar or "iso-morphic" with one another (DiMaggio and Powell 1983). Driving uniform adoption by organizations are mimetic, normative, and coercive institutional processes. Organizations tend to mimic those that are perceived as more success-ful. They adopt models and practices that are viewed as standards, which for consultants even included specific dress codes. There are also formal rules often prescribed by the state to which all organizations within a field are expected to conform. The outcome is greater homogenization among organizations as a field matures (DiMaggio and Powell 1983).

This overarching theme notwithstanding, there has been greater recognition that even in mature fields there can be diversity as well as divergent change (Fligstein and McAdam 2012). This means that fields are not necessarily characterized by taken-for-granted beliefs, common norms and rules but are rather sites that entail contestation and struggle among field participants (Wooten and Hoffman 2008) – a feature very common within the management consulting field, where firms with different backgrounds constantly jostled for position (Kipping 2002).

Change within organizational fields may come about, on the one hand, due to exogenous shocks or interventions by powerful external actors. These may lead to far-reaching field-level transformations, as they did for the business education field in the US, for example, in the aftermath of World War II and, in particular, with the involvement of the Ford Foundation (see, e.g., Augier and March 2011). On the other hand, change may emerge in an endogenous manner resulting from interactions among actors within the field. This can come about as field participants try to improve their legitimacy, status, or relative positions. The French schools of commerce, for example, strove to emulate the well-established and high-status engineering *grandes écoles* from the outset and particularly after the 1960s (see Kipping, Üsdiken, and Puig 2004). It may also originate from the activities of so-called institutional entrepreneurs, defined as "actors who have an interest in particular institutional arrangements and who leverage resources to create new institutions or to transform existing ones" (Maguire, Hardy, and Lawrence 2004: 657). Religious orders and organizations like the Jesuits and *Opus Dei* as well as the state served as institutional entrepreneurs, for instance, re-shaping the organizational field of business education in Spain after World War II by creating schools of business inspired by those in the US (Kipping, Üsdiken, and Puig 2004).

Characteristics of Fields: Structures and Logics

In addition to being viewed as contexts influencing organizational forms and action, fields can also be considered as entities in themselves, embodying particular structural and cultural characteristics. These field-level features may vary temporally and across similar fields in different national settings. Book publishing, for example, saw major structural changes recently, especially in the US, with mergers, acquisitions, and the blurring of boundaries. As a consequence, university presses there retreated, while at the same time those in the UK, namely Oxford and Cambridge, expanded their range and revenues (see, e.g., Thompson 2005).

The processes of structuration mentioned above involves the creation of stratification as particular organizations come to occupy more central positions and thus command greater status and influence over the field – a role played for almost a century by the Harvard Business School for example. This hierarchical differentiation among field participants can be described as a center–periphery structure, as Greenwood and Suddaby (2006), for example, have done in their study of what they referred to as the "professional business services" field in Canada by identifying the "big five" international accounting firms as occupants of the center (see also Shils 1975). Relative to organizations placed in peripheral or marginal positions, those that are perceived as located at the center are likely to be more resource-rich and seen as best in representing the core ideas, norms, and rules of the field. Governance structures may also exist through which particular actors can exercise coercive or normative controls over field participants (Scott 2014). Examples of such governance bodies would be public agencies or the state at large, legal systems and courts, as well as trade or professional associations. The latter, for example, have existed in the business school and consulting fields since the 1910s and 1930s, albeit with changing objectives and jurisdictions.

In addition to such structural characteristics, an important concept that captures the cultural–cognitive and normative framing of organizational fields is the notion of institutional logics. Again, a variety of definitions exist. Friedland and Alford (1991: 248), who have introduced this particular term, define institutional logics as "a set of material practices and symbolic constructions which constitutes its organizing principles and which is available to organizations and individuals to elaborate." Logics are significant because they provide "templates for organizing" within fields (Wooten and Hoffman 2008). They define the appropriate ways of structuring and conducting organizational activities: On the one hand, they limit the options that can be considered or viewed as proper and worthy, while, on the other, they provide opportunities for developing organizational forms and practices that are viewed as legitimate.

It may be that a single logic permeates a field and is constitutive of shared understandings among field participants. However, logics are history dependent (Thornton, Ocasio, and Lounsbury 2012). They can become altered over time due to pressures from the outside or from within the field. A dominant logic may

28 Approach

wane as it becomes challenged and replaced wholly or in part by an alternative logic. Thornton and Ocasio (1999), for example, showed that the higher education publishing field in the US shifted from what they called an "editorial" logic, dominant in the 1950s and the 1960s, to a "market" logic during the 1970s. Such change may not necessarily involve the complete eradication of an old logic, which may persist among a subset of field actors despite the advent of a new one (see, e.g., Reay and Hinings 2005). Similar findings have increasingly led to the view that organizational fields are quite often characterized not by a single but multiple logics. Dunn and Jones (2010), for example, have identified two competing logics in the US field of medical education, namely, "care" and "science." Likewise, while consulting firms today are clearly driven by a commercial logic, remnants of a professional logic are still present – at least in linguistic terms (Kipping 2011). As Greenwood et al. (2011) suggest, especially when such plurality involves incompatible beliefs and assumptions, this is likely to lead not only to tensions for organizations but also to struggles and contestation within the field.

Relations and Interactions between Fields

Fields can also be conceived as open systems that are influenced by actors and forces at the wider international and societal levels as well as adjacent fields (Scott 2014: 224). They can serve as "intermediate systems," which mediate the relations between organizations and macro structures and changes at that level (Scott 2014: 236–238). Hence, models that gain currency at international and societal levels are likely to become transformed or translated as they diffuse into specific organizational fields (see, e.g., Sahlin and Wedlin 2008). The MBA degree, for example, which is increasingly used as a label internationally, continues to be implemented in many parts of the world as a shorter version of the two-year archetypal model in the US, where it originated and became institutionalized (see, e.g., Üsdiken 2004).

Organizational fields are also in relationship with other proximate fields. Relations and interactions with such adjoining fields may be of a vertical or horizontal nature (Fligstein and McAdam 2012). Vertically, fields can be viewed as nested in what may be considered super-ordinate fields (Fligstein and McAdam 2012). Business schools, for example, are embedded within national fields of higher education. Such vertical relationships imply that superordinate fields in which organizational fields are located as well as the changes in the former are likely to influence how lower-level fields are formed and evolve over time, though influence may flow in the reverse direction as well. For example, that, at the beginning, schools of commerce could become a part of the university in the US, whereas they had to be established as stand-alone schools outside the university sector in much of Europe, was due to the different ways that higher education fields were becoming structured in each of these settings during the nineteenth century (Engwall, Kipping, and Üsdiken 2010). Horizontal relations with other fields arise because of "resource dependence, mutual beneficial inter-actions, sharing of power, information flows, and legitimacy" (Fligstein and McAdam 2012: 59). These relationships may be cooperative and symbiotic or characterized by dependence – and thus power – of one field over the other. Such cooperative and symbiotic relationships, for instance, have been character-istic of the management-fashion-setting community of which the three authorities form an integral part (see Chapter 2). Relations among fields also vary with respect to the degree of closeness, i.e., the extent of linkages. Close relationships arise typically from geographical proximity but also – and increasingly so – due to the density of social ties (Fligstein and McAdam 2012).

Interactions between fields may also involve overlaps. These overlaps arise when actors – organizations or individuals – within a field cross boundaries and operate in multiple adjacent fields. They occur, for example, when actors expand their activities internationally and enter into similar fields in other countries or when a particular organization or individual engages with distinct but related fields – like the involvement of universities in publishing or of business school professors in consulting. Outcomes of these connections vary. They may con-tribute to the internationalization of previously national fields. Or, they may lead to a blurring of boundaries between proximate fields, as more actors from one organizational field become a part of others. This may also result in the penetra-tion of institutional logics prevalent in one field to others and thus serve to increase similarities between otherwise distinct fields.

A Historical, Comparative, and Integrative Perspective

The Development of the Three Fields

A historical approach allows charting the ways in which the three present-day authorities on management have come to be constructed over a period that dates back to the late nineteenth century. The importance and the value of such his-torical sensitivity lies in demonstrating that what are now often viewed as char-acteristic aspects of business schools, management consultants, and business media have not remained unchanged since they emerged. The accounts provided in this book all begin with the rudimentary origins of the three sets of actors and the organizational fields that they came to constitute. These early days were not only in many ways different from the organizational forms, practices, and labels that are often taken-for-granted today but invariably involved struggles on the part of the early movers to gain legitimacy and to carve out distinct fields for themselves. The narratives for each of the three sets of actors then show how they expanded and also look at the changes that have come about within each of these fields – often gradually and at times in a transformational manner. As will be seen in later chapters, there have been some similarities in the way business schools, manage-ment consultants, and business media have developed as organizational fields over time. These parallel patterns have had to do mainly with the events and changes in broader political, economic, and business environments. There have also been differences among the three fields due to the nature of their respective activities as well as the higher-level fields that they have been embedded in both nationally and internationally.

So, for instance, what are commonly referred to today as business schools – a term borrowed from the US – were not even in the US originally known by this label but as "schools of commerce." And at the time they were struggling, on the one hand, to distinguish themselves from private, for-profit commercial schools and, on the other, to become recognized as "professional" schools within US universities. Neither was there any reference to management education, again a common label today, but rather to commercial education or education for business. Likewise, those that offered advice to corporations were not called management consultants. They were typically referred to as "efficiency experts" or "efficiency engineers" and often operated as individuals. And when it came to publishing academic articles pertaining to business, this had to be done in economics journals – with the appearance of those with "business," let alone "management" in their titles having to await the 1920s.

Since these early days new claims, new logics, new labels, new organizational forms, and new practices and activities have appeared. Not only have there been changes but also increasing institutionalization – and internationalization – particularly of labels and to some extent organizational forms and practices, though with a considerable degree of cross-national variation still persisting. Nowadays, the terms "business school" and "MBA," as its flagship program, have become well established in many parts of the world – at least as labels. And management education has come to be the standard way to refer to what business schools do. Likewise, the terms management consultant and management consulting are now widely used, having become commonplace since World War II. Similarly, academic journals, carrying the term management or administration in their titles began to appear in the 1950s, with increasingly specialized outlets following since the 1970s and the 1980s. They have nowadays become highly institutionalized fixtures of business and management academia – together with their practitioner-oriented companions.

Cross-national Comparisons and Linkages

The historical perspective of the book is accompanied by a comparative approach, which attends to the development of business schools, management consultants, and business media within different societal contexts, though admittedly only to the extent that the extant literature and its largely North American and Western European focus permits. Doing so includes, first, considering a selected range of countries to compare the emergence and evolution of each of these fields with a view to showing differences and similarities. Second, it involves examining the ways and the extent to which there has been internationalization in the sense of (i) a cross-national extension of organizational activities, (ii) cross-border influences and transfers and (iii) the international expansion of field boundaries.

Variation – as well as parallels – among countries can be examined by extending the center–periphery model mentioned above from the field level to the international level, as has been done in some of the sociology and political economy literatures (see, e.g., Shils 1972; Wallerstein 1974). At the international level too, the center–periphery model points to inequalities among countries. Core or central countries are distinguished by economic and political power and/ or creativity, accomplishments, and the intensity of activity in cultural spheres such as science, literature, and the arts (Shils 1972). This international center–periphery structure may also include intermediate strata that could be referred to as "secondary center" or "semi-periphery." Within this center–periphery configuration two sets of conditions and processes have been at play in shaping the emergence and evolution of the respective national fields of business schools, management consultants, and business media. First, the industrial revolutions and in particular the emergence of large-scale organizations in the US and a few other settings paved the way and provided the opportunities for the initial appearance of these three sets of actors. There have been parallels as well as some degree of diversity among the first movers and their followers in the initial stages of development of the three fields. With ensuing economic growth these countries have continued to build on their early lead, though the US was occupying a central position across the three fields almost from the outset – albeit with some degree of variation and contention.

Thus, while there were some consulting activities elsewhere, namely by accountants, a separate field first emerged in the US related to the development of what became widely known as "scientific management." And while the content of management consulting and those providing it changed over time, the US clearly remained its dominant center. Likewise, while there were similarities between the US and various European countries in the way that publishers turned to publishing business books, a business press was created first in the US and the UK. At the outset, greater variety – and balance – existed between the US and various European countries in the ways the fields of commercial education emerged – partly due to Germany occupying a position of center vis-à-vis much of Europe and even Japan for the first three decades of the twentieth century. Nevertheless, like in consulting and publishing, the central position of the US was to become consolidated after World War II in business education too, which meant that, in this new international configuration, the other economically developed countries were turning into secondary centers or semi-peripheries in all three fields.

Within this emerging international stratification, the second process at play in shaping national trajectories in the three fields since the mid-nineteenth century has been the spread of models and practices from the center(s) to other parts of the world. The conditions and ways in which such diffusion occurred have varied

32 Approach

across the three fields. Nevertheless, a main idea in the center–periphery model is that when a country or countries are perceived as the center, they become a source of reference and international influence. In addition, the center may also take an active role in disseminating its organizational models, practices, and services abroad. This is best exemplified by the forceful involvement of US aid agencies, philanthropic organizations, and universities in exporting US models for business education to other parts of the world in the aftermath of World War II, a process often dubbed "Americanization" (see, e.g., Üsdiken 2004). Similar processes are at play when secondary centers exercise some degree of influence over their periphery. An example are several French consultants, usually spawned by US firms, developing, even – temporarily – "colonizing" the Spanish market. While the response to the center in this international stratification often involves deference or emulation, the periphery and, in particular, the semi-periphery can also be a source of resistance or challenge – seeking change and improvements in their marginal position.

As the preceding discussion has shown, the issue of cross-national differences and similarities is inextricably linked with processes of internationalization. With respect to the three fields examined in this book, internationalization can be addressed at three interrelated levels, namely (i) the cross-national extension of the activities of individual organizations; (ii) exporting and importing of templates and practices among different countries; and (iii) the extent to which each of these fields have moved beyond national boundaries and come to be defined and perceived as international.

Expanding what an organization does beyond its home country has been considered as the most typical route to internationalization – though there are a variety of ways as to how this has been done. Variation exists, for example, with respect to the commitment involved in reaching out to foreign contexts. For the three fields, internationalization could range from limited levels of involvement like attempting to access resources, e.g., students, clients or readers, outside the home environment, to establishing campuses or branches in other countries. In relation to business schools for instance, Engwall and Kipping (2013: 322) distinguish between "insourcing," "outsourcing" and "foreign direct investment." Insourcing involves attracting foreign students and/or faculty members. Outsourcing includes various forms of partnerships with or among schools from different countries to provide students with international exposure. And finally, foreign direct investment entails setting up – though not always with success (see, e.g., Alajoutsijärvi, Juusola, and Lamberg 2014) – educational facilities abroad singularly or in collaboration with local providers (Datar, Garvin, and Cullen 2010). This last mode is likely to be the more typical form of internationalization of management consulting and business media, though both may also be engaged in "exporting" their services to clients abroad or their publications to foreign audiences.

In line with the center–periphery model discussed above, Engwall and Kipping (2013) also refer to the importation or its counterpart, exportation, of organizational and program templates as well as educational content in the case of business schools, which occurs for instance through the widespread use of international, namely Anglo-American textbooks. Another case in point was the above mentioned engagement of US universities in advising the creation of schools of business or business programs in many countries following World War II. It can be considered as internationalization both for the US universities and those at the receiving end, though clearly as an example of attempts by the center to influence the periphery. Nevertheless, as also pointed out above, national fields have almost always operated as mediating systems that have led to alterations in the transfer of foreign models and practices.

Finally, internationalization may take the form of expanding field boundaries cross-nationally and possibly to the transnational level (e.g., Meyer et al. 1997). This can occur very much in the manner that DiMaggio and Powell (1983: 148) have suggested with respect to the formation and structuration of fields. It happens as organizations from different countries become more aware of one another, as competitive or collaborative interactions among them increase and the patterns of domination and dependence discussed above emerge at the international level. Organizational manifestations for such transformations are the proliferation of multinational actors and the expansion of international associations, some of which may begin to operate as rule-setting authorities, as the accreditation agencies and the various rankings by the media have done in the case of business schools more recently.

Interactions among the Fields and with Practice

The organizational fields of business schools, management consultants, and business media have not developed as closed systems but in interaction with one another. These interactions have historically been multi-faceted. They have included resource exchanges involving the flow of people and the transfer of ideas. This points to a potentially symbiotic relationship as actors within one field meet the needs of those in others. Yet, connections among the three fields have not always been of a collaborative kind involving mutually beneficial exchange relationships. They have also involved the infringement of boundaries, competition, and the exercise of influence.

With respect to collaborative ties, business schools, for example, serve as a source of recruitment for management consulting firms. Indeed, as will be discussed in the following chapters, the latter have been major employers of MBAs, especially since the 1960s – though there have been claims that, more recently, there has been a movement towards the employment of undergraduates (Pfeffer and Fong 2002). Which schools these MBAs – or undergraduates – come from and which consulting firms they go to have additionally served as ways of increasing reputations for actors in the respective fields, contributing to the stratification within both of them (Pfeffer and Fong 2002). These graduates are also

34 Approach

carriers of language and concepts developed and taught in business schools – incidentally blamed by some observers for recent corporate scandals (e.g., Ferraro, Pfeffer, and Sutton 2005).

The relationship is not one-way though. Thus, models and systems developed by management consultants, such as the Boston Consulting Group (BCG) portfolio matrix, provide teaching material for business education. Former consultants have also joined business school faculties. A recent example is Pankaj Ghemawat, who received a Ph.D. from Harvard, then joined McKinsey before returning to Harvard as a business school professor and later holding professorships at IESE Business School in Spain and New York University's Stern School of Business (IESE, 25 September 2015). And among his various awards are also two sponsored by consulting firms: the Booz Eminent Scholar Award of the International Management Division of the Academy of Management and the McKinsey Award for the best article published in the *Harvard Business Review*. Moreover, under pressure from the rankings, business schools are now bringing in consultants to advise them on image building or help students develop their interview skills (Podolny 2009).

As far as the business media are concerned, there has for a long time been a link to business schools. Publishers thus always had a strong interest to connect to faculty members as prospective authors or as gatekeepers in the selection of textbooks and other teaching aids (see, e.g., Apple 1989). Yet again, the relationship is reciprocal as academic authors look for publishers too and publishers provide the material to be used in business school teaching. A mutually beneficial form of collaboration is related to journal editing. Thus, publishers provide opportunities for editing journals or launching new ones (see, e.g., Cummings and Frost 1985), while at the same time taking advantage of the willingness of faculty members to carry out editorial tasks with minor, if any compensation – other than the prestige and power such an editorial role can bestow. Equally notable, the relationship between the business press and business schools has become of paramount importance since the advent of rankings in the late 1980s. For the former, rankings have turned into opportunities for increasing circulation. For business schools they have become a primary source of attention in promoting and protecting their reputation (Zell 2001; Wedlin 2006).

In terms of the relationship between business media and management consulting, there is a long history of consultants attempting to spread their ideas – and promote their business – through the publications of books (e.g., Furusten 1999). A well-known early example is Frederick W. Taylor's *The Principles of Scientific Management*, which soon after its initial publication in 1911 was translated into many languages. A more recent example is *In Search of Excellence* by two McKinsey consultants (Peters and Waterman 1982), which sold more than five million copies. It has been followed by numerous other titles authored by consultants associated with the big consulting firms. Some of these firms even publish their own journals, such as the *McKinsey Quarterly*, in an effort to gain academic legitimacy and prestige.

However, as pointed out above, the relationships between the three fields have not always been of a collaborative kind. There have been overlapping activities and competition. Faculty members, for example, have been involved in consulting since the emergence of business schools, a practice that continues to the present day (Augier and March 2011). More notably perhaps, there has been competition between business schools and consulting firms in post-experience education, since it has become a lucrative market in many parts of the world (Friga, Bettis, and Sullivan 2003). University publishers have long competed with publishing firms. And with the introduction of rankings the business press has come to gain considerable power over business schools leading to increasing concerns with teaching, student satisfaction, and public relations (Zell 2001; Augier and March 2011). Some schools have actually expressed concerns about inappropriate and hidden metrics employed in these rankings, namely the one by the *Financial Times* (*FT*), seen to harm their positioning (Byrne 2015). Interestingly enough, in the creation of its ranking the UK-based *FT* had originally collaborated with the leading European business schools, interested in combatting their exclusion from US-based rankings (Wedlin 2006).

The three fields also interact with management practice. Indeed what this book tries to show is how these sets of the actors have expanded their authority in defining what initially "business" and later "management" is and what its practice does and should involve. Thus, business schools claim to provide well-prepared graduates, offer valuable post-experience education for executives, and generate knowledge for more effective practice and better outcomes. Management consultants allege to be offering advice with similar ends. And the business media not only supply economic information to practice through the business press, but also make similar claims in the books, papers, magazines, and journals they publish.

All these linkages to practice also involve some degree of reciprocity. What business schools teach is based, not negligibly, on actual management practice. Practitioners have long served as instructors (Friga, Bettis, and Sullivan 2003). Teaching of practitioners in business schools was significant in early stages of development and is experiencing a revival in recent years as the pressures of business school rankings have prompted deans to lighten the teaching loads of their publishing stars with practitioners taking their place in the classroom (Zell 2001). Management consultants tend to learn from their clients and in turn use their knowledge in other organizations, which in some cases will lead to a link back to business schools. Like business school faculty members and consultants, who provide media with manuscripts, so do practitioners, namely former top executives, generally through autobiographies (e.g., Sorensen 1956; Sloan 1964; Iaccoca 1984; Welch 2014). In terms of media consumption, people in top positions appear to limit their reading to the business press and popular books (Pfeffer and Fong 2002).

Yet, very much like the connections among the three fields their links to practice have not always been of a congenial nature either. In its early stages, business education enjoyed only a lukewarm reception from practitioners almost everywhere. Although they gained considerable legitimacy over time, business schools

36 Approach

have continued to be criticized with respect to the practical relevance of their research and teaching (e.g., Bennis and O'Toole 2005). Management consulting firms have been sued by their clients due to allegedly unfulfilled promises (see, e.g., O'Shea and Madigan 1997). And the critical scrutiny of corporations by the business press has become a significant part of the media–practice relationship. This in turn has meant that managers have taken steps to defend and promote their image in the media, with most corporations establishing specific communication units, usually staffed by former journalists (Engwall and Sahlin 2007; Engwall 2014).

The various brief examples presented throughout this chapter are intended as illustrations for both the conceptual framework, based on organizational fields, and the historical, comparative, and integrative approach taken in this book. The subsequent chapters will examine the development of the three authorities over more than a century in all its complexities.

References

Alajoutsijärvi, K., Juusola, K., and Lamberg, J. A. (2014) "Institutional logic of business bubbles: Lessons from the Dubai business school mania," *Academy of Management Learning & Education*, 13(1): 5–25.

Apple, M. W. (1989) "Textbook publishing: The political and economic influences," *Theory into Practice*, 28(4): 282–287.

Augier, M. and March, J. G. (2011) *The Roots, Rituals, and Rhetorics of Change: North American business schools after the Second World War*, Stanford, CA: Stanford University Press.

Bennis, W. G. and O'Toole, J. (2005) "How business schools lost their way," *Harvard Business Review*, 83(5): 96–104.

Byrne, J. A. (2015) "The vertigo in the Financial Times 2015 Ranking," *Poets & Quants*, 26 January. http://poetsandquants.com/2015/01/26/the-vertigo-mba-ranking-of-the-financial-times (accessed 23 September 2015).

Clark, B. R. (1995) *Places of Inquiry: Research and education in modern universities*, Berkeley, CA: University of California Press.

Cummings, L. L. and Frost, P. J. (eds) (1985) *Publishing in the Organizational Sciences*, Homewood, IL: Irwin.

Datar, S. M., Garvin, D. A., and Cullen, P. G. (2010) *Rethinking the MBA: Business education at a crossroads*, Boston, MA: Harvard Business Press.

DiMaggio, P. J. and Powell, W. W. (1983) "The iron cage revisited: Collective rationality and institutional isomorphism in organizational fields," *American Sociological Review*, 48(2): 147–160.

Dunn, M. B. and Jones, C. (2010) "Institutional logics and institutional pluralism: The contestation of care and science logics in medical education, 1967–2005," *Administrative Science Quarterly*, 55(1): 114–149.

Engwall, L. (2014) "Corporate governance and communication," in J. Pallas, L. Strannegård, and S. Jonsson (eds), *Organizations and the Media: Organizing in a mediatized world*, London: Routledge, pp. 220–233.

Engwall, L. and Kipping, M. (2013) "The internationalization of international management education and its limitations," in D. Tsang, H. Kazeroony, and G. Ellis (eds), *The Routledge Companion to International Management Education*, London: Routledge, pp. 319–343.

Engwall, L., Kipping, M., and Üsdiken, B. (2010) "Public science systems, higher education, and the trajectory of academic disciplines: Business studies in the United States and Europe," in R. Whitley, J. Gläser, and L. Engwall (eds), *Reconfiguring Knowledge Production*, Oxford: Oxford University Press, pp. 325–353.

Engwall, L. and Sahlin, K. (2007) "Corporate governance and the media: From agency theory to edited corporations," in P. Kjaer and T. Slaatta (eds), *Mediating Business: The expansion of business journalism*, Copenhagen: Copenhagen Business School Press, pp. 265–284.

Ferraro, F., Pfeffer, J., and Sutton, R. I. (2005) "Economics language and assumptions: How theories can become self-fulfilling," *Academy of Management Review*, 30(1): 8–24.

Fligstein, N. and McAdam, D. (2012) *A Theory of Fields*, Oxford: Oxford University Press.

Friedland, R. and Alford, R. R. (1991) "Bringing society back in: Symbols, practices and institutional contradictions," in W. W. Powell and P. J. DiMaggio (eds), *The New Institutionalism in Organizational Analysis*, Chicago, IL: University of Chicago Press, pp. 232–263.

Friga, P. N., Bettis, R. A., and Sullivan, R. S. (2003) "Changes in graduate management education and new business school strategies for the 21st century," *Academy of Management Learning & Education*, 2(3): 233–249.

Furusten, S. (1999) *Popular Management Books: How they are made and what they mean for organizations*, London: Routledge.

Goodall, K., Warner, M., and Lang, V. (2004) "HRD in the People's Republic: The MBA with 'Chinese characteristics?'" *Journal of World Business*, 39(4): 311–323.

Greenwood, R., Oliver, C., Sahlin, K., and Suddaby, R. (2008) "Introduction," in R. Greenwood, C. Oliver, K. Sahlin, and R. Suddaby (eds), *The SAGE Handbook of Organizational Institutionalism*, London: SAGE, pp. 1–46.

Greenwood, R., Raynard, M., Kodeih, F., Micelotta, E. R., and Lounsbury, M. (2011) "Institutional complexity and organizational responses," *Academy of Management Annals*, 5(1): 317–371.

Greenwood, R. and Suddaby, R. (2006) "Institutional entrepreneurship in mature fields: The big five accounting firms," *Academy of Management Journal*, 49(1): 27–48.

Iaccoca, L. (1984) *Iacocca: An autobiography*, New York: Bantam Books.

IESE, 25 September 2015. www.iese.edu/en/faculty-research/professors/faculty-director y/pankaj-ghemawat.

Khurana, R. (2007) *From Higher Aims to Hired Hands: The social transformation of American business schools and the unfulfilled promise of management as a profession*, Princeton, NJ: Princeton University Press.

Kipping, M. (2002) "Trapped in their wave: The evolution of management consultancies," in T. Clark and R. Fincham (eds), *Critical Consulting*, Oxford: Blackwell, pp. 28–49.

Kipping, M. (2011) "Hollow from the start? Image professionalism in management consulting," *Current Sociology*, 59(4): 530–550.

Kipping, M., Üsdiken, B., and Puig, N. (2004) "Imitation, tension, and hybridization: Multiple 'Americanizations' of management education in Mediterranean Europe," *Journal of Management Inquiry*, 13(2): 98–108.

Maguire, S., Hardy, C., and Lawrence, T. B. (2004) "Institutional entrepreneurship in emerging fields: HIV/AIDS treatment advocacy in Canada," *Academy of Management Journal*, 47(5): 657–669.

Marshall, L. C. (1928) "The American collegiate school of business," in L. C. Marshall (ed.), *The Collegiate School of Business: Its status at the close of the first quarter of the twentieth century*, Chicago, IL: University of Chicago Press, pp. 3–44.

38 Approach

Meyer, J. W., Boli, J., Thomas, G. M., and Ramirez, F. O. (1997) "World society and the nation-state," *American Journal of Sociology*, 103(1): 144–181.

O'Shea, J. and Madigan, C. (1997) *Dangerous Company: The consulting powerhouses and the businesses they save and ruin*, New York: Times Business.

Peters, T. J. and Waterman, R. H., Jr (1982) *In Search of Excellence: Lessons from America's best-run companies*, New York: Harper and Row.

Pfeffer, J. and Fong, C. T. (2002) "The end of business schools? Less success than meets the eye," *Academy of Management Learning & Education*, 1(1): 78–95.

Podolny, J. M. (2009) "The buck stops (and starts) at business school," *Harvard Business Review*, 87(6): 62–67.

Reay, T. and Hinings, C. R. (2005) "The recomposition of an organizational field: Health care in Alberta," *Organization Studies*, 26(3): 351–384.

Sahlin, K. and Wedlin, L. (2008) "Circulating ideas: Imitation, translation and editing," in R. Greenwood, C. Oliver, K. Sahlin, and R. Suddaby (eds), *The SAGE Handbook of Organizational Institutionalism*, London: SAGE, pp. 218–242.

Scott, W. R. (2008) "Approaching adulthood: The maturing of institutional theory," *Theory and Society*, 37(5): 427–442.

Scott, W. R. (2014) *Institutions and Organizations: Ideas, interests and identities*, 4th edn, Thousand Oaks, CA: Sage.

Shils, E. (1972) "Metropolis and province in the intellectual community," in E. Shils (ed.), *The Intellectuals and the Powers, and Other Essays*, Chicago, IL: University of Chicago Press, pp. 355–371.

Shils, E. (1975) *Center and Periphery: Essays in macrosociology*, Chicago, IL: University of Chicago Press.

Sloan, A. P. (1964) *My Years with General Motors*, New York: Doubleday.

Sorensen, C. E. (1956) *My Forty Years with Ford*, New York: Collier.

Suchman, M. C. (1995) "Managing legitimacy: Strategic and institutional approaches," *Academy of Management Review*, 20(3): 571–610.

Taylor, F. W. (1911) *The Principles of Scientific Management*, New York: Harper and Brothers.

Thompson, J. B. (2005) *Books in the Digital Age: The transformation of academic and higher education publishing in Britain and the United States*, Cambridge: Polity Press.

Thornton, P. H. and Ocasio, W. (1999) "Institutional logics and the historical contingency of power in organizations: Executive succession in the higher education publishing industry, 1958–1990," *American Journal of Sociology*, 105(3): 801–843.

Thornton, P. H., Ocasio, W., and Lounsbury, M. (2012) *The Institutional Logics Perspective: A new approach to culture, structure and process*, Oxford: Oxford University Press.

Üsdiken, B. (2004) "Americanization of European management education in historical and comparative perspective: A symposium," *Journal of Management Inquiry*, 13(2): 87–89.

Wallerstein, I. M. (1974) *The Modern World-System*, New York: Academic Press.

Wedlin, L. (2006) *Ranking Business Schools: Forming fields, identities, and boundaries in international management education*, Cheltenham: Edward Elgar.

Welch, J. (2014) *Jack: What I've learned leading a great company and great people*, London: Hachette UK.

Wooten, M. and Hoffman, A. J. (2008) "Organizational fields: Past, present and future," in R. Greenwood, C. Oliver, K. Sahlin, and R. Suddaby (eds), *The SAGE Handbook of Organizational Institutionalism*, London: SAGE, pp. 130–147.

Zell, D. (2001) "The market-driven business school: Has the pendulum swung too far?" *Journal of Management Inquiry*, 10(4): 324–338.

PART I

Diverse Origins

The period covered in the first part of this book ranges, broadly speaking, from the late eighteenth century through World War I with a particular focus on the turn of the century.

Economically, it was marked by two industrial revolutions, the first starting in Britain toward the end of the eighteenth century and then quickly expanding to the rest of Western and Central Europe and across the North Atlantic. It centered on textiles, where mechanization and the associated factory system led to unparalleled increases in productivity followed by more general economic expansion. The second had its hub in the United States, where growing markets and scale-intensive technologies prompted large-scale manufacturing of packaged consumer goods and, later on, automobiles together with the necessary machinery and raw materials. Other countries followed in a somewhat lagged and uneven way with yet others being left behind for various reasons, leading to what is today called the "great divergence" in economic development.

Socially, while the first industrial revolution saw the emergence of a working class and an associated and ongoing struggle for better working and living conditions, the second, in particular, was marked by the expansion of a new and quickly internally diversifying group of "managers," whose "visible hand" was instrumental in running the growing number of ever larger corporations. At the outset, many of them had a background in engineering, which shaped "management" during this period both in practical and ideological terms. These engineers formed professional associations at national levels and were also connecting and exchanging ideas internationally. Moreover, managers relatively quickly came to influence society and societal culture in the United States due to the absence of established elites – a process that often took much longer elsewhere.

40 Diverse Origins

Politically, this period was marked by colonialism and imperialism, with the early industrializing countries establishing their hegemony, either by creating outright political and military rule over some parts of the world or opening other countries, like China and Japan, up for commerce and investment. Combined with (i) innovations in transportation and communication; (ii) relatively unhindered movement of people from the poorer to the richer countries; and (iii) financial stability through the so-called "gold standard," this led to what is now called the "first global economy." It was marked by some multinational enterprises drawing raw materials from less developed parts of the world, while others established production in the more developed ones. World War I brought these developments to a halt and also constituted a first affirmation for the increasingly dominant role of the United States in economic, social, and – albeit reluctantly – political terms.

4

THE EMERGENCE OF SCHOOLS OF COMMERCE

Schools of commerce claiming to provide higher education appeared in different parts of the world towards the end of the nineteenth century. By the 1920s, one could speak about emerging fields of commercial education in countries such as the US, Germany, and France. The ways in which higher commercial education was organized differed however. In the US they were established as parts of universities or colleges whereas in Germany and France as well as in other European countries and elsewhere they were created outside the universities. Almost everywhere, the initial efforts to carve a space for commerce within higher education fields involved struggles due to skepticism and resistance on the part of both universities and business people. Nevertheless, in these national contexts, schools of commerce did manage to expand and gain legitimacy, serving, in turn, as models for early initiatives in other countries.

Organizing Higher Commercial Education

Redlich (1957: 79) observed that between 1890 and 1920 there was an "international trend" towards establishing what he called "academic education for business." Although there had been earlier initiatives, it was in this period that schools, institutes or academies of "commerce" appeared in various countries. What made Redlich consider this period as constituting the beginnings of academic business education was that these schools were set up with the intention of, or were moving toward, providing higher education. Within this international trend schools of commerce took one of two main forms: They were either university-based or stand-alone, i.e., specialized schools. In the United States (US) they became a part of universities and colleges either in the form of separate schools or as departments (Marshall 1928). Early developments in the United

42 Diverse Origins

Kingdom (UK) were similar to those in the US. In other European countries, and elsewhere, the schools of commerce were created outside the universities (Engwall, Kipping, and Üsdiken 2010).

The emergence of these two distinct patterns of founding was associated mainly with the different ways in which the organizational field of higher education was becoming structured during the nineteenth century in the US and within and outside Europe. The super-ordinate higher education fields, as they were developing in respective countries indigenously or by importation, provided the bounds within which commercial education could seek entry and the models that it could follow. Differences in higher education fields shaped the forms that schools of commerce could take as well as their educational features such as duration, curricula, and pedagogy. The motives and the purposes that these schools could proclaim varied accordingly. So did the ways through which they could aim to obtain legitimacy. This struggle also required drawing boundaries between higher commercial education and its precursors, which included – variably across countries – for-profit, or secondary commercial schools.

United States: Inclusion into Universities

Dating back to the colonial era, the college was the locus of higher education in the US, though there were also increasing numbers of freestanding or for-profit schools, for example in medicine and law (Ruml 1928; Thelin 2004). Traditionally, collegiate education rested on classical or liberal arts instruction of four years leading to a bachelor's degree, which typically comprised languages, literature, humanities, science, and mathematics with a view to developing character rather than imparting any specialized knowledge. Although the liberal arts college persisted, a shift began toward the university in the last two decades of the nineteenth century – increasingly leading to its dominance in US higher education (Thelin 2004).

The transition from the college to the university involved the addition of what in American parlance came to be labelled professional schools, such as divinity, medicine, law, and somewhat later, engineering (Thelin 2004). Openness to the professions also had to do with the forms of funding and governance that has characterized universities in the US not only at the turn of the century but up to the present day. Financing of both private and public universities came from a variety of sources, including, in particular, student tuitions and philanthropy (Clark 1995). Moreover, limited involvement by the federal government within the field as a rule-making authority and provider of funds was coupled with a university or college governance structure whereby an external board and the president had strong powers. These financial and governance conditions made universities in the US more open to outside influences and served to curb the power of the liberal arts faculty members to resist the entry of professional subjects (Engwall, Kipping, and Üsdiken 2010). Nonetheless, the strong legacy of college education as understood in the US led to the uniquely American invention of the graduate school as a new layer on top of the bachelor's degree. This new tier was to serve as the organizational unit both for advanced study in the so-called learned professions and for research. It was, thus, a response at once to the strong foothold of liberal arts education in the US and the research-based German university, which served as a model at the time (Clark 1995).

The inclusion of commercial education into the universities took place somewhat belatedly within this developmental trajectory. Becoming a part of the university was in fact the only way through which commerce or business, as it was also occasionally referred to, could be a subject for study within higher education in the US. The model to be emulated for gaining entry had already been set by the earlier absorption of law and medicine as well as engineering and agriculture as professional schools (Ruml 1928). Thus, only two sets of issues had to be tackled by those promoting higher commercial education. One was whether commerce should be taught at the undergraduate or the graduate level. The other had to do with whether it could be organized as a separate school or be included in a college as a department or a division.

Champions of higher commercial education in the US were varying coalitions of businessmen, trustees, university administrators, and faculty members. In some of the earliest and somewhat later initiatives, individual businessmen played a prominent role as benefactors, though they were always dependent on the support of insiders from the university (see, e.g., Sass 1982, Broehl 1999). When the idea originated from within the university, the initiators were, in turn, dependent on funding that could be obtained from the business community – not always an easy task as businessmen at the time often had strong reservations about the value of higher commercial education (Gleeson, Schlossman, and Allen 1993).

The early initiatives to introduce commerce into the universities came at a time when private, for-profit commercial schools were burgeoning and public and private secondary commercial schools were expanding. The private, for-profit schools were often small operations offering short and typically evening programs for clerical jobs – "the private, elementary, unendowed, unassisted and uninspected educational undertaking," as Edmund James phrased it in 1899 (quoted in Ruml 1928: 244). Nevertheless, while in 1850 there were at best 20 of them, by the 1890s their numbers had risen to around 250, leading Haynes and Jackson (1935: 26), for example, to conclude that in this period commercial education was dominated by these types of schools. Their numbers continued to increase and in 1912 a National Association of Accredited Commercial Schools was established (Lyon 1923: 306–10).

Hence, for early proponents of higher commercial education in the US, the question was not only to justify that commerce was worthy of study at a university or college but also to set it apart from the training provided by private, for-profit schools. The main claim in attempting to deal with both of these

44 Diverse Origins

challenges was that business was as much a calling as the more established professions such as law and medicine and, therefore, required a similar form of education (see James 1901). Allegedly, collegiate education differed from the private, for-profit schools in preparing for higher-level rather than clerical positions as well as in developing cultured individuals with greater social awareness and a sense of societal welfare (e.g., Marshall 1913). The professional claim has since persisted, though interpreted in different ways over time, as will be discussed in later chapters. The social or moral dimension was particularly pronounced in this formative period and until the mid-twentieth century, linked as it was with the tradition of general or liberal education within the American university or college. The emphasis on this moralizing or liberalizing mission in educating future businessmen was also a move to gain acceptance in the university. In parallel however – and differently from many other parts of the world, it was a source of much curricular tension for many years to come and, indeed, a main element in the birth of the graduate school of business.

Europe: Left on the Outside

Unlike the US, there was much greater state involvement in Europe in funding, shaping, and governing higher education. Moreover, in most of Europe higher education had initially developed on the basis of a binary division. Universities constituted one of the two sectors within respective higher education fields. The other sector was made up of a variety of schools, which provided training for practical careers – such as engineering – that were not included within the university. It was only the UK that proved to be an exception moving towards a singular university-based organizational field before World War I by merging specialized schools into colleges and universities. Higher education in the UK also involved a division though, namely the separation between, on the one hand, the ancient universities of Oxford and Cambridge and, on the other, the old universities in Scotland and the universities that were created during the course of the nineteenth century in part through private and/or local authority funding (Rüegg 2004). The late-coming universities turned out to be more open to the inclusion of new and practical subjects, as in the US (Smith 1928; Locke 1984).

France and Germany have been the earliest examples of the binary structure within higher education. Moreover, the binary division in these two countries, as well as their universities and schools, has had the greatest influence on the structuring of higher education fields elsewhere in Europe as well as beyond. In both France and Germany universities contained similar faculties, i.e., organizational units that typically included humanities, sciences, theology, law, and medicine. Again in both cases, engineering developed in separate schools outside the university (Clark 1995). Yet, a major difference had taken shape in the position of these schools in French and German higher education fields. Most of the engineering schools in France known as the *grandes écoles* dated back to the mid-eighteenth century and already in the following century gained a more central position in the organizational field relative to the universities. This happened mainly because they were able to supersede the university in training the country's elite engineers and administrators for the military and civil service due to increasingly selective admissions through competitive examinations (Locke 1989).

In Germany, on the other hand, universities emerged as the bastion of research in the nineteenth century, as they developed a strong *Wissenschaft* or science tradition. State funding and self-governance also created extensive autonomy (Fehling 1926). One outcome of these features of the German university was strong resistance to the inclusion of subjects that were considered vocational. Thus, engineering education was left to the purview of the so-called *Technische Hochschulen*. These schools were also a part of the higher education field but in the German case were perceived as of lower standing relative to the high status and the concomitant central position enjoyed by the universities (Locke 1989).

Thus, neither in France nor in Germany was the university a target to accommodate commercial education as it was in the US. It had to be developed outside the university, though motivations differed due to the ways in which the organizational fields of higher education had come to be structured in the two countries. In France, the engineering *grandes écoles* did not only provide a model but also an aspiration for the emergent schools of commerce. In the case of Germany, higher commercial education had to be developed through separate schools, as there was no way that it would be accepted in the universities. Notably, some of the early champions actually preferred for these schools to be established outside universities, as the latter were perceived as too academic (Redlich 1957). At the end of the nineteenth century it was only in the UK that higher commercial education could be conceived as a part of the university.

Pioneering Initiatives and Early Expansion

United States: Failed and Successful Foundations

For the US, the Wharton School founded in 1881 is generally accepted to be the first collegiate school of business, though originally it was called School of Finance and Economy (see Box 4.1). Indeed it is, though in the sense of being the first that has survived since. There were actually a number of earlier but failed attempts. The school of commerce established within the University of Louisiana, now Tulane University, in 1851 appears to have been the very first, though it was discontinued in 1857 – to be re-established only in 1914 (Haynes and Jackson 1935: 83–84). The same was the case with the commerce program founded in 1868 within the University of Illinois, which was named "school of commerce" in 1870 but was closed in 1880, as the trustees thought that the "attempt [had] proven unsuccessful" (Lockwood 1938: 132). A new program was set up in this university in 1902, which expanded into a College of Commerce and Business

46 Diverse Origins

Administration in 1915 (Pierson 1959: 40). Likewise, there was a proposal to establish a commercial school in Washington College, now Washington and Lee University, in 1869, but when its president General Robert Lee, who made the proposal, died in 1870 the school could not become operational and had to wait until 1906 to be established (Marsh 1926; Ruml 1928). These failed initiatives point to the difficulties that university-based commercial education in the US had to contend with in the second half of the nineteenth century. Neither were the early years easy for the Wharton School, which did, however, manage to survive (see Box 4.1).

BOX 4.1 WHARTON SCHOOL OF FINANCE AND ECONOMY: THE FIRST THREE DECADES

The founding of the Wharton School at the University of Pennsylvania, originally under the name Wharton School of Finance and Economy was made possible by a gift of $100,000 by a businessman, Joseph Wharton, which he raised to $500,000 by the time of his death. However, as Edmund James, who was in charge of the school from 1886 until 1895, pointed out, after the first two years "there was talk of handing back the endowment to Mr. Wharton, on the ground that there seemed to be no special demand for such instruction" (1901: 162). There was a renewed impetus in 1883, as the word "economy" in the name of the school was replaced by "commerce," new faculty members were hired and courses were expanded. The new curriculum was believed to be one "which it would be worth the while of a future business man to complete before he took up the actual work [...], in the same sense [...] of the physician to take the medical course or the lawyer to take the legal course" (James quoted in Ruml 1928: 247). Rise in student demand helped and the program was extended to four years in 1894. However, getting accepted in the university was still a problem, as "other departments in the university and most of the faculty were bitterly opposed to the whole project" (James quoted in Haynes and Jackson 1935: 89). It was only in 1912 that the school became a separate unit, though its new dean, Roswell McCrea, still complained that faculty more "interested in the liberal arts" served as a "controlling group" (1913: 116). He hoped that with the expansion of the "knowledge of business technique" "increasingly specialized vocational work" could be developed, which actually turned out to be the direction that Wharton took until the 1960s.

Sources: James (1901); McCrea (1913); Lyon (1923: 364–369); Ruml (1928); Haynes and Jackson (1935: 88–91); Redlich (1957); Pierson (1959: 35–42); Sass (1982).

Within this context, it took almost two decades for followers of Wharton to appear, with two new schools established at the universities of Chicago and California in 1898 and five others in 1900 (James 1901; Ruml 1928). Growth until 1910 was slow but was followed by a steady expansion including during World War I, so that by 1918, according to Bossard and Dewhurst (1931: 253, 259–261), 62 additional universities had introduced some form of commercial education, though not all as separate schools and some only as evening programs (see, e.g., Hotchkiss 1913). Total enrollments also grew, available reports indicating an increase from 1,100 registered students in 1903 to around 17,000 in 1918 (Bossard and Dewhurst 1931: 250).

This expansion was almost entirely at the undergraduate level. Only the Amos Tuck School of Administration and Finance established at Dartmouth College in 1900 had ventured into providing graduate education. However, this was in the form of an undergraduate-graduate or 3+2 arrangement, which involved a two-year program after three years of liberal arts study in college or a bachelor's degree (Ruml 1928; Bossard and Dewhurst 1931). It took a couple of years to find a label for the new master's degree, until the trustees decided that it should be called the Master of Commercial Science, which persisted at Dartmouth until 1953 (Broehl 1999: 43–44).

It was the opening of the Harvard Graduate School of Business Administration in 1908 only as a graduate school that marked a departure from the prevalent undergraduate orientation in the US at the time (see Box 4.2). The school, then a uniquely American form of organizing business education, was modelled after the schools of law and medicine that already existed at Harvard University (Khurana 2007). Forming a graduate school was not only a way of strengthening the claim to being a professional school but also a recipe for overcoming the resistance arising from the stronghold of liberal arts education at the undergraduate level. It was also at this school that the now widespread Master of Business Administration (MBA) title was invented (Gleeson, Schlossman and Allen 1993). In fact, with Harvard's graduate school, the business school as it is generally understood today was born, though it took more than half a century for this particular form to get established even in the US. The reach of the graduate degree, including the MBA, also remained very limited during this period. Altogether 110 master's degrees were awarded in 1919–1920, relative to about 1,500 bachelor's degrees (Gordon and Howell 1959: 21; Pierson 1959: 711).

48 Diverse Origins

BOX 4.2 HARVARD GRADUATE SCHOOL OF BUSINESS ADMINISTRATION: THE FIRST DECADE

Differently from the Wharton School, the graduate school at Harvard was an initiative of university administrators and a few faculty members. In the US context, a graduate school provided a better reconciliation of liberal arts and commercial education, as students could now have a full four years of college experience before beginning their two-year MBA program. It also served as a stronger basis for the claim to educate "business leaders," indicated by bringing together for the first time the words "administration" and "business" in the name of the school. However, there was apparently some hesitation, as the school was founded only as a graduate department and with a five-year experimental term. Although the school did survive the experimentation stage and did become separate, the first decade was fraught with difficulties, student demand and tuition income as well as funding by business remaining below expectations. Neither were the courses taught in any notable way distinct from those at the undergraduate level elsewhere. Faculty members were mostly practitioners. The school still remained fragile at the end of its first decade. Its fortunes were to change, however, after World War I. And already in 1911 the Harvard school had taken one of the earliest steps towards authority building by establishing a Bureau of Business Research. This was a pioneering move toward increasing legitimacy as a professional graduate school purportedly indicating the aim of developing a "scientific" basis.

Sources: Gay (1927); Gleeson, Schlossman, and Allen (1993); Khurana (2007: 111–115).

Europe: Multiple Moves and Influences

The nineteenth century saw the appearance of schools of commerce in various parts of Europe (for even earlier plans and initiatives see Redlich 1957). The early ones in particular were more like secondary schools at the beginning. The demarcation between secondary and higher education started to become somewhat clearer only toward the end of the nineteenth century, though perhaps more so in intent than in what was actually taught (Redlich 1957). The *École Spéciale de Commerce et d'Industrie*, founded in Paris in 1819 by two silk merchants, has been credited as being the oldest school (Redlich 1957). It was taken over by the Paris Chamber of Commerce in 1869, gaining its current name: *École Supérieure de Commerce de Paris* (ESCP). In the meantime two other schools – one public, one private – were established in Antwerp, followed by schools in Vienna, Mulhouse, and Venice (see Table 4.1). According to Redlich (1957: 71), already by 1870 the public school in Antwerp was seen by the Belgian government "as the equivalent of a genuine university." Likewise, for Longobardi (1927: 40) the school in Venice was "an institute of university grade."

Schools of Commerce 49

TABLE 4.1 Schools (and Faculties) of Commerce Established in Europe, 1819–1919

Year	School/Faculty	Country	Year	School/Faculty	Country
1819	École Spéciale de Commerce et d'Industrie, Paris (ESCP, 1869)[a]	France	1900	ESC Nantes	France
1852	Institut Supérieur de Commerce de l'Etat, Antwerp	Belgium	1901	HH Cologne (University of Cologne, 1919)	Germany
1852	Institut Supérieur de Commerce Saint Ignace, Antwerp	Belgium	1901	Academie für Sozial- und Handelswissenschaft, Frankfurt (University of Frankfurt, 1914)	Germany
1858	Wiener Handelsakademie, Vienna	Austria	1901	Faculty of Commerce, University of Birmingham	UK
1866	ESC Mulhouse (closed down in 1872)[b]	France	1902	ESC Toulouse	France
1868	Regia Scuola Superiore di Commercio, Venice	Italy	1902	Istituto Superiore di Commercio Luigi Bocconi, Milan	Italy
1871	ESC Rouen (closed down in 1872, re-opened 1895)	France	1903	Faculty of Commerce and Administration, University of Manchester	UK
1871	ESC Le Havre	France	1903	École de Commerce Solvay, Brussels	Belgium
1872	ESC Lyon	France	1905	Institut Commercial de Nancy	France
1872	ESC Marseille	France	1906	HH Berlin	Germany
1874	ESC Bordeaux	France	1906	R. Istituto Superiore di Studi Attuariali, Coloniali e Commerciali, Rome	Italy
1881	École des Hautes Etudes Commerciales (HEC), Paris	France	1906	R. Istituto Superiore di Sc. Econ. e Comm., Turin	Italy
1883	Hamidiye Ticaret Mektebi, Istanbul	Turkey	1907	Institut Economique, Paris (ESSEC, 1913)	France
1884	Regia Scuola Superiore di Applicazione per gli Studi Commerciali, Genoa	Italy	1908	HH Mannheim	Germany
1886	R. Istituto Superiore di Sc. Econ. e Comm., Bari	Italy	1909	Handelshögskolan i Stockholm	Sweden
1892	ESC Lille	France	1910	HH Munich	Germany
1895	London School of Economics and Political Science (commerce degree in 1919)	UK	1910	Department of Commerce, University of Liverpool	UK
1896	ESC Nancy	France	1911	Helsingin kauppakorkeakoulu	Finland
1897	ESC Montpellier	France	1913	Nederlandsche Handelshoogeschool, Rotterdam	Netherlands
1898	HH Leipzig[c]	Germany	1915	HH Königsberg	Germany

50 Diverse Origins

Year	School/Faculty	Country	Year	School/Faculty	Country
1898	HH Aachen (closed down in 1908)	Germany	1916	*Universidad Comercial de Deusto*, Bilbao	Spain
1898	*Akademie für Handel, Verkehr und Verwaltung*, St. Gallen	Switzerland	1918	Department of Commerce, University of Edinburgh	UK
1898	*Exportakademie*, Vienna (*Hochschule für Welthandel*, 1919)	Austria	1918	Department of Commerce, University of Aberdeen	UK
1899	*Kereskedelmi Akadémia*, Budapest	Hungary	1919	HH Nürnberg	Germany
1900	ESC Dijon	France	1919	ESC Clermont	France

Sources: Fehling (1926); Longobardi (1927); Smith (1928); Engwall and Zamagni (1998); Fauri (1998); Meyer (1998); Kipping, Üsdiken, and Puig (2004); Blanchard (2012).

[a] Original names of schools are listed, other than when available sources only mentioned a later title (e.g., Bari and Turin, Italy). Major name and organizational form changes as well as closures and re-openings during the period covered by the table are indicated in parentheses.
[b] ESC – *École Supérieure de Commerce*
[c] HH – *Handelshochschule*

Following these pioneers, there was a surge of similar schools toward and after the end of the nineteenth century. The founding and sponsorship of these schools varied across and within countries. In some cases they were private initiatives by individual businessmen or, more commonly, local chambers of commerce. They would also be founded by religious groups. There were varying degrees of state involvement, often at the provincial or city level. Some of them could be outright public schools set up and administered by the state. Quite often the schools of commerce were established anew and as independent entities, but there were also cases where they grew out of or had ties to secondary commercial schools, as well as instances where there was some form of cooperation with a university. In Italy, for example, the impetus initially came from groups of academics, politicians, and businessmen, together with some support by city authorities. However, they soon became essentially state schools (Longobardi 1927). The same was very much the case in Spain and Turkey. Nevertheless, in Italy and Spain private ones were also established such as *Luigi Bocconi* in Milan and *Deusto* in Bilbao, the former by a businessman and the latter by the Jesuits (Fauri 1998; Kipping, Üsdiken, and Puig 2004; Longobardi 1927; see also Table 4.1).

Differently from these countries, the schools of commerce in France were all private. It was individual businessmen and, particularly, the chambers of commerce that took a major role in establishing the *écoles supérieures de commerce* (ESC) in various provincial cities (Table 4.1). They were officially recognized by a government decree in 1890, which also brought some degree of regulation. The legitimacy attained by state recognition led to a second wave of establishments by chambers of commerce in other cities as well as an additional one in Paris by the

Jesuits, which became *École Supérieure des Sciences Économiques et Commerciales* (ESSEC) in 1913 (Table 4.1). Despite the designation *supérieure* however, these were more like secondary schools.

It was the founding of the *École des Hautes Études Commerciales* (HEC) in 1881 by the Paris Chamber of Commerce that can be considered the beginning of higher commercial education in France. Armed with state recognition, all of the schools of commerce, including HEC attempted to emulate their prime model, the engineering *grandes écoles*, by introducing in 1897 the *concours*, competitive examinations for student recruitment (Blanchard 2012: 79). This turned out to be short-lived however, as a government decree liberated entry into these schools in 1906. That HEC was better positioned relative to the other *écoles* even at the turn of the century is indicated by the number of students that it was able to attract to the *concours*. HEC's claim to a distinctive status was officially recognized in 1914, together with the right to establish special preparatory classes in secondary schools for its entrance examination, which could not be carried out at that time however due to the war (Blanchard 2012).

In Germany too, the creation of the schools of commerce, *Handelshochschulen* as they were called, was based mainly on private initiatives (see Box 4.3). Individual businessmen, chambers of commerce and/or business associations took the lead, together with the support and endorsement of city authorities. After they were established, the German schools also benefited from public funding provided by the city and the state in which they were located (Fehling 1926; Tribe 1995). The first *Handelshochschulen* (HH) were created in 1898 in Leipzig and Aachen and were followed in the next 20 years by seven others, which were founded in major commercial centers (Table 4.1). The HH Leipzig was established by cooperation between an existing secondary commercial school and the university in the city. The Aachen initiative was different in that it was developed within the local *Technische Hochschule* – turning out to be an unsuccessful venture however and having to close down in 1908. The school established in Cologne in 1901 was the first entirely independent one with its own staff, accompanied by the one founded in Frankfurt in the same year, both of which also had sections for training civil servants (Fehling 1926).

Student numbers grew until World War I, surpassing those studying economics (Meyer 1998: 25). Differently from the college- and university-based schools in the US, women were also admitted, though at a proportion that went up to and remained around 10 percent in the war years (Fehling 1926). By 1920 the holders of the HH qualification exceeded 4,000 (Tribe 1995: 99). The *Handelshochschulen* had an immediate impact, as already in 1908 six percent and in 1913 eight percent of the "directors" in German firms were graduates of these schools (Lindenfeld 1990: 225).

52 Diverse Origins

BOX 4.3 THE GERMAN *HANDELSHOCHSCHULEN*

From the very beginning, the German *Handelshochschulen* (HH) were distinctly post-secondary schools. *Diplom-Kaufmann*, the HH qualification, created with the founding of the first school in Leipzig, initially required two years of study. The main aim was seen as educating young people for business and training teachers for secondary commercial schools. At the beginning there was the issue of general vs. commercial education, partly because the aspiration was to train business leaders and partly due to a limited base in teaching commerce. Yet, in the German case general education was more narrowly construed relative to the US, referring mostly to economics and law. The founding of the schools in Cologne and Berlin re-orientated the emergent organizational field, leading to greater priority given to commerce. This focus on commerce was made possible through the development of a new discipline, eventually labelled *Betriebswirtschaftslehre* (BWL) or business economics. Gaining any degree of legitimacy within the German higher education field required a claim to being scientific. But to deal with the reservations of the business community a delicate balance had to be maintained between science and a practical orientation. So, while the *Handelshochschulen* drew on practitioners as teachers in subjects like commerce and law, they turned toward the university as a frame of reference, taking the same path as the *Technische Hochschulen* had done earlier. Already by World War I, the *Handelshochschulen* had achieved some degree of parity with the universities, having become more "scientific" and were therefore distinct from the schools of commerce elsewhere in the world. Ironically in a sense, the drive to become more academic and research-based sowed the seeds of a major subsequent change with the *Handelshochschulen* disappearing as an organizational form and becoming amalgamated into newly established or already existing universities (see Chapter 7).

Sources: Fehling (1926); Redlich (1957); Locke (1984: 199–241, 1989: 56–112); Lindenfeld (1990); Tribe (1995: 95–139); Meyer (1998).

Within the European context, the UK constituted an exception in that, like in the US, both technical and commerce education was housed by the universities. Inclusion of commerce into the university was part of the process of creating the so-called civic universities and university colleges at the turn of the century (Tribe 2003). The earliest Faculty of Commerce, the counterpart of college or school in US terminology, was the one founded in the University of Birmingham (1901), which began to offer a three-year Bachelor of Commerce (B.Com.) degree in 1902 (Smith 1928; Engwall and Zamagni 1998; Fauri 1998). Again, like in the US there was a claim to general education, not least due to the prominence historically attached to culture and liberal education. William Ashley, brought back from Harvard University to lead the Faculty at Birmingham, for example, expressed the belief that the program, the "course" in British terminology, "will not only give information – though this is important enough – but also train the reasoning powers and strengthen the judgment" (Ashley 1903: 38). This approach was in line with the aspirations of the faculty, which were, as Ashley saw it, "the education, not of the rank and file, but of the officers of the industrial and commercial army" (quoted by Tribe 2003: 685).

Birmingham's example was followed by universities in provincial industrial and commercial centers as well as the old universities in Scotland (see Table 4.1). Likewise, the London School of Economics and Political Science (LSE) established in 1895 with the explicit purpose of training the "business or official administrator" was incorporated into the University of London in 1900 and a commerce degree was introduced in 1919 (Redlich 1957: 74; see also Smith 1928). Of these universities, Birmingham, Manchester, and Liverpool also offered a master's (M.Com.) degree which involved one or two years of additional study, not too different in that sense from the one initiated shortly before in the US by Dartmouth College (Smith 1928; Tribe 2003). Notably, the prestigious old universities of Oxford and Cambridge stayed away from commerce, indeed for many decades to come. Moreover, despite the increase in universities offering commerce degrees as well as the introduction of evening studies at Manchester and the LSE for example, the number of graduates remained very modest in this formative period (Engwall and Zamagni 1998).

International Circulation of Models

As the claims to higher-level commercial education emerged and developed in the US and Europe during the nineteenth century there was some degree of international influence and borrowing of models. This is not surprising in that all of the initiatives faced questions of not only devising content and establishing particular forms of organizing but also had to deal with issues of legitimacy and acceptance into pre-existing or evolving higher education fields in their respective contexts. Among the earliest initiatives, the school founded in Antwerp apparently served as an exemplar for those in Venice, Genoa, and Cologne, as well as for the provincial commercial schools in France – indeed more so than the ones already established in Paris (Longobardi 1927; Redlich 1957). Redlich (1957: 60) also notes that during the founding of the HH Berlin visits were made not only to existing schools in Germany but also to Paris, London, Antwerp, and Vienna.

As the latter examples suggest, awareness of initiatives in other countries appears to have increased toward the end of the century, including between the US and Europe (Redlich 1957). This is best indicated by the visits of the champions of commercial schools from one continent to the other. For example, Edmund James from Wharton (see Box 4.1) was sent in 1892 by the American Bankers' Association to visit and study commercial education in Europe (James

54 Diverse Origins

1893). Likewise, Ignaz Jastrow, the lead figure in the founding of the HH Berlin, was funded by the association of Berlin merchants to visit the US in 1904, based on the belief that the US was the most advanced country in higher education for commerce (Tribe 1995: 117). One could thus reckon that there was some flow of ideas through such visits and that what was observed was employed in justifying and legitimizing commercial education in home settings (see, e.g., James 1901). But while Jastrow, for example, was impressed by the American idea that higher education in commerce needed to be general rather than focused on technique, he did not think that the university schools of commerce in the US could serve as a model for Germany (Redlich 1957; Tribe 1995). Overall, the modelling effects across the two continents remained very limited at this formative stage, mainly due to the major differences, discussed above, in the ways in which respective higher education fields had come to be shaped with respect to what universities did or did not encompass.

The schools in France and, even more so, the ones in Germany did have, however, a considerable impact on other European countries as well as further afield. The lower level French *écoles de commerce*, for example, provided the model for Spain, as did the HEC in Paris for the school founded in Istanbul two years later (Kipping, Üsdiken, and Puig 2004). The *Handelshochschulen* had their most powerful influence on the Nordic countries, where Germany was serving as the model for higher education at large (see Table 4.1). The first commercial school was established in Sweden in 1909 by private initiative, presently known as the Stockholm School of Economics. It also started with a two-year program initially employing German professors (Engwall 2009). Next, was the school established very much along similar lines in Helsinki in 1911, later known as the Helsinki School of Economics and now Aalto University School of Business – though in the beginning within an already existing secondary school (Kettunen 2013). In 1917, based on an initiative of the association of merchants and bankers, came a *Handelshøjskolen* in Copenhagen, presently known as Copenhagen Business School. A similar school was founded in Rotterdam in 1913, also based on the initiative of the business community and the German model. Called *Nederlandsche Handels-Hoogeschool* (NHH) at the time, it became the origin for the present day Erasmus University (Engwall and Zamagni 1998).

The influence of the early schools in Europe also extended to other parts of the world. The establishment of an *école supérieure de commerce* in Algiers in 1900 was due to colonial ties (Blanchard 2012: 82). Similarly, university-affiliated public commercial colleges were founded in India, first in Mumbai in 1913, then in Delhi in 1920 (Hill et al. 1973). The French *grandes écoles* also served as the model for the first full-fledged post-secondary school of commerce in Canada, the *École des Hautes Études Commerciales de Montréal*, which became operational in 1910. It was established as a separate school upon the initiative of the city's francophone chamber of commerce but was funded by the Quebec government. It was also heavily influenced by the school of commerce at Antwerp due mainly

Schools of Commerce **55**

to the administrators and teaching staff being recruited from Belgium (Harvey 2000). For the University of Toronto, on the other hand, which started out in 1901 with a two-year diploma program that was extended to four years in 1909 and turned into a B.Com. degree in 1921 though not into a separate Faculty, the model was the University of Birmingham (Boothman 2000).

The Antwerp school also served as a source of inspiration for the first private school established, initially at the secondary level, in Tokyo as early as 1875 – eventually leading to present day Hitotsubashi University. The link with Antwerp again came about through the employment of Belgian teachers as well as students sent to Belgium (Nishizawa 1996). The school in Tokyo, as well as companion ones established in Osaka and Kobe, and later in Yamaguchi, Nagasaki, and Otaru, were officially recognized in 1903 as higher-level business colleges or *Jitsugyo Senmon Gakko* that remained outside the imperial universities (Nishizawa 1998). At that time, these schools increasingly came under the influence of the *Handelshochschulen* and their business economics discipline, mainly through students sent to study in Germany. Since demand steadily increased, these Japanese higher commercial schools could become more selective, with the school in Tokyo for example admitting only around 10 percent of more than 4,000 applicants in 1919 (Nishizawa 1998: 87).

Apart from such cases of borrowing models, in this formative period organizational fields of commercial education developed very much in nationally bounded ways – perhaps with the exception of the German *Handelshochschulen*. Especially the schools in Berlin and Leipzig became so reputable internationally that foreigners, mostly from Eastern Europe, Russia, and the Balkan countries, made up more than a third of the students in the former in 1913 and about half in the latter in particular years (Fehling 1926: 573; Tribe 1995: 118).

By the end of World War I then, fields of higher commercial education had emerged in the first mover countries, namely the US, Germany, and France, and were incubating in many other places. As will be examined in Chapter 7, the organizational patterns and field structures that had taken shape during this formative period continued largely in the same manner during the interwar years, though a major change did take place in Germany with the involvement of the universities – a change, which then had effects in a number of other countries.

References

Ashley, W. J. (1903) "The universities and commercial education," *The North American Review*, 176(554): 31–38.

Blanchard, M. (2012) *Socio-histoire d'une entreprise éducative: Le développement des écoles supérieures de commerce en France (fin du XIXe siècle – 2010)*, Unpublished Ph.D. dissertation, Paris: École des Hautes Études en Sciences Sociales.

Boothman, B. E. C. (2000) "Culture of utility: The development of business education in Canada," in B. J. Austin (ed.), *Capitalizing Knowledge: Essays on the history of business education in Canada*, Toronto: University of Toronto Press, pp. 11–86.

Bossard, J. H. S. and Dewhurst, J. H. (1931) *University Education for Business: A study of existing needs and practices*, Philadelphia: University of Pennsylvania Press.

Broehl, W. G., Jr (1999) *Tuck and Tucker: The origin of the graduate business school*, Hanover, NH: University Press of New England.

Clark, B. R. (1995) *Places of Inquiry: Research and education in modern universities*, Berkeley, CA: University of California Press.

Engwall, L. (2009) *Mercury Meets Minerva: Business studies and higher education – the Swedish case*, 2nd edn, Stockholm: EFI, The Economic Research Institute.

Engwall, L. and Zamagni, V. (1998) "Introduction," in L. Engwall and V. Zamagni (eds), *Management Education in Historical Perspective*, Manchester: Manchester University Press, pp. 1–18.

Engwall, L., Kipping, M., and Üsdiken, B. (2010) "Public science systems, higher education, and the trajectory of academic disciplines: Business studies in the United States and Europe," in R. Whitley, J. Gläser, and L. Engwall (eds), *Reconfiguring Knowledge Production*, Oxford: Oxford University Press, pp. 325–353.

Fauri, F. (1998) "British and Italian management education before the Second World War: A comparative analysis," in L. Engwall, and V. Zamagni (eds), *Management Education in Historical Perspective*, Manchester: Manchester University Press, pp. 34–49.

Fehling, A. W. (1926) "Collegiate education for business in Germany," *Journal of Political Economy*, 34(5): 545–596.

Gay, E. F. (1927) "The founding of the Harvard business school," *Harvard Business Review*, 4(4): 397–400.

Gleeson, R. E., Schlossman, S., and Allen, D. G. (1993) "Uncertain ventures: The origins of graduate management education at Harvard and Stanford, 1908–1939," *Selections*, 9(3): 9–37.

Gordon, R. A. and Howell, J. E. (1959) *Higher Education for Business*, New York: Columbia University Press.

Harvey, P. (2000) "The founding of the École des Hautes Études Commerciales de Montréal," in B. J. Austin (ed.), *Capitalizing Knowledge: Essays on the history of business education in Canada*, Toronto: University of Toronto Press, pp. 87–100.

Haynes, B. R. and Jackson, H. P. (1935) *A History of Business Education in the United States*, Cincinnati, OH: South-Western Publishing.

Hill, T. M., Haynes, W. W., Baumgartel, H., and Paul, S. (1973) *Institution Building in India: A study of international collaboration in management education*, Boston, MA: Harvard University.

Hotchkiss, W. E. (1913) "The Northwestern University School of Commerce," *Journal of Political Economy*, 21(3): 196–208.

James, E. J. (1893) *Education of Business Men in Europe*, New York: American Bankers' Association.

James, E. J. (1901) "Relation of the college and university to higher commercial education," *Publications of the American Economic Association*, 3rd Series, 2(1): 144–165.

Kettunen, K. (2013) *Management Education in a Historical Perspective: The business school question and its solution in Finland*, Ph.D. dissertation, Oulu: University of Oulu.

Khurana, R. (2007) *From Higher Aims to Hired Hands: The social transformation of American business schools and the unfulfilled promise of management as a profession*, Princeton, NJ: Princeton University Press.

Kipping, M., Üsdiken, B., and Puig, N. (2004) "Imitation, tension, and hybridization: Multiple 'Americanizations' of management education in Mediterranean Europe," *Journal of Management Inquiry*, 13(2): 98–108.

Lindenfeld, D. F. (1990) "The professionalization of applied economics: German counterparts to business administration," in G. Cocks and K. H. Jarausch (eds), *German Professions, 1800–1950*, Oxford: Oxford University Press, pp. 213–231.

Locke, R. (1984) *The End of the Practical Man: Entrepreneurship and higher education in Germany, France and Great Britain*, Greenwich, CT: JAI Press.

Locke, R. (1989) *Management and Higher Education since 1940: The influence of America and Japan on West Germany, Great Britain, and France*, Cambridge: Cambridge University Press.

Lockwood, J. (1938) "Early university education in accountancy," *Accounting Review*, 13(2): 131–144.

Longobardi, E. C. (1927) "Higher commercial education in Italy," *Journal of Political Economy*, 35(1): 39–90.

Lyon, L. S. (1923) *Education for Business*, 2nd edn, Chicago, IL: University of Chicago Press.

Marsh, C. S. (1926) "General Lee and a school of commerce," *Journal of Political Economy*, 34(5): 657–659.

Marshall, L. C. (1913) "The College of Commerce and Administration of the University of Chicago," *Journal of Political Economy*, 21(2): 97–110.

Marshall, L. C. (1928) "The American collegiate school of business," in L. C. Marshall (ed.), *The Collegiate School of Business: Its status at the close of the first quarter of the twentieth century*, Chicago, IL: The University of Chicago Press, pp. 3–44.

McCrea, R. C. (1913) "The work of the Wharton School of Finance and Commerce," *Journal of Political Economy*, 21(2): 111–116.

Meyer, H.-D. (1998) "The German Handelshochschulen, 1898–1933: A new departure in management education and why it failed," in L. Engwall and V. Zamagni (eds), *Management Education in Historical Perspective*, Manchester: Manchester University Press, pp. 19–33.

Nishizawa, T. (1996) "Business studies and management education in Japan's economic development – An institutional perspective," in R. P. Amdam (ed.), *Management, Education and Competitiveness: Europe, Japan and the United States*, London: Routledge, pp. 96–110.

Nishizawa, T. (1998) "The development of managerial human resources in Japan: A comparative perspective," in L. Engwall and V. Zamagni (eds), *Management Education in Historical Perspective*, Manchester: Manchester University Press, pp. 83–94.

Pierson, F. C. (1959) *The Education of American Businessmen: A study of university-college programs in business administration*, New York: McGraw-Hill.

Redlich, F. (1957) "Academic education for business: Its development and the contribution of Ignaz Jastrow (1856–1937) – in commemoration of the hundredth anniversary of Jastrow's birth," *Business History Review*, 31(1): 35–91.

Ruml, F. (1928) "The formative period of higher commercial education in American universities," *Journal of Business*, 1(2): 238–263.

Rüegg, W. (2004) "Themes," in W. Rüegg (ed.), *A History of the University in Europe. Vol. III: Universities in the Nineteenth and Early Twentieth Centuries (1800–1945)*, Cambridge: Cambridge University Press, pp. 3–31.

Sass, S. A. (1982) *The Pragmatic Imagination: A history of the Wharton School, 1881–1981*, Philadelphia, PA: University of Pennsylvania Press.

Smith, J. G. (1928) "Education for business in Great Britain," *Journal of Political Economy*, 36(1): 1–52.

Thelin, J. R. (2004) *A History of American Higher Education*, Baltimore, MD: Johns Hopkins University Press.

Tribe, K. (1995) *Strategies of Economic Order: German economic discourse, 1750–1950*, Cambridge: Cambridge University Press.

Tribe, K. (2003) "The faculty of commerce and Manchester economics, 1903–1944," *Manchester School*, 71(6): 680–710.

5

ACCOUNTANTS AND EFFICIENCY ENGINEERS AS EARLY CONSULTANTS

Compared to business schools and business media, management consulting as an organizational field and even as a clearly defined and delineated activity was a latecomer – the actual term only becoming commonplace after World War II. While accountants provided some advisory services since the early nineteenth century, consulting as a visible and distinguishable activity originated in the United States at the turn of the twentieth century, linked to engineering and in particular to so-called scientific management and its figurehead, Frederick W. Taylor. As part of efforts to disseminate their ideas, Taylor and his multiple collaborators and competitors also offered paid advice – in a role often referred to as "consulting engineers" or "efficiency experts." Among them, Harrington Emerson was the first to adopt a more commercial logic, establishing a – still rather small – multi-office organization, founded in 1907. While scientific management quickly spread around the globe, its related consulting activities only saw a very limited emulation outside the US before World War I.

Situating the Origins of Consulting: A Variety of Views

It is close to impossible to identify relatively specific starting dates for management consulting activities in different countries, since this organizational field is less clearly defined and delineated than the other two covered in this book – especially at the outset. Not surprisingly therefore, the relevant literature has offered divergent views on the origins of management consulting as well as the names of the first consultants and consulting firms.

Some go back to ancient times and even invoke biblical characters. Thus, Moses' father-in-law Jethro has been seen as the "first management consultant," since he apparently "helped design the organization through which Moses ruled the Hebrews

60 Diverse Origins

in the desert" (Pindur, Rogers, and Kim 1995: 59). In her overview of the early consultants Marsh (2009: Chapter 2) points to a number of individuals in ancient Egypt, Greece, Rome, and China, who played such a role. Among the Greek antecedents she quite extensively discusses Plato and "his views about the process of advice-giving to rulers" (pp. 35–39, quote p. 36) but, somewhat surprisingly, omits Socrates, whose "Socratic method" is actually still being used by consultants today (see, e.g., Gronke and Häußner 2006). Marsh (2009) also mentions, as do others, Niccolò Machiavelli (1469–1527), who had summarized his advice in the posthumously published book *The Prince* (see Chapter 2). Notably, the recipients of advice in these early examples were generally the "rulers," and "the advice proffered from ancient times was twofold: how to help the prince stay in power and how to be a virtuous leader" (Marsh 2009: 30). This also reflects the fact that the largest organizations at those times were public administrations or, even when they had a productive purpose like the Venice shipbuilding arsenals or the French *manufactures*, served the interests of the rulers (see Chapter 2).

Most observers would therefore situate the beginning of management consulting in more recent periods, namely in the late eighteenth and nineteenth centuries, when the first and second industrial revolutions created privately owned organizations employing thousands and then tens or even hundreds of thousands of people. Klein (1977: 14), for example, characterizes British pottery entrepreneur Josiah Wedgewood (1730–1795) as a "proto-consultant," because he, together with a few others, "laid down the foundations of the idea that the manufacturing process could be organized into [a] system that would use, and not abuse, the men harnessed to it"; "proto," because Klein draws a more or less direct line to Frederick W. Taylor (1856–1915), characterized as the "Father of Scientific Management" and a kind of grandfather of management consulting (e.g., Klein 1977: 21–25; Tisdall 1982: 15–16; see also Box 5.1). He and those who followed were referred to as "consulting engineers," "efficiency engineers" or, more broadly, "efficiency experts" at the time. Most tended to work alone, which is why many authors (e.g., Fink and Knoblach 2003) point to Arthur D. Little (ADL), founded in 1886, as the first management consulting *firm*. But this is mistaken, since ADL carried out contract research, namely in chemistry, and developed management consulting activities only much later (Kahn 1986; see also Chapter 11).

Some recent authors place the origins of management consulting in the interwar period – in parallel with the first uses of the actual label. Since they cannot ignore earlier consulting activities, they distinguish them through a labeling of their own – referring to the newer firms, like Booz Allen Hamilton, McKinsey, and A.T. Kearney, as "modern" (McKenna 1995), implicitly downplaying the others as pre-modern; or by contrasting their "professional form" with a purely commercial one, exemplified by consulting bad boy, the "flamboyant" George S. May and his "aggressive, high-pressure sales tactics" (David, Sine, and Haveman 2013: 363). These firms did indeed become dominant during the post-World

War II decades and also managed to obtain a significant definitional power over what is until today understood as management consulting (see Chapters 8 and 11). However, some of these "modern" and "professional" consulting firms have now disappeared, while others are in decline. More importantly, such a focus on a limited – while admittedly important – part of the consulting field misses longer-term trends and changes in its development, namely the significant role played by firms with roots in engineering (see Wright and Kipping 2012) as well as the accounting origins of those that dominate the industry today, at least in terms of revenues (see Chapter 14).

Accountants as Invisible Frontrunners

Thus, while it is helpful to identify the origins of the "management consultant" label, it is equally important to trace similar activities carried out under different labels and the efforts by their providers at legitimation and institutionalization. When looking at these more broadly defined activities, which refer to external advice given to those in charge of the enterprises of the first and second industrial revolutions, probably the earliest to provide these kinds of services were accountants. For the most part however, their consulting activities remained hidden at least until the interwar period.

Accounting itself has a long history, going back to ancient times, with double-entry bookkeeping as a major innovation codified in fifteenth-century Italy (see Chapter 2), from where it gradually spread elsewhere. In parallel with economic developments, i.e. the first industrial revolution, accounting saw a surge in the United Kingdom since the late eighteenth century. It was originally carried out by individual practitioners, who gradually amalgamated into larger partnerships (see Figure 5.1 for the multiple origins of Arthur Young, which in 1989 merged with Ernst & Whinney to form one of today's "Big Four" and abbreviated its name to EY in 2013). British investments in the US also brought accountants from the UK there. Price Waterhouse for example, which goes back to a firm founded in London in 1849 by Samuel Lowell Price, established an office in the US in 1890. It quickly became an independent partnership, a development repeated elsewhere – resulting in a very loose international federation operating under a common name (Jones 1995; Allen and McDermott 1993: Chapter 1).

During the late nineteenth century, accounting institutionalized and became a recognized profession (see, for a summary, Coffee 2006: Chapter 5). In the UK, where the Joint Stock Companies Act of 1844 already stipulated an annual audit, accountants formed local associations during the 1870s in order to improve their public standing and achieve control over those exercising the activity. They combined into the Institute of Chartered Accountants in England and Wales (ICAEW) and received government recognition through a Royal Charter in 1880. A competing body formed in 1885 with the Society of Incorporated Accountants. Both of them eventually merged in 1957. In the US, the American

62 Diverse Origins

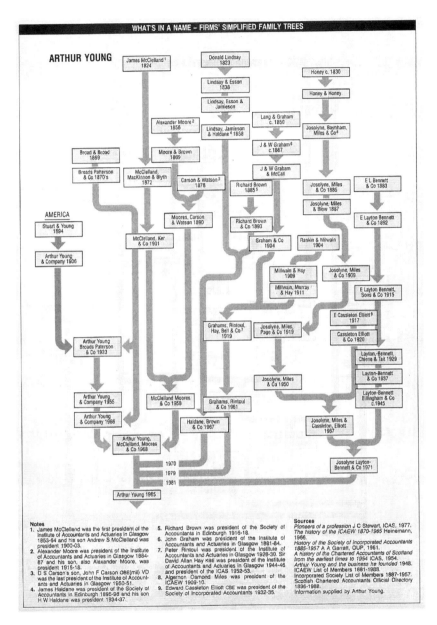

FIGURE 5.1 Arthur Young family tree
Source: *Accountancy*, January 1989, p. 102. www.icaew.com/~/media/corporate/files/library/subjects/accounting%20history/family%20trees/family%20tree%20arthur%20young.ashx; reproduced with permission.

Association of Public Accountants, which later became the American Institute of Certified Public Accountants (AICPA), was established in 1887. But companies were not required to file certified balance sheets and profit-and-loss statements until the adoption of the Securities Act of 1933. For the consulting activities of these firms the fact that they were part of their own professionalized field was both a blessing and a curse. A blessing because it gave them legitimacy as well as easy client access, due to what today is referred to as cross-selling of services. A curse because it forced them to fulfill the certification requirements in accounting and made it very difficult to develop their own identity and/or independent organizational field, causing significant internal strife as these activities became important, even preponderant from the 1970s onwards (see McDougald and Greenwood 2012; Chapters 11 and 14).

None of this was yet visible or even predictable in the nineteenth and early twentieth century, when the consulting activities carried out by accountants were still marginal. Judging from the rather rare accounts in the extant histories of the larger firms that gradually came to dominate the profession during the latter half of the twentieth century, their early advisory work seems to have happened on an occasional, even accidental rather than frequent and systematic basis, and was often tagged on to their primary activity (see, for examples of such "special assignments" at Price Waterhouse in the UK, Jones 1995: 57–58). Often, these consulting activities appear to have been related to bankruptcy and insolvency work. A good example is given in the history of the Canadian firm Clarkson Gordon, which goes back to a trustee and receivership business established by Thomas Gordon in Toronto in 1864 and became allied with Arthur Young in 1944. After the founder's death, the business was continued by his son Edward Roper Curzon (E. R. C.) Clarkson (1852–1931), whose "*advice and counsel* were particularly sought by financial institutions" (MacKenzie 1989: 19; emphasis added), because, according to the company's own history:

> [h]e was able to wind up insolvent businesses quickly and realize cash for the creditors. However, he did not think this policy was good for the banks and other large creditors, or indeed the country as a whole. He finally persuaded one of the banks to let him manage a company that was in difficulty, instead of winding it up. His success in guiding the enterprise out of trouble was vitally important to the small community where it was located and, at the same time, saved a profitable client for the bank.

Other examples are related to the provision of external expertise. This was the case of Charles Waldo Haskins and Elijah Watt Sells who, between 1893 and 1895, served as experts to the so-called Dockery–Cockrell Commission, which aimed at examining and improving the accounting systems and organization of the US government (Kraines 1954). They subsequently established a partnership offering similar services, which eventually, in the 1970s, combined with the UK firm Deloitte.

64 Diverse Origins

Despite their marginality at the outset, these activities deserve to be mentioned here for two reasons: First of all, accountants remained a constant among those providing consulting services – gradually moving from the margins of the field to its center. Second and relatedly, the complex and often contentious relationship between accounting as an established profession and the emerging and evolving management consulting field had its origins in this period. Nevertheless, during the late nineteenth and early twentieth century the consulting activities of the accounting firms paled in comparison to another professionalized group, the engineers.

Scientific Management and the "Efficiency Experts"

The United States as the Seedbed

As noted above, the first more visible development of management consulting activities occurred in conjunction with the emergence of so-called scientific management in the United States and is usually tied to the ideas and activities of Frederick W. Taylor. The US became the birthplace of scientific management mainly due to its leading role in the creation of large-scale organizations in the second industrial revolution, which supplied fast growing urban markets with packaged consumer goods, including many food items, and, from the early twentieth century onwards, automobiles, and also produced the necessary inputs, such as steel and machinery (see Chapter 2). The challenge of distance – between the sources of supply, located within the country, and demand, mainly situated on its coast – was overcome through the construction of an extensive railway as well as telegraph and, later on, telephone network. The railways – and their need for close coordination and control – also became a kind of training ground for those carrying out these tasks. Managers, usually trained as engineers, became "the visible hand" coordinating the speedy flow from raw materials to manufacturing based on capital-intensive technologies, followed by the distribution and marketing of both producer and consumer goods. The self-perception and underlying ideology of this new social group quickly penetrated not only these corporations but also everyday life and society.

Engineering has probably even deeper historical roots than accounting – in its simplest manifestations being as old as humanity. Likewise, it developed and increasingly diversified in conjunction with the industrial revolutions – with chemical and electrical engineering following the earlier civil, i.e., construction, and mechanical engineering. All of them formed professional associations (see, e.g., Noble 1977). The establishment of the American Society of Mechanical Engineers (ASME) in 1880 is of particular interest in this context, since its meetings became the forum for discussions on how to best address the increasing tensions between engineering trained managers and workers in the sprouting large corporations. Increasingly organized and unionized workers collectively demanded higher wages and/or individually reduced their effort, leading to lower productivity. There was no obvious solution since mechanization was capital intensive and standard piece-rates – increasingly introduced in lieu of time-based wages – were largely arbitrary and potentially wrong.

Various ASME members therefore developed and presented more sophisticated systems to increase efficiency, while determining an appropriate as well as fair remuneration of workers (see for this and the following, among others, Noble 1977; Kanigel 1997). Taylor was not the first, when proposing his time-study-based "piece-rate system" in 1895 – followed by "shop management" in 1903. He was preceded by others, including Henry R. Towne and his ideas for "gain-sharing" in 1889 and Frederick Arthur Halsey with "the premium plan" in 1891. All three were originally published in the society's *Transactions* and re-printed together by the American Economic Association (Towne, Halsey, and Taylor 1896).

In order to increase efficiency, Towne (1844–1924), an industrialist, advocated a more systematic management as well as profit sharing. Halsey (1856–1935) had graduated in mechanical engineering from Cornell University, became the long-time editor of the influential *American Machinist* magazine, and, incidentally, was instrumental in preventing the adoption of the metric system in the US. His premium plan went beyond the extant remuneration of workers in terms of daily wages, piece-work or profit-sharing, all of which he criticized. But it lacked the sophistication of subsequent systems in relying solely on "previous experience" when determining the time required for each piece and paying workers a premium for reducing this time. As a result, it could be implemented more easily and without external assistance – explaining both its subsequent popularity (see Chapter 8) and the lack of related consulting activities. It was Taylor and his ideas, which became widely popular and led to the gradual development of a management consulting field (see Box 5.1).

There is no definite answer in the relevant literature as to why Taylor became the figurehead for all these efforts (e.g., Merkle 1980; Nelson 1980; Kanigel 1997). His popularity probably resulted from a combination of factors, including the social connections from his upbringing in a wealthy Philadelphia family and, more importantly, his credibility due to an extensive practical experience as a worker, supervisor, and manager as well as consultant. There was also his suggestion, if not promise that the proposed system would be "a partial step toward the solution of the labor problem," so the sub-title to his 1895 paper and a theme more fully developed in his 1911 book *The Principles of Scientific Management* (Taylor 1911). Moreover, his system received increasing public visibility. Thus, in 1910 future Supreme Court judge Louis Brandeis referred to it when arguing before the Interstate Commerce Commission for an increase in efficiency rather than an increase in rail freight rates. Incidentally, it was at this occasion that Brandeis coined the term "scientific management," which Taylor then used in his book. Moreover, in 1912 Taylor was invited as a witness to the congressional hearings about the resistance from workers at the government-owned Watertown Arsenal against the implementation of his system (Aitken 1960).

BOX 5.1 FREDERICK WINSLOW TAYLOR: THE GRANDFATHER OF MANAGEMENT CONSULTING

Taylor was born to a wealthy Quaker family in Philadelphia in 1856. His father was a lawyer, educated at Princeton, and his mother, born Winslow, drew her ancestry back to one of the pilgrims on the Mayflower. Originally home-schooled, Taylor studied and travelled in Europe before entering a private academy in New Hampshire in 1872 to prepare for the entrance examinations to Harvard. He passed them in 1874 and could have followed in his father's footsteps as a lawyer but, for reasons still being debated, he chose a very different path and entered a pump-making company in Philadelphia, owned by family friends. After completing his apprenticeship there in 1878, he started a career at the Midvale Steel Works, which were part-owned by another family friend, Edward Clark, whose son Clarence married Taylor's sister. Benefitting from this relationship, Taylor quickly rose through the ranks: machine-shop laborer, time clerk, machinist, gang boss, foreman, research director, and, finally, chief engineer. It was as a foreman that Taylor apparently realized the workers' tendency toward "soldiering," i.e., producing less than possible, and began to study ways to improve efficiency focusing on both men and machines. Meanwhile, he continued his high-society life, winning, for instance, together with his brother-in-law, the doubles tournament at the first US national tennis championships in 1881. In 1883, he obtained a mechanical engineering degree by correspondence from the Stevens Institute of Technology in Hoboken, NJ, and, in 1884, got married. When Edward Clark sold his share in Midvale in 1890, Taylor was forced to leave and began his career as an independent consultant, while trying to systematize and disseminate his ideas, namely through presentations at ASME. In 1898 he joined Bethlehem Steel to deal with a capacity problem, which he and his team solved by developing "high speed steel." Disagreements with other managers prompted him to leave less than three years later. Subsequently, he focused exclusively on speaking, writing, and consulting, reaching much wider audiences after the Eastern Rate case in 1910 and the congressional hearings about the Watertown Arsenal strikes in 1912 brought him and his system nationwide notoriety (see below). He also lectured regularly at the newly established Harvard Business School and Dartmouth's Tuck School. Aged 59, he died of pneumonia in March 1915.

Sources: Urwick and Brech (1945: Chapter III); Nelson (1980); Kanigel (1997).

Last not least, there was Taylor's early death, which made others focus on the myth rather than the man. He had also created an institutional structure that was to preserve and perpetuate his legacy. After having been its – somewhat controversial – president in 1906–1907, Taylor became increasingly estranged from ASME and, with like-minded efficiency engineers, in 1911 established the "Society to Promote the Science of Management," which was renamed Taylor Society after his death (see also Chapter 8). Moreover, the engineers promoting his or their own ideas as independent consultants also contributed to a propagation of scientific management – or, as it also came to be called, Taylorism – first in the US and then, increasingly, elsewhere.

Consulting Emergent: Many Individuals and One Firm

Taylor's own activity as a consultant was limited to the period between 1890 and 1898, when he first worked as in-house adviser for a Philadelphia-based investment company that owned and operated paper mills in Wisconsin and Maine. From 1893 onwards he worked independently, with a business card stating: "Consulting Engineer – Systematizing Shop Management and Manufacturing Costs a Specialty" (Kanigel 1997: 269). But he never saw consulting as his major activity – and neither did he depend on it financially given his family wealth. His main interest lay in developing and disseminating his ideas in different ways, namely through publications and lectures. It was others who tried to implement his system in a wide range of organizations, including the Watertown Arsenal. But even their success was limited. Thus, a survey conducted after Taylor's death in 1915 showed that only 113 plants applied the full system (Thompson 1917). A more recent analysis covering the 1920s came to similar conclusions, also pointing to the fact that it was most used, not surprisingly, in labor-intensive and batch production (Nelson 1991).

Nevertheless, Taylor and his system did matter, since they inspired others in the broad scientific management movement to also disseminate their ideas through consulting – a necessity rather than an option for many of them. Among the early pioneers with a lasting impact was Henry L. Gantt (1861–1919), who graduated as a mechanical engineer from the Stevens Institute of Technology, initially worked in industry, including at Midvale Steel as an assistant to Taylor, with whom he maintained a lifelong association. Between 1902 and his early death in 1919, aged 58, he offered his services as, in his words, "a consulting engineer for economical shop management and for time-, cost-, and record-keeping," carrying out a total of about 50 assignments, based on his own "task and bonus" scheme. He is most famous though for his "Gantt Chart," a graphical tool to monitor the progress of projects, designed during World War I while working for the US government to increase the effectiveness of war production (Urwick and Brech 1945: Chapter VII; see also Chapter 8).

68 Diverse Origins

The Gilbreths, Frank Bunker (1868–1924) and Lillian Moller (1878–1972), are another interesting example (see Box 5.2). Unbeknownst to many, they have been immortalized in the books *Cheaper by the Dozen* and *Belles on their Toes* (Gilbreth and Carey 1948, 1950) written by two of their 12 children, recounting their lives and showing how they applied scientific management to run such an extensive family. Urwick and Brech (1945: 126) characterized Frank Gilbreth "with Taylor and Gantt as the third point in the triangular foundation on which the full science of management was built," pointing in particular to his development of "motion studies" (Urwick and Brech 1945: Chapter XII; see also Tisdall 1982: 16–20). Despite being admitted to the Massachusetts Institute of Technology, Gilbreth chose to become a bricklayer's apprentice and, similar to Taylor, quickly moved up the ranks while observing and improving work practices. Influenced by Brandeis and Taylor, he became a consultant in 1912, soon joined by his spouse, who had a strong academic background and interest in psychology (see Box 5.2), which complemented his own practical experience. Together they developed a classification of 18 movements called "therblig," i.e., Gilbreth spelled backwards with 'th' transposed, which they applied to develop optimal motions that minimized worker fatigue – an approach they also tried to clearly distinguish from Taylor's (Price 1992). Both offered their advice to companies in the US and Europe (see below). After her husband's early death, aged 54, Lillian Gilbreth continued to globally promote these ideas – and scientific management more generally – as a writer, teacher, and consultant for almost five additional decades (see also Chapter 8).

And there was Clarence Bertrand Thompson (1882–1969), who had written the above mentioned survey on Taylor's ideas and their application (Thompson 1917; see for the following Wren et al. 2015). Grandson of a slave, he obtained a law degree from the University of California and also graduated in Sociology and in Economics from Harvard. He became a Unitarian minister but left service and wrote a book on *The Churches and the Wage Earner* (Thompson 1909). Having been introduced to Taylorism by Boston department store owner Edward A. Filene, he began researching scientific management and, in 1910, joined the recently established Harvard Business School (HBS) as a lecturer in manufacturing. Thompson subsequently published many books and articles on Taylor and Taylorism, including in the *Quarterly Journal of Economics* (e.g., Thompson 1915) – some of them critical of Taylor for his alleged "elitist" approach. Thompson seemed destined for an academic career but, in 1916, turned down a full professorship offered by HBS, opting instead for his consulting activities, which he pursued in France after the end of World War I (see Chapter 8).

BOX 5.2 LILLIAN GILBRETH: FIRST LADY OF MANAGEMENT

Lillian Gilbreth was born in 1878 as the daughter of a well-to-do family in Oakland, California. She studied English at the University of California and received a Master's degree with a thesis on Ben Jonson's *Bartholomew Fayre*. In 1904 she married the 10-year older Frank Bunker Gilbreth, whom she had met accidentally. They developed a close collaboration, where he brought in the methods to save labor he had developed in the construction industry and she contributed knowledge in psychology. In 1911 she completed her doctoral thesis, "The Psychology of Management," at the University of California. However, since she had not complied with residency requirements, she was not awarded a Ph.D. The thesis was nevertheless published in the *Industrial Engineering Magazine* in 1912–1913 and, again, in 1914 as a monograph by L. B. Gilbreth – to hide the fact that the author was a woman. In the meantime, she worked on a second dissertation at Brown University, and received her Ph.D. there in 1915 with a thesis on "Some Aspects of Eliminating Waste in Teaching." She was also working with Frank in the consulting business he had started in 1912. Together, they published a number of books such as *Fatigue Study* (1916), *Applied Motion Study* (1917) and *Motion Study for the Handicapped* (1920). After Frank's death in 1924, she continued their joint work as well as caring for their remaining 11 children. She even took his place at conferences in Europe shortly after he died. In addition, she replaced him as visiting lecturer at Purdue University and, between 1935 and 1948, was Professor of Management there. In her later work she focused on home economics through publications such as *The Home-Maker and Her Job* (1927) and *Management in the Home* (1954) and through consulting. She remained active well beyond "normal" retirement and died in 1972, aged 93. Quite tellingly, one observer (Graham 1996: 1607) called her the "First Lady of Management."

Sources: Graham (1996); Lancaster (2004).

All of these, like hundreds of lesser-known efficiency engineers, operated on their own or as small, ad-hoc, and temporary networks (Nelson 1991). The notable exception was the firm established in 1907 by Harrington Emerson (1853–1931), which became the first more substantial consulting organization and, by 1918, employed 30 engineers in five "agencies" located in New York, Pittsburgh, Chicago, Philadelphia, and Tacoma, while also drawing on a variety of "affiliated specialists" for different projects (Quigel 1992: 289–294; see also Wright and Kipping 2012). Like Taylor, Emerson was born into an affluent family in Trenton, New Jersey in 1853. His father was a Professor of Political Science and his mother the daughter of a US Congressman and Treasury Secretary. And, again like Taylor, he spent part of his school years in Europe, and then

70 Diverse Origins

studied engineering in Munich between 1872 and 1875. Upon his return he became Professor of Modern Languages at the University of Nebraska but was dismissed in 1882, apparently for his overly progressive views on education. He remained in the West, trying his hand at a wide range of jobs, including as a tax agent, frontier banker, and land speculator – with little success. He returned to the East in 1897 and worked for the Electric Storage Battery Company in New York, but left again to join in the Alaskan Gold Rush of 1899 – once again to no avail.

Upon his return to New York, Emerson decided to focus on the emerging area of scientific management, which he had followed as a member of the American Society of Mechanical Engineers and seen applied in some of the ventures he was involved in. He gradually developed his own ideas, which he published in various articles and books, including, in 1919, *Efficiency as a Basis for Operation and Wages* (for a comparison with Taylor, see Witzel 2002). His first important client was the Santa Fe Railroad, where he introduced an incentive and bonus system between 1904 and 1907, helped by his brother Samuel and other time study engineers (Quigel 1992: Chapter 3). The visibility of this project drew new clients, which eventually came to include household names like the Aluminum Company of America (Alcoa), Bethlehem Steel, and General Motors. In 1907, he hired additional efficiency engineers and established a firm under the name "Emerson Company Engineers," changed to "Emerson Efficiency Engineers" in 1913 (Quigel 1992: Chapter 5). It had a deliberately commercial orientation, focusing on "achieving immediate gains and meeting the specific needs of clients," which according to Quigel (1992: 279), "not only facilitated management's acceptance of efficiency engineering but *also expanded the role of the consulting engineer*" (emphasis added).

Thus, Emerson set up the first large – by the standards of the time – multi-office consulting organization. Equally if not more importantly, his "Emerson Efficiency Engineers" also stood out, because they were the first to pursue a predominantly commercial logic – as compared to what could be called the ideological, or even missionary logic that drove most other proponents of scientific management, who mainly saw consulting as *one* way to disseminate their systems and underlying beliefs. This might, incidentally, be the reason why Taylor disdained Emerson's ideas (Quigel 1992: 146) and why Urwick and Brech (1945) left him off the list of scientific management pioneers. Both logics also expanded abroad – albeit in different ways.

Spreading the Gospel – and the Business

Given the almost missionary zeal with which many of the proponents of scientific management aimed at disseminating their ideas, including through consulting, it should not come as a surprise that they also came to spread them outside the US (see especially Merkle 1980). These ideas fell on fertile ground, since engineers in many countries had been struggling with similar issues. Taylor's *Principles of*

Accountants and Efficiency Engineers 71

Scientific Management was quickly translated and published in a wide range of countries (see Guillén 1994 and Chapter 6). The rapid expansion of Taylorism beyond its country of origin was facilitated by the global network of engineers, many of whom travelled internationally, met at world exhibitions – like the one in Paris in 1900 – or participated in international standards bodies.

Among the countries particularly receptive to Taylor's ideas was France, which also became a secondary center for their spread in countries like Spain and Turkey. The technically oriented French engineers were initially drawn to Taylor because of the "high speed steel" he had developed, but also came to espouse his more general suggestions because of their "rational" nature (see Moutet 1975; Merkle 1980: Chapter 5; and, in detail, Henry 2012). Among his early acolytes was the renowned chemist Henry Le Châtelier (1850–1936), who published translations of Taylor's writings, initially in the *Revue de métallurgie*, then as separate books, and also invited Taylor to France in 1913. While Le Châtelier was soon joined by other enthusiastic engineers and industrialists, the application of Taylor's and other systems was often resisted by workers due to its "speed-up." Moreover, Taylor's French followers had to contend with those espousing the ideas of French mining engineer Henri Fayol (1841–1925), whose suggestions on industrial and general administration or *Administration industrielle et générale*, first published in 1916, aimed beyond the shop floor and came closer to what we today understand as management – with a focus on planning, coordinating and controlling (see Chapter 2). But despite the significant interest in Taylorism in France – as well as the UK and Germany, there is little evidence to suggest that the activities of consulting engineers in these countries went much beyond technical advice (Kipping 1997).

When it came to the international diffusion of scientific management, there was also some "insourcing," namely people travelling to the US from other parts of the world to acquaint themselves with the new ideas and systems. Take the case of Japan – a country that had started to industrialize only in the late nineteenth century (see, for the following, Tsutsui 1998: Chapter 1). The pioneers in introducing the new methods were companies, like Nippon Electric, that had US joint venture partners and – not surprisingly – the railways in their repair shops. Interest was such that a narrative booklet promoting American methods for efficiency improvement published by a former Japanese employee of Wrigley Chewing Gum, who had toured the US in 1911, sold more than one million copies. That same year, another Japanese visitor, Hoshino Yukinori from Kajima Trust Bank, obtained Taylor's permission to translate and publish *The Principles of Scientific Management*. This translation, which appeared in 1913, was followed by others, including Gilbreth's *Motion Study* (Gilbreth 1911), prompting one observer to state that "efficiency increase" had "become an expression very much in vogue" in the country (quoted in Tsutsui 1998: 19). Possibly even more important in the long run were a large number of fellowships sponsored by the government for Japanese to learn Western commercial and technological skills, with

72 Diverse Origins

over two hundred of them sent to the US. Upon their return, most went back to their companies, but some also operated as individual consultants in the subsequent period (see Chapter 8).

Even more consequential in hindsight was the trip by the Italian engineer A. M. Morrini to the US to study the various efficiency systems there during the winter of 1912–1913. He toured factories on the East coast, then went with a few Emerson engineers to Paris, setting up a small consulting office there – apparently the first of its kind in France (Christy 1984: 27–35; see also Moutet 1975: 31–33, who characterized Morinni [sic] as American). After the outbreak of World War I, they closed the operation and returned to the US. This case is worth mentioning, because it illustrates the notoriety of the Emerson system and consulting firm as well as the international flow of consulting engineers. It had an even more important – somewhat serendipitous – impact, because the person who accompanied Morrini on his US tour and the Emerson engineers to France as an assistant and interpreter, was Charles E. Bedaux (1886–1944). Building on the knowledge and relationships gained in this role, Bedaux would create the largest, internationally active consulting firm during the subsequent period (see Chapter 8).

Thus, at the outset of World War I a management consulting field had started to take shape in the US – largely populated by professional engineers, who tried to promote scientific management with a kind of missionary zeal. This period also saw the modest beginnings of a somewhat more commercial logic in the form of the Emerson Efficiency Engineers. And while scientific management as an idea quickly expanded internationally – mainly through interchanges between engineers and their travels, outside the US consulting as an activity remained largely confined to a more technical side. The war brought a temporary halt to the international flows, but it also prompted a growing interest in efficiency – an interest that formed the basis for renewed expansion during the interwar period encompassing both the missionary logic and, increasingly, the commercial one.

References

Aitken, H. (1960) *Taylorism at Watertown Arsenal: Scientific management in action, 1908–1915*, Cambridge, MA: Harvard University Press.

Allen, D. G. and McDermott, K. (1993) *Accounting for Success: A history of Price Waterhouse in America 1890–1990*, Boston, MA: Harvard Business School Press.

Christy, J. (1984) *The Price of Power: A biography of Charles Eugène Bedaux*, Toronto: Doubleday.

Coffee, J. C. (2006) *Gatekeepers: The professions and corporate governance*, Oxford: Oxford University Press.

David, R. J., Sine, W. D., and Haveman, H. A. (2013) "Seizing opportunity in emerging fields: How institutional entrepreneurs legitimated the professional form of management consulting," *Organization Science*, 24(2): 356–377.

Emerson, H. (1919) *Efficiency as a Basis for Operation and Wages*, New York: The Engineering Magazine.

Fayol, H. (1916) "Administration industrielle et générale: prévoyance, organisation, commandement, coordination, contrôle," *Bulletin de la Société de l'Industrie minérale*, Saint-Étienne: Société de l'industrie minérale.

Fink, D. and Knoblach, B. (2003) *Die grossen Management Consultants: Ihre Geschichte, ihre Konzepte, ihre Strategien*, Munich: Franz Vahlen.

Gilbreth, F. B. (1911) *Motion Study: A method for increasing the efficiency of the workman*, London: Constable.

Gilbreth, F. B., Jr and Carey, E. G. (1948) *Cheaper by the Dozen*, New York: T.Y. Crowell.

Gilbreth, F. B., Jr and Carey, E. G. (1950) *Belles on Their Toes*, London: Heinemann.

Gilbreth, F. B. and Gilbreth, L. M. (1916) *Fatigue Study*, New York: Sturgis & Walton.

Gilbreth, F. B. and Gilbreth, L. M. (1917) *Applied Motion Study*, New York: Sturgis & Walton.

Gilbreth, F. B. and Gilbreth, L. M. (1920) *Motion Study for the Handicapped*, New York: Macmillan.

Gilbreth, L. M. (1927) *The Home-Maker and Her Job*, New York: D. Appleton.

Gilbreth, L. M., Thomas, O. M., and Clymer, E. (1954) *Management in the Home: Happier living through saving time and energy*, New York: Dodd, Mead.

Graham, P. (1996) "Gilbreth, Frank Bunker (1868–1924) and Gilbreth, Lillian Evelyn Moller (1878–1972)," in M. Warner (ed.), *International Encyclopedia of Business & Management*, London: Routledge, pp. 1606–1611.

Gronke, H. and Häußner, J. (2006) "Socratic coaching in business and management consulting practice," *Practical Philosophy*, 8(1): 28–38.

Guillén, M. F. (1994) *Models of Management: Work, authority and organization in a comparative perspective*, Chicago, IL: University of Chicago Press.

Henry, O. (2012) *Les guérisseurs de l'économie: Ingénieurs-conseil en quête de pouvoir*, Paris: CNRS Éditions.

Jones, E. (1995) *True and Fair: A history of Price Waterhouse*, London: Hamish Hamilton.

Kahn, E. J., Jr (1986) *The Problem Solvers: A history of Arthur D. Little, Inc.*, Boston, MA: Little, Brown and Company.

Kanigel, R. (1997) *The One Best Way: Frederick Winslow Taylor and the enigma of efficiency*, New York: Viking.

Kipping, M. (1997) "Consultancies, institutions and the diffusion of Taylorism in Britain, Germany and France, 1920s to 1950s," *Business History*, 39(4): 67–83.

Klein, H. J. (1977) *Other People's Business: A primer on management consultants*, New York: Mason/Charter.

Kraines, O. (1954) "The Dockery-Cockrell Commission, 1893–1895," *The Western Political Quarterly*, 7(3): 417–462.

Lancaster, J. (2004) *Making Time: Lillian Moller Gilbreth, a life beyond "Cheaper by the dozen,"* Boston, MA: Northeastern University Press.

MacKenzie, D. (1989) *The Clarkson Gordon Story, 1864–1989*, Toronto: Clarkson Gordon.

Marsh, S. (2009) *The Feminine in Management Consulting: Power, emotion and values in consulting interactions*, Basingstoke: Palgrave Macmillan.

McDougald, M. S. and Greenwood, R. (2012) "Cuckoo in the nest? The rise of management consulting in large accounting firms," in M. Kipping and T. Clark (eds), *The Oxford Handbook of Management Consulting*, Oxford: Oxford University Press, pp. 93–116.

McKenna, C. D. (1995) "The origins of modern management consulting," *Business and Economic History*, 24(1): 51–58.

Merkle, J. E. (1980) *Management and Ideology: The legacy of the international scientific management movement*, Berkeley, CA: University of California Press.

Moutet, A. (1975) "Les origines du système de Taylor en France: Le point de vue patronal (1907–1914)," *Le mouvement social*, 93 (October–December): 15–49.

Nelson, D. (1980) *Frederick W. Taylor and the Rise of Scientific Management*, Madison, WI: University of Wisconsin Press.

Nelson, D. (1991) "Scientific management and the workplace, 1920–1935," in S. Jacoby (ed.), *Masters to Managers*, New York: Columbia University Press, pp. 74–89.

Noble, D. F. (1977) *America by Design: Science, technology, and the rise of corporate capitalism*, New York: Alfred A. Knopf.

Pindur, W., Rogers, S. E., and Kim, P. S. (1995) "The history of management: A global perspective," *Journal of Management History*, 1(1): 59–77.

Price, B. (1992) "Frank and Lillian Gilbreth and the Motion Study Controversy, 1907–1930," in D. Nelson (ed.), *A Mental Revolution: Scientific management since Taylor*, Columbus, OH: Ohio State University Press, pp. 58–76.

Quigel, J. P. (1992) *The Business of Selling Efficiency: Harrington Emerson and the Emerson efficiency engineers, 1900–1930*, Doctoral dissertation, State College, PA: Pennsylvania State University.

Taylor, F. W. (1911) *The Principles of Scientific Management*, New York: Harper and Brothers.

Thompson, C. B. (1909) *The Churches and the Wage Earners: A study of the causes and cure of their separation*, New York: Charles Scribner's Sons.

Thompson, C. B. (1915) "Scientific management in practice," *Quarterly Journal of Economics*, 29(2): 262–307.

Thompson, C. B. (1917) *The Theory and Practice of Scientific Management*, Boston, MA: Houghton Mifflin.

Tisdall, P. (1982) *Agents of Change: The development and practice of management Consultancy*, London: Heinemann.

Towne, H. R., Halsey, F. A., and Taylor, F. W. (1896) "The adjustment of wages to efficiency: Three papers on gain-sharing, the premium plan, a piece rate system," *Economic Studies*, 1(2), New York: Macmillan.

Tsutsui, W. M. (1998) *Manufacturing Ideology: Scientific management in twentieth-century Japan*, Princeton, NJ: Princeton University Press.

Urwick, L. and Brech, E. F. L. (1945) *The Making of Scientific Management*, vol. I: *Thirteen Pioneers*, London: Management Publications Trust.

Witzel, M. (2002) "A short history of efficiency," *Business Strategy Review*, 13(4): 38–47.

Wren, D. A., Greenwood, R. A., Teahen, J., and Bedeian, A. G. (2015) "C. Bertrand Thompson and management consulting in Europe, 1917–1934," *Journal of Management History*, 21(1): 15–39.

Wright, C. and Kipping, M. (2012) "The engineering origins of management consulting and their long shadow," in M. Kipping and T. Clark (eds), *The Oxford Handbook of Management Consulting*, Oxford: Oxford University Press, pp. 29–49.

6

MODEST BEGINNINGS FOR BUSINESS PUBLISHING

This chapter will examine how commercial *publishers* that today play a significant role emerged in the nineteenth and the early twentieth century as small private ventures and trace their first steps into the printing and distribution of business and management publications, a field they soon came to share, for academic output, with a number of university presses. The chapter will also look at the *business press*, which originally aimed to disseminate economic information and analysis on growing stock and commodity markets. And it will discuss how certain *academic journals*, namely in economics, emanating from professional organizations or academic presses, became the first to publish texts related to business and management, particularly in their review sections. Moreover, these academic journals took an interest in the curricula for the teaching in schools of commerce, which, as the chapter will also show, is only one example of the multiple interplays between publishing and the other two authorities during this period.

Frontrunners in Business and Management Publishing

The Origin of Four Significant Publishing Houses

In the nineteenth century a number of publishing houses, which later on would become significant for business and management publishing, were established as small family businesses taking the names of their often rather young founders (Table 6.1): Wiley (1807), Harper (1817), Macmillan (1843), and McGraw-Hill (1889). While originally focusing on other areas, they eventually came to realize the potential for books in what would become management, in particular those related to "scientific management" and its figurehead Frederick W. Taylor (see Chapter 5).

76 Diverse Origins

TABLE 6.1 Foundations of Four Early Publishers in Management

Name	Founded	Founder(s)	Location	Early publications
Wiley	1807	Charles Wiley	New York	Taylor and Thompson (1905) and Taylor (1912)
Harper	1817	James and John Harper	New York	Taylor (1911a and b)
Macmillan	1843	Daniel and Alexander Macmillan	London	Hoover (1916)
McGraw-Hill	1889	James H. McGraw and John Hill	New York	Going (1911), Diemer (1914)

Sources: Exman (1967); Moore (1982); Abbott (2001); James (2002); Jacobson et al. (2007); McGraw Hill Financial, 5 May 2015.

The oldest among them, Wiley, was started in 1807 by Charles Wiley (1782–1826), who in his mid-20s set up a printing shop on Manhattan in New York (see further Moore 1982; Jacobson et al. 2007). Originally oriented towards the publication of American literature, he began in the 1820s to publish titles in science, technology, and medicine. The latter profile was further developed by the founder's sons, who for obvious reasons changed the name of the company to the present one: Wiley & Sons. Through its orientation towards scientific publications Wiley in the early 1900s had become a leading publisher in the United States in science and technology. The company was therefore well prepared to move into the publishing of texts in the social sciences and business (Wiley 5 May 2015). Early manifestations of this were two books by Frederick W. Taylor, who would become the "guru" of scientific management (see Box 5.1), on the use and costs of concrete (Taylor and Thompson 1905; Taylor 1912). According to a reviewer, the first of these contained a text "on time study and valuable tables of unit times determined in accordance with the Taylor method" (Jacobson et al. 2007: 129).

Harper was started nine years after Wiley, in 1817, by two brothers in their 20s: James Harper (1795–1869) and John Harper (1797–1875) (see, for this and the following Exman 1967 and Abbott 2001). Like Charles Wiley they started up their printing business on Manhattan. They became well-known through their publishing of popular magazines like *Harper's New Monthly Magazine* (1850), *Harper's Weekly* (1857), *Harper's Bazaar* (1867), and *Harper's Young People* (1879). Their publishing also included authors of fiction, Mark Twain among others, as well as non-fiction. Harper's foray into business and management is once again related to Frederick W. Taylor, since it published two of his – subsequently most widely spread – books in 1911: *Shop Management* and *The Principles of Scientific Management* (Taylor 1911a and 1911b).

On the other side of the Atlantic, Macmillan was founded in London in 1843 by the two Scottish brothers Daniel Macmillan (1813–1857) and Alexander

Macmillan (1818–1896) (see, for details, James 2002). They managed to attract a number of authors, who came to fame through their publications, including Lewis Carroll, Charles Kingsley, Rudyard Kipling, and Francis Turner Palgrave. Macmillan also launched *Macmillan's Magazine*, which eventually became today's highly prestigious scientific journal *Nature*. Like the other publishers mentioned above, they started including business-related books in the early twentieth century, publishing, among others, *The Nature of Capital and Income* by the neo-classical economist Irving Fisher (Fisher 1906), Lillian Gilbreth's first doctoral dissertation from 1911, *The Psychology of Management* (Gilbreth 1914), and Simon Robert Hoover's *The Science and Art of Salesmanship* (Hoover 1916). Among these authors, Gilbreth is particularly worth noting, since she has been characterized as the "First Lady of Management" (see Box 5.2).

McGraw-Hill has its roots in railway industry publishing in 1888, when James H. McGraw (1860–1948) bought the *American Journal of Railway Appliances*, and his partner-to-be John Hill (1858–1916) was working as an editor at the *Locomotive Engineer* (see McGraw Hill Financial 5 May 2015). Around 1900 they both founded publishing companies carrying their names, combining their book departments in 1909 and merging the two companies in 1917. Based on their earlier interest in railways they published Charles Buxton Going's *Principles of Industrial Engineering* (Going 1911) and Hugo Diemer's *Factory Organization and Administration* (Diemer 1914).

The Four Publishing Houses in Context

Another feature of the period was that universities started their own presses. This development had its origins in the United Kingdom in the sixteenth century through the foundations of Cambridge University Press and Oxford University Press (see Box 6.1).

In the nineteenth century a number of universities, particularly in the United States, followed in their footsteps (Jagodzinski 2008): Cornell in 1869, Johns Hopkins in 1878, Chicago in 1891, Stanford in 1892, the University of California, Columbia, and Northwestern in 1893 as well as Liverpool University in the UK in 1899. In the early twentieth century further establishments of university presses were made by the universities of Manchester in 1904, Princeton in 1905, Yale in 1908, Harvard in 1913, Washington in 1915, and New York in 1916 (see Table 6.2). These organizations aimed at facilitating the publication of the work of their faculty members. As will be pointed out below, two of them – University of Chicago Press and Cambridge University Press – were early to publish journals in economic sciences.

78 Diverse Origins

BOX 6.1 CAMBRIDGE UNIVERSITY PRESS AND OXFORD UNIVERSITY PRESS

Cambridge University Press (CUP) and Oxford University Press (OUP) constitute two significant players in publishing with long traditions. For CUP it started in 1534 with Henry VIII granting to print "all manner books," and the publishing of the first book in 1584. This makes CUP the oldest still existing publisher in the world. Oxford University Press followed closely after CUP, receiving its printing grant in 1586, and has since then developed into the largest university press in the world. During the early centuries CUP published academic texts as well as other texts, among them the Bible. The printing of the Bible was also a fundamental base for OUP after it had received the right in the seventeenth century to print the King James Authorized Version of the Bible. Later on in the 1870s and 1880s OUP collaborated with CUP to publish the revised version of the Bible. In the late nineteenth century both presses started an expansion by broadening their publishing. Cambridge University Press turned into a significant educational and academic publisher, publishing in 2015, according to its web page, "over 50,000 titles covering academic research, professional development, over 350 research journals, school-level education, English language teaching and Bible publishing." As far as OUP is concerned, also according to its web page, it puts out 6,000 titles a year world-wide and publishes more than 300 academic journals, many of the latter in collaboration with professional associations. Both CUP and OUP have over time become quite active in the publishing of management texts (see below, particularly Chapter 15). Nowadays, they are highly internationalized with offices around the globe. In relation to the rest of the actors in the media business the two British university presses have the particular advantage of being part of their universities – meaning they have not been subject to the mergers and acquisitions that have become so common within the media industry (see Chapter 15).

Sources: Sutcliffe (1978); Cambridge University Press 28 September 2015; Oxford University Press 28 September 2015.

In addition to the above mentioned publishers, a number of others were founded in the early period. Some of them – like the German Springer, established in Berlin in 1842 (Götze 1996), the Dutch Elsevier, founded in Amsterdam in 1880, and the German Walter de Gruyter, again in Berlin in 1919 – later on became significant actors in scientific publishing, management included (see further Chapters 9, 12, and 15). Others – like Longman, founded in London in 1724, Collins, in Glasgow in 1819 (Keir 1952), Routledge, in London in 1851, and Blackwell, in Oxford in 1879 – have later on been acquired by larger publishing companies. And, so have Harper, Macmillan, and McGraw-Hill as well as two additional publishers of early business texts, Appleton and the Ronald Press.

Business Publishing **79**

TABLE 6.2 Year of Foundation for Early University Presses

Name	Year of foundation
Cambridge University Press	1584
Oxford University Press	1632
Cornell University Press	1869 (inactive 1884–1930)
Johns Hopkins University Press	1878
University of Chicago Press	1891
Stanford University Press	1892
University of California Press	1893
Columbia University Press	1893
Northwestern University Press	1893
Liverpool University Press	1899
Manchester University Press	1904
Princeton University Press	1905
Yale University Press	1908
Harvard University Press	1913
University of Washington Press	1915
New York University Press	1916

Sources: Sutcliffe (1978) and Jagodzinski (2008).

Appleton, established in New York in 1831, became known for publishing the US edition of *Alice in Wonderland* and the works by Rudyard Kipling as well as by scholars like Charles Darwin, Thomas Huxley, Herbert Spencer, and John Tyndall. Early titles focusing on management were John C. Duncan's *The Principles of Industrial Management* (Duncan 1911) and Robert Franklin Hoxie's *Scientific Management and Labor* (Hoxie 1915), both dealing with management of factory work. The Ronald Press was also established in New York, uncertain when. The founder was probably Hugh Ronald Conyngton, who was an active author of the company, in some cases using his own name (see, e.g., Conyngton 1902 on the modern corporation) and in other cases writing under the pseudonym Francis Cooper (see, e.g., Cooper 1907 on business finance). The titles published were mainly in auditing and accounting (e.g., Montgomery 1912; Nicholson 1913; Esquerre 1914) but also on how to influence men in business (Scott 1911).

The foundings discussed above constitute a modest beginning for today's business publishing – a field that has since undergone considerable restructuring and concentration, particularly in the most recent period, with an exponential expansion in the supply of texts especially in the area of management (see, further Jacobson et al. 2007: 218 and 272). During the early period, by comparison, the share of texts related to business and management, while growing, was still marginal in what can at best be considered an incipient organizational field.

80 Diverse Origins

The Business Press: Specialized Challengers to the Established Newspapers

Four Significant Entrants

Another feature of the early period was that a number of economically oriented newspapers and magazines were started. They aimed at being complementary to general newspapers, which long since had provided economic information on shipping, commodity prices, stock markets, etc. The main establishments in that direction were the *Economist* in 1843 and the *Financial Times* in 1888 in the United Kingdom, and the *Wall Street Journal* in 1889 and *Forbes* in 1917 in the United States (Table 6.3).

The *Economist* was started by James Wilson (1805–1860), a Scotsman raised in a Quaker family (see Edwards 1993). After a business career in London with varying success he began to write on economic issues for newspapers such as the *Manchester Guardian*. This led him in 1843 to establish the *Economist*, where he was especially supporting liberal economic ideas in the capacity of chief editor until 1857. However, already in 1847 he had become a Member of Parliament and soon occupied various government positions. He therefore engaged the philosopher Herbert Spencer (1820–1903) as sub-editor in the 1848–1853 period. By 1900 the *Economist* had gained a position in political and business circles.

Almost half a century later, in 1888, the second now widely acknowledged business publication, the *Financial Times* was founded (Kynaston 1988). It was first named the *London Financial Guide* but almost immediately changed its name to the present one. Founders were the journalist James Sheridan and the financier Horatio Bottomley (1860–1933). At its foundation the *Financial Times* had been preceded a few years by the *Financial News*, a title which would be merged with the *Financial Times* in 1945 (see further Chapter 9). In order to distinguish itself from its competitor, the *Financial Times* chose to start printing on pink paper – a practice which over time has been taken up by other business newspapers. In the early years the *Financial Times* was a four-page publication, almost exclusively addressing the London financial community, but it gradually came to include more and more business news (see Chapters 9, 12, and 15).

TABLE 6.3 Four Economically Oriented Publications Founded in the Early Period

Name	*Country*	*Type*	*Founded*
Economist	United Kingdom	Weekly	1843
Financial Times	United Kingdom	Daily	1888
Wall Street Journal	United States	Daily	1889
Forbes	United States	Weekly	1917

Interestingly enough, the third title in Table 6.3, the *Wall Street Journal* (*WSJ*) was founded in the US in 1889, only one year after the *Financial Times* (see, further Rosenberg 1982; Wendt 1982; Scharff 1986). Similar to the *Financial Times*, the *WSJ* was aimed at providing information to the actors on the financial markets in a four-page newspaper. Behind the project were three journalists in their 30s: Charles Dow (1851–1902), Edward Jones (1856–1920), and Charles Bergenstresser (1858–1923). Of these, Dow and Jones had already in 1882 started today's very well-known company Dow Jones. In 1896 they introduced the Dow Jones Industrial Average, an index of stock market prices, still used today. In 1902 Charles Barron (1855–1928) bought the *WSJ* and became a key figure in developing financial journalism.

Finally, *Forbes* was founded in 1917 by Bertie C. Forbes (1880–1954), who at the time worked as the financial editor of the *New York American* (see further Parsons 1989; Kurtz 2000). *Forbes* was, and still is, published bi-weekly and has a more popular orientation than the other three titles. The latter is underlined by its original title: *Forbes: Devoted to Doers and Doings*.

The Entrants in Context

It is important to point out that the titles in Table 6.3 were established in a field, where there already were a number of established players. In the United Kingdom the *Times* had been in operation since 1785, the *Manchester Guardian* since 1821 and the *Daily Telegraph* since 1855. Similarly, in the United States the *New York Times* has been published since 1851, the *Boston Globe* since 1872 and the *Washington Post* since 1877. Likewise the French have been able to read *Le Figaro* since 1826 and the Swiss had their *Neue Zürcher Zeitung* since 1780. In addition, there were also a number of local titles in both Europe and the United States. In this context the four titles, as indicated above, played on differentiation, i.e., addressed specialized audiences in a world where economic information, particularly on the expanding stock markets, became increasingly demanded.

In relation to all the media outlets, it is important to also mention the suppliers of information, i.e., news agencies. Among these, one international news agency is particularly worthy of attention: Reuters. It was started already in 1849 by Paul Reuter (1816–1899), who by means of telegraphy and carrier pigeons distributed news. In 1851 he founded Reuter's Telegram Company, which was focusing on providing news services to commercial actors. As will be shown in later chapters, Reuters has developed into a very significant player in the market for information (Storey 1969; Lawrenson and Barber 1985; Read 1992; Mooney and Simpson 2003). A similar initiative was taken in Asia. Today's publisher of the Nikkei index for the Tokyo Stock Exchange, *Nihon Kezai Shimbun*, has its roots in the early period through the foundation, in 1876, of an internal weekly for market quotations within the Mitsui Company. It became a company of its own in 1882, turned into a daily publication in 1885, and took its present name after World War II. In 2015 it was the world's largest financial newspaper with a circulation of three million copies. And in July 2015 its owner acquired the *Financial Times* (*Wall Street Journal* 28 July 2015).

Thus, the business press that today constitutes a significant part of the business media started to develop in the early period – largely in response to an emerging demand for economic information resulting from industrialization. In this context the new titles, i.e., the *Economist*, the *Financial Times*, the *Wall Street Journal*, and *Forbes*, provided differentiated services compared to the earlier general newspapers and magazines. At the same time companies that would be significant for the provision and handling of information, namely the US *Dow Jones*, the British *Reuters*, and the Japanese *Nikkei*, also came into being. Similar to the publishing of business and management books, the business press was an emergent field in the United States, the United Kingdom, and other industrialized countries during this period.

Academic Journals: Early Steps Towards Institutionalization

Points of Departure

The establishment of academic journals constitutes a significant indicator for the institutionalization of scientific disciplines. As shown in Figure 6.1, based on Engwall and Hedmo (2016), such establishments can be seen as part of an organizing process. At an early stage, innovators – in different places, at the same time, but independently of each other – move in new directions. After having met resistance in their own academic community, they find like-minded colleagues abroad and informal networks are formed. Over time these networks develop into formal organizations with statutes, boards, fees, and professional meetings. A significant further step is then the launching of a journal. And, as will also be seen in the subsequent chapters on business media, professional associations have played an important role when new journals have been started.

Looking at the emergence of academic journals in business and management we have chosen to focus on those journals that have today become acknowledged in the field. Such an acknowledgment can be measured in many ways. The corresponding chapters in this book have defined it by looking at the list of 45 journals that the *Financial Times* has selected for its rankings of business schools

FIGURE 6.1 A model of the organizing of scientific disciplines

(Financial Times 5 May 2015), since they cover all areas of the increasingly specialized academic discipline of management and include journals that are published outside the US as well.

Five American Frontrunners

On the *FT*45 list there are five titles – all appearing in the United States – that were first published during the early period (Table 6.4): the *Quarterly Journal of Economics* (1886), the *Journal of the American Statistical Association* (1888), the *Journal of Political Economy* (1892), the *American Economic Review* (1911), and the *Journal of Applied Psychology* (1917). Of these five journals, three were the outcomes of the organizing process summarized in Figure 6.1. They were launched by three professional associations founded earlier, i.e., the American Statistical Association, established in 1839, the American Economic Association, in 1885, and the American Psychological Association, in 1892. The remaining two, the *Quarterly Journal of Economics* and the *Journal of Political Economy*, were the result of academic initiatives, started by two universities: Harvard University and the University of Chicago, respectively. The Chicago initiative is particularly remarkable, since it occurred just two years after the foundation of the university in 1890, and six years before the foundation of the business school in 1898 (see Chapter 4).

As their titles indicate, three of the five journals were mainly oriented toward economics. However, they also had some relation to business. Thus, in the first volumes of the *Quarterly Journal of Economics*, the oldest of the economics journals, there were articles on the sources of business profits (Walker 1887), profit-sharing (Giddings 1887), and the theory of capital (Giddings 1890). The same journal also had contributions in two of the early issues on the design of academic studies in

TABLE 6.4 Academic Journals on the *FT*45 List Founded in the Early Period

Name of journal	*Founded*	*First publisher*	*Present publisher*
Quarterly Journal of Economics	1886	Harvard University	Oxford University Press
Journal of the American Statistical Association[a]	1888	American Statistical Association	Taylor & Francis
Journal of Political Economy	1892	University of Chicago	University of Chicago
American Economic Review	1911	American Economic Association	American Economic Association
Journal of Applied Psychology	1917	American Psychological Association	American Psychological Association

[a] Published originally as *Publications of the American Statistical Association* (1888–1912) and *Quarterly Publications of the American Statistical Association* (1912–1921).

84 Diverse Origins

economics (Taussig 1888; Dunbar 1891). Similarly, the *Journal of Political Economy* published in its very first issue a piece on the study of political economy in the United States (Laughlin 1892). And for the later development of what would become business education a paper on the relation of sociology to economics (Small 1895) is particularly noteworthy. Already in the late nineteenth century therefore some contents in the business media, in this case academic journals, were linked to business education (see, in general, Chapter 3).

The *American Economic Review* had right from the beginning an even clearer link to business issues through the permanent book review subheading "Accounting, Business Methods, Investments, and the Exchanges." Under this title, the very first issue contained a review of *Work, Wages, and Profits* by H. L. Gantt (1910), who in the words of the reviewer, C. W. Mixter, "was long associated with Mr. F. W. Taylor, the man of genius who originated the whole movement [of scientific management]." The reviewer even described this movement as a "new art or profession slowly developing in obscurity for some years [having] suddenly come into the full light of publicity" (Mixter 1911: 103). Scientific management is also dealt with in later issues. First, by John R. Commons, who discussed the attitudes of organized labor toward industrial efficiency (Commons 1911), and then in a review (Jones 1911) of three contributions on scientific management (Brandeis 1911; Duncan 1911; Taylor 1911b). Again Frederick W. Taylor is mentioned with admiration as "the man who has done most to bring into existence the system of scientific shop management" (Jones 1911: 833). This piece is followed by another (Gilman 1911), which provides a further link to business: a review of William Morse Cole's book *Accounting and Auditing* (Cole 1911). Thus, already in the first volume of the journal there are reflections of the emerging education for business and many references to the "father of scientific management" and his ideas (see Box 5.1).

As could be expected, the *Journal of the American Statistical Association* – called *Publications of the American Statistical Association* at the time – mainly contained articles on statistical matters not related to business, particularly on demographic issues. Exceptions in the early volumes were papers on retail prices in Boston and its vicinity (Cook 1890), on bankruptcies (Stevens 1891), on the cost of production (Wright 1891), and on net profits of manufacturing in the state of Massachusetts (Hawley 1892).

By contrast, in the foreword to the first issue of the *Journal of Applied Psychology* the editors clearly highlighted the relationship between psychology and business. They started out by pointing to "an unprecedented interest in the extension of the application of psychology to various fields of human activity," and moved on to state that "perhaps the most strikingly original endeavor to utilize the methods and the results of psychological investigation has been in the realm of business" (Hall, Baird, and Geissler 1917: 5). They supported this assertion by mentioning the use of psychology in advertising, sales, and the selection of personnel. Nevertheless, the first issue – with the exception of a book review of *The*

Science and Art of Salesmanship (Hoover 1916) – lacked articles with a business orientation. In the second issue however, there were papers on human engineering, the human element in business, and the psychology of efficiency. Papers in later issues continued this interest in efforts to improve business by means of scientific methods – and constitute an early sign of the "scientization" of management by taking advantage of psychology (see Chapter 5).

The Five Frontrunners in Context

In addition to the above mentioned five journals that are now on the *FT*45 list there were also a number of other foundings of business-related academic journals during the early period outside the Anglo-Saxon context. At the same time, some of the early business and management texts were published in already established journals with a practical or engineering orientation – not surprising given the dominance of engineers among the early managers (see Chapters 2 and 5). For instance, Henri Fayol's treatise on industrial and general administration (Fayol 1916) was first published in the French mining industry's *Bulletin de la Société de l'Industrie minérale*.

One particularly significant country for academic publishing in business was Germany, where, as shown in Chapter 4, many schools of commerce were created during this period. Two journals are particularly worth mentioning, the *Zeitschrift für handelswissenschaftliche Forschung* and the *Zeitschrift für Handelswissenschaft und Handelspraxis*. What is very notable here is that, in contrast to the US journals discussed above, both were specifically oriented towards business, or commerce as it was usually referred to at the time. The first of these journals was established in 1906 by Eugen Schmalenbach (1873–1955), professor at the *Handelshochschule* in Cologne, founded only five years prior. He had been promoted to full professor the very same year, and over time became "one of the most influential scholars for teaching, research, and accounting practice in Germany and Continental Europe" (Schoenfeld 1996: 514; see further Box 6.2). However, in the early years the interest for the journal was limited and the editor himself became a major contributor. He even considered closing it down in 1915, but G. A. Gloeckner, a major German publisher of business texts (e.g., Schär 1911; Schmalenbach 1919, 1927; Schmidt 1921), supported a continued publication (Schmalenbach 1931). The journal survived and, since 2000, is published as *Schmalenbachs Zeitschrift für betriebswirtschaftliche Forschung* with an English version: *zfbf Schmalenbachs Business Review*. The *Zeitschrift für Handelswissenschaft und Handelspraxis*, which started its publication in 1908, had even more problems. It was discontinued in 1929 but reappeared as *Die Betriebswirtschaft* between 1930 and 1943 to have another revival in 1977 as *Die Betriebswirtschaft (DBW)*.

86 Diverse Origins

BOX 6.2 EUGEN SCHMALENBACH: NESTOR OF GERMAN BUSINESS ECONOMICS

Schmalenbach was born in 1873 in the city of Halver in North-Rhine Westphalia. In his early years his family moved around and his schooling was therefore irregular. In 1894, at the age of 21, he started to work in his father's firm with the intention that he would take over within three years. However, in 1898 the commercial school in Leipzig (*Handelshochschule Leipzig*) started and Eugen Schmalenbach, against his father's will, became one of its first students. He graduated in 1900 and then turned to studies of economics. Three years later he was appointed associate professor (*Dozent*) at the Cologne school of commerce (*Handelshochschule Köln*) founded in 1901. He became full professor in 1906 and, in 1919, a university professor after the *Handelshochschule* had been merged into the University of Cologne as a Faculty of Business Economics (*Betriebswirtschaftslehre* or BWL). In 1933 he was forced to retire at the age of 60, since his wife Marianne, whom he had married in 1901, was Jewish. After World War II, he returned to his position for a few years. Between 1906 and 1933 he published extensively: 14 books, many of which were published in several editions, and some 150 papers in journals and edited volumes (Kruk, Potthoff, and Sieben 1984: 443, 450–5). His publications are oriented towards various kinds of accounting problems in business, with *Grundlagen dynamischer Bilanzlehre* (1919) the most widely known. It was published in 13 editions – from the third edition with the title *Dynamische Bilanz* – and was translated into Japanese (1950), Spanish (1953), English (1959), and French (1961). Another widely spread volume is *Der Kontenrahmen* (1927), which has been published in six editions and has been translated into Russian (1928) as well as Japanese (1953). In addition, his book *Finanzierungen* (1915) has appeared in nine editions and *Grundlagen der Selbstkostenrechnung und Preispolitik* (1925) in eight. His influence is also demonstrated by the very existence of the Schmalenbach Society, which was founded in 1932. He died in 1955 at the age of 82.

Sources: Kruk, Potthoff, and Sieben (1984); Forrester (1993); Schoenfeld (1996); see also Box 7.2 regarding *Betriebswirtschaftslehre*.

As evident from their titles, these German journals were more explicitly oriented toward business than the five *FT*45 journals discussed above – even if the latter already in the beginning had some contributions on business and management related topics. All in all therefore, maybe with the exception of Germany, academic journals in business and management was still a rather weakly institutionalized field at the time. Here, like in the publishing of business and management books and the business press the subsequent period would see a further process of institutionalization.

References

Abbott, J. (2001) *The Harper Establishment: How books are made*, New Castle, DE: Oak Knoll Press.

Brandeis, L. D. (1911) *Scientific Management and Railroads: Being part of a brief submitted to the Interstate Commerce Commission*, New York: The Engineering Magazine.

Cambridge University Press, 28 September 2015. www.cambridge.org/about-us/who-we-are/glance.

Cole, W. M. (1911) *Accounting and Auditing*, Chicago, IL: Cree Publishing Company.

Commons, J. (1911) "Organized labor's attitude toward industrial efficiency," *American Economic Review*, 1(3): 463–472.

Conyngton, T. (1902) *The Modern Corporation: A concise statement of the objects, methods and advantages of the business corporation*, New York: Ronald Press.

Cook, W. F. (1890) "The study of retail prices in Boston and vicinity," *Publications of the American Statistical Association*, 2(11–12): 116–119.

Cooper, F. (1907) *Financing an Enterprise: A manual of information and suggestion for promoters, investors, and business men generally*, 2nd edn, New York: Ronald Press.

Diemer, H. (1914) *Factory Organization and Administration*, New York: McGraw-Hill.

Dunbar, C. F. (1891) "The academic study of political economy," *Quarterly Journal of Economics*, 5(4): 397–416.

Duncan, J. C. (1911) *The Principles of Industrial Management*, New York: Appleton.

Edwards, R. D. (1993) *The Pursuit of Reason: The Economist, 1843–1993*, Boston, MA: Harvard Business School Press.

Engwall, L. and Hedmo, T. (2016) "The organizing of scientific fields: The case of corpus linguistics," *European Review*, 24 (forthcoming).

Esquerre, P.-J. (1914) *The Applied Theory of Accounts*, New York: Ronald Press.

Exman, E. (1967) *The House of Harper*, New York: Harper & Row.

Fayol, H. (1916) "Administration industrielle et générale: Prévoyance, organisation, commandement, coordination, contrôle," *Bulletin de la Société de l'Industrie minérale*, Saint-Étienne: Société de l'industrie minérale.

Financial Times, 5 May 2015. www.ft.com/cms/s/2/3405a512-5cbb-11e1-8f1f-00144fea bdc0.html#axzz37GX5Hu73.

Fisher, I. (1906) *The Nature of Capital and Income*, New York: Macmillan.

Forrester, D. A. R. (1993) *Eugen Schmalenbach and German Business Economics*, New York: Garland.

Gantt, H. L. (1910) *Work, Wages, and Profits: Their influence on the cost of living*, New York: Engineering Magazine.

Giddings, F. H. (1887) "The theory of profit-sharing," *Quarterly Journal of Economics*, 1(3): 367–376.

Giddings, F. H. (1890) "The theory of capital," *Quarterly Journal of Economics*, 4: 172–206.

Gilbreth, L. M. (1914) *The Psychology of Management: The function of the mind in determining, teaching and installing methods of least waste*, New York: Macmillan.

Gilman, S. W. (1911) "Review of *Accounting and Auditing* by William Morse Cole," *American Economic Review*, 1(4): 836–839.

Going, C. B. (1911) *Principles of Industrial Engineering*, New York: McGraw-Hill.

Götze, H. (1996) *Springer-Verlag: History of a scientific publishing house*, Berlin: Springer.

Hall, G. S., Baird, J. W., and Geissler, L. R. (1917) "Foreword," *Journal of Applied Psychology*, 1(1): 5–7.

88 Diverse Origins

Hawley, F. B. (1892) "Net profits of manufacturing industries in the state of Massachusetts," *Publications of the American Statistical Association*, 3(17): 38−64.

Hoover, S. R. (1916) *The Science and Art of Salesmanship*, New York: Macmillan.

Hoxie, R. F. (1915) *Scientific Management and Labor*, New York: Appleton.

Jacobson, T. C., Smith, G. D., Wright, R. E., Wiley, P. B., Spilka, S. B., and Heaney, B. L. (2007) *Knowledge for Generations: Wiley and the global publishing industry, 1807–2007*, New York: Wiley.

Jagodzinski, C. M. (2008) "The university press in North America: A brief history," *Journal of Scholarly Publishing*, 40(1): 1−20.

James, E. (ed.) (2002) *Macmillan: A publishing tradition*, Basingstoke: Palgrave.

Jones, E. D. (1911) "Review of *The Principles of Scientific Management* by Frederick W. Taylor; *The Principles of Industrial Management* by John C. Duncan; *Scientific Management and Railroads: Being Part of a Brief Submitted to the Interstate Commerce Commission* by Louis D. Brandeis," *American Economic Review*, 1(4): 833−836.

Keir, D. (1952) *The House of Collins: The story of a Scottish family of publishers from 1789 to the present day*, London: Collins.

Kruk, M., Potthoff, E., and Sieben, G. (1984) *Eugen Schmalenbach: Der Mann, sein Werk, die Wirkung*, Stuttgart: Schäffer.

Kurtz, H. (2000) *The Fortune Tellers: Inside Wall Street's game of money, media, and manipulation*, New York: Free Press.

Kynaston, D. (1988) *The Financial Times: A centenary history*, London: Viking.

Laughlin, J. L. (1892) "The study of political economy in the United States," *Journal of Political Economy*, 1: 1−19.

Lawrenson, J. and Barber, L. (1985) *The Price of Truth: The story of the Reuters £££ Million*, Edinburgh: Mainstream.

McGraw Hill Financial, 5 May 2015. www.mhfi.com/about/our-history.

Mixter, C. W. (1911) "Review of *Work, Wages, and Profits: Their influence on the cost of living*," *American Economic Review*, 1(1): 103−104.

Montgomery, R. H. (1912) *Auditing Theory and Practice*, New York: Ronald Press.

Mooney, B. and Simpson, B. (2003) *Breaking News: How the wheels came off at Reuters*, Oxford: Capstone.

Moore, J. H. (1982) *Wiley: One hundred and seventy five years of publishing*, New York: Wiley.

Nicholson, J. L. (1913) *Cost Accounting: Theory and practice*, New York: Ronald Press.

Oxford University Press, 28 September 2015. http://global.oup.com/about/publishing?cc=se.

Parsons, W. (1989) *The Power of the Financial Press: Journalism and economic opinion in Britain and America*, Aldershot: Elgar.

Read, D. (1992) *The Power of News: The history of Reuters 1849–1989*, Oxford: Oxford University Press.

Rosenberg, J. M. (1982) *Inside the Wall Street Journal: The history and the power of Dow Jones & Company and America's most influential newspaper*, New York: Macmillan.

Schär, J. F. (1911) *Allgemeine Handelsbetriebslehre*, Leipzig: Gloeckner.

Scharff, E. E. (1986) *Worldly Power: The making of the Wall Street Journal*, New York: Beaufort Books.

Schmalenbach, E. (1915) *Finanzierungen*, Leipzig: Gloeckner.

Schmalenbach, E. (1919) *Grundlagen dynamischer Bilanzlehre*, Leipzig: Gloeckner.

Schmalenbach, E. (1925) *Grundlagen der Selbstkostenrechnung und Preispolitik*, Leipzig: Gloeckner.

Schmalenbach, E. (1927) *Der Kontenrahmen*, Leipzig: Gloeckner.

Schmalenbach, E. (1931) "25 Jahre," *Zeitschrift für handelswissenschaftliche Forschung*, 25(1): 1–4.

Schmidt, F. (1921) *Die organische Tageswertbilanz*, Leipzig: Gloeckner.

Schoenfeld, H. M. (1996) "Schmalenbach, Eugen (1873–1955)," in M. Chatfield and R. Vangermeersch (eds), *History of Accounting: An international encyclopedia*, New York: Garland Publishing, pp. 514–516.

Scott, W. D. (1911) *Influencing Men in Business: The psychology of argument and suggestion*, New York: Ronald Press.

Small, A. W. (1895) "The relation of sociology to economics," *Journal of Political Economy*, 3(2): 169–184.

Stevens, A. C. (1891) "The commercial death rate," *Publications of the American Statistical Association*, 2(13): 186–194.

Storey, G. (1969) *Reuters: The story of a century of news-gathering*, reprint of the 1st edn from 1951, New York: Greenwood Press.

Sutcliffe, P. (1978) *The Oxford University Press: An informal history*, Oxford: Clarendon.

Taussig, F. W. (1888) "A suggested rearrangement of economic study," *The Quarterly Journal of Economics*, 2(2): 228–232.

Taylor, F. W. and Thompson, S. E. (1905) *A Treatise on Concrete, Plain and Reinforced: Materials, construction, and design of concrete and reinforced concrete*, New York: Wiley.

Taylor, F. W. (1911a) *Shop Management*, New York: Harper.

Taylor, F. W. (1911b) *The Principles of Scientific Management*, New York: Harper.

Taylor, F. W. (1912) *Concrete Costs*, New York: Wiley.

Walker, F. A. (1887) "The source of business profits," *The Quarterly Journal of Economics*, 1(3): 265–288.

Wall Street Journal, 28 July 2015. http://blogs.wsj.com/briefly/2015/07/23/5-things-to-know-about-nikkei-after-financial-times-deal.

Wendt, L. (1982) *The Wall Street Journal: The story of Dow Jones & the nation's business newspaper*, Chicago, IL: Rand McNally.

Wiley, 5 May 2015. http://eu.wiley.com/WileyCDA/Section/id-301697.html.

Wright, C. D. (1891) "A basis for statistics of cost of production," *Publications of the American Statistical Association*, 2(14): 257–277.

PART II

In Search of Directions

The period covered in the second part of this book ranges from World War I through World War II with a focus on the interwar period and both wars as important transitions.

Economically, it was marked by significant turmoil following first the Great War and then the Great Crash of 1929. The former crippled most of Europe financially and economically – a situation aggravated by the latter, following a brief respite during the "roaring twenties." It was the build-up to World War II and war production itself that eventually provided a kick-start to the global economy. The economic leadership of the United States had already become apparent in the earlier period and now mass production and mass consumption started to spread internationally. But the US model was questioned during the Great Depression – and revamped with Roosevelt's New Deal. It was also challenged more directly by different forms of economic organization, most of which involved technocratic control – often combined with authoritarian if not totalitarian regimes.

Socially, the new class of managers had now become highly visible in the United States – a development not uniformly welcomed though. By contrast, old elites continued to dominate in most of Europe, but were largely eradicated in Russia by the communist October Revolution in 1917, the subsequent civil war – fomented by foreign intervention, and the Stalinist purges. While totalitarian regimes elsewhere also led to some social change, it was World War II that proved transformative in this respect with massive casualties, mass murder, and displacements of large numbers of people. It also – by default, not design – opened the workforce to women at a large scale. And its outcome questioned and partially removed extant elites in the defeated countries, while asserting the US economic, political, social, and cultural model – albeit ultimately rivalled by the opposing Soviet one, usually imposed by force.

92 In Search of Directions

Politically, this period was marked by the opposition between the democratic capitalist and a wide range of totalitarian and nationalistic models – the latter gaining further ground following the Great Depression and expanding aggressively already before World War II often driven by a quest for resources. Efforts at global governance were stunted by the isolationist stance of the US government after World War I and therefore largely driven by other actors: businesses that (re)established international cartels, individuals and their philanthropic foundations and the networks, mainly of engineers, that continued to roam the globe. Most of these contacts and exchanges were slowed but not entirely stopped in the build-up to the war and even persisted to some extent during the actual hostilities.

7

ESTABLISHING A PLACE FOR BUSINESS EDUCATION

The interwar years were in many ways an extension of the patterns set in the preceding formative period, though there were some notable changes, particularly in the case of Germany. In the US, it was a period of expansion and increasing diversity. Along the way, the search for purpose and content continued, as did the struggle to establish legitimacy within the university and the business world. There was more scrutiny about what was on offer. Concerns and criticisms also started to be voiced for the first time. As pointed out in Chapter 4, it was mainly in Germany that major changes took place towards strengthening the claim of turning the study of business into a science. These advances were accompanied by a structural transformation, as the *Handelshochschulen* became incorporated into universities and virtually disappeared by the early 1930s. The changes in Germany had some impact on its European periphery as well as Japan. They had literally no influence, however, on the USA, France, and the UK.

The Struggle for Recognition as a Professional School in the United States

Changing Nomenclature, Continuing Diversity

After World War I the naming of the field and the purported domain of the constituent schools began to go through a chequered transition from "commerce" to "business" and then to "business administration." Greater reference to business came after the creation of the Association of Collegiate Schools of Business in 1916, which then became the AACSB with the addition of "American" (see Chapter 13; Box 13.1). By establishing the AASCB, schools of commerce were following the pattern set by other professional schools in US

94 In Search of Directions

universities (Marshall 1928). Also, with the words "collegiate" and "business" in the title, the AACSB was an attempt to distinguish university-based schools from the private, for-profit commercial schools which had already established a national association and continued to enroll large numbers of students (Lyon 1923; Haynes and Jackson 1935; see also Chapter 4).

The term "business administration," on the other hand, had been introduced by the graduate school at Harvard. The word "administration" had been employed before then, as the school established at the University of Chicago, for example, had added it to its name in 1902. Yet, this was separate from "commerce," indicating the intention to train "social workers" and "civil servants" as well as "business men" (Marshall 1913: 100). Adjoining it with "business," as done by Harvard, was novel and was soon to capture others' imagination, so that Jones, for example, was already in 1913 referring to "university instruction in business administration" without at all mentioning the term "commerce" (Jones 1913). Many newly founded schools also adopted the term "business administration" in their names with or without "commerce" (see Marshall 1928: 4–7; and the list of AACSB members in Bossard and Dewhurst 1931: 265–266). Although some continued to label the field "higher commercial education" (see, e.g., Ruml 1928), it was increasingly replaced by "education for" or "schools of" business (though not "business schools") as indicated by various articles or books published in the 1920s and the 1930s (e.g., Lyon 1923; Marshall 1928; Bossard and Dewhurst 1931; Haynes and Jackson 1935). The reference to "commerce" had not disappeared altogether even by the end of World War II, as it remained in the names of schools and degrees (see, e.g., Phelps 1946). Nevertheless, it was clearly overtaken by "business" in describing the field and the stage was set, not least because of Harvard, for some degree of consensus to appear around the label "business administration" in the post-World War II decade (see Gordon and Howell 1959).

The diversity in curricular and administrative structuring that had taken shape during the emergence of the field continued after World War I in much the same way. Marshall (1928: 11–12), for example, identified four main types of organizational arrangements by the mid-1920s, all of which had their roots in the formative period (see Chapter 4): the graduate, the undergraduate-graduate, the two-year undergraduate, and the four-year undergraduate schools. Those representing the first two categories were the fewest. Harvard's graduate school was joined only by the one established at Stanford in 1925, the two remaining the sole cases until the end of World War II. Dartmouth, founded as the first undergraduate-graduate school, which admitted students after three or four years in college, was followed at the time only by the University of Michigan – though there were also other undergraduate schools, which awarded the master's degree (Marshall 1928). The two- and four-year undergraduate programs constituted the bulk, differing amongst themselves as to whether they admitted students after two years of college or directly to a four-year program in business – though in the latter case too, the first two years were largely based on liberal arts subjects.

These alternative arrangements possibly had to do in part with faculty availability and local funding conditions (Khurana 2007). More importantly perhaps, they manifested – within the rather unique university and college context in the US – attempts to reconcile in different ways the stronghold of liberal arts education with training for business. Controversy and tension as to whether and how this could be done persisted throughout, coupled with the search for what the purpose of business education should be (Khurana 2007). The struggle for enhancing legitimacy also continued through attempts to strengthen the profession claim and to address what were seen as pressing problems of quality.

As mentioned in Chapter 4, the contention that, differently from the private, for-profit commercial ones, the collegiate schools were educating for "higher levels" had been there from the outset. There was now a search for more specific aims, formulated sometimes in normative terms like preparing students to become "business executives" or "professional or technical experts," the latter typically exemplified as accountants and statisticians (Marshall 1928: 19; see also Heilman et al. 1928; Ruml 1928). Although more rarely, there was also reference to training "managers" or "business administrators" (e.g., Jones 1915; Lyon 1923). Some thought that "administration" was a higher-level task than "management" and schools of business would do their best to try and cater to the latter category (see Hotchkiss 1920). Grander formulations were also there, with the aim defined at times as educating "business leaders" – though often actually equated with "training for executive positions" (Bossard and Dewhurst 1931: 268; Donham 1927a: 417). This claim was a key element in the struggle to be accepted as a professional school, expressed most overtly perhaps by Edwin F. Gay (1927: 399), when he said that Harvard's school of business – of which he was the founding dean – "should seek to train business executives and be satisfied with nothing less [otherwise forfeiting] its right to stand on the same level with the older professional schools."

Claims toward "Profession" and "Science"

The promotion of the profession theme continued throughout the interwar years. Parallels were drawn with the older professional schools, such as divinity, law, and medicine: Ruml (1928), for example, already made reference to the famous Flexner (1910) report on US medical schools, which re-gained currency during the post-World War II transformation of the schools of business (see further Chapter 10). The claim to being a profession was built on the two footings that had emerged in the early period, namely, science and social consciousness. As highlighted in Chapter 4, Dartmouth College had named the first ever master's degree "commercial science." Somewhat later, in describing the ambitions of their schools – Northwestern and Chicago respectively, Hotchkiss (1913: 196) referred to "business science" and Marshall (1913: 103) to adding to "the bounds of existing scientific knowledge." And, again as mentioned in Chapter 4, in 1911 Harvard's school of business had set up, for the first time, a bureau of business research.

In the 1920s and the 1930s, the science claim was voiced even more strongly in the unending endeavor to gain greater legitimacy within the university. Hotchkiss (1920: 90–91) was now arguing, for example, that "no body of subject-matter can justify a permanent place in the curriculum except on the basis of embodying scientific principles." A doctoral program was started for the first time at the University of Chicago's school of commerce in 1920, followed by the one at Harvard which began in 1922 to confer what was called the "doctor of commercial science" degree (Khurana 2007: 171; Augier and March 2011: 153). Legitimacy was also sought by increasing reference to theory and research. Thus, Wallace B. Donham (1922a), dean of the Harvard school, for example, talked about the necessity and the possibility of "executive theory" or a "theory of business." Bureaus of business research began to spread, especially among the larger universities (Dickinson 1925). So, already by the early 1930s Bossard and Dewhurst (1931: 24) were expressing the hope of marrying science with management by pointing to the "heavy responsibility" of the business school "in training its students in the principles of the sciences underlying human relationships and in their application to the solution of management problems."

While some had begun to complain in AACSB meetings that too much attention was being devoted to research at the expense of teaching (Dirksen and Kroeger 1966), it is important to understand what was meant by "science" and "research" at the time (see also Sass 1982). Donham (1922a: 5), for example, thought that "the conception that scientific studies should be approached through the collection and classification of facts and through the development from recorded facts of generalizations and theories into which the facts fit, is the basis of all science." Yet, for Donham (1922a), not the natural sciences but law had to serve as the model for schools of business – a predilection that has since characterized the school of business at Harvard (Augier and March 2011). So, the case method, which had been imported from Harvard Law School, was considered not only as a distinctive feature of graduate instruction but also as providing an empirical basis for generalization (see Box 7.1).

Even more strongly pronounced, perhaps, was the claim that being – or becoming – a profession meant public responsibility and service to society. Again, the older professions served as the main reference. Business was deemed to be not only about personal gain and money-making. As a profession it required ethical values and a sense of responsibility to others as well as to the country as a whole. These were ideas that had been voiced earlier. Drawing analogies with the legal and medical professions, Marshall (1913: 101), for example, had argued that "the most important task of all is to aid in promoting the progress and welfare of society." They were now put more forcefully when Donham (1927a: 406), for instance, unreservedly claimed that "the development, strengthening, and multiplication of socially minded business men is the central problem of business." And he argued that it was the university-based schools of business that could deal with this "problem" by cultivating the ethical, moral, and social values of the "emergent" profession – a contention strengthened in the aftermath of the Great Depression (see, e.g., Donham 1933).

BOX 7.1 DEAN DONHAM AND THE "CASE METHOD" AT HBS

Although the case method has been and is understood and used in different ways, it typically involves the discussion of a "real-life" situation that an organization has faced. The written description contains facts and views about the issues at hand and the context. Students are expected to analyze and discuss this information and to recommend courses of action. While there had been earlier mentions of problem-based courses, it was Wallace B. Donham who championed the case method for the teaching of business after he became dean of the Harvard Business School (HBS) in 1919. Donham was inspired by the widespread use of this method in legal education, introduced for the first time in 1870 at the Harvard Law School. Cases, Donham believed, brought teaching closer to the realities of business and to training in established professional schools such as law and medicine. It was also a way of moving away from the view that business was essentially applied economics and for going beyond specialist viewpoints. And, in Donham's conception, the most important task of the business man was decision-making, which was an art and could thus be learned best by being exposed to as many and as varied business situations as possible that executives faced. So, already by the mid-1920s the MBA at HBS became almost entirely based upon the case method. During Donham's long tenure HBS invested huge amounts of resources into the development of cases, making the case method a hallmark of the school. Donham also believed that evidence collected through cases could provide a basis for generalization and, thus, the development of a science or theory of business. However, the case method became associated predominantly with an art as opposed to a science-based view of studying business. Nevertheless, given the prestige that Harvard enjoyed at the time, the case method began to spread among schools of business in the US – expanding also to parts of undergraduate programs and eventually to executive training. It still remains part and parcel of business school teaching in the US and in various other parts of the world.

Sources: Donham (1922a, 1922b); Fraser (1931); McNair (1954); Pierson (1959: 48–50, 245–148); Gleeson, Schlossman, and Allen (1993); Khurana (2007); Augier and March (2011: 193–204).

98   In Search of Directions

As the preceding comments indicate, in the 1920s and the 1930s the profession theme was essentially built around the view that business was a profession (Donham 1927b; Ruml 1928; Bossard and Dewhurst 1931). This broad construction helped not only in calls for professional school status but also served a range of other aims, such as elevating the low esteem attributed to business, which was thought to have made it "a dumping ground into which in the case of many families inferior sons are advised to go" (Donham 1927a: 417). It was also proposed as a way of fostering self-regulation so that the need for government intervention could be reduced (Donham 1927b). Somewhat differently, reference was also made to so-called "business professions," which, as mentioned above, was taken to mean technical experts such as accountants or statisticians. These "professional men" were distinguished and treated separately from "business executives" for which being a professional was not insinuated (see, e.g., Heilman et al. 1928). It was only in the latter part of the 1930s that Donham (1936: 409), for example, proclaimed that "administration should become a profession" and that a "theory of administration" needed to be developed. The shift from "business" to "administration" in Donham's way of identifying the profession possibly had to do with the presence and the influence at Harvard of Elton Mayo, who was the key figure in the famous Hawthorne studies, which served to introduce human relations ideas into the business literature (see Chapters 2 and 9). For Donham's successor Donald K. David the profession was "business administration" (see his preface to McNair 1954). It was still not "management" that was referred to as a profession. This had to wait another couple of decades (see Chapter 10).

Expansion, Increasing Stratification, First Critiques

The search for a clarification of purpose and a definition of the profession was taking place in a context of expansion. Growth in the number of schools had already gained further pace after World War I. By 1925 there were more than 180 universities or colleges with schools, departments, or divisions variously named as "commerce," "business" or "business administration" (Marshall 1928: 4; see pp. 4–9 for a comprehensive list with founding dates). The upward surge continued thereafter so that by the beginning of World War II all major public universities had a program under one of these labels (Pierson 1959). For 1940–1941, Phelps (1946: 185) identified 110 schools within universities. In addition there were 405 four-year colleges, which offered, in Phelps' words, "business administration" as a concentration for the bachelor's degree.

Seeing this fast growth as a problem, Marshall (1928) had already observed in the late 1920s that quite often the motive behind setting up schools or programs in business was to generate revenue through tuitions and donations from businessmen or to secure funds from state legislatures. With expansion, stratification also began to emerge within the organizational field, mainly in two ways. First, there was the Harvard Business School (HBS), as it was now beginning to be called by its administrators – apparently again with inspiration from the university's Law School (see, e.g., Gay 1927; Donham 1933). Harvard Business School was not only distinct as the first exclusively graduate school but also because of the reputation of its parent university. Moreover, by the 1920s, the school had begun to attract an increasing number of applicants as well as sizable financial resources, which provided a stronger basis for distinguishing itself from and influencing others (Gleeson, Schlossman, and Allen 1993). A second source of stratification was the AACSB, which had been initiated by prominent universities (see Zammuto 2008: 260 for the list). In order to become a member of the AACSB, a school or program had to fulfil at least a set of modest standards that were related only to the undergraduate degree (see Box 13.1). And, although AACSB membership did grow to 55 before World War II (Flesher 2007: 13), it remained small relative to the large number of schools and departments within the organizational field and therefore continued to serve as a basis for distinguishing the better or the acceptable from those deemed of lower quality.

Together with the growth and the stratification that was taking shape, there seemed to be an increasing awareness that not all was well, as indicated by Marshall's (1928) observations mentioned above. Studies on the state of the field began to appear, such as the ones by Heilman et al. (1928), Ruml (1928), and Bossard and Dewhurst (1931). Criticisms were being voiced from within, though always phrased delicately. Concerns were expressed particularly about the fast pace of growth, the unwieldy proliferation of courses and weaknesses in quality (Bossard and Dewhurst 1931). Claims to a science basis notwithstanding, there appeared to be an overall drift toward a practical orientation, due both to an over-reliance on practitioners and the extensive involvement of full-time faculty in outside consulting (Pierson 1959; Locke 1989). There was a parallel trend toward greater specialization (Bossard and Dewhurst 1931). Even Harvard and Stanford succumbed to a stronger practical and specialist orientation. The MBA, as a result, was not becoming particularly distinct from the undergraduate degree (Gleeson, Schlossman, and Allen 1993). The scientific basis was not forthcoming either, as available research mostly consisted of case writing and contract work typically carried out by bureaus of business research (Gleeson 1997). Doctoral education also remained limited. After the granting of the first ever degree in 1926, business doctorates averaged around 35 annually in the 1930s, climbing to about 50 only in the early 1940s (Phelps 1946: 186; Gordon and Howell 1959: 21). Neither were these doctoral programs particularly geared toward developing researchers (Augier and March 2011).

In one sense, however, there was little to worry about since student demand was rising, given the fertile environment provided by US business for career opportunities. Summarizing the growth over the entire interwar period, Pierson (1959: 7) noted that business had gone up from 3 percent of the first degrees conferred in the United States in 1919–1920 to 10 percent in 1939–1940, making business more popular than engineering and second only to education among the so-called professional schools (Pierson 1959: 8 and 711). Notably though, evening and extension courses played a significant part in this expansion. Bossard and Dewhurst (1931: 261), for example, reckoned that, in the late 1920s, about half of the students were attending evening classes – a form of instruction that continued during the interwar years (Pierson 1959). In any case, Phelps' (1946: 187) estimate for 1941–1942 was that around 140,000 students were enrolled in business programs, of which 105,000 were in separately organized schools of business within universities and colleges. Already by the end of World War II business education was referred to as an "industry" in the US (e.g., Phelps 1946: 183).

Like in the previous period however, the growth in enrollment occurred overwhelmingly at the undergraduate level. There was some increase in master's degrees too. As mentioned in Chapter 4, 110 master's degrees were conferred in 1919–1920. This figure had gone up to over a thousand in 1939–1940. However, the bachelor's degrees awarded in the same year exceeded 18,000. As a matter of fact, throughout the interwar years, master's degrees in business corresponded on average only to about seven percent of the bachelor's degrees (Gordon and Howell 1959: 21). Moreover, unlike today, most of the master's programs were not the two-year MBA but rather a master of science or a master of arts, involving one year of study after an undergraduate degree in business (Pierson 1959: 265). And, even the MBA remained essentially a program for pre-experience students. In fact, Bossard and Dewhurst (1931: 260 and 271), for example, thought that "graduate work" was a misnomer for the MBA. For them, "graduate" meant advanced study after an undergraduate grounding in business.

Despite concerns with the ways in which the organizational field at large was evolving, schools that enjoyed greater status were developing aspirations for claiming authority – helped not least by the sentiments of the post-depression era (Khurana 2007). The university-based schools were now viewed as having the capacity to deal with both business and societal problems. Not surprisingly, Harvard's administrators were most vocal in that respect (see, e.g., Donham 1933). A further indicator of building authority was the step taken by the Massachusetts Institute of Technology (MIT) to train junior executives with a one-year full-time program which was started in 1931. Demand turned out to be limited though and a total of only 78 managers had attended the program until it was adjourned in 1942 (Andrews 1959). Nevertheless, this program and the 15-week one for more senior executives, which HBS started in 1943 – at the same time as Stanford – upon the request of the US Office of Education and which then turned into its Advanced Management Programme, were heralding a new line of activity that was to gain pace in the 1950s and become a major "business" for schools of business.

Probably not unrelated to these conditions, the organizational field of business education in the US increasingly became inward-looking during the interwar years. Seeking legitimacy from and reference to commercial education in Europe had all but disappeared. This likely had to do also with the self-perception that the US had passed "to a position of world dominance and world leadership" (Bossard and Dewhurst 1931: 260). That this view was shared, to some extent, by those outside the US is indicated by Harvard starting to attract foreign students already in the late 1920s (Khurana 2007: 139).

Diverging Developments in Europe and Elsewhere

Turning into a "Science" and a Faculty in Germany

As pointed out in Chapter 4, the German *Handelshochschulen* or commercial schools had already embarked on a trajectory different from their counterparts in France and the university-based faculties in the UK. The need to develop subject matter that would be distinct from what was taught in secondary trade schools and the struggle against opposition by universities resulted in the creation of a new discipline that was finally to be named *Betriebswirtschaftslehre* (BWL) or business economics (see Box 7.2).

That building legitimacy for a new organizational form within the German higher education field required a research orientation had been recognized earlier. Thus, Eugen Schmalenbach, one of the founding fathers of BWL, already wrote in 1906 that "it would be essential to do research in the science of commerce" and that the new schools had to "prove that they are capable of conducting research" (quoted in Üsdiken, Kieser, and Kjaer 2004: 385; see also Box 6.2). So, with the advances leading to BWL in the early 1920s and with growing research activities and publications, the *Handelshochschulen* were becoming increasingly similar to the universities. The *Diplom-Kaufmann* and the associated qualification for teaching at the secondary trade schools, the *Diplom-Handelslehrer*, paved the way for the creation in 1923 of a comparable qualification in economics, the *Diplom-Volkswirt*, which until then was only available at the doctoral level (Tribe 1994). To achieve equivalence with this new degree the duration of study for the *Diplom-Kaufmann* was extended to three years in 1924 (Fehling 1926; Tribe 1995). The *Handelshochschule* in Berlin became a public corporation in 1926 and, despite opposition by the universities, obtained the right to grant doctorates, which Cologne and Frankfurt had already gained by becoming university faculties (Meyer 1998). Mannheim and Nuremberg followed in 1929 and Leipzig and Königsberg in 1930 (Tribe 1994). However, while the schools were becoming stronger and more legitimate academically, student demand began to fall after the mid-1920s, especially in the larger ones with greater nationwide reach, possibly providing an additional explanation for why most ended up becoming parts of universities (Tribe 1994).

102 In Search of Directions

BOX 7.2 THE GERMAN *BETRIEBSWIRTSCHAFTSLEHRE* (BWL)

The first steps toward BWL were taken when commercial courses were brought together under a subject group called *Handelstechnik* or commercial technique in HH Cologne and *Handelswissenschaft* or commercial science in HH Berlin. Although there was some controversy as to whether the discipline was actually a science, *Wissenschaft*, or a craft, *Kunstlehre*, the commerce part of the instruction then became labelled *Privatwirtschaftslehre* (PWL), "private" in the sense of focusing on the rational operation of individual economic units. Thus, it was distinct from economics or *Volkswirtschaftslehre*, which dealt with the entire economy and issues of economic welfare. The aim of the change to PWL was a transition from bookkeeping and commercial calculation to an economic analysis of the business enterprise or, put differently, from "commercial science" to "business economics." This re-definition was also construed as gaining autonomy from economics taught in the universities. Though not without contestation by some university professors, by the end of World War I PWL had come to be recognized as a distinct branch of economics. Soon after, the name turned to *Betriebswirtschaftslehre* (BWL), as the word private appeared to be strongly associated with profit-making as the central concern. The word *Betrieb*, enterprise or firm, was regarded as more neutral, since it was defined in a way that encompassed all types of units of economic activity. Thus, by the 1920s BWL had become established as the core component of the curricula for business education in Germany and the label for the new discipline that was created – persisting until the present day. In BWL, the *Betrieb* was studied as an entity. Bookkeeping, calculation, and organization constituted the main topics with an overall focus on efficiency. Despite the science emphasis, a practical orientation prevailed, the main concern being to show how business could be made more effective. Nevertheless, with its integrated content and research backing BWL was, arguably, ahead of what was taught in the US and the rest of Europe at the time.

Sources: Redlich (1957); Locke (1984: 155–241; 1989: 88–96); Lindenfeld (1990); Tribe (1994, 1995: 95–139); Üsdiken, Kieser, and Kjaer (2004).

The organizational transformation that occurred in Germany in the aftermath of these developments had actually started already earlier. Thus, the school in Frankfurt was converted into a faculty and became a founding part of a new university established in this city in 1914. The same happened in Cologne in 1919. That this could happen despite the negative attitude of German universities towards the *Handelshochschulen* was because there were no universities at the time in these two cities (Meyer 1998). Nonetheless, the pattern continued, mainly because of the depletion of initial funding and due to post-World War I economic difficulties. The school in Munich was bought by the Bavarian state in

Establishing a Place for Business Education **103**

1920 and was attached to the *Technische Hochschule* (Fehling 1926). Then, in 1931, the ones in Leipzig and Berlin were incorporated into the universities in these cities (Meyer 1998). Finally, the school in Mannheim merged with the University of Heidelberg in 1933 (Tribe 1994). As a result, the *Handelshochschulen* had all but disappeared as an organizational form before World War II. Nevertheless, despite the decline in demand, by 1933 the total number of their graduates had increased to around 16,000 (Locke 1984: 200; Tribe 1995: 99).

The Nazi regime did not reverse the integration into universities, but business education came under attack for instilling a liberal, capitalist spirit and prioritizing self-interest. The Nazis also forced a large number of professors to resign or emigrate – mainly because they or their spouses were Jewish, causing an important brain drain (Üsdiken, Kieser, and Kjaer 2004; see Box 6.2 for Schmalenbach).

Fragile Developments in France and the United Kingdom

In France, the patterns set before World War I continued very much in the same manner. There was some revival of student interest, which led to the founding of additional *écoles de commerce* in provincial towns such as Clermont, Reims, and Strasbourg (Blanchard 2012: 86). The schools became attached to the Ministry of Education in 1920, which also brought about some further degree of procedural uniformity (Blanchard 2012). Nevertheless, the lower-level image and local character of the provincial ones did not change much during the interwar years (Locke 1989). Enrollment rose until 1930, followed by a sharp decline in the next five years, when it went down to around 1,100 – with ESCP in Paris faring somewhat better (Blanchard 2012: 95). Difficulties in attracting students also meant that the schools were financially fragile, as state support was not forthcoming either. A reform attempt initiated by the state in 1937 – aiming to bring them closer to HEC, could not be implemented due to the outbreak of the war (Blanchard 2012).

HEC had officially affirmed its "superior" status in 1923. It also regained the right to institute preparatory classes in secondary schools for the competitive entrance examinations or *concours* not only in Paris but also in the provinces (Blanchard 2012; see also Chapter 4) – becoming more selective in admitting students. Curricular changes were also introduced, reducing the share of law and including more courses in commerce (Locke 1989). Nevertheless, as the *Wissenschaft* tradition did not prevail within the French higher education field, even HEC did not move in the direction of becoming more academic and research oriented. In fact, it did not have any full-time faculty until well after World War II. Teaching was carried out by professors from the university, businessmen, and civil servants in ways that were very much oriented to practice (Locke 1989). Although there was the intention, the school could not reach out to industry, remaining confined to commerce and banking. Its number of graduates was small relative to the German *Handelshochschulen* (Locke 1984). And the extension of the duration of study to three years took longer than in Germany and was achieved at

104 In Search of Directions

HEC only in 1938 – the others continuing with a two-year program (Blanchard 2012: 100). Nevertheless, HEC graduates did manage to rise in the managerial hierarchies of French business. But despite being advanced relative to the other ESCs, HEC remained second-tier and not a serious challenger to the engineering *grandes écoles* (Kipping and Nioche 1998).

Like in France, limited changes took place in the UK. There were some additions, such as the university colleges in Exeter, Nottingham, Reading, and Southampton, which offered courses leading to the University of London's B.Com. degree, as well as a school of economics and commerce founded in Dundee in 1931 (Smith 1928; Murphy 1953). Moreover, in 1926–1927 the University of Manchester introduced a division, which created two B.A. degrees, one in administration and one in commerce, reinvigorating its founding aim of educating students also for public administration (Smith 1928). Notably, the resistance of Oxford and Cambridge continued, indeed of academics more generally (Locke 1989). Lyndall Urwick, a prominent author and a long-time advocate of business education in the UK (see Chapter 2 and Box 8.1), for example, complained in 1938 about the negative attitude, especially by the ancient universities: "Why it should be considered academically respectable to traverse the foundations in various sciences necessary as a preparation for medicine, but dangerously vocational to attempt a similar preparation for those who are adopting careers involving administrative leadership, is a paradox which the older universities in Great Britain have not explained" (quoted in Murphy 1953: 39).

There was also skepticism on the part of the business community (Smith 1928). The widespread belief was that business was an art rather than a science and that managers were born not bred. As Locke (1989: 97) argued however, this conviction had more to do with the value attached to "social qualifications" rather than innate abilities, serving to protect the leadership positions of the privileged classes. According to Smith (1928: 50), for example, "the curriculum of the faculty of commerce of a British university, therefore, must aim at providing a general training while affording choice of optional vocational subjects to the comparatively small number of its students whose future careers are outlined for them before they come to the university." Given this kind of an environment, UK universities shared with the French *écoles de commerce* the problem of low student demand. During the interwar years an average of only 12 students graduated, for example, from Birmingham, twice that from Manchester and around 30 from Edinburgh (Smith 1928: 40).

Diverse Influences, Different Outcomes in Other Parts of the World

The interwar developments in the rest of Europe and elsewhere occurred in a number of different directions, as there were now a multitude of models, both historically and contemporaneously. A major source of influence was Germany, both with its earlier stand-alone schools and the more recent university-based faculties as well as the science of business economics or BWL that had been developed there.

The Nordic countries continued to follow the earlier *Handelshochschulen* model, with the school established previously in Stockholm serving as an exemplar (see Chapter 4). A second school in Sweden was founded in 1923 in Gothenburg, again supported by private funding and with German professors at the beginning. Though somewhat belatedly, these two schools were following the German ones when they extended their period of study from two to three years in 1939 (Engwall 2009). Swedish commercial schools were also opened in Helsinki and Turku in 1927 for the Swedish-speaking population in Finland (Engwall 1998; Kettunen 2013). In the meantime, the school in Copenhagen began a two-year full-time program in commercial science in 1924. Here, *driftsøkonomi* or business economics soon became an important element of the curriculum and an area of specialization in 1929 (Üsdiken, Kieser, and Kjaer 2004). A similar school followed in 1939 in Aarhus. Norway was a latecomer, with the *Norges Handelshøyskole* (NHH) eventually established in Bergen in 1936. The NHH also started out with a two-year BWL-based program – which was in place until 1946, adding a year in 1938 for those who wanted to be teachers in secondary commercial schools. A second school called *Bedriftsøkonomisk Institutt* (BI) was opened in Oslo in 1943. Initially a private consulting firm, which also offered short evening courses, BI set up a two-year program after the end of the war (Amdam 1996).

In some other countries, while stand-alone schools continued to exist and to increase, commerce or business economics was also made part of the university. In the Netherlands, for example, another stand-alone Catholic school was founded in 1927 in Tilburg – the origin of present day Tilburg University. Already earlier, in 1921, a Faculty of Commerce was established within what was then the Municipal University of Amsterdam. This Faculty was renamed "Economic Sciences" in 1935, accompanied by a similar name change at the Rotterdam school in 1935 (van Baalen and Karsten 2010). Likewise in Turkey, BWL was granted a chair in 1937 in the newly founded Faculty of Economics within the University of Istanbul. Although the new faculty was to gain greater prestige rather quickly, the French-inspired commercial school from the previous century also continued to exist (Üsdiken, Kieser, and Kjaer 2004; see also Chapter 4).

In Italy, where BWL had also been imported, there was a definitive turn, like in Germany, toward accommodating commercial or BWL education entirely within the universities, sealed by a law passed in 1934 (Fauri 1998; Kipping, Üsdiken, and Puig 2004). In Japan, by contrast, the dual structure persisted. Thus, the Universities Act of 1918 enabled earlier alternative forms to be recognized as universities – with the earliest commercial school becoming the Tokyo University of Commerce for instance (see Chapter 4). And the government also established higher commercial schools in various cities (Nishizawa 1998). At the same time, other universities began to set up Faculties of Commerce or Economics, which relied heavily upon the German BWL (Saitō 1995). By 1930, the number of these faculties reached 20 with an enrollment exceeding 11,000 students.

106 In Search of Directions

Very little is known about what transpired during the interwar years outside Europe and Japan. Among the sparse literature available, Byrt (1989), for example, mentions that, reminiscent of those in the UK, a Faculty of Commerce was inaugurated in 1924 within the University of Melbourne in Australia to offer a B.Com. degree. Again not differently from the UK, most students were part-time, with full-time students not exceeding a quarter even by 1939. In Canada, on the one hand, an *École Supérieure de Commerce de Québec* was established in 1937 affiliated to *Université Laval*; on the other, commerce education that developed in universities like McGill, Queen's, and Western Ontario in the 1920s was very much influenced by US exemplars. The University of Toronto also introduced a two-year master of commerce degree in 1938, mainly for part-time students. Altogether only 62 students had graduated from this program by 1950 (Sawyer 2000). Overall, there was strong resistance to commerce education in Canada originating both from within and outside the university and enrollments could not reach the proportions they did in the US (see Boothman 2000).

There are also indications that there were encounters with the US model, leading to sporadic and limited importation in Europe. A graduate program was set up in Milan Polytechnic, for example, with funding from an association of managers in industry. The initiative was inspired by its director's visit to the US and in particular the Harvard Business School. The program appears to have been received well, attracting on average 150 participants per year between 1934 and 1944 (Fauri 1998). A similar contact was also established between George Doriot, an HBS faculty member of French origin, and the Paris Chamber of Commerce (see also Box 10.2 on Doriot). According to then HBS dean Wallace B. Donham (1931: 6), there was the belief "that the chamber itself should start a school in Paris under its own aegis, and that this school should be modelled as closely as possible after the Harvard Business School." The end result was the founding of the *Centre de Préparation aux Affaires* (CPA) in 1930 to offer short post-experience programs for practitioners, relying, as could be expected, upon the case method (Kipping and Nioche 1998). However, these small-scale initiatives to bring in US-based content and methods had very limited, if any, influence on higher business education in those countries. Such an impact had to await the much stronger thrust of the post-World War II period (see Chapter 10).

References

Amdam, R. P. (1996) "National systems versus foreign models in management education: The Norwegian case," in R. P. Amdam (ed.), *Management, Education, and Competitiveness: Europe, Japan and the United States*, London: Routledge, pp. 19–37.

Andrews, K. R. (1959) "University programs for practicing executives," in F. C. Pierson, *The Education of American Businessmen: A study of university-college programs in business administration*, New York: McGraw-Hill, pp. 577–608.

Augier, M. and March, J. G. (2011) *The Roots, Rituals, and Rhetorics of Change: North American business schools after the Second World War*, Stanford, CA: Stanford University Press.

Blanchard, M. (2012) *Socio-histoire d'une entreprise éducative: Le développement des écoles supérieures de commerce en France (fin du XIXe siècle–2010)*, unpublished Ph.D. dissertation, École des Hautes Études en Sciences Sociales, Paris.

Boothman, B. E. C. (2000) "Culture of utility: The development of business education in Canada," in B. J. Austin (ed.), *Capitalizing Knowledge: Essays on the history of business education in Canada*, Toronto: University of Toronto Press, pp. 11–86.

Bossard, J. H. S. and Dewhurst, J. F. (1931) *University Education for Business: A study of existing needs and practices*, Philadelphia: University of Pennsylvania Press.

Byrt, W. (1989) "Management education in Australia," in W. Byrt (ed.), *Management Education: An international survey*, London: Routledge, pp. 78–103.

Dickinson, Z. C. (1925) "Bureaux for economic and 'business' research in American universities," *Economic Journal*, 35(139): 398–415.

Dirksen, C. J. and Kroeger, A. (1966) "Summary of the major events of the association from 1916–1966," in *The American Association of Collegiate Schools of Business, 1916–1966*, Homewood, IL: Richard D. Irwin, pp. 181–252.

Donham, W. B. (1922a) "Essential groundwork for a broad executive theory," *Harvard Business Review*, 1(1): 1–10.

Donham, W. B. (1922b) "Business teaching by the case system," *American Economic Review*, 12(1): 53–65.

Donham, W. B. (1927a) "The social significance of business," *Harvard Business Review*, 5(4): 406–419.

Donham, W. B. (1927b) "The emerging profession of business," *Harvard Business Review*, 5(4): 401–405.

Donham, W. B. (1931) "The cooperative arrangement recently completed between the French school of commerce and the Harvard Business School," *Bulletin of the Business Historical Society*, 5(1): 4–8.

Donham, W. B. (1933) "The failure of business leadership and the responsibility of the universities," *Harvard Business Review*, 11(4): 418–435.

Donham, W. B. (1936) "The theory and practice of administration," *Harvard Business Review*, 14(4): 405–413.

Engwall, L. (1998) "The making of Viking leaders: Perspectives on Nordic management education," in L. Engwall and V. Zamagni (eds), *Management Education in Historical Perspective*, Manchester: Manchester University Press, pp. 66–82.

Engwall, L. (2009) *Mercury Meets Minerva: Business studies and higher education – the Swedish case*, 2nd edn, Stockholm: EFI, the Economic Research Institute.

Fauri, F. (1998) "British and Italian management education before the Second World War: A comparative analysis," in L. Engwall and V. Zamagni (eds), *Management Education in Historical Perspective*, Manchester: Manchester University Press, pp. 34–49.

Fehling, A.W. (1926) "Collegiate education for business in Germany," *Journal of Political Economy*, 34(5): 545–596.

Flesher, D. L. (2007) *The History of the AACSB International, Vol. 2: 1966–2006*, Tampa, FL: AACSB.

Flexner, A. (1910) *Medical Education in the United States and Canada*, New York: Carnegie Foundation for the Advancement of Teaching.

Fraser, C. (ed.) (1931) *The Case Method of Instruction: A related series of articles*, New York: McGraw-Hill.

Gay, E. F. (1927) "The founding of the Harvard Business School," *Harvard Business Review*, 4(2), 397–400.

Gleeson, R. E. (1997) "Stalemate at Stanford, 1945–1958: The long prelude to the new look at Stanford Business School," *Selections*, 13(3): 6–23.

Gleeson, R. E., Schlossman, S., and Allen, D. G. (1993) "Uncertain ventures: The origins of graduate management education at Harvard and Stanford, 1908–1939," *Selections*, 9(3): 9–37.

Gordon, R. A. and Howell, J. E. (1959) *Higher Education for Business*, New York: Columbia University Press.

Haynes, B. R. and Jackson, H. P. (1935) *A History of Business Education in the United States*, Cincinnati, OH: South-Western Publishing.

Heilman, R. E., Kiekhofer, W. H., Ruggles, C. O., Sharfman, I. L., and Marshall, L. C. (1928) "Collegiate education for business," *Journal of Business*, 1(1): 1–59.

Hotchkiss, W. E. (1913) "The Northwestern University School of Commerce," *Journal of Political Economy*, 21(3): 196–208.

Hotchkiss, W. E. (1920) "The basic elements and their proper balance in the curriculum of a collegiate business school," *Journal of Political Economy*, 28(2): 89–107.

Jones, E. D. (1913) "Some propositions concerning university instruction in business administration," *Journal of Political Economy*, 21(3): 185–195.

Jones, E. D. (1915) "The relation of education to industrial efficiency: The study of the general principles of administration," *American Economic Review*, 5(1) (supplement): 209–226.

Kettunen, K. (2013) *Management Education in a Historical Perspective: The business school question and its solution in Finland*, Ph.D. dissertation, Oulu: University of Oulu.

Khurana, R. (2007) *From Higher Aims to Hired Hands: The social transformation of American business schools and the unfulfilled promise of management as a profession*, Princeton, NJ: Princeton University Press.

Kipping, M. and Nioche, J.-P. (1998) "Much ado about nothing? The US productivity drive and management training in France, 1945–1960," in T. R. Gourvish and N. Tiratsoo (eds), *Missionaries and Managers: American influences on European management education*, Manchester: Manchester University Press, pp. 50–76.

Kipping, M., Üsdiken, B., and Puig, N. (2004) "Imitation, tension, and hybridization: Multiple 'Americanizations' of management education in Mediterranean Europe," *Journal of Management Inquiry*, 13(2): 98–108.

Lindenfeld, D. F. (1990) "The professionalization of applied economics: German counterparts to business administration," in G. Cocks and K. H. Jarausch (eds), *German Professions, 1800–1950*, Oxford: Oxford University Press, pp. 213–231.

Locke, R. R. (1984) *The End of Practical Man: Entrepreneurship and higher education in Germany, France and Great Britain*, Greenwich, CT: JAI Press.

Locke, R. R. (1989) *Management and Higher Education since 1940: The influence of America and Japan on West Germany, Great Britain, and France*, Cambridge: Cambridge University Press.

Lyon, L. S. (1923) *Education for Business*, 2nd edn, Chicago, IL: The University of Chicago Press.

Marshall, L. C. (1913) "The College of Commerce and Administration of the University of Chicago," *Journal of Political Economy*, 21(2): 97–110.

Marshall, L. C. (1928) "The American collegiate school of business," in L. C. Marshall (ed.), *The Collegiate School of Business: Its status at the close of the first quarter of the twentieth century*, Chicago, IL: The University of Chicago Press, pp. 3–44.

Meyer, H.-D. (1998) "The German Handelshochschulen, 1898–1933: A new departure in management education and why it failed," in L. Engwall and V. Zamagni (eds),

Management Education in Historical Perspective, Manchester: Manchester University Press, pp. 19–33.

McNair, M. P. (ed.) (1954) *The Case Method at the Harvard Business School: Papers by present and past members of the faculty and staff*, New York: McGraw-Hill.

Murphy, M. E. (1953) "Education for management in Great Britain," *Journal of Business*, 26(1): 37–47.

Nishizawa, T. (1998) "The development of managerial human resources in Japan: A comparative perspective," in L. Engwall and V. Zamagni (eds), *Management Education in Historical Perspective*, Manchester: Manchester University Press, pp. 83–94.

Phelps, O. W. (1946) "The case for an active association of collegiate schools of business," *Journal of Business*, 19(3): 183–193.

Pierson, F. C. (1959) *The Education of American Businessmen: A study of university-college programs in business administration*, New York: McGraw-Hill.

Redlich, F. (1957) "Academic education for business: Its development and the contribution of Ignaz Jastrow (1856–1937) – in commemoration of the hundredth anniversary of Jastrow's birth," *Business History Review*, 31(1): 35–91.

Ruml, F. (1928) "The formative period of higher commercial education in American universities," *Journal of Business*, 1(2): 238–263.

Saitō, T. (1995) "Americanization and postwar Japanese management: A bibliographical approach," *Japanese Yearbook on Business History*, 12: 5–22.

Sass, S. A. (1982) *The Pragmatic Imagination: A history of the Wharton School, 1881–1981*, Philadelphia, PA: University of Pennsylvania Press.

Sawyer, J. A. (2000) "From commerce to management: The evolution of business education at the University of Toronto," in B. J. Austin (ed.), *Capitalizing Knowledge: Essays on the history of business education in Canada*, Toronto: University of Toronto Press, pp. 146–166.

Smith, J. G. (1928) "Education for business in Great Britain," *Journal of Political Economy*, 36(1): 1–52.

Tribe, K. (1994) "Business education at the Mannheim Handelshochschule, 1907–1933," *Minerva*, 32(2): 158–185.

Tribe, K. (1995) *Strategies of Economic Order: German economic discourse, 1750–1950*, Cambridge: Cambridge University Press.

Üsdiken, B., Kieser, A., and Kjaer, P. (2004) "Academy, economy and polity: Betriebswirtschaftslehre in Germany, Denmark and Turkey before 1945," *Business History*, 46(3): 381–406.

van Baalen, P. and Karsten, L. (2010) "The social shaping of the early business schools in the Netherlands: Professions and the power of abstraction," *Journal of Management History*, 16(2): 153–173.

Zammuto, R. F. (2008) "Accreditation and the globalization of business," *Academy of Management Learning & Education*, 7(2): 256–268.

8

OLD CERTAINTIES AND NEW DEPARTURES IN CONSULTING

During the interwar period, engineers, who continued applying various shades of scientific management, still dominated the consulting field. They expanded significantly both in the United States and particularly in Europe. While cooperative efforts were increasing at national and international levels – with Germany a particularly noteworthy example, the consulting field overall became more commercially oriented. Most successful was the firm founded by Charles E. Bedaux – expanding first throughout the US, then worldwide. Consulting activities by accountants also progressed but still remained largely invisible. During this period a different, more generally oriented type of consulting activity emerged in the US – often referred to as "management engineering." These firms grew fast during the Great Depression and World War II, mainly based on restructuring and government projects, respectively. While commercially driven, they also laid the groundwork for a professional logic, which came to dominate the field after the war.

Scientific Management: Still on a Mission, Now Also Internationally

Expanding Taylorist Ideology and Practice

The interwar period saw a significant expansion of scientific management nationally and internationally based on what one scholar referred to as "the 'scientizing' and utopian impulses at its core." It no longer focused only on work processes, but developed a more general "ethos of organizational efficiency through expert research and functional prescription," with its application moving beyond the industrial enterprise to other sectors of the economy as well as to

Old Certainties and New Departures in Consulting **111**

education and public administration (Alchon 1992: 102; see also Maier 1970). This expansion was more systematic than in the previous period. While involving a number of known individuals, it was increasingly organized through a variety of associations. Most of these efforts continued to be driven by a "missionary" logic though.

Thus, in the US many of the individuals mentioned in Chapter 5 continued to spread the efficiency gospel through publications, presentations, teaching as well as consulting. Among the additional actors was the social scientist Luther H. Gulick (1892–1993), who obtained a Ph.D. from Columbia University in 1920 and was a professor there from 1931 to 1942 (Blumberg 1981). He became instrumental for the introduction of scientific management in the US public sector, namely through the Institute for Public Administration, which he presided from its foundation in 1921 until 1962. He also was part of the three-person "President's Committee on Administrative Management," which made recommendations for the reorganization of the executive branch of the federal government to President Roosevelt in 1937 (see Chapter 2; also Fesler 1987).

Another important individual was the socially progressive Boston-based department store owner Edward A. Filene (1860–1937) (Stillman 2004; see also Chapter 5). In 1916, he created the international Retail Research Association, whose members "regularly travelled around the world visiting member stores in their efforts to spread innovations in management" (Jeacle 2004: 1167). And in 1919 Filene established the not-for-profit Cooperative League – renamed Twentieth Century Fund (TCF) in 1922 – to promote his ideas of a more socially responsible capitalism both in the US and outside. One of the TCF's board members was Henry S. Dennison, another Boston-based industrialist. In 1922, Dennison helped establish the Manufacturers' Research Association (MRA) – a small and locally based grouping, which included a dozen firms as well as the Harvard Business School and exchanged information to solve common management problems. This local effort eventually came to have global repercussions, following the visit of British chocolate producer Seebohm Rowntree to the US in 1926 (Briggs 1961; Brech, Thomson, and Wilson 2010: 38–46). Impressed by the MRA, he decided to start similar regional – and ultimately national – forums for the discussion and exchange of ideas in the UK. The task to create what came to be called Management Research Groups (MRG) was entrusted to Lyndall Urwick (1891–1983), who had joined Rowntree in 1922 and was to become one of the most influential management thinkers of the twentieth century (see Box 8.1).

112 In Search of Directions

BOX 8.1 LYNDALL FOWNES URWICK (1891–1983): PROLIFIC PROPAGATOR OF MANAGEMENT

Urwick was born into a family-owned glove-making business in the English country town of Malvern. After completing his studies in history at Oxford, he was drafted into the army during World War I and saw active as well as staff duty, apparently reading Taylor's *Shop Management* in the trenches. Decommissioned in 1919 at the rank of Major, he initially joined his father's firm but left in 1922 to work for Seebohm Rowntree in the company's organization office. At the latter's behest, he started to establish the Management Research Groups in 1926 before being asked to direct the International Management Institute in Geneva in 1928. Upon its closure in 1933, Urwick returned to the UK, where he co-founded, with a former Bedaux consultant, Urwick, Orr and Partners (UOP), which was to become one of the leading management consulting firms in the country (see below). Playing a largely reputational and relational role in UOP, Urwick participated actively in the promotion of management education in the UK, chairing, for instance, a government committee on "Education for Management" in 1945–1946, leading a productivity mission to the US on the same topic in 1951 and becoming a founding member and, eventually, chairman of the tripartite British Institute of Management. Probably even more importantly, he was a very prolific writer, publisher, and presenter. Among his over 200 publications are *Papers on the Science of Administration*, edited with Luther Gulick (1937), later criticized as unscientific by Herbert Simon, and the three-volume book on *The Making of Scientific Management* (see Chapter 2). While his initial interest was sparked by Taylor, he also publicized the work of authors providing alternative views, namely Mary Parker Follett, whose writings he edited, and Henri Fayol, whose ideas he introduced to the English-speaking audience. Even after his retirement, he continued to give lectures and teach courses in North America and Australia, where he died in 1983.

Sources: Brech, Thomson, and Wilson (2010); Parker and Ritson (2011).

In addition to these individual initiatives there was also some degree of organized activity. The most developed association in the US at the time was the Taylor Society, founded in 1911 as the Society to Promote the Science of Management and renamed in Taylor's honor after his death in 1915 (see Chapter 5). The Taylor Society became involved in efforts to spread the scientific management gospel internationally, including a conference held in Prague in the summer of 1924 with the participation of 50 leading figures from the US. The organizers' declared intention was "the building up of a single world-system of activity for the scientific management of work" (quoted by Bloemen 1996: 111). They established a permanent International Committee of Scientific Management

(*Comité Internationale de l'Organisation Scientifique du Travail* or CIOS), with additional conferences taking place in Brussels (1925), Rome (1927), Paris (1929), Amsterdam (1932), London (1935), and Washington (1938). Attended by a total of over 9,000 participants, including many practitioners, these conferences served to foster exchanges and create a community among proponents of scientific management during the interwar period (Bloemen 1996).

The CIOS also became part of probably the most ambitious – but ultimately failed – initiative to organize the dissemination of Taylorism at an international level, the International Management Institute (IMI), established in Geneva in 1927. The proposal came from the French Socialist Albert Thomas (1878–1932), who headed the permanent secretariat of the International Labour Organization (ILO) established in Geneva in 1919 to further dialog between business, trade unions, and governments. The initial funding was provided by the ILO, Filene's Twentieth Century Fund, and the Rockefeller Foundation. When the IMI's first director resigned in 1928, Urwick was appointed as successor and started to establish MRGs at a European level. But for a variety of reasons funding dried up and the IMI was forced to close in 1933 (Wrege et al. 1987; Boyns 2007).

Waning Efforts in Japan, China, and Russia

As mentioned in Chapter 5, scientific management had become very "fashionable" in Japan before World War I. The "efficiency craze" continued after the war with a particularly prominent role played by Yōichi Ueno (1883–1957), who came to be known as the "father of the Japanese Efficiency Movement" (see, for this and the following, Tsutsui 2001). A graduate of Tokyo University in psychology, Ueno visited the US in 1921 and met many of the movement's luminaries, including Emerson and the Gilbreths. Like his Western counterparts, he subsequently tried to promote these broadly conceived ideas through presentations, publications, and consulting, He also helped establish a variety of associations including a Japanese branch of the Taylor Society in 1924 and the Japan Efficiency Federation in 1927. But consulting never became institutionalized and he and the few other "efficiency peddlers" were increasingly side-lined as the movement and the related associational structure became controlled by the dominant business groups, the *zaibatsu*, and the government, which focused on the more technical aspects of efficiency in the interest of armaments and war production.

Similarly, individuals who had studied or worked in the United States and other Western countries also drove the introduction of scientific management in interwar China. A good example is Cao Yunxiang (1881–1937), sometimes referred to as China's Taylor. His trajectory apparently included studies at Yale, an MBA from the Harvard Business School, and a stint in the Chinese Foreign Service. Upon his return to China, he served as a director of British American Tobacco there and was president of Tsinghua University in Beijing between 1922

114 In Search of Directions

and 1928 (Morgan 2004: 16). In 1930 he became the founding director of the Chinese Institute of Scientific Management (*Zhongguo gongshang guanli xiehui*). Membership came from business, government, and academia and included many who had also studied in the US. The Institute and other, similar associations seem to have focused mainly on "setting professional standards, educating members, and providing a forum for the exchange of ideas both in person and through the pages of the journals that many of these societies also published" (Morgan 2004: 8). The Japanese invasion of 1937 put an end to all these efforts.

In Russia engineers had already discussed Taylorism in their professional journals before the October Revolution in 1917. Not surprisingly, interest in ways to improve production and productivity persisted under the new communist regime (see, e.g., Merkle 1980: Chapter 4). A crucial individual in this respect was the revolutionary trade unionist and poet Aleksei Gastev (1882–1939), who envisioned a kind of "machine age," where – independent of the dominant political regime – "[m]achines from being managed will become managers" (quoted by Bailes 1977: 378). His vision and ideas found an organizational base with the creation, in 1920, of the Central Institute of Labour (*Centralnij Institut truda* or CIT), which studied simple motions in detail and recommended training workers to carry out repetitive tasks in a robot-like fashion as the best way to increase productivity. Gastev's vision and the CIT's recommendations were, quite naturally, controversial within the communist party and its relevant organs. While prevailing initially, they fell by the wayside after Stalin tightened his grip on power in the late 1920s and promoted "Stachanovism," i.e., the heroic human efforts to vastly exceed production targets, as the main method of increasing output. Gastev as well as the CIT were eliminated during the Stalinist purges in the late 1930s, marking the end for a Soviet version of scientific management.

Building an Alternative: Germany's Cooperative Logic

Like in other European countries, there had been considerable interest in scientific management in Germany already before World War I – even if its application was often met with resistance (see Chapter 5). The war itself brought some cooperative efforts, culminating in the establishment of a committee for efficient production (*Ausschuß für wirtschaftliche Fertigung* or AWF) in February 1918. But it was the defeat, the related loss of all overseas subsidiaries and trademarks as well as the resurgence of the US that prompted German business and political leaders to launch additional initiatives to promote *Rationalisierung* or rationalization – a term that indicated a more encompassing understanding of efficiency. In 1921 they established the National Efficiency Board (*Reichskuratorium für Wirtschaftlichkeit* or RKW) with the objective to increase national prosperity through cost reductions and an improvement in the quantity and quality of products (Kipping 1997). It published a monthly newsletter with a circulation of 12,000 in 1932, a book series, and, since 1928, a comprehensive and frequently updated handbook covering different aspects of rationalization. It also compiled performance indicators for a growing number of sectors, allowing each company to – in today's parlance – benchmark themselves against competitors.

In addition, the RKW served as an umbrella for a wide range of more specific associations, including, since 1923, the above mentioned AWF. Most important among these with respect to consulting-type activities was the National Committee for Work Time Determination or *Reichsausschuß für Arbeitszeitermittlung* (REFA), founded in 1924 by companies in metalworking and mechanical engineering but quickly extending its reach to other sectors (Kipping 1997). Since 1928, REFA also published a handbook, detailing the methods for determining "standard times" for a wide range of tasks. By 1933 REFA had trained over 10,000 work study engineers in these methods, most of whom worked within companies rather than as external consultants. After coming to power in 1933, the Nazis initially rejected rationalization – widely blamed for high unemployment. But they soon realized the importance of efficiency enhancements for their rearmament and war efforts and therefore brought the existing apparatus under their control. The RKW quickly increased the number of benchmarking surveys, covering over 100 sectors by 1940; and REFA accelerated the training of work study engineers, adding another 30,000 by 1945. The number of independent consultants was marginal by comparison, even if it also grew from about 100 in the mid-1920s to over 300 in 1942 and close to 700 by 1944 (Kipping 1997).

These associative structures, which have to be seen as part of Germany's specific form of capitalism, often referred to as "organized" or "co-operative" (e.g., Chandler 1990), proved highly beneficial for those sharing information and, ultimately, for the country as a whole (Kipping 1999b). Their advantages did not escape the US consulting engineers either. A group of REFA-trained engineers visiting the US after World War II as part of the so-called "productivity missions" – designed to inspire Europeans to emulate the American model reported their opinion as follows (quoted in Kipping 1999b: 31–32): "Anyone [in the US] who feels competent or sees a commercial opportunity develops his theories, his methodology and, which is the worst, his own terminology. […] Because of this situation, those American engineers who are involved in our field out of interest are envious of our REFA organisation." However, it was actually the commercial logic that expanded rapidly in the US and elsewhere during this period.

Efficiency as a Growing Business

US Consulting Engineers at Home and Abroad

As noted in Chapter 5, most of the scientific management pioneers saw consulting as one of several ways to spread the gospel of scientific management – with the Emerson Efficiency Engineers founded by Harrington Emerson in 1907 the notable exception. Following World War I, the company tried to broaden its commercial appeal, including renaming itself Emerson Engineers – moves apparently resisted by the founder. Conflicts seem to have continued until 1925, when Emerson was pushed out completely by his brother Samuel and younger firm members (Quigel 1992: 288). He returned, quite tellingly, to promoting the cause of scientific management on an individual basis, namely by providing advice on transportation policy to various foreign governments (Quigel 1992). By 1930 the firm's payment-by-results system was the third most widely used in the US (see below).

Other scientific management consultants established permanent presences abroad, namely in Europe. One example is Taylor follower and critic C. Bertrand Thompson (see Chapter 5), who moved to France in 1917, following an invitation by Henry Le Châtelier, to help the Ministry of Armaments increase efficiency in munitions production (for this and the following, see Moutet 1997; Wren et al. 2015). He remained after the war to sell what he called the "Taylor-Thompson System" and tried to increase his notoriety through newspaper ads and lectures at engineering schools and associations. While his own operation remained rather small, it contributed to the development of local consulting firms. A case in point is Paul Planus, who met Thompson at the Ministry of Armaments, then became his first consultant after the war, but left in 1929 to establish his own consulting firm. Planus employed close to 40 consultants on the eve of World War II, mainly based on projects in the public sector, including the Postal Service.

Another internationally active US consultant was Henry Wallace Clark (1880–1948). After graduating in economics and sociology from the University of Cincinnati in 1902 he joined the Remington Typewriter Company's Asian operations, then worked for a number of other companies before re-joining Remington's New York headquarters as an assistant to the president in 1907 (for this and the following, see Moutet 1997; Wren 2015). There, he met Taylor disciple Henry L. Gantt (see Chapter 5), who had been asked to streamline operations in the company's factories and head office. In 1917, Clark joined Gantt to help with war-related projects and stayed on afterwards. After Gantt's death in 1919, Clark founded his own firm of "consulting management engineers" in New York (Wren 2015: 313), which initially carried out work for the federal government, including a study of the US Patent Office. But he was most successful in proselytizing the Gantt chart as a management tool through various publications, including a book (Clark 1922), and his consulting work. Clark expanded to Europe following his participation in a 1926 US mission to develop a stabilization plan for Poland. Subsequently, he carried out various projects for the Polish government and, in 1927, opened an office in Paris, where his clients included well-known firms such as Renault. Clark consulted companies in many other European countries, including state monopolies in Romania and Turkey, and established an additional office in London (Wren 2015: Table 1). In 1939, Clark returned to the US, where he became the progenitor of another well-known consultant: quality guru Joseph Juran, who joined Clark's firm and then set up on his own after the latter's death in 1948 (see Chapter 11).

France is an interesting case, because it shows how US consultants became instrumental in establishing a national management consulting field with sufficient legitimacy to attract many large and reputable firms as clients (see Kipping 1997; Moutet 1997; Henry 2012). Their expansion might have been facilitated by the absence of a strong cooperative alternative, like it existed in Germany. As shown in Chapter 5, the French engineering community was marked by internal rivalries, namely between the followers of Taylor and Fayol. Both set up their own associations, which in 1926 merged with a third one to form the *Comité national de l'organisation française* (CNOF) or National Committee of French Organization. The CNOF resembled the German RKW in that it published a newsletter, established a training center for work study engineers in 1934, and a center for time and methods research in 1938. But it was soon challenged by a new rival, supported by leading industrialists, the peak employers association, and the government: the *Commission générale de l'organisation scientifique du travail* (CGOST) or General Commission on Scientific Management, renamed *Commission Générale d'Organisation Scientifique* (CEGOS) in 1936. At the outset CEGOS established working parties on different topics – a bit like the British Management Research Groups. After World War II it morphed into a professional development consulting firm which is still operational today with about 1,000 employees worldwide (CEGOS 6 October 2015).

Thus, in the emerging national consulting fields, one can still find evidence of two logics, one more commercially oriented, represented by the internationalizing US consultants; the other more cooperative, where ideas and best practices were shared not sold. The latter dominated in Germany and, for different reasons, in Japan, China, and the Soviet Union. It also drove the – ultimately unsuccessful – initiatives at an international level. And it retained some presence in France and the UK. Moreover, there were still remnants of the earlier ideological or missionary logic even among the US consulting firms – evidenced, for instance by the struggles within the Emerson Engineers or by Thompson's and Clark's multiple publications. But this period also saw the emergence of firms that were purely – and unashamedly – commercial.

Paling Them All: Charles E. Bedaux and His Firm

The firm that (re)shaped management consulting fields around the world during this period had been founded in 1916 by French immigrant Charles Eugène Bedaux (1886–1944). After rather tumultuous beginnings (see Box 8.2), Bedaux capitalized on the familiarity he had gained with scientific management when working as an assistant and interpreter for an Italian efficiency engineer in the US and France before World War I (see Chapter 5). Upon his return, he developed and codified his own system of work study (Bedaux 1917), selling it through the firm established originally in Grand Rapids, Michigan, then moved to Cleveland, Ohio in 1918.

118 In Search of Directions

BOX 8.2 CHARLES E. BEDAUX: SELF-MADE MAN, SOCIALITE, AND NAZI AGENT?

Bedaux's story is a rags-to-riches fairy tale, albeit with a bad ending and ongoing controversies among its chroniclers up until this day. Born to a railway engineer in a Paris suburb in 1886, he dropped out of high school and became involved in the Paris red light district, eventually forced to leave in a hurry, opting for the United States as the destination. After toiling in menial jobs, including the construction of the Hudson tunnel, he found the get-rich quick scheme he was looking for by developing and selling his own system of efficiency improvements. His rapidly expanding consulting firm brought him fortune and fame. He increased the latter through a number of widely publicized expeditions in the Sahara and the sub-arctic Rocky Mountains. And he used the former to acquire an estate in North Carolina, a hunting lodge in Scotland, property in North Africa, and, in 1927, the Château de Candé in the Loire Valley – marking a triumphant return to his country of origin. At Candé Bedaux and his second wife, the American Fern Lombard (1892–1972), held retreats for his consultants and social gatherings, which cemented and increased Bedaux's reach into the international business élite at the time. They also hosted the wedding of divorcee Wallis Simpson, a friend of Fern, with the former British King Edward VIII in 1937. A seeming highpoint, it ultimately spelt trouble when Bedaux organized the highly controversial trip of the Duke of Windsor to Nazi Germany, which caused bad publicity in the UK and the US, with the Duke having to cancel his planned trip there. After the German invasion of France in 1940, Bedaux stayed but, because he was a US citizen, transferred ownership of the consulting firm to his brother Gaston. Travelling to North Africa in November 1942 to examine the potential for a trans-Saharan pipeline and railway, he was captured by the advancing allied troops, returned to the US and accused of treason, committing suicide on February 14, 1944, while awaiting trial in Miami. Controversy continues as to whether he was indeed a Nazi agent or rather an American spy, trying to protect his wife, who had remained in France.

Sources: Flanner (1945); Christy (1984); Kipping (1999a).

One measure of Bedaux's success is a survey of payment methods conducted by the National Industrial Conference Board of the United States in 1,214 plants, employing a total of almost 800,000 workers (NICB 1930). Among those remunerated based on an incentive system – rather than paid by time or pieces – Bedaux came first by a wide margin: 33,177 workers as compared to 9,953 for the second placed Halsey and 9,252 for Emerson. During the 1920s, Bedaux had already opened additional offices in Boston, Chicago, and Portland and, in 1930, moved his headquarters to the recently completed, iconic Chrysler building in the country's financial capital New York. Growth was even faster during the 1930s with the number of plants applying his system increasing almost tenfold to reach 500 by 1937 (see Table 8.1). His clients included many household names of US industry including Eastman Kodak, Du Pont, and General Electric (Kreis 1992).

Part of the reason for his commercial success can be found in the system itself, which was based on the direct observation of worker efforts and standardized *all* tasks to the so-called "B" unit, comprised of a fraction of a minute of activity plus a fraction of a minute of rest, with workers receiving bonuses for more than 60B per hour. The system allowed comparisons across the whole organization and could be applied for "general management purposes, as well as for technical cost-accounting purposes" – a flexibility, which, according to contemporary observers, distinguished it from competing systems (Sanders 1926, quote p. 19). Another important factor were Bedaux's remarkable sales and self-promotion skills as well as his visibility and social connections (see Box 8.2). Moreover, he increased the legitimacy and reputation of his firm by hiring consulting engineers with degrees from highly regarded institutions, including the French *grandes écoles* and MIT.

Moving Abroad and Engendering Local Firms

Bedaux established his first office outside the US in London in 1926, using work for one of his main US clients, Eastman Kodak, as a "bridge" (Kipping 1999a). As Table 8.1 shows, the consulting firm quickly expanded to other European countries, encountering varied success.

It was most impactful in the UK, not only because of the number of clients, but because it more or less kick-started the consulting field there through a number of spin-offs (see also Tisdall 1982; Kipping 1997, 1999b). Thus, in 1934 a former Bedaux client hired one of his managers to establish Production

TABLE 8.1 The International Expansion of the Bedaux Consulting Firm during the 1930s

Country	Office opened	Plants with the Bedaux System	
		1931	1937
United States	1916/18	52	500
British Isles	1926	30	225
Germany	1927	5	25
Italy	1927	21	49
France	1929	16	144

Source: Kipping (1999a: 198).

120 In Search of Directions

Engineering (P-E); that same year its sales manager Leslie Orr teamed up with Lyndall Urwick to form Urwick, Orr and Partners (UOP) (see Box 8.1). After the controversies surrounding Bedaux's association with the Duke of Windsor, his own British subsidiary forced him out of ownership, became quoted on the London Stock Exchange and changed its name to Associated Industrial Consultants (AIC) in 1938. Another spin-off – with hindsight the most important one – occurred in 1943, when former AIC consultant Ernest Button established Personnel Administration (PA). Together, these consulting firms became known as the "Big Four" and dominated the UK field into the 1970s (see Chapter 11).

Bedaux established his French subsidiary somewhat later but it quickly surpassed all the other US and domestic consultants there and, on the eve of World War II, had advised a total of 350 companies and employed close to 80 consulting engineers (Moutet 1997: 211–216). He was somewhat less successful in Italy and Germany, despite having Fiat as well as tire producers Pirelli and Continental among his first clients there. In Germany, this was due to the preponderance of the REFA system, while a certain hostility of the Fascist regime held back his Italian operations. When building a presence in these countries, Bedaux used a similar approach, hiring consulting engineers from reputable engineering schools or universities, and placing well-connected industrialists on the boards of the various national subsidiaries, including in the Italian case Giovanni Agnelli and Piero Pirelli (Kipping 1999a).

Bedaux's consulting firm also became active outside the core countries in Europe, expanding for instance to Scandinavia, advising the Greek government on how to improve efficiency after the country defaulted on its foreign debt in 1932 [sic] and visiting the Soviet Union. Bedaux expanded even farther, with a project in Belgian Congo, a short-lived presence in Japan and a more permanent one in Australia, all controlled from an international holding, which moved from New York to Amsterdam (see, further, Christy 1984; Kipping 1999a). The Netherlands, incidentally, was a country where engineering-based management consulting also expanded quite rapidly during this period, albeit mainly based on domestic service providers. Among them, Ernst Hijmans (1890–1987) was the best known, namely for applying scientific management in office settings, and also well connected internationally (Hellema and Marsman 1997).

The rearmament and war efforts led to a boom for all these consulting activities, seen as essential for increases in production and productivity. Scientific management systems were also a response to the replacement of skilled male workers, drafted into military service, with a largely unskilled female workforce. In the UK for instance, AIC conducted almost 300 projects during the war years, compared to 375 for the period between 1926 and 1939. And in the US, despite the damage caused by the Duke of Windsor's cancelled trip, Bedaux's consulting operations continued to thrive. Their managing director, Albert Ramond made public speeches and published at least two books, trying to promote the Bedaux system as a way to improve efficiency as well as the cooperation between management and the unions (Anon. 1942). After Bedaux's suicide in 1944, he changed the name of the firm to Albert Ramond and Associates. In addition to the well-established engineering-based consulting firms, several newcomers also benefitted from the war.

The "Others": Ongoing Trends and New Developments

During the interwar period management consulting was clearly dominated by scientific management in terms of content and by engineers in terms of the background of consultants and consulting firms. But there were new developments outside engineering, some of which, as we know from hindsight, ended up shaping the future of the field.

Still in the Shadows: Accounting and HR Consulting

During this period the accounting profession continued to grow and so did their – still marginal and largely invisible – consulting activities. Among the most active in this respect seems to have been Peat, Marwick, Mitchell & Co. It was formed in 1925 through the merger of the UK firm of William Barclay Peat & Co., formally established in 1891, and the US firm founded in 1897 by fellow Scotsmen and University of Glasgow graduates James Marwick and Roger Mitchell. The US firm claims to have carried out management advisory activities since 1907 and started using the "management consulting" label shortly after World War II (Higdon 1969: 275). The firm that went even further in terms of centralized organization and control was the one founded by Arthur E. Andersen (1885–1947) in Chicago in 1913 (see Moore and Crampton 2000; Squires et al. 2003). Orphaned at age 16, Andersen trained as an accountant, joined Price Waterhouse in 1907 and moved to the Schlitz brewing company in Milwaukee as a comptroller in 1910. He also studied part-time toward a business degree at Northwestern University's new School of Commerce, which, upon graduation in 1912, he joined as an assistant, then full professor and head of the Accounting Department. In 1917 he published a textbook entitled *Complete Accounting Course* (Andersen 1917).

But in 1922 Andersen resigned from the school to devote himself to his fast growing accounting practice, for which he had often hired his own students. Subsequently, it opened six additional offices, including New York and Los Angeles. While appointing new partners, Andersen retained 50 percent of equity and made all the major – and often minor – decisions. He introduced internal training to ensure the uniformity of know-how as well as values. While focusing on accounting, the firm also offered consulting under the label "financial and industrial investigation services." It achieved national notoriety and reputation by signing up well-known clients, including retailer Montgomery Ward.

122 In Search of Directions

More consulting-type activities – and visibility – ensued from the Great Depression, when Andersen was asked to supervise the restructuring of the near-bankrupt utility empire assembled by Anton Insull. Such activities, it should be noted, were not confined to the US. Accountants elsewhere also offered their services as consultants. A case in point is Oskar Sillén (1883–1965), who was professor of *handelsteknik*, a direct translation of the German *Handelstechnik* (see Box 7.2) at the Stockholm School of Economics (SSE) between 1912 and 1951. Initially, he also led the Industrial Office – a consulting organization established by the Federation of Swedish Industries. But, unlike Andersen, he eventually opted for his academic career, while continuing to provide advice to companies and public agencies on an individual basis (Engwall, Furusten, and Wallerstedt 2002).

Another type of consulting firm also emerged during this period – related to what today is subsumed under the human resources (HR) label. Small at the time, they remained on the margins of the field even in the long run. Their stories are noteworthy, because they show again a division between those disseminating new management ideas based on a "missionary" logic and others turning them into commercial success. In this case, it was the increasingly popular body of thought about human relations developed by Elton Mayo and others in the 1920s and 1930s (see Chapter 2). Its progenitors did provide some individual consulting services even if, like Taylor, they were more interested in dissemination via education and publication. Mayo, for instance, was a professor at the Harvard Business School and published numerous books (see Chapters 7 and 9). A firm focusing on the "human element," which would become a global leader in HR consulting, was the one founded by Edward N. Hay (1891–1958) in Philadelphia in 1943.

Many of the other consulting firms occupying this space today – which, it should be stressed, remains marginal with respect to the management consulting field – are related to pension and employee benefits consulting. Given the state provision of social and old age security in most of Europe, this was almost exclusively a US phenomenon, greatly accelerated in the 1930s as a consequence of the New Deal. The Social Security Act of 1937 in particular drew in both established and new firms. Among the former was the insurance agency Marsh & McLennan, which had its origins in the nineteenth century and was formally established in Chicago in 1905 (Marsh & McLennan Companies 6 October 2015); it changed its name to Mercer in 1959 following the acquisition of a similar firm founded by William M. Mercer in Vancouver, Canada in 1945. Among the newcomers were Towers, Perrin, Forster & Crosby, established in Philadelphia in 1934 (Towers Watson 7 October 2015), and the firm founded by Edwin "Ted" Hewitt in Lake Forest, Illinois in 1940, both moving from insurance brokerage into pension and benefit plans and advice.

During this period, the US also became the cradle of another type of consulting firm providing more general business advice rather than focusing on productive efficiency, accounting-related issues, or human resources.

What the Future Would Bring: A Professional Vision for the Field

Probably the earliest example of the new type of management consulting was the firm set up in Chicago in 1914 by Edwin G. Booz (1887−1951), who had graduated from Northwestern University first in economics, then in psychology (see, for this and the following, Higdon 1969: Chapter 5; Kleiner 2004; McKenna 2006). Working with psychology professor Walter Dill Scott, an authority on personnel selection and advertising (see Chapter 9), Booz evaluated human resources, conducted executive searches, but also carried out market research and even land surveys. Drafted in 1917, he re-joined Scott in developing a system for the classification of Army personnel. Decommissioned in 1919, Booz went back into consulting, first trying to tap into the still dominant efficiency engineering services, but quickly changing the firm's name (see Table 8.2) to reflect the survey work he did for the majority of his clients.

TABLE 8.2 Booz: Changing Names and Identity?

Year	Name
1914	The Business Research Service
1916	The Business Research and Development Co.
1919	Edwin G. Booz, Business Engineering Service
1921	Edwin G. Booz Service, Business Surveys
1924	Edwin G. Booz Surveys
1935	Edwin G. Booz and Fry Surveys
1936	Booz, Fry, Allen and Hamilton
1943	Booz, Allen & Hamilton

Source: Kleiner (2004: 20).

As the business grew, Booz partnered with two other Northwestern graduates, George S. Fry in 1925 and James L. Allen in 1929. In 1935 they were joined by former executive Carl L. Hamilton, who brought and developed many new relationships. For much of the 1930s Booz conducted projects at retailer Montgomery Ward, but eventually fell out with the company's CEO. World War II brought more business and visibility, when the firm was asked to help reorganize first the US Navy and then the Army (Kleiner 2004: Chapter 2; McKenna 2006). It also prompted two spin-offs: 1942 saw the departure of Fry, who objected to the government focus; and in 1946 three consultants, who had become friends during these wartime projects, left to establish Cresap, McCormick & Paget (see Chapter 11). The firm nevertheless thrived, also because Allen insisted on turning the collection of individuals into a more structured organization. Incidentally, he was apparently one of the first to describe himself as a "management consultant" in a brochure in the early 1930s (Kleiner 2004: 14), even if the Navy in the early 1940s still referred to Richard Paget as a "management engineer" (p. 25).

124 In Search of Directions

The firm founded by James O. McKinsey (1889–1937) in 1926 experienced a similar trajectory during this period (see Higdon 1969; Wolf 1978; McKenna 2006; McDonald 2013). McKinsey obtained bachelor degrees in pedagogy and law, before focusing on accounting, initially lecturing in bookkeeping at the University of St. Louis. He then completed another bachelor's, at the University of Chicago's School of Commerce and Administration, joining its accounting faculty in 1917. After serving in the army during the war, in 1919 he completed a masters in accounting as well as his CPA exam, and started authoring many accounting- and finance-related textbooks (see also Chapter 9). In 1923–1924, he became vice president, then president of the American Association of University Instructors in Accounting, predecessor of today's American Accounting Association. As such, he played an important role in separating it from the American Economic Association and establishing the *Accounting Review*. But his ambitions and his vision went beyond accounting and in 1926 he established his own firm called "James O. McKinsey and Company, Accountants and Management Engineers" and was named Professor of Business Policy – a position he held concurrently until 1931.

His consulting activities received a boost from the Great Depression, when companies or their creditors required help with restructuring – a service he standardized with the creation of a 30-page "General Survey Outline." This tool was also used by many of his competitors and, as one of them, Stevenson, Jordan & Harrison, put it, "appraises the effectiveness of management, checks the organization procedures, the nature of records, the standards, budgets, quotas, and the like" (quoted by McKenna 2006: 67). McKinsey hired additional consultants. With hindsight two stand out: in 1929, Andrew Thomas "Tom" Kearney (1892–1962), who had been director of commercial research at meat packers Swift & Co.; and, in 1933, Marvin Bower (1903–2003), who had both a law degree and an MBA from Harvard and previously worked at the Cleveland-based law firm Jones Day (see Chapter 11).

In 1935 McKinsey joined one of his clients, the loss-making department store Marshall Fields, as Chairman and CEO in order to manage the implementation of his suggestions. To ensure the survival of his firm during his absence, in 1936 he agreed to a merger with the Boston-based accounting and consulting firm Scovell, Wellington & Company. The consulting activities of the combined firm operated under the McKinsey, Wellington & Co. name, employing 22 consultants in Chicago, 17 in New York and five in Boston (McDonald 2013: 31). However, professional and personal tensions appeared almost from the outset and came to a head after McKinsey died unexpectedly from pneumonia in 1937. Accounting and consulting firms split, Oliver Wellington was ousted and the offices started operating as a loose association rather than an integrated firm, even if they jointly opened an office in San Francisco in 1944. Commercially the firm thrived though (McDonald 2013: 41–53): participating in a study to reorganize US Steel; hiring a former labor relations manager from Procter & Gamble to help

Old Certainties and New Departures in Consulting   **125**

companies deal with the resurgent unions; and, during World War II, working for the federal government and for corporate clients adjusting to wartime production.

The above mentioned reorganization project for US Steel in the mid-1930s was worth 1.5 million US dollars in billings – a huge sum at the time. It was led by engineering consultants Ford, Bacon & Davis, who brought in various sub-contractors including McKinsey and Cleveland-based Robert Heller & Associates (Higdon 1969: 141). A Harvard trained economist, Heller had acquired a reputation in consulting on marketing and distribution (Anon. 1944: 145) and achieved even more visibility when asked to prepare a recommendation for the reorganization of US Congress during World War II (McKenna 2006: 67). The role and success of all these "management engineering" firms should not be overestimated though – easily done by focusing too much on what we know today. Thus, McKinsey employed a total of only 44 consultants in 1936 – compared to say Bedaux's 80 consultants in France alone (see above).

What they did do, however, was set up a professional association – not unusual for newcomers and challengers. Discussions among a dozen or so firms, including Booz Allen Hamilton, Ford, Bacon & Davis, Heller as well as McKinsey, started in 1929 and eventually led to the formation of the Association of Consulting Management Engineers (ACME) in 1933 (Higdon 1969, esp. Appendix D). By adopting a "Code of Professional Ethics," ACME was partially and officially aimed at making a distinction with some very aggressive consultants, like the "business engineering" firm founded by former bible salesman George S. May (1890–1962) in Chicago in 1925. It literally bombarded potential clients with promotional material vaunting the improvements introduced by its consultants – sending up to 4,800 letters a day (Anon. 1944: 213; see also Higdon 1969: Chapter 7; and Chapter 11). But equally, if not more importantly, ACME also tried to create visibility and legitimacy for this new group of firms.

As mentioned, World War II provided a significant boost to consulting activities. Thus, a 1944 *Fortune* article estimated the number of what they called "business consultants" in the US to have grown by about 50 percent since 1938, reaching a total of 7,000 (Anon. 1944: 142). The same article also displayed the increasing diversity of the field: Exemplary consultants discussed in some detail included, among others, Edwin G. Booz, Wallace Clark as well as the managing partner of McKinsey's New York office, Horace G. Crockett (pp. 144–146) – with George S. May mentioned separately as the "company [that] takes in more money than any other in the business-advisory field" (p. 213). Its concluding remarks showed that consultants had become institutionalized – at least as an occupation, and confirmed their predominantly commercial orientation: "The consulting field is now so promising that executives may well give up industrial jobs for what will possibly be more lucrative and almost certainly will be more exhilarating careers as advisers to other executives" (p. 213). Most importantly, using a medical metaphor, the article's title – "Doctors of Management" – also

126 In Search of Directions

highlighted their growing role and recognition as an authority. All of these trends would develop further in the subsequent period – in the US and, increasingly, elsewhere – with some shifts in terms of the most visible and authoritative firms.

References

Alchon, G. (1992) "Mary Van Kleeck and Scientific Management," in D. Nelson (ed.), *A Mental Revolution: Scientific management since Taylor*, Columbus, OH: Ohio State University Press, pp. 102–129.

Andersen, A. E. (1917) *Complete Accounting Course*, New York: Ronald Press.

Anon. (1942) "Bedaux Reformed," *Time*, 39(3), 19 January.

Anon. (1944) "Doctors of Management," *Fortune*, 30(1): 142–213.

Bedaux, C. E. (1917) *The Bedaux Efficiency Course for Industrial Application*, Grand Rapids, MI: Bedaux Industrial Institute.

Bailes, K. (1977) "Aleksei Gastev and the Soviet Controversy over Taylorism," *Soviet Studies*, 24(3): 386–391.

Brech, E., Thomson, A. and Wilson, J. F. (2010) *Lyndall Urwick, Management Pioneer: A biography*, Oxford: Oxford University Press.

Briggs, A. (1961) *Social Thought and Social Action: A study of the work of Seebohm Rowntree, 1871–1954*, London: Longman.

Bloemen, E. (1996) "The movement for scientific management in Europe between the wars," in J.-C. Spender and Hugo Kijne (eds), *Scientific Management: Frederick Winslow Taylor's gift to the world?*, Boston, MA: Kluwer, pp. 111–131.

Blumberg, S. K. (1981) "Seven decades of public administration: A tribute to Luther Gulick," *Public Administration Review*, 41(2): 245–248.

Boyns, T. (2007) "Lyndall Urwick at the International Management Institute, Geneva, 1928–1934: Right job, wrong man?" paper presented at the EBHA Conference in Geneva, 13–15 September. www.ebha.org/ebha2007/pdf/Boyns.pdf (accessed 2 January 2016).

CEGOS, 6 October 2015. www.cegos.com.

Chandler, A. D., Jr (1990) *Scale and Scope: The dynamics of industrial capitalism*, Cambridge, MA: Belknap Press.

Christy, J. (1984) *The Price of Power: A biography of Charles Eugène Bedaux*, Toronto: Doubleday.

Clark, W. (1922) *The Gantt Chart: A working tool of management*, New York: Ronald Press.

Engwall, L., Furusten, S., and Wallerstedt, E. (2002) "The changing relationship between management consulting and academia: Evidence from Sweden," in M. Kipping and L. Engwall (eds), *Management Consulting*, Oxford: Oxford University Press, pp. 36–51.

Fesler, J. W. (1987) "The Brownlow Committee Fifty Years Later," *Public Administration Review*, 47(4): 291–296.

Flanner, J. (1945) "Annals of collaboration: Equivalism I–III," *New Yorker*, 21 (22 September): 28–47; (6 October): 32–45; (13 October): 32–48.

Gulick, L. and Urwick, L. (eds) (1937) *Papers on the Science of Administration*, New York: Columbia University.

Hellema, P. and Marsman, J. (1997) *De organisatie-adviseur: De opkomst en groei van een nieuw vak in Nederland 1920–1960*, Meppel: Boom.

Henry, O. (2012) *Les guérisseurs de l'économie: Ingénieurs-conseil en quête de pouvoir*, Paris: CNRS Éditions.

Higdon, H. (1969) *The Business Healers*, New York: Random House.

Jeacle, I. (2004) "Emporium of glamour and sanctum of scientific management: The early twentieth century department store," *Management Decision*, 42(9): 1162–1177.

Kipping, M. (1997) "Consultancies, institutions and the diffusion of Taylorism in Britain, Germany and France, 1920s to 1950s," *Business History*, 39(4): 67–83.

Kipping, M. (1999a) "American management consulting companies in Western Europe, 1920 to 1990: Products, reputation and relationships," *Business History Review*, 73(2): 190–220.

Kipping, M. (1999b) "British economic decline: Blame it on the consultants?" *Contemporary British History*, 13(3): 23–38.

Kleiner, A. (2004) *Booz Allen Hamilton: Helping clients envision the future*, Old Saybrook, CT: Greenwich Publishing.

Kreis, S. (1992) "The diffusion of scientific management: The Bedaux Company in America and Britain, 1926–1945," in D. Nelson (ed.), *A Mental Revolution: Scientific management since Taylor*, Columbus, OH: Ohio State University Press, pp. 156–174.

Maier, C. S. (1970) "Taylorism and technology: European ideologies and the vision of industrial productivity in the 1920s," *Journal of Contemporary History*, 5(2): 27–61.

Marsh & McLennan Companies, 6 October 2015. www.mmc.com/about-us/about-history/about-timeline.html.

McDonald, D. (2013) *The Firm: The story of McKinsey and its secret influence on American business*, New York: Simon & Schuster.

McKenna, C. D. (2006) *The World's Newest Profession: Management consulting in the twentieth century*, New York: Cambridge University Press.

Merkle, J. (1980) *Management and Ideology: The legacy of the international scientific management movement*, Berkeley, CA: University of California Press.

Moore, M. V. and Crampton, J. (2000) "Arthur Andersen: Challenging the status quo," *Journal of Business Leadership* (Fall): 71–89. www.anbhf.org/pdf/moore_crampton.pdf (accessed 2 January 2016).

Morgan, S. L. (2004) "Professional associations and the diffusion of new management ideas in Shanghai, 1920–1930s: A research agenda," *Business and Economic History On-Line*. www.thebhc.org/sites/default/files/Morgan_1.pdf (accessed 2 January 2016).

Moutet, A. (1997) *Les Logiques de l'entreprise: La rationalisation dans l'industrie française de l'entre-deux-guerres*, Paris: Éditions de l'EHESS.

NICB (1930) *Systems of Wage Payment*, New York: National Industrial Conference Board.

Parker, L. D. and Ritson, P. (2011) "Rage, rage against the dying of the light: Lyndall Urwick's scientific management," *Journal of Management History*, 17(4): 379–398.

Quigel, J. P., Jr (1992) *The Business of Selling Efficiency: Harrington Emerson and the Emerson Efficiency Engineers, 1900–1930*, unpublished Ph.D. dissertation, Pennsylvania State University.

Sanders, T. H. (1926) "Wage systems: An appraisal," *Harvard Business Review*, 5(1): 11–20.

Squires, S. E., Smith, C. J., McDougall, L., and Yeack, W. R. (2003) *Inside Arthur Andersen: Shifting values, unexpected consequences*, London: FT Press.

Stillman, Y. (2004), "Edward Filene: Pioneer of social responsibility," *Jewish Currents*, September. www.jewishcurrents.org/2004-sept-stillman.htm (accessed 2 January 2016).

Tisdall, P. (1982) *Agents of Change: The development and practice of management consultancy*, London: Heinemann.

Towers Watson, 7 October 2015. www.towerswatson.com/en/about-us/history.

Tsutsui, W. M. (2001) "The way of efficiency: Ueno Yōichi and scientific management in twentieth-century Japan," *Modern Asian Studies*, 35(2): 441–467.

Wolf, W. B. (1978) *Management and Consulting: An introduction to James O. McKinsey*, Ithaca, NY: Cornell University.

128 In Search of Directions

Wrege, C. D., Greenwood, R. G., and Hata, S. (1987) "The International Management Institute and political opposition to its efforts in Europe, 1925−1934," *Business & Economic History*, 2nd series, 16: 249−265.

Wren, D. A. (2015) "Implementing the Gantt chart in Europe and Britain: The contributions of Wallace Clark," *Journal of Management History*, 21(3): 309–327.

Wren, D. A., Greenwood, R. A., Teahen, J., and Bedeian, A. G. (2015) "C. Bertrand Thompson and management consulting in Europe, 1917−1934," *Journal of Management History*, 21(1): 15−39.

9

BROADENING AUDIENCES FOR BUSINESS PUBLICATIONS

The interwar period saw increasing efforts in business-oriented publishing. The four publishers presented in Chapter 6, and particularly McGraw-Hill, extended their activities in business and management, while multiple new actors entered the field. The period also witnessed a change in terms of the contents of the books and articles from a focus on shop-floor efficiency toward finance, marketing, and the human aspects of management – with publications based on the Hawthorne studies and Chester Barnard's discussion of the functions of executives particularly influential for the future development of management thinking. And, so was the publishing of Peter Drucker, which started in the late 1930s and continued until the late 1990s, and that of Henri Fayol. During this period the business press continued to develop on both sides of the Atlantic in terms of an increasing circulation of the established titles and the addition of new ones. Likewise, a number of academic journals were launched by universities and professional associations.

Publishers: New Actors and Increasing Numbers of Management Books

Wiley, Harper, Macmillan, and McGraw-Hill

During the interwar period, the emerging field for business and management books continued to grow within the broader field of book publishing – with established publishers expanding their offering and others entering the field. The four publishers founded in the previous period, Wiley, Harper, Macmillan, and McGraw-Hill (see Chapter 6), kept adding new titles to their management portfolios as shown in Table 9.1, which is based on searches in library catalogs.

130 In Search of Directions

TABLE 9.1 A Selection of Management Publications Published in the Interwar Period

Year	Title	Publisher	Reference
1917	Applied Methods of Scientific Management	Wiley	Parkhurst (1917)
1917	Manufacturing Costs and Accounts	McGraw-Hill	Church (1917)
1923	Frederick W. Taylor	Harper	Copley (1923)
1923	Personnel Management	McGraw-Hill (Shaw)	Scott and Clothier (1923)
1925	Office Management	McGraw-Hill	Leffingwell (1925)
1927	Time and Motion Study and Formulas for Wage Incentives	McGraw-Hill	Lowry, Maynard, and Stegemerten (1927)
1928	Scientific Purchasing	McGraw-Hill	Gushee and Boffey (1928)
1928	A Scientific Approach to Investment Management	Harper	Rose (1928)
1931	Industrial Engineering and Management	McGraw-Hill	Barnes (1931)
1932	Common Sense Applied to Motion and Time Study	McGraw-Hill	Mogensen (1932)
1933	Introduction to Sales Management	McGraw-Hill	Tosdal (1933)
1933	The Human Problems of an Industrial Civilization	Macmillan	Mayo (1933)
1940	Industrial Organization and Management	Harper	Davis (1940)
1940	Industrial Management	Wiley	Lansburgh and Spriegel (1940)
1943	Management of Manpower	Macmillan	Knowles and Thomson (1943a)
1943	Production Control	Macmillan	Knowles and Thomson (1943b)
1943	Textbook of Office Management	McGraw-Hill	Leffingwell and Robinson (1943)
1944	Industrial Management	Macmillan	Knowles and Thomson (1944)
1945	Top-Management Planning	Harper	Hempel (1945)
1945	Management of Inspection and Quality Control	Harper	Juran (1945)
1945	Budgeting for Management Control	Harper	Rowland (1945)
1945	Industrial Organization and Management	McGraw-Hill	Bethel (1945)
1945	Business Executive's Guide	McGraw-Hill	Lasser (1945)

In terms of content, Wiley continued in the scientific management tradition and had books on industrial management both in the beginning (Parkhurst 1917) and toward the end of the period (Lansburgh and Spriegel 1940). Similarly, Harper published a book on Frederick W. Taylor in the beginning of the period (Copley 1923) and at the end (Davis 1940). The vitality of Taylor's ideas is also demonstrated by two books from Macmillan (Knowles and Thomson 1943a, 1944) and four from McGraw-Hill (Lowry, Maynard, and Stegemerten 1927; Barnes 1931; Mogensen 1932; Bethel 1945). Related titles from Macmillan (Knowles and Thomson 1943b) and Harper (Juran 1945) dealt with production control and quality control, respectively. In addition, scientific management was also applied to purchasing in a book from McGraw-Hill (Gushée and Boffey 1928). At the same time, the human aspects in management received increasing attention. Already in the 1920s McGraw-Hill printed books on personnel management (Scott and Clothier 1923) and office management (Leffingwell 1925), while Macmillan published Elton Mayo's *The Human Problems of an Industrial Civilization* (Mayo 1933). At the end of the period the same publishing house brought out four titles on the relationship with employees (Leffingwell and Robinson 1943; Cantor 1945; Gardiner 1945; Hill and Hook 1945).

All in all, these four publishing houses brought out a number of publications in the management area both related to the traditions of scientific management and to new business issues. Table 9.1 also shows the increasing activity of McGraw-Hill in the business and management area in relation to the other three publishers. However, it is evident from the accounts of the histories of the four companies that, at the time, genres other than business publishing dominated their publication lists. The titles mentioned above therefore appear more as exceptions rather than the rule. Jacobson et al. (2007: 110 and 149) thus report that less than 10 percent of the Wiley publications between 1865 and 1956 were in the business area, while engineering and science accounted for the majority. For the interwar period, the Harper biography (Exman 1965: Chapter 20) does not even mention business and management texts at all. The history of the UK publisher Macmillan (James 2002) shows a prominent connection to the economic sciences. After an economic controversy with Cambridge University Press, John Maynard Keynes (1883–1946) went to Macmillan and they accepted his manuscript (Moggridge and Keynes 1992: 219–21). As result, a number of Keynes' publications, among them the highly influential *The General Theory of Employment, Interest and Money* (Keynes 1936), came to be published by Macmillan.

Other Early Entrants: The Ronald Press and University Presses

The Ronald Press continued to add new titles to its business list (see Chapter 6), including textbooks, particularly in accounting, such as Arthur Andersen's *Complete Accounting Course* (Andersen 1917), Roy Kester's *Accounting Theory and Practice* (Kester 1917) and *Budgetary Control* (1922) by James O. McKinsey (see

132 In Search of Directions

Chapter 8). Other titles were *The Economics of Retailing* by the marketing pioneer, and subsequent first editor of the *Journal of Marketing* (see below), Paul H. Nystrom (1915), *Developing Executive Ability* by Enoch Burton Gowin (1919) as well as one of the internationally most influential books during this period, presenting *The Gantt Chart* as a management tool by Wallace Clark (1922) (see Chapter 8). The Ronald Press even published a journal in 1921−1923: *Administration: The Journal of Business Analysis and Control* (see Ronald Press Company 12 October 2015).

Among the university presses founded earlier, the University of Chicago Press was particularly open for business books. In 1921 it published Leon C. Marshall's *Business Administration*, a textbook of more than 900 pages. Three years later, *Managerial Accounting* by James O. McKinsey came off their press (McKinsey 1924). They also published books on overhead costs (Clark 1923), social control of business (Clark 1926), business forecasts (Cox 1929), business cycles (Barnett 1941), and a statistical analysis of costs in a chain of shoe stores (Dean and Warren 1942). A similar orientation toward more quantitative approaches was demonstrated by the Bureau of Business Research in the School of Business Administration at the University of Michigan through the publication of Merwin H. Waterman's *Public Utility Financing 1930−35* (Waterman 1936). However, the most significant publication among the quantitatively oriented university press publications was no doubt John von Neumann's and Oskar Morgenstern's path-breaking *Theory of Games and Economic Behaviour* (Neumann and Morgenstern 1944). It paved the way for game theory not only in the economic sciences but also more generally.

At Harvard a number publications appeared from the business school. Two of these, published in the early 1930s, came to be particularly influential: Edwin Chamberlin's *The Theory of Monopolistic Competition* (Chamberlin 1933) and Fritz J. Roethlisberger's and William J. Dickson's *Management and the Worker* (Roethlisberger and Dickson 1934). The first of these books, together with another book published in the same year by Joan Robinson (1933), radically changed ideas about markets. In a similar way, the second book, which reported on the experiments at Western Electric's Hawthorne plant, changed the focus from scientific management toward human relations, particularly in the United States (see also Chapter 2). In an edited volume a few years later (McNair and Lewis 1938) Harvard faculty members published chapters on business and modern society. That same year Harvard University Press also published what was to become another highly influential management classic: *The Functions of the Executive* by Chester Barnard (Barnard 1938), which was based on the author's personal experience (for Harvard University Press, see Hall 1986).

Four Additional Publishers

In addition to the above mentioned publishers, there were a number of new entrants − new in the sense that they started publishing business-related books during this period. One of them is Prentice-Hall, which had been started in 1913 by the law professor Charles W. Gerstenberg (1882–1948) and his student Richard P. Ettinger (1893–1971) – and named by combining the maiden names of their mothers (Thomas 1996). Their first publication in business was Gerstenberg's *Financial Organization and Management of Business* in 1924 (Gerstenberg 1924), which would, over time, be published in five editions (1924, 1932, 1939, 1951, and 1959). These repeated editions can be seen as an early indication of a growing textbook market with successive revisions of old texts. Gerstenberg's book was followed among Prentice-Hall titles in 1931 by John William Wingate's *Manual of Retail Terms* (Wingate 1931) and Dale Yoder's *Personnel Management and Industrial Relations* (Yoder 1942). As their titles indicate, these three books show, like the titles in Table 9.1, the development of the field from an engineering efficiency focus toward broader issues like finance, marketing, and human aspects of management. As will be seen in Chapters 12 and 15, they were just a modest start for a much more significant development of the management book publishing field in the future.

Another significant event in the interwar period for the later development was the move in 1921 by Pearson – originally founded in 1844 as a construction company – into media by purchasing and combining a number of local UK newspapers into the Westminster Press. Pearson was eventually to become a very significant multinational media group (Pearson 5 May 2015a; see further Chapters 12 and 15; Box 12.2). A similar story is provided by the media empire of the Thomson family, which started its media business in 1931 through the acquisition of the Canadian newspaper *Timmins Press*. Through further acquisitions it would subsequently become very influential in the business media field, not least as the owner of Reuters (Thomson Reuters 5 May 2015; see further Box 15.2). A third entrant in the interwar period was Addison-Wesley, created in 1942 and named after the first, and not – as most others had done – the last names of its founders. In the 1960s it started to publish management titles but was eventually acquired in 1988 by the above mentioned Pearson group (Pearson 5 May 2015b). Finally, this period also saw the foundation of Random House in 1925 by Bennett Cerf and Donald Klopfer, which eventually became the world's largest general-interest publisher – owned, since 1998, by the German Bertelsmann AG (Funding Universe 5 May 2015).

The university presses, finally, saw the emergence of a new member in the mid-1920s when MIT Press published its first piece: a lecture series entitled *Problems of Atomic Dynamics* given by the visiting German physicist and later Nobel Laureate, Max Born (1926). Six years later, in 1932, MIT's publishing operations were formally constituted with the creation of an imprint called Technology Press. Between 1937 and 1962 its editorial and marketing functions were undertaken by Wiley (MIT Press 5 May 2015). Although primarily oriented toward science and engineering, it later on also published a few titles in management such

134 In Search of Directions

as Alfred Chandler's *Strategy and Structure* (Chandler 1962) and Jay Galbraith's *Designing Complex Organizations* (Galbraith 1973).

The Emergence of General Management Books

Chester Barnard (1886–1961) became very influential despite the fact that he did not publish much in addition to the 1938 book (see above). This is in contrast to another management author, Peter Drucker (1909–2005), whose publishing record spanned more than six decades starting in the late 1930s (see further Box 9.1). His first book, published by the British company Heinemann, founded in 1890, was entitled *The End of Economic Man* and critically discussed the leadership of Henry Ford (Drucker 1939). Three years later, the US publisher John Day Co., founded in 1926, brought out *The Future of Industrial Man*, which developed a basic social theory (Drucker 1942). These two books were the start of a stream of about 30 management books (among others, Drucker 1946, 1954, 1974, 1985, and 1999). Most of these were published by Harper in its different constellations (see Chapters 12 and 15).

Outside the Anglophone world, an important management book was published by the French publisher Dunod et Pinat, founded in Paris in 1905: Henri Fayol's *Administration industrielle et générale* (Fayol 1917), which had first been published as a journal article the year before, and then published in an English translation in 1930 by the British publisher Pitman. However, it was only the publication of a second English edition in 1949 with a foreword by Lyndall Urwick – which, it should be noted as highly indicative, translated *administration* to "management" – that made it more widely known (Fayol 1949; see also Box 8.1). Much faster were transfers of American publications to Europe. For example, Taylor's *The Principles of Scientific Management* (Taylor 1911) was available in a Swedish translation already two years after its original publication (Taylor 1913). Likewise Frank B. Gilbreth's *Primer of Scientific Management* (Gilbreth 1912) was published in German by Springer five years after the original publication (Gilbreth and Ross 1917) (see, for additional translations, Guillén 1994). These examples underline the emerging internationalization, or rather Americanization, in the management book publishing field during the interwar period.

BOX 9.1 PETER F. DRUCKER: PHILOSOPHER OF MANAGEMENT

Drucker was born in Vienna in 1909. His father was a prominent lawyer with a number of intellectual friends, such as Joseph Schumpeter, who impressed the young Peter. After school he worked mainly as a journalist and studied law at the University of Frankfurt where he received a Ph.D. in international law in 1931. Of Jewish descent, he emigrated to England in 1933 and, another three years later, moved to the United States, where he became Professor of Politics and Philosophy at Bennington College in 1942. He stayed there until 1949, when he was recruited as Professor of Management to New York University. His tenure there lasted until 1971, when he moved to the Claremont Graduate University in California. Drucker was a very productive author. His bibliography lists 39 books, many of them translated into other languages, and a large number of articles in outlets like *Harper's Magazine*, the *Harvard Business Review*, and the *Wall Street Journal*. His writings have been described as a move from scientific management toward management as philosophy. A central idea in that context was "management by objectives," i.e. the notion that managers should use goals instead of detailed instructions. More generally, Drucker argued for decentralization and outsourcing but also for the social responsibility of corporations. An early book was *Concept of Corporation* (1946), based on two years of observations at General Motors. It did not become popular among GM top executives but brought Drucker a large number of consulting engagements. Subsequent books included *The Practice of Management* (1954), *Managing for Results* (1964), *The Effective Executive* (1967). His last book *The Daily Drucker* (Drucker and Maciariello 2004) was published the year before he died in 2005 at the age of 95. Through his work as a consultant to major corporations and through his writings he is by many considered to have been a significant actor for the shaping of modern ideas of management. In the words of Witzel (1996: 1060): "Drucker's philosophy of management has pervaded management thinking at all levels, from the highest reaches of business academia to the lowest levels of even small companies."

Sources: Tarrant (1976); Witzel (1996); Beatty (1998); Flaherty (1999).

It can thus be concluded that the four major publishers identified in Chapter 6 as well as the university presses continued to publish management-oriented texts. The number of titles had increased compared to the previous period, but was still not a significant part of their overall publication lists. Additional growth occurred through a small number of new entrants. In terms of content, the publications in the interwar period reflect the development of the business literature from a rather narrow focus on the efficient organization of work and the workflow to include issues of human relations, marketing, financing, etc. Toward the end of the period there were also a number of publications that looked specifically at management in a broader sense, namely by Barnard and Drucker.

Expansion of the Business Press: Higher Circulation and New Titles

Similar to book publishing, the business press field also saw an expansion through an increase in circulation of the extant papers and the launching of a number of new

136 In Search of Directions

titles. While still part of the overall field of periodic publications, the economic and business press became increasingly discernible and independent.

In the UK, William and Gomer Berry, who since 1915 were the owners of the *Sunday Times*, in 1919, also took over the *Financial Times*. During their ownership the *Financial Times* kept a sober style and became, according to Kynaston (1988), "the stockbroker's Bible." At the same time their competitor from the very beginning, the *Financial News*, tried to address a broader audience – albeit without much success, taking it to the brink of bankruptcy. In this situation, in 1945 William Berry sold the *Financial Times* to its competitor, who combined the two papers, though understandably retaining the *Financial Times* title (Kynaston 1988).

In the US, the *Wall Street Journal* was for the first part of the interwar period run by Clarence W. Barron, who developed the contents of the journal as well as increased its circulation. In 1903, the year after Barron had taken over, the paper sold 11,957 copies. Circulation more than doubled to 27,925 by 1925, and again almost doubled to 52,047 by 1930 (Wendt 1982: 88, 167, 204). However, Barron himself neither experienced the last of these figures nor the Great Crash of 1929, since he died in October 1928. Under the leadership of Kenneth C. Hogate (1890–1947) the *Wall Street Journal* managed to survive the Great Depression. Then, in the early 1940s, it was radically reshaped by the new managing editor Bernard Kilgore (1908–1967). According to Wendt (1982: 299), "he and his staff had totally revised the paper from front to back." Most important was probably the new design of the front page: no photos, no ads, and six columns, of which those to the very left and very right were the lead stories (Scharff 1986: 78–79; see also Rosenberg 1982).

Clarence W. Barron was not only successful in running Dow Jones & Co and the *Wall Street Journal*. In 1921, he also launched a business weekly, *Barron's National Financial Weekly*, nowadays just *Barron's*. As its original name indicates, it provided information and analyses for investors. In this way he added a competitor to the UK-based *Economist* and to *Forbes*. Of these the *Economist* succeeded, particularly during the war years, to increase its circulation considerably. At the turn of the century, it had sold around 3,500 copies, a figure that had risen to 6,000 in 1920 and reached 17,744 in 1945 (Edwards 1995: 951, 617, 875). By contrast, the circulation of *Forbes*, which was edited by its founder B. C. Forbes until 1954, only took off in the late 1950s.

The *Economist, Forbes*, and *Barron's* got an additional competitor in 1929, when the publishing company McGraw-Hill launched *Business Week* – shortly before the Wall Street Crash. Somewhat surprisingly, it was followed four months after the Crash, in 1930, by the launching of the monthly magazine *Fortune*. Its founder was Henry R. Luce (1898–1967), who, in 1923, together with his friend Briton Hadden (1898–1929) started to publish the news magazine *Time*. After Hadden's death in 1929 Luce launched not only *Fortune* but also *Life* in 1934 and *Sports Illustrated* in 1954. In this way Luce became a significant publisher of magazines. *Fortune* became particularly known for its listings of the largest companies in the United States and other parts of the world from 1955 onwards (see, for *Fortune*, Baughman 1987; for the financial press in general, Parsons 1989; Kurtz 2000).

Similar trends to the Anglophone field could also be observed in other countries. For instance, in Germany the business weekly *Wirtschaftswoche* appeared in 1926 and in France *Les Échos*, founded in Paris as a monthly publication in 1908 by Robert and Émile Servan-Schreiber, turned into a daily in 1928. The same year the Swedish business economics magazine *Tidskrift för affärsekonomi* started to be published, presenting articles by business professors for practitioners. It had been preceded by the Nordic Magazine on Organization or *Nordisk tidskrift i organization*, published between 1919 and 1922, which included many articles inspired by scientific management. Similar publications were also started in other countries.

During the interwar period the national fields encompassing the periodic publishing of business news and management ideas clearly came into their own and were increasingly distinct from the general press. Thus, several additional specialist titles were launched in the US and new ones also emerged in many other industrialized countries. In addition, most of the earlier publications increased their circulation numbers quite significantly. Together these developments reflect the growing interest in business and management as well as in information on stock markets – an interest that, maybe somewhat surprisingly, does not seem to have been dented by the Great Crash of 1929.

Academic Journals: New Initiatives from Universities and Professional Associations

Four Interwar Entrants

The interwar period saw a growth in the field of academic journal publishing with the foundation of four titles, which today are included in the *FT*45 list (Table 9.2): the *Harvard Business Review* (1922), the *Accounting Review* (1926), *Econometrica* (1933) and the *Journal of Marketing* (1936). The first was published by the Harvard Business School, while the other three were launched by professional associations, similar to what had happened in the previous period.

In the *Harvard Business Review*, although it is primarily addressing practitioners, the bulk of the authors are academics, mainly prominent professors at the Harvard Business School (see further Box 9.2). Widely cited papers in the first five years were Melvin T. Copeland's "Relation of consumers' buying habits to marketing methods" (Copeland 1923), and three articles by the second Harvard Business School dean Wallace B. Donham (1919–42) entitled "Essential groundwork for a broad executive theory," "The social significance of business," and "The emerging profession of business" (Donham 1922, 1927a and 1927b), which reflect his

138 In Search of Directions

TABLE 9.2 Academic Journals on the *FT*45 Founded in the Interwar Period

Name of journal	Founded	First publisher	Present publisher
Harvard Business Review	1922	Harvard Business School	Harvard Business School Publishing
Accounting Review	1926	American Accounting Association	American Accounting Association
Econometrica	1933	Econometric Society	Blackwell-Wiley
Journal of Marketing	1936	American Marketing Association	American Marketing Association

overall vision for business and the role of the business school (see Chapter 7 for details).

The *Accounting Review* started its publication in 1926. As already pointed out in Chapter 8, James O. McKinsey, who founded his consulting firm in the same year, played an important role in its establishment. The journal was launched after intense discussions in the American Association of University Instructors of Accounting, which was renamed American Accounting Association in 1935. Already in 1919 there had been a proposal to start a *Quarterly Journal of Accountics*, but it took seven years to materialize due to internal controversies regarding the scientific standards of accounting. During the early decades the articles in *Accounting Review* were to a large extent devoted to education and accounting problems in particular contexts. From 1929 to 1943 a practitioner, Eric Kohler (1892–1976), served as the editor (Heck and Jensen 2007: 117–118).

The third title in Table 9.2, *Econometrica*, was founded in 1933 as a quarterly journal by the Econometric Society, which in turn had been created two years earlier. Its first editor was the 1969 Nobel Laureate Ragnar Frisch (1895–1973), who in his first editorial stressed "the quantitative aspect of economic problems." He went on to point out that econometrics implied the integration of economic statistics, general economic theory and the application of mathematics to economics, and that *Econometrica* aimed at being a clearing-house for econometric work (Frisch 1933). After this editorial followed, among others, articles by Joseph Schumpeter on the common sense of econometrics (Schumpeter 1933), and by Frisch's co-Laureate Jan Tinbergen (1933, in French) on the use of equations and complex numbers in economic research. Although this journal was primarily directed toward economists, it has relevance here due to their role as faculty members in business schools. *Econometrica* is presently published by Blackwell-Wiley for the Econometric Society.

BOX 9.2 THE *HARVARD BUSINESS REVIEW*

The first issue of the *Harvard Business Review* was published in October 1922, and this was the only issue that year. The opening article "Essential groundwork for a broad executive theory" was authored by the then dean of the Business School, Wallace B. Donham. It was followed by some dozen articles on various topics, a summary of research and case studies as well as book reviews. In the following year the number of issues was increased to four, a number which was increased in 1948 to six and doubled in 2002 to the present 12 issues per year. Over time the *HBR* has become more and more practitioner oriented. One important sign of this is the collaboration since 1959 with the consulting firm McKinsey in giving awards to each year's two most significant *HBR* articles. Among past winners have been a number of Harvard faculty members like Clayton M. Christensen, Theodore Levitt, Rosabeth Moss Kanter, and Michael Porter. Among the rewarded authors are also the above mentioned Peter Drucker (see Box 9.1), a non-Harvard faculty member, who received the award as many as seven times. One of the award winners, Theodore Levitt, is also considered to have been instrumental in transforming the *HBR* during his editorship in the early 1980s "from a dry academic journal to a readable management magazine that featured cartoons" (Guru: Theodore Levitt 28 May 2015). This transformation was reinforced still further when the former deputy director of *Time* magazine, Adi Ignatius, was recruited as editor-in-chief in 2009. He has since then made further efforts to address a broader audience. In 2015 the *HBR* had a circulation of about 250,000 copies in English. In addition it publishes global editions in 11 countries or areas outside the United States: Brazil, China, France, Germany, Italy, Japan, Poland, Russia, South Asia, South Korea, and Taiwan. As a result the *HBR* has been mentioned as the "fourth most influential magazine in the world" (*HBR* Under Review 28 May 2015) and as having "a significant impact on the scientific discourse in management research" (Schulz and Nicolai 2015) – good indicators for it having gained definitional power over management.

Sources: PdfSR.com 5 May 2015; HBR Under Review 28 May 2015; Guru: Theodore Levitt 28 May 2015; *Harvard Business Review* 28 May 2015; various *HBR* issues.

The *Journal of Marketing*, finally, was founded in 1936 after a merger between the American Marketing Society and the National Association of Marketing Teachers (also in the US). They both had their own journals – the *American Marketing Journal*, published in 1934–1936, and the *National Marketing Review*, published in 1935–1936, which now were combined into one publication with issues in January, April, July, and October. The first editor was the Columbia marketing professor, Paul H. Nystrom (1878–1969) (Agnew and Coutant 1936). Like the *Accounting Review*, the *Journal of Marketing* constitutes a clear sign of the increasing specialization and institutionalization of the field of academic business journals. Both journals also show the significance of teachers for the formation of the field. The development in the marketing area is also consistent with Fligstein's (1990: 161) findings that "the sales and marketing conception of control dominated the tactics of the largest firms from the Depression until the mid-1950s" (see also Chapter 2).

Impact and Orientation of the Nine FT45 Journals

At the end of the interwar period, in total, nine of the *FT*45 journals thus had been founded. An analysis of the impact of papers published in these nine journals (Table 9.3) reveals both differences in terms of citations and the content of the most cited papers. For natural reasons the most cited papers in the journals founded in the early period, with one exception, have higher citation figures than their followers in the interwar period. The exception, the *Journal of Applied Psychology*, was only cited about 50 times, a circumstance that can be seen as an indication of a weaker integration of the field at the time. Among those founded in the interwar period, the *Harvard Business Review* is the one that received most attention.

Out of the authors of the papers in Table 9.3, there were a number of currently highly regarded economists: John Maynard Keynes in the *Quarterly Journal of Economics*, Milton Friedman in the *Journal of the American Statistical Association*, Harold Hotelling in the *Journal of Political Economy*, and Friedrich von Hayek in the *American Economic Review*, but also an authority in the developing field of marketing: Melvin T. Copeland in the *Harvard Business Review*.

In terms of their content, the most cited articles from the period in the economics-oriented journals dealt with issues such as employment (Keynes 1937), rank correlation (Friedman 1937), environmental issues (Hotelling 1931), knowledge in society (Hayek 1945), and urban economics (Clark 1945). The most cited papers in the four more business-oriented journals dealt with work organization (Poffenberger 1928), consumer behavior (Copeland 1923), amortization (Preinreich 1937), and the development of marketing (Converse 1945). We can thus see a clear difference between the groups of journals in terms of study objects: the economists are focussing on macro-level issues, while the business scholars direct their interest toward more micro-level questions involving organizations, their workers, and their customers.

Broadening Audiences for Business Publications **141**

TABLE 9.3 The Most Cited Papers in July 2014 from the Interwar Period in the Nine *FT*45 Journals

Name of journal	Start	Most cited	Title	Cited
Quarterly Journal of Economics	1886	Keynes (1937)	The general theory of employment	2,876
Journal of the American Statistical Association	1888	Friedman (1937)	The use of ranks to avoid the assumption of normality implicit in the analysis of variance	1,987
Journal of Political Economy	1892	Hotelling (1931)	The economics of exhaustible resources	4,152
American Economic Review	1911	Hayek (1945)	The use of knowledge in society	10,675
Journal of Applied Psychology	1917	Poffenberger (1928)	The effects of continuous work upon output and feelings	55
Harvard Business Review	1922	Copeland (1923)	Relation of consumers buying habits to marketing methods	670
Accounting Review	1926	Preinreich (1937)	Valuation and amortization	157
Econometrica	1933	Clark (1945)	The economic functions of a city in relation to its size	98
Journal of Marketing	1936	Converse (1945)	The development of the science of marketing: an exploratory survey	131

Sources: Search at Google Scholar in July 2014 on most cited papers in the nine journals published between 1916 and 1945.

The *FT45* Journals in Context

In addition to the four journals in Table 9.2, there was also another business-oriented journal that started its publication in the interwar period: the *Journal of Business* published by the University of Chicago Press in collaboration with Cambridge University Press (London), the Maruzen Co. (Tokyo), and the Commercial Press (Shanghai). It actually began publication in 1922 under the title *The University Journal of Business*, changed to *The Journal of Business of the University of Chicago* in 1928 and eventually, in 1954, to the *Journal of Business*. It can be seen as a complement to the *Quarterly Journal of Economics* published since 1892 by the University of Chicago Press. According to *JSTOR*, it was "the first scholarly journal to focus on business-related research and played a pioneering role in fostering serious academic research about business" (*JSTOR* 5 May 2015). It was published four times a year until 2006, when the publication was terminated due to the difficulties of competing in a field characterized by increasing specialization. During its existence though the *Journal of Business* published several highly

142 In Search of Directions

cited papers, including several ones authored by later Nobel Laureates, such as Fama (1965), Sharpe (1966), McFadden (1980), as well as Tversky and Kahneman (1986). If the publication of the *Journal of Business* had continued, it probably would have been part of the *FT*45 list. Nevertheless, the decision to close down a journal with a general orientation constitutes a strong reminder of the increasing specialization within this field.

Yet another journal published in Chicago from 1940 onwards, the *Public Administration Quarterly*, constitutes a further example for a scientific association – in this case the American Society for Public Administration – launching its own journal. As the name indicates, it was directed toward public administration, something clearly demonstrated by the second issue focusing on the executive office of the president – which had been subject to a review by the so-called Brownlow Committee a few years earlier (see Chapters 2 and 8). Subsequently, the journal published papers highly cited by management scholars, including Herbert A. Simon's "Decision-making and administrative organization" (Simon 1944) and Charles E. Lindblom's "The science of 'muddling through'" (Lindblom 1959).

For the business- and management-related academic journals it has again been demonstrated how professional associations were important for the launching of new journals in line with the model presented in Chapter 6. In addition, like in the previous period, the University of Chicago Press was active in creating a new outlet for scholarly work, this time a journal focusing explicitly on business. It has also been evident that faculty members were significant in the shaping of the field of academic business journals, while at the same time contributing to its fragmentation in line with the increasing specialization in business academia. Many of these emerging trends would continue and take more definite forms in the subsequent period.

References

Agnew, H. E. and Coutant, F. R. (1936) "The Journal of Marketing makes its bow," *Journal of Marketing*, 1(1): 2.

Andersen, A. (1917) *Complete Accounting Course*, New York: Ronald Press.

Barnard, C. I. (1938) *The Functions of the Executive*, Cambridge, MA: Harvard University Press.

Barne, R. M. (1931) *Industrial Engineering and Management: Problems and policies*, New York: McGraw-Hill.

Barnett, P. (1941) *Business-cycle Theory in the United States, 1860–1900*, Chicago, IL: University of Chicago Press.

Baughman, J. L. (1987) *Henry R. Luce and the Rise of the American News Media*, Boston, MA: Twayne Publishers.

Beatty, J. (1998) *The World According to Drucker: The life and work of the world's greatest management thinker*, London: Orion Business.

Bethel, L. L. (1945) *Industrial Organization and Management*, New York: McGraw-Hill.

Born, M. (1926) *Problems of Atomic Dynamics*, Cambridge, MA: MIT Press.

Cantor, N. F. (1945) *Employee Counseling: A new viewpoint in industrial psychology*, New York: McGraw-Hill.

Chamberlin, E. (1933) *The Theory of Monopolistic Competition*, Cambridge, MA: Harvard Economic Studies.

Chandler, A. D., Jr (1962) *Strategy and Structure: Chapters in the history of the American industrial enterprise*, Cambridge, MA: MIT Press.

Church, A. H. (1917) *Manufacturing Costs and Accounts*, New York: McGraw-Hill.

Clark, C. (1945) "The economic functions of a city in relation to its size," *Econometrica*, 13(2): 97–113.

Clark, J. M. (1923) *Studies in the Economics of Overhead Costs*, Chicago, IL: University of Chicago Press.

Clark, J. M. (1926) *Social Control of Business*, Chicago, IL: University of Chicago Press.

Clark, W. (1922) *The Gantt Chart*, New York: Ronald Press.

Converse, P. D. (1945) "The development of the science of marketing: An exploratory survey," *Journal of Marketing*, 10(1): 14–23.

Copeland, M. T. (1923) "Relation of consumers' buying habits to marketing methods," *Harvard Business Review*, 1(3): 282–289.

Copley, F. B. (1923) *Frederick W. Taylor: Father of scientific management*, New York: Harper.

Cox, G. V. (1929) *An Appraisal of American Business Forecasts*, Chicago, IL: University of Chicago Press.

Davis, R. C. (1940) *Industrial Organization and Management*, New York: Harper.

Dean, J. and Warren, J. R. (1942) *The Long-run Behavior of Costs in a Chain of Shoe Stores: A statistical analysis*, Chicago, IL: University of Chicago Press.

Donham, W. B. (1922) "Essential groundwork for a broad executive theory," *Harvard Business Review*, 1(1): 1–10.

Donham, W. B. (1927a) "The emerging profession of business," *Harvard Business Review*, 5(4): 401–405.

Donham, W. B. (1927b) "The social significance of business," *Harvard Business Review*, 5(4): 406–419.

Drucker, P. F. (1939) *The End of Economic Man: A study of the new totalitarianism*, London: Heinemann.

Drucker, P. F. (1942) *The Future of Industrial Man: A conservative approach*, New York: Day.

Drucker, P. F. (1946) *Concept of Corporation*, London: John Day.

Drucker, P. F. (1954) *The Practice of Management*, New York: Harper & Row.

Drucker, P. F. (1964) *Managing for Results*, New York: Harper & Row.

Drucker, P. F. (1967) *The Effective Executive*, New York: Harper & Row.

Drucker, P. F. (1974) *Management: Tasks, responsibilities, practices*, New York: Harper & Row.

Drucker, P. F. (1985) *Innovation and Entrepreneurship: Practices and principles*, New York: Harper & Row.

Drucker, P. F. (1999) *Management Challenges for the 21st Century*, New York: Harper.

Drucker, P. F. and Maciariello, J. A. (2004) *The Daily Drucker*, New York: HarperBusiness.

Edwards, R. D. (1995) *The Pursuit of Reason: The Economist, 1843–1993*, Boston, MA: Harvard Business School Press.

Exman, E. (1965) *The Brothers Harper: A unique partnership and its impact upon the cultural life of America from 1817 to 1853*, New York: Harper & Row.

Fama, E. F. (1965) "The behavior of stock-market prices," *Journal of Business*, 38(1): 34–105.

Fayol, H. (1916) "Administration industrielle et générale: prévoyance, organisation, commandement, coordination, contrôle," *Bulletin de la Société de l'Industrie minérale*, Saint-Étienne: Société de l'industrie minérale.

Fayol, H. (1917) *Administration industrielle et générale: prévoyance, organisation, commandement, coordination, contrôle*, Paris: Dunod et Pinat.

Fayol, H. (1930) *Industrial and General Administration*, London: Pitman.

Fayol, H. (1949) *General and Industrial Management*, London: Pitman.

Flaherty, J. E. (1999) *Peter Drucker: Shaping the managerial mind: How the world's foremost management thinker crafted the essentials of business success*, San Francisco, CA: Jossey-Bass.

Fligstein, N. (1990) *The Transformation of Corporate Control*, Cambridge, MA: Harvard University Press.

Friedman, M. (1937) "The use of ranks to avoid the assumption of normality implicit in the analysis of variance," *Journal of the American Statistical Association*, 32(200): 675–701.

Frisch, R. (1933) "Editor's note," *Econometrica*, 1(1): 1–4.

Funding Universe, 5 May 2015. www.fundinguniverse.com/company-histories/random-house-inc-history.

Galbraith, J. (1973) *Designing Complex Organizations*, Reading, MA: Addison-Wesley.

Gardiner, G. (1945) *When Foreman and Steward Bargain*, New York: McGraw-Hill.

Gerstenberg, C. W. (1924) *Financial Organization and Management of Business*, New York: Prentice-Hall.

Gilbreth, F. B. (1912) *Primer of Scientific Management*, New York: D. Van Nostrand.

Gilbreth, F. B. and Ross, C. (1917) *Das ABC der wissenschaftlichen Betriebsführung = Primer of Scientific Management*, Berlin: Springer.

Gowin, E. B. (1919) *Developing Executive Ability*, New York: Ronald Press.

Guillén, M. F. (1994) *Models of Management: Work, authority and organization in a comparative perspective*, Chicago, IL: University of Chicago Press.

Guru: Theodore Levitt, 28 May 2015. www.economist.com/node/13167376.

Gushée, E. T. and Boffey, L. F. (1928) *Scientific Purchasing*, New York: McGraw-Hill.

Hall, M. (1986) *Harvard University Press: A history*, Cambridge, MA: Harvard University Press.

Harvard Business Review, 28 May 2015. https://hbr.org.

HBR Under Review, 28 May 2015. www.forbes.com/2009/07/24/harvard-business-review-business-media-ignatius.html.

Hayek, F. A. (1945) "The use of knowledge in society," *American Economic Review*, 38(4): 519–530.

Heck, J. L. and Jensen, R. E. (2007) "An analysis of the evolution of research contributions by the *Accounting Review*, 1926–2005," *Accounting Historians Journal*, 34(2): 109–141.

Hempel, E. H. (1945) *Top-management Planning: Methods needed for postwar orientation of industrial companies*, New York: Harper.

Hill, L. H. and Hook, C. R. (1945) *Management at the Bargaining Table*, New York: McGraw-Hill.

Hotelling, H. (1931) "The economics of exhaustible resources," *Journal of Political Economy*, 39(2): 137–175.

Jacobson, T. C., Smith, G. D., Wright, R. E., Wiley, P. B., Spilka, S. B., and Heaney, B. L. (2007) *Knowledge for Generations: Wiley and the global publishing industry, 1807–2007*, New York: Wiley.

James, E. (ed.) (2002) *Macmillan: A publishing tradition*, Basingstoke: Palgrave.

JSTOR, 5 May 2015. www.jstor.org/page/journal/jbusiness/about.html.

Juran, J. M. (1945) *Management of Inspection and Quality Control*, New York: Harper.

Kester, R. B. (1917) *Accounting Theory and Practice*, New York: Ronald Press.

Keynes, J. M. (1936) *The General Theory of Employment, Interest and Money*, London: Macmillan.

Keynes, J. M. (1937) "The general theory of employment," *Quarterly Journal of Economics*, 51(2): 209–223.

Knowles, A. S. and Thomson, R. D. (1943a) *Industrial Management*, New York: Macmillan.

Knowles, A. S. and Thomson, R. D. (1943b) *Production Control*, New York: Macmillan.

Knowles, A. S. and Thomson, R. D. (1944) *Management of Manpower*, New York: Macmillan.

Kurtz, H. (2000) *The Fortune Tellers: Inside Wall Street's game of money, media, and manipulation*, New York: Free Press.

Kynaston, D. (1988) *The Financial Times: A centenary history*, London: Viking.

Lansburgh, R. H. and Spriegel, W. R. (1940) *Industrial Management*, New York: Wiley.

Lasser, J. K. (1945) *Business Executive's Guide: A check list on problems of organization, finance, taxes & management*, New York: McGraw-Hill.

Leffingwell, W. H. (1925) *Office Management: Principles and practice*, New York: McGraw-Hill.

Leffingwell, W. H. and Robinson, E. M. (1943) *Textbook of Office Management*, New York: Published for the United States Armed Forces Institute by McGraw-Hill.

Lindblom, C. E. (1959) "The science of 'muddling through'," *Public Administration Review*, 19(2): 79–88.

Lowry, S. M., Maynard, H. B., and Stegemerten, G. J. (1927) *Time and Motion Study and Formulas for Wage Incentives*, New York: McGraw-Hill.

Marshall, L. C. (1921) *Business Administration*, Chicago, IL: University of Chicago Press.

Mayo, E. (1933) *The Human Problems of an Industrial Civilization*, New York: Macmillan.

McFadden, D. (1980) "Econometric models for probabilistic choice among products," *Journal of Business*, 53(3, part 2): S13–S29.

McNair, M. P. and Lewis, H. T. (1938) *Business and Modern Society: Papers by members of the faculty of the Graduate School of Business Administration, Harvard University*, Cambridge, MA: Harvard University Press.

McKinsey, J. O. (1922) *Budgetary Control*, New York: Ronald Press.

McKinsey, J. O. (1924) *Managerial Accounting*, Chicago, IL: University of Chicago Press.

MIT Press, 5 May 2015. http://mitpress.mit.edu/about/history.

Mogensen, A. H. (1932) *Common Sense Applied to Motion and Time Study*, New York: McGraw-Hill.

Moggridge, D. E. and Keynes, J. M. (1992) *Maynard Keynes: An economist's biography*, London: Routledge.

Neumann, J. von and Morgenstern, O. (1944) *Theory of Games and Economic Behavior*, Princeton, NJ: Princeton University Press.

Nystrom, P. H. (1915) *The Economics of Retailing*, New York: Ronald Press.

Parkhurst, F. A. (1917) *Applied Methods of Scientific Management*, New York: Wiley.

Parsons, W. (1989) *The Power of the Financial Press: Journalism and economic opinion in Britain and America*, Aldershot: Elgar.

PdfSR.com, 5 May 2015. http://pdfsr.com/pdf/mckinsey-award-winners-for-best-hbr-articles.

Pearson, 5 May 2015a. http://timeline.pearson.com.

Pearson, 5 May 2015b. http://wayback.archive.org/web/20060711035850/http://www.pearson.com/index.cfm?pageid=14.

Poffenberger, A. T. (1928) "The effects of continuous work upon output and feelings," *Journal of Applied Psychology*, 12(5): 459–467.

Preinreich, G. A. D. (1937) "Valuation and amortization," *Accounting Review*, 12(3): 209–226.

Robinson, J. (1933) *The Economics of Imperfect Competition*, London: Macmillan.

Roethlisberger, F. J. and Dickson, W. J. (1934) *Management and the Worker: Technical vs. social organization in an industrial plant*, Boston, MA: Graduate School of Business Administration, Harvard University.

Ronald Press Company, 12 October 2015. https://openlibrary.org/publishers/The_Ronald_press_company#.

Rose, D. C. (1928) *A Scientific Approach to Investment Management*, New York: Harper.

Rosenberg, J. M. (1982) *Inside the Wall Street Journal: The history and the power of Dow Jones & Company and America's most influential newspaper*, New York: Macmillan.

Rowland, F. H. (1945) *Budgeting for Management Control*, New York: Harper.

Scharff, E. E. (1986) *Worldly Power: The making of the Wall Street Journal*, New York: Beaufort Books.

Schulz, A.-C. and Nicolai, A. T. (2015) "The intellectual link between management research and popularization media: A bibliometric analysis of the *Harvard Business Review*," *Academy of Management Learning & Education*, 14(1): 31–49.

Schumpeter, J. (1933) "The common sense of econometrics," *Econometrica*, 1(1): 5–12.

Scott, W. D. and Clothier, R. (1923) *Personnel Management: Principles, practices, and point of view*, Chicago, IL: Shaw.

Sharpe, W. (1966) "Mutual fund performance," *Journal of Business*, 39(1, part 2): 119–138.

Simon, H. A. (1944) "Decision-making and administrative organization," *Public Administration Review*, 4(1): 16–30.

Tarrant, J. J. (1976) *Drucker: The man who invented the corporate society*, London: Barrie & Jenkins.

Taylor, F. W. (1911) *The Principles of Scientific Management*, New York: Harper and Brothers.

Taylor, F. W. (1913) *Rationell arbetsledning* (Swedish translation of *Scientific Management*), Stockholm: Aktiebolaget Nordiska Bokhandeln.

Thomas, R. M., Jr (1996) Richard P. Ettinger Jr., 73, Publisher Who Helped Indians, *New York Times*, 5 May. www.nytimes.com/1996/05/05/us/richard-p-ettinger-jr-73-publisher-who-helped-indians.html.

Thomson Reuters, 5 May 2015. http://thomsonreuters.com/about-us/company-history.

Tinbergen, J. (1933) "L'utilisation des équations fonctionnelles et des nombres complexes dans les recherches économiques," *Econometrica*, 1(1): 36–51.

Tosdal, H. R. (1933) *Introduction to Sales Management*, New York: McGraw-Hill.

Tversky, A. and Kahneman, D. (1986) "Rational choice and the framing of decisions," *Journal of Business*, 59(4, part 2): S251–S278.

Waterman, M. H. (1936) *Public Utility Financing, 1930–35*, Ann Arbor, MI: University of Michigan, School of Business Administration, Bureau of Business Research.

Wendt, L. (1982) *The Wall Street Journal: The story of Dow Jones & the nation's business newspaper*, Chicago, IL: Rand McNally.

Wingate, J. W. (1931) *Manual of Retail Terms*, New York: Prentice-Hall.

Witzel, M. (1996) "Drucker, Peter F. (1909-)," in M. Warner (ed.), *International Encyclopedia of Business & Management*, London: Routledge, pp. 1057–1061.

Yoder, D. (1942) *Personnel Management and Industrial Relations*, New York: Prentice-Hall.

PART III

Post-World War II Expansion

The period covered in the third part of this book ranges from World War II to the early 1980s, with a focus on the immediate post-war decades.

Economically, this period initially saw strong growth in the developed economies with the US providing a model based on the combination of big business, big science, and big government – seen as crucial for the US victory in the war and ongoing superiority. The alternative, communist model also expanded though with the Soviet Union increasing its sphere of influence, namely in Central and Eastern Europe after World War II, Mao gaining power in China in 1949 and the newly independent India experimenting with a planned economy – albeit combined with a democratic political system. The US decartelized German and Japanese industries and more general efforts were made to liberalize trade though multilateral agreements both at international and regional levels, the latter in particular in Western Europe with the formation of the European Economic Community or Common Market. The 1970s saw increasing turmoil with the breakdown of the so-called Bretton Woods financial system based on the US dollar, the successive shocks induced by skyrocketing oil prices, and growing competition from Japanese companies.

Socially, managers and management largely benefitted from the war and the view of US superiority being based on superior public and private administration. The US also actively promoted such a view by inviting managers, workers, and public administrators to experience its system first hand as well as using a variety of organizations and associations to promote it abroad. While the US was marked by the returning GIs looking for opportunities, established elites in many European economies – and not only in the defeated ones, became questioned and were increasingly sidelined and replaced by a new generation of more "Americanized" leaders, while the middle class also increased. In communist countries new, closed

148 Post-WWII Expansion

elites were established based on the single-party system – with partial renewals following recurrent internal purges, while military regimes in many of the developing countries tended to serve the interests of an established economic elite.

Politically, this period was marked by decolonization and the Cold War between the US and the Soviet Union, both of which attempted to expand their respective zones of influence through a variety of means. In many Western countries as well as Japan, communist parties and/or trade unions initially had a strong presence but their influence waned as prosperity increased and the oppressive nature of communist regimes became apparent. But the late 1960s saw renewed contestation, driven also but not only by a rejection of the Vietnam War, continuing into the 1970s now mainly due to the malaise inflicted by slower growth and recurring crises.

10

MAKING BUSINESS EDUCATION SCIENTIFIC

The post-World War II period saw a major drive to make business education science-based, culminating in the US business school as it is known today. On the way, there was a move toward the archetypal two-year post-experience MBA, purportedly as the ultimate degree for "professional management." As this so-called "New Look" school of business administration was in the making, American influence began to radiate to different parts of the world. Within the Cold War environment this was driven very much by the financial support of US government agencies and philanthropic foundations together with assistance by US schools of business. By the time such sponsorship weakened, the US had become the center of the world in business research and was serving as the main source of reference. Nevertheless, despite strong US influence, organizational fields of business education developed in variable ways across recipient countries, as institutional legacies also came into play. Thus, unlike the shift in the US toward the MBA, education in business expanded mainly at the first-degree level, the US-type MBA making little inroads even by the late 1980s.

Post-war Transformation in the United States

In the wake of World War II, a considerable degree of unease persisted about the quality of business education in the US. Nevertheless, enrollments were booming, fuelled in part by the so-called GI Bill of 1944, which, among other benefits, provided financial aid to war veterans to attend university. Schools and departments of business were also increasing. Pierson (1959: 723), for example, identified a total of 587 universities and colleges offering business programs in the mid-1950s. With about 50,000 undergraduate degrees awarded at the end of the decade, business constituted 13 to 14 percent of all bachelor's degrees in the US.

Doctoral programs had expanded too and were now offered in 20 or so universities, which altogether produced on average more than a hundred Ph.D.s a year in the latter part of the 1950s (Gordon and Howell 1959: 21 and 27). Master's degrees also increased, though still remaining at the level of 9 to 10 percent of the undergraduate degrees (Gordon and Howell 1959: 21). Business education in the US was still predominantly at the undergraduate level.

It was within this context that the Ford Foundation stepped in as a promoter of change in the US field of higher education for business. The aspiration was to make business education more scientific and research-based. Allusion to science had been around for quite a while. This time, however, it was different. The aim was to bring the social sciences as well as mathematical and statistical modelling into the study of and the search for solutions to business problems (Carroll 1959). This was meant to provide a scientific grounding for more advanced training, enabling schools of business to become at par with other professional schools – a long-time ambition as shown in Chapters 4 and 7, now with medicine serving as the main model. The claim to being a profession was shifting to a "science" basis rather than making reference to social awareness and service to society.

Ford Foundation involvement began in 1954 with grants for the expansion of the doctoral program at the newly founded Graduate School of Industrial Administration (GSIA) at the Carnegie Institute of Technology and the one at the Harvard Business School (HBS) (Carroll 1959). The former school in particular was regarded as the epitome of the transformation that the Foundation wanted to bring about in American business education (see Box 10.1). Obtaining the involvement of HBS was important due to its dominant position within the organizational field, despite its prevailing orientation toward a law school model, rather than science-based education (Augier and March 2011). Since then and until 1966, the GSIA and the HBS as well as an additional select group including Columbia, Chicago, and Stanford received generous grants (Gleeson and Schlossman 1995). Although there was particular emphasis on strengthening doctoral education, some of this funding was also geared toward reforming graduate as well as undergraduate programs. The main idea was to provide financial support to schools that were thought to be or believed to have the potential to become a model. They were expected to serve as exemplars for the diffusion of what came to be labelled in Ford Foundation circles as the "New Look" (Khurana 2007). To this end, a variety of activities were sponsored, such as summer seminars and fellowships for faculty members for advanced study in mathematical and statistical methodologies (Carroll 1959).

BOX 10.1 SHOWCASE OF THE "NEW LOOK": THE GSIA AT THE CARNEGIE INSTITUTE OF TECHNOLOGY

The Graduate School of Industrial Administration – now the Tepper School of Business – was founded in Pittsburgh, PA in 1949 in a not well-known engineering school at the time, the Carnegie Institute of Technology – since 1967 Carnegie Mellon University – with a six million dollar donation by William L. Mellon, the main entrepreneur behind the Gulf Oil Company. It was named a school of "industrial administration" as the initial aim was to admit only students with engineering and science backgrounds. More importantly perhaps, the name also signified a divergence from its two predecessors, Harvard and Stanford. The difference from the latter two schools was not only in the name. Initially, the degree offered by the GSIA was an MS in Business rather than an MBA. Even more importantly, the GSIA was the very first initiative to make graduate instruction in business analytical and scientifically based. The behavioral sciences, economic analysis, and quantitative methods constituted the backbone of the program. A broad management view was taken with a focus on decision making, implementation, and control. The quantitative social-scientific approach characterized faculty research as well as the contract work that the GSIA carried out for corporations and government agencies. Led by the founding dean Leland Bach, the GSIA brought together a core group of social science oriented faculty, including William Cooper, Richard Cyert, James March, and Herbert Simon, among others. In all, the GSIA stood for and served as the model until the early 1960s for the transformation that the Ford Foundation wanted to create in the US organizational field of business education. It was generously funded by the foundation and the GSIA's dean and faculty took an active role in guiding and disseminating the New Look. The school's final contribution after the early 1960s was through the dispersion of its faculty and doctoral students to prominent US business schools.

Sources: Bach (1958); Gleeson and Schlossman (1995); Khurana (2007: 251–256); Augier and March (2011: 123–144); Fourcade and Khurana (2013).

Perhaps the most influential Ford Foundation initiative to disseminate the New Look across the entire organizational field was the commissioning to two economics professors at the University of California and at Stanford, Robert A. Gordon and James E. Howell respectively, of a study on the state of business education in the US in 1956. The Flexner (1910) report on medical schools again served as an exemplar (see Chapter 7). The publication of the Gordon and Howell (1959) study was followed a few months later by a similar one contracted by the Carnegie Corporation to Frank Pierson (1959) from Swarthmore College.

152 Post-WWII Expansion

These two reports served, according to Augier and March (2011), as the "manifesto" for the "revolution" that was called for.

Although the two studies had their differences, they were broadly at one in what they saw as the deficiencies of business education in the US and the recommendations that they made. Both reports were careful in pointing out that the suggestions were not meant to be a straightjacket and should be adapted to local conditions. Nevertheless, they also contained a clear agenda as to the ways to proceed. Business education had to shift to the graduate level with a focus on the MBA, though not as a fifth year of study but as a distinct two-year "professional" degree that would prepare students for practice and for their entire career rather than the first job. Curricula therefore had to be made more rigorous with a stronger scientific basis. For this to happen, the quality of faculty members had to be increased. Thus, doctoral programs had to be expanded and strengthened, particularly with respect to developing methodological knowledge and skills. The scientific grounding of graduate training also required a strong research orientation on the part of schools of business. Research characterized until then by description or case studies had to turn toward quantitative analysis in which "both hypothesis forming and testing [were] essential" (Gordon and Howell 1959: 379). Student quality had to be raised too, through more rigorous screening procedures, possibly together with requiring some prior work experience. The call for a shift toward the MBA notwithstanding, it was deemed appropriate that the undergraduate degree should continue, though with curricula that were devoted entirely to the liberal arts in the first two years. Less able students needed to be directed to junior colleges.

Although there was some resistance, the impetus that the Ford Foundation had generated began to have its effects in the 1960s (see, e.g., Gleeson 1997 on the arduous process of change at Stanford). This was despite the fact that the Foundation was stepping back in the earlier part of the decade. As Gordon and Howell (1959: 118) conceded, there did not appear to be a "strong preference" at the time in US business circles for a graduate degree. Yet, schools of business had taken on board the Ford Foundation message and the organizational field was becoming transformed in the direction envisaged by the two reports. The long-standing aspiration to become at par with other professional schools in the American university appeared to be coming true. Science and practice were believed to be wedded together to be put to the service of the "profession" through the synthesis that the school of business was to provide (see Box 10.1).

The New Look "Business School" and the MBA in the United States

That there was student demand and adequate resources helped the transition (Augier and March 2011). Undergraduate enrollments continued to rise in the two decades that followed. About 200,000 bachelor's degrees were conferred annually in the early 1980s (Edfelt 1988: 346). Particularly notable though was the turn toward the master's degree, the MBA in particular. By the mid-1970s, almost all major universities and colleges were offering the degree (Gleeson and Schlossman 1995). Not unlike today, consulting and banking were becoming the industries that predominantly recruited MBAs (Khurana 2007). The master's degrees in business – mostly but not entirely MBAs – awarded in the early 1980s were in the order of 60,000 annually, with 650 US universities and colleges estimated to be offering them (Edfelt 1988: 341 and 346). The ten to one proportion between undergraduate and master's degrees in business in the late 1950s went down to five to one in 1970 and then to less than three and a half to one during the 1980s (NCES 1993: 85–86).

The quality of students in MBA programs was rising too, especially in the better known schools as they could now become more selective in their admissions (Gleeson 1997). The proportion of students with prior experience, for example, increased (Daniel 1998). In fact, a small group of business schools led by HBS approached the Educational Testing Service (ETS) to develop a special test for admissions (see Schmotter 1993). The so-called Admission Test for Graduate Study in Business (ATGSB) was administered for the first time in 1954 to about 7,000 students. Membership remained confined to an elite group to which only 21 schools belonged in the mid-1960s. Nevertheless, the ATGSB was increasingly becoming a standard within the organizational field with around 100,000 students taking the test in the early 1970s (Schmotter 1993).

In parallel, the quest for a shift from "commercial education" to "business administration" that dated back to the founding of the graduate school at Harvard and that gained further strength during the interwar years was turning toward the claim to train for "management." The accent on administration as being the closest to a professional status in business and the need for a managerial approach was already in the foundation reports. It was particularly apparent in GSIA's conception of the MBA degree (see Box 10.1). It had even found its way into the media, as a *Business Week* article proclaimed in 1952 that "the day of the truly professional general management man isn't here yet, but it is not far away. That man will be trained for management in general, rather than in any one phase of business. He'll learn his technique in school, rather than on the job" (quoted in Fourcade and Khurana 2013: 140). Nevertheless, the widespread establishment of the perception that the main purpose of graduate business schools and the MBA was to train for management took longer – indeed well into the 1970s (Edfelt 1988). That this has been the case is perhaps best indicated by the naming and renaming of the entity that was established in 1970 to take over the administration of the ATGSB from ETS. It was initially called the Graduate Business Admission Council (GBAC), but was renamed Graduate Management Admission Council (GMAC) in 1976, together with a change in the name of the test from ATGSB to GMAT or Graduate Management Admission Test (Schmotter 1993).

The broad science thrust in the 1950s as well as the two foundation reports had fit well with the aspirations of the schools of business to ameliorate their low status within the university. During the 1960s and the 1970s, a stronger research orientation began to take hold especially in schools within prominent research universities, as they began to recruit faculty members trained in the social sciences and in quantitative methods. The character of research was changing too, as it was now directed toward theory testing through rigorous quantitative analysis. Again, this was very much internally driven, mainly to gain academic legitimacy and respectability, not because it was particularly demanded by business circles. Doctoral programs also expanded. By the early 1980s around 800 to 900 Ph.D.s were awarded annually (Edfelt 1988: 344). Equally, if not more importantly, the curricula were altered very much along the lines of the foundation reports to include a much greater emphasis on research and advanced analysis.

The transformation was not uniform across the entire organizational field however. Indeed, the post–Ford Foundation era extended and coagulated the stratification within the field that had emerged in the interwar years (see Chapter 7). At the center, now beyond HBS, were the business schools that were favored by the Ford Foundation and a number of others in the major research universities that had quickly joined them. Then there were the large, often regional but AACSB accredited schools, constituting together with the central ones about a third of all US business schools. And there was still a third-tier, which included a large number of smaller colleges and universities that were also offering the MBA but in ways that were not markedly different from the pre–World War II period (Khurana 2007).

Nevertheless, overall the archetypal two-year full-time MBA and the idea of the research-driven (graduate) business school had become institutionalized in the US by the 1980s, the former becoming the flagship program of the latter. Various part-time and executive versions of the MBA had also appeared. And there was some expansion of non-degree executive programs, though confined largely to the leading schools (Porter and McKibbin 1988). Business education was already being perceived in the US as a big business that was predominantly driven by market forces (see, e.g., Harris 1984: 125–126). Moreover, the international attractiveness of the US as the place to study business had increased, with nine percent of master's and 20 percent of doctoral degrees estimated to be awarded to foreign citizens (Edfelt 1988: 349).

Yet, all was not quiet on the business school front. Some from within and outside university circles began to question the course that US schools of business had taken after the Carnegie Corporation and Ford Foundation reports. Thus, they were implicated by some authors in the decline of US competitiveness (e.g., Hayes and Abernathy 1980). Already by the mid-1980s, Cheit (1985: 50–51) could identify four main indictments, namely, that (i) the MBA model was wrong, namely too quantitative and theoretical, not least because of overreliance on economics; (ii) the development of behavioral skills and an international outlook were ignored; (iii) society's needs were not met, and (iv) undesirable attitudes were fostered, such as short-termism and risk aversion. A study commissioned by the AACSB to address such criticisms – viewed as comparable in intent to the two reports – provided a broadly favorable assessment (Porter and McKibbin 1988). Still, even these authors pointed to the lack of diversity in degree programs, the narrowness of analysis-focused MBA education, little international orientation, the overspecialization of faculty members, limited appeal of research to the business community, and strongly recommended, yet again, the emulation of the medical school model. All in all however, these criticisms were to have little, if any, impact, at least until media rankings of business schools began to gain greater saliency during the 1990s (see Chapter 13).

American-style Business Education Moves Abroad

The Post-war US Offensive

American influence had begun to penetrate into other parts of the world even before the Ford Foundation embarked on the New Look project within the US. The official launch of the European Recovery Program – widely known as the Marshall Plan – in 1948 provided the basis for massive aid geared toward strengthening and re-structuring Western European economies as well as thwarting the spread of communism. The early orientation toward industrial modernization gave way, after the early 1950s, to greater attention toward increasing productivity and closing what was perceived to be a "management gap" between the US and Europe (McGlade 1998). Thus, the focus turned to organizing training activities and to providing aid for reforming and expanding higher education in business. The Cold War environment led to the concurrent involvement of the US in "development assistance" to various countries in the Middle East, Asia, and Latin America, parts of which were geared toward exporting American-style business education.

Post-war US financial and technical aid to Europe and to other regions lasted mainly through the 1950s and the 1960s. Initially, the main agency was the Economic Cooperation Administration (ECA) set up in 1948 to monitor the implementation of the Marshall Plan, which morphed into the International Cooperation Administration (ICA) and eventually became in 1961 the Agency for International Development (AID). There was also the European Productivity Agency (EPA) that existed between 1953 and 1961, which promoted and guided the establishment of national productivity centers. Supplementing the aid agencies

156 Post-WWII Expansion

were private philanthropic foundations, in particular the Ford Foundation (Gemelli 1998). American universities were heavily involved in both of these types of aid as contractors. They also took part by running training programs for foreign faculty members and sending out visiting professors (Boel 2003). One estimate suggests that US universities had received more than 9,200 faculty members from abroad by 1966 (McGlade 1998: 29).

What and who initiated the transfer of American-style business education into a country varied. There were often political considerations, such as the strength of communist movements or the perceived threat of encroachment by the Soviet Union. So in some cases it was the US aid agencies or philanthropic foundations that made the first move in providing funds and guidance. Initiatives could come from local actors too, as importing US models and know-how was viewed as a way for promoting economic development and social change. The local "modernizing" agents could be, on the one hand, governments and public agencies and, on the other, the business community and, in some cases, religious orders (Kipping, Üsdiken, and Puig 2004). Notably though, the enthusiasm at the receiving end had to do not only with an increasingly heightened belief in the supremacy of American business education but also with the availability of US grants that made importation cheaper and easier (Leavitt 1957). US influence could also be indirect as local actors took the US as a reference and source of learning, when they went ahead – largely on their own – in developing higher business education.

Whatever the particular mechanism, these attempts involved bringing American program formats as well as educational content and methods into higher education fields abroad, which had their own established forms of organizing and institutional frameworks. As discussed in Chapters 4 and 7, the university-based school of business was an alien organizational form to much of the world, as was a separate graduate degree like the MBA. The influx of American business education into recipient countries occurred mainly in two ways, namely, through the creation of stand-alone schools outside the university sector or by incorporation into universities. Table 10.1 presents a list of stand-alone or university-based educational units formed in different parts of the world in the two decades that followed World War II.

The Stand-alone Schools

Although the US was the main source of reference and guidance, the stand-alone school did not exist as an organizational form within the US. The creation of such schools was similar to the manner in which higher commercial education had emerged in Europe in the late nineteenth and early twentieth century (see Chapter 4). Not only was this a way of circumventing resistance on the part of public universities but it also enabled, indeed ensured the involvement of business or other private interests (see Table 10.1 for notable examples and Box 10.2 for

Making Business Education Scientific 157

TABLE 10.1 Examples of Post–World War II Schools and Institutes Established with US Technical Assistance or Inspired by US Models, 1945–1969[a]

Year	School/Institute	Country	Ownership	Form	Level[b]
1946	Centre d'Etudes Industrielles (CEI)	Switzerland	Private	Stand-alone	Executive
1952	Istituto Post-universitario per lo Studio dell'Organizzazione Aziendale (IPSOA)	Italy	Private	Stand-alone	Graduate
1954	İşletme İktisadi Enstitüsü (IIE), Istanbul Üniversitesi	Turkey	Public	U-based[c]	Executive/ Graduate
1954	Institute of Administrative Sciences, University of Tehran	Iran	Public	U-based	Graduate
1954	Institute of Business Administration, University of Karachi	Pakistan	Public	U-based	Graduate
1954	Escola de Administração de Empresas de São Paulo (FGV-EAESP)	Brazil	Quasi-Private	Stand-alone	Executive/ First degree/ Graduate
1955	Escuela de Organización Industrial (EOI)	Spain	Public	Stand-alone	Graduate
1955	Institut d'Administration des Entreprises (IAE)[d]	France	Public	U-based	Graduate/ Executive
1955	Institut d'Administration des Entreprises (IAE), Université d'Alger	Algeria	Public	U-based	Graduate
1956	Istituto Superiore per Imprenditori e Dirigenti d'Azienda (ISIDA)	Italy	Private	Stand-alone	Graduate
1956	Instituto Católico de Administración y Dirección de Empresas (ICADE)	Spain	Private	Stand-alone	Graduate/First degree
1957	Institut pour l'Etude des Méthodes de Direction de l'Entreprise (IMEDE)	Switzerland	Private	Stand-alone	Executive
1957	Escuela Nacional de Contabilidad y Administración, Universidad Nacional Autónoma de México (UNAM)	Mexico	Public	U-based	First degree/ Graduate
1958	Escuela Superior de Administración de Empresas (ESADE)	Spain	Private	Stand-alone	Graduate/First degree
1958	Instituto Superior de Estudios de la Empresa (IESE), Universidad de Navarra	Spain	Private	U-based	Executive/ Graduate
1959	Institut Européen d'Administration des Affaires (INSEAD)	France	Private	Stand-alone	Graduate/ Executive
1959	Escuela de Administración de Empresas (EAE)	Spain	Public	Stand-alone	Graduate/ Executive

158 Post-WWII Expansion

Year	School/Institute	Country	Ownership	Form	Level[b]
1960	*Escuela de Administración y Finanzas* (EAF; EAFIT in 1962)	Colombia	Private	Stand-alone	Graduate/First degree
1960	*Escola de Administração, Universidade Federal da Bahia*	Brazil	Public	U-based	First degree/ Executive
1960	*Instituto de Administração, Universidade Federal do Rio Grande do Sul*	Brazil	Public	U-based	Executive/ First degree
1961	Indian Institute of Management, Calcutta	India	Public	Stand-alone	Executive/ Graduate
1962	College of Business Administration, Seoul National University	South Korea	Public	U-based	First degree
1962	Indian Institute of Management, Ahmedabad	India	Public	Stand-alone	Executive/ Graduate
1962	*Escuela Superior de Contabilidad y Administración, Instituto Politécnico Nacional* (IPN)	Mexico	Public	U-based	First degree/ Graduate
1963	*Escuela de Administración de Negocios para Graduados* (ESAN)	Peru	Private	Stand-alone	Graduate
1963	Graduate School of Business Administration, Korea University	South Korea	Private	U-based	First degree/ Graduate
1964	*Instituto Centroamericano de Administración de Empresas* (INCAE)	Guatemala/ Nicaragua	Private	Stand-alone	Executive/ Graduate
1964	*Escuela de Graduados en Administración, ITESM*	Mexico	Private	U-based	Graduate
1965	London Graduate School of Business Studies, University of London	UK	Public	U-based	Executive/ Graduate
1965	Manchester Business School, Manchester University	UK	Public	U-based	Executive/ Graduate
1965	*Instituto de Estudios Superiores de Administración* (IESA)	Venezuela	Private	Stand-alone	Graduate
1965	*Graduate School of Business Administration, Yonsei University*	South Korea	Private	U-based	First degree/ Graduate
1967	*Instituto Panamericano de Alta Dirección de Empresa* (IPADE)	Mexico	Private	Stand-alone	Executive/ Graduate
1968	Asian Institute of Management (AIM)	Philippines	Private	Stand-alone	Graduate

[a] Based on available secondary sources: AID (1971); Bátiz-Lazo (2013); Davila (1991); Gemelli (1996); Hill et al. (1973); Kipping and Nioche (1998); Park and Choi (2011); Puig (2003); Sass (1982); Taylor (1968); Üsdiken (2011); Whitley, Thomas and Marceau (1981).
[b] Indicates the types of programs offered within the time period covered by the table.
[c] University-based.
[d] Seven of these IAE were created in 1955 in different universities. By 1957 the number had increased to 15.

INSEAD). The stand-alone schools were typically set up to provide graduate programs, often preceded by or in parallel with shorter courses for practicing managers. The priority given in these schools to executive and graduate education – often based on advice by American sponsors – had to do both with similar developments in the US at the time and the hope of creating immediate impact at the receiving end.

BOX 10.2 AN AMERICAN SCHOOL IN FONTAINEBLEAU: INSEAD

L'Institut européen d'administration des affaires (INSEAD) was created in a context when European unification was on the agenda, the Treaty of Rome having been signed in 1957. The main champion of the idea was George Doriot who had also acted as a bridge with the Harvard Business School in the founding of the CPA in Paris in 1930 (see Chapter 7). In this case too, Harvard was the model and was there to help right from the beginning, continuing to do so later by training some of INSEAD's prospective faculty members. The aspiration was to build an international school that would also have a strong practical orientation and would, in Doriot's view, be "a bastion of defence for free enterprise" (quoted in Barsoux 2000: 42), which might also explain the choice of its location in the same town as the NATO headquarters at the time. The Paris Chamber of Commerce provided the initial funding and INSEAD was formally established in 1959 as a "foreign non-profit association" (Barsoux 2000: 35). Additional grants were obtained from the EPA and Fulbright and, eventually, the Ford Foundation, which extended its support until the early 1970s. In the early stages, a sizable financial contribution was also made by the French authorities for the construction of the campus. For quite a few years, there were also donations by American multinational firms, including, for example, McKinsey. Still, a core full-time faculty could only be established toward the end of the 1960s. INSEAD started out with a pre-experience graduate program which was only a year long, unlike the two-year version becoming typical at the time in US business schools. Moreover, the program was not called an MBA. By the late 1960s INSEAD had also moved toward offering shorter executive courses – invariably run in cooperation with US business schools – and, in the early to mid-1970s, customized programs. In 1975, the one-year graduate program was finally labelled an MBA. Despite growing recognition, INSEAD remained a teaching school. Only in the mid-1980s was there a serious move toward research, which eventually culminated in opening a doctoral program in 1989 (see Barsoux 2000 as well as Fragueiro and Michelini 2014 for the later development of the school).

Sources: Whitley, Thomas, and Marceau (1981); Gemelli (1996); Barsoux (2000); Fragueiro and Michelini (2014).

The model of the stand-alone school extended far beyond Europe. The Ford Foundation, for example, encouraged the establishment of two government-sponsored Indian institutes of management (IIMs), one in Calcutta and the other in Ahmedabad, linking them, respectively, with the Sloan School of Management at MIT and the Harvard Business School (Hill et al. 1973). An Asian Institute of Management was also established in Manila, Philippines, though not by the government but as a joint initiative of two Catholic universities, again with the financial support of the Ford Foundation and the AID (AID 1971: 199).

The entry of American-type business education into Latin America was largely through stand-alone schools too. The first in line was the quasi-private FGV-EAESP founded in São Paulo, Brazil with funding by AID, later augmented by the Ford Foundation, and academic support by Michigan State University (MSU) (Taylor 1968). Various other Latin American countries followed the same path during the 1960s, often with a private stand-alone school in each, such as EAF in Colombia, ESAN in Peru, IESA in Venezuela and INCAE for Central America (see, Table 10.1). These schools benefited from the academic support of US universities – Syracuse, Stanford, Northwestern, and Harvard, respectively, which were financed through US development assistance (Davila 1991). In addition, as another initiative by the Catholic organization *Opus Dei*, IPADE was founded in Mexico, modelled on IESE established by the same organization in Spain, as well as Harvard (Bátiz-Lazo 2013).

Penetration into the University

Unlike the stand-alone schools, making business a subject of study within public universities was typically initiated or supported by governments, though there were also cases where private universities served as a primary conduit. Inclusion into the university was either in the form of graduate "institutes" annexed to a faculty or through the creation of first-degree programs (undergraduate in Anglo-American terminology). The former were somewhat akin to the graduate business school in the US and were likely to be established with aims similar to those of the stand-alone schools.

In France, for example, a decree by the Ministry of National Education in 1955 stipulated the establishment of institutes, the so-called *instituts d'administration des entreprises* (IAE), attached to faculties of law and economics of various universities to offer graduate programs (Table 10.1). This initiative also benefited from a grant by the AID-precursor ICA and the advice of Northwestern University (Adams and Garraty 1960). Similar institutes were established even before in public universities of various countries in which the US had geopolitical interests, such as Turkey, Iran, and Pakistan (Table 10.1). The institute in Istanbul was generously sponsored by the Ford Foundation to obtain assistance from HBS, while the ones in Tehran and Karachi were aided by the ICA and, respectively, the University of Southern California and the Wharton school (AID 1971; Sass 1982; Üsdiken 2011).

Making Business Education Scientific **161**

Differently from the preceding cases, in some countries business education entered the university as a first degree. This was the case in Sweden and Finland, for example, where commerce education had, until then, been outside the universities (Engwall 2009; Kettunen 2013). In some Latin American countries too, the same happened soon after the founding of the private stand-alone schools. In Brazil, for example, the introduction of the first degree in business at FGV-EAESP in 1955 was soon followed by two public universities, which were also included in the AID-funded MSU project mentioned above (Table 10.1). By the mid-1960s, the first degree in business had begun to spread to other public universities as well as private ones run by religious orders, mostly in the form of departments within faculties of economics (Taylor 1968). In contrast, in the case of Mexico the sequence was reversed since it were the private universities, such as ITESM, which brought in the American-style first degree as early as the end of the 1940s (Bátiz-Lazo 2013).

Schools or departments of business administration began to be established in Japan too, the first at Kobe University in 1949 and later at Meiji University in 1953, to offer the first degree (Nishizawa 1998). Growth occurred after the mid-1960s mainly in private universities, the proportion of first-degree students specializing in business or commerce reaching 10 percent in the 1980s (Edfelt 1988).

As these examples indicate, already in the 1950s and the 1960s business education outside the US had begun to turn toward the first degree. Other than the cases cited above, the MBA – or even graduate study in general – could not make inroads before the end of the 1960s. Actually, even when the explicit aim was to introduce the American MBA, almost everywhere it had to be shortened – like in the Italian IPSOA or the French IAE and INSEAD – and often could only be offered part-time as was the case in EOI, ICADE, and ESADE in Spain (see Table 10.1). Obtaining official recognition for a graduate degree in business quite often turned out to be difficult, so that not a degree but only a "certificate" could be awarded like in the French IAE or the IIE in Turkey, the FGV-EAESP in Brazil and the IIMs in India – with rare reference to the MBA label.

The University-based Graduate Business School and the MBA

One country in which the American-style university-based graduate school of business could be established was the UK – though somewhat belatedly. Actually, an Administrative Staff College (Henley) had been founded in 1947 as a private entity to provide post-experience courses for senior managers. It was not, however, based on US exemplars but rather on the army staff colleges in the UK (Warner 1987). Similar to what happened in many other European countries, the University of Cambridge was offered funds through Marshall Plan aid to start business education – but the university was not eager to do so (Williams 2010). Another stand-alone school, the Ashridge Management College was established in 1959, as a companion and then a competitor to Henley. Eventually, two university-based graduate schools of business were founded in London and Manchester in

1965 – with financial support from government as well as business and some funding by the Ford Foundation. The explicit intention was to be like the schools in the US, to become the "British Harvards" (Whitley, Thomas, and Marceau 1981: 48). Together with executive education, two-year graduate programs were launched in 1966 in London and in 1968 in Manchester – though only in the latter case was it labelled an MBA from the outset. The University of Oxford also established a "management centre" in 1965, though this was extended to undergraduate and graduate education only after the early 1980s (Williams 2010).

The MBA could also be introduced in countries where commerce education had earlier become a part of the university under British or American influence and where there were no regulatory constraints regarding graduate degrees (see Chapter 7). However, this was not always together with a separate graduate school. In Australia, for example, full- or part-time variants of the MBA – or the MAdmin as it was called in some cases – were launched in the 1960s. The founding of graduate schools of business, however, had to await the 1970s (Byrt 1989). In Canada, the MBA was introduced as early as the 1950s in universities such as Western Ontario and British Columbia, the former very much patterned after Harvard and referred to as "Harvard North" (Boothman 2000a: 68). Likewise, the University of Toronto changed its master of commerce degree that dated back to the late 1930s (see Chapter 7) to an MBA in 1960, though more as a one-year extension of the B.Com. degree. In the same year albeit, the Institute of Business Administration that was founded within the graduate school in 1950 was converted into a graduate school of business (Sawyer 2000).

Growth in Business Education Outside the US and its Limitations

US grants were largely drained after the 1960s, becoming confined to bursaries for doctoral studies offered by American universities or governmental programs such as the Fulbright. There were only occasional cases such as the funding provided by the Ford Foundation for the European Institute for Advanced Studies in Management (EIASM) in Brussels founded in 1971 (Durand and Dameron 2008). Likewise, the Foundation extended its grants to the CEI in Geneva through the 1970s, not least because this school could reach out to managers from Eastern Europe (David and Schaufelbuehl 2015; see also Table 10.1).

Despite reduced involvement by US agencies and foundations, American influence continued in educational content and, to some degree, in instructional methods. Yet, while the 1970s and the 1980s were marked by the expansion of business education elsewhere in the world, it did not closely follow the pattern in the US where, as shown above, the MBA had an increasingly higher share. Growth in other places was mainly at the first-degree level – though still not near the US even in relative terms (see Edfelt 1988: 346).

The first degree continued to be dominant in much of Continental Europe. There was some variation across countries, however, with respect to the role of private – often stand-alone – schools and the public universities. In France for example, the graduate IAEs became more significant and were followed by the founding in 1968 of a university in Paris, called *Dauphine*, which specialized in "management and applied economics." However, the more marked expansion of the first degree occurred at the private schools of commerce (Blanchard 2012: 128). The latter also began to reform their curricula along American lines. By 1990, the number of these schools had grown to 46 – and to over 200 including the ones that were not officially recognized. It was however the Parisian ones, HEC, ESSEC, and ESCP in particular, that garnered greater prestige within the field by becoming more and more selective (Blanchard 2012: 214–216).

In contrast, in some other European countries, the organizational field of business education either remained or came almost entirely under the purview of the state. In Germany, for example, the first degree at the public university (*Diplom-Kaufmann*) continued as the sole form of higher business education. American influence was confined to the introductin of content and the resultant fragmentation in BWL along functional lines, together with private post-experience seminars modelled on the Advanced Management Program at HBS (Kipping 1998; Kieser 2004). There was a shift toward the university in the Netherlands too, as the former stand-alone schools in Rotterdam and Tilburg were turned into universities. Differently from Germany, however, the US influence led to the creation of a first degree in business separate from the conventional business economics degree (de Man 1996). As pointed out above, in Sweden and Finland – and later Denmark – business had already been included within the public university. The originally private stand-alone schools also became more reliant on state funds or were incorporated into the university, as in the case of the Gothenburg school in Sweden, or, as in Finland, converted into public entities in the 1970s (Engwall 2009; Kettunen 2013).

In Spain and Italy too, the first degree in business was introduced into public universities in the early 1970s, as an amalgam of the prior German BWL tradition and American content (Kipping, Üsdiken, and Puig 2004). There was a turn to the first degree in some of the private stand-alone schools too. The ones run by the Jesuits, i.e., ICADE, ESADE, as well as *Deusto* (see Table 10.1 and Chapter 4), did so to cater to students coming out of their own secondary schools. The same broad pattern of development occurred in much of Latin America, though with private universities playing a greater part. There was an explosive growth at the first-degree level in that by the mid-1980s students in business accounted for around 10 percent of those in higher education within the region (Davila 1991). In this expansion, however, it was a relatively small number of mostly private, university-based or stand-alone schools that managed to become selective and came to be distinguished as the "elite." With the exception of some cases such as Chile and Argentina, where graduate programs were late-coming, most of these schools were established in the 1950s and the 1960s and focused more on graduate and executive education – though almost all also had the first degree (Davila 1991; see also Table 10.1).

In Asia, business education expanded in the 1970s and the 1980s very much along the lines it had become structured after World War II. The MBA did not appear in Japan, for example. Keio University, which had been the sole exception, remained so. It extended in 1978 the program that it had started in 1969 to two years so that it could officially be recognized as a master's degree (Ishida 1997). In India, on the other hand, the IIMs, with two later additions, stuck to their graduate programs, becoming highly selective and increasingly prestigious. Yet, their degrees were still not called an MBA, with the master's in the universities that followed them also often referred to as the M.Com. (Koenig and Tapie 2008).

So, even by the end of the 1980s the MBA label was in use outside the US only in a few contexts and mainly in two kinds of organizational settings. On the one hand, it had taken hold in the UK, Canada, Australia, and New Zealand. As pointed out above, these were the countries where American-type university-based schools of business either already existed or were established in the 1970s (Byrt 1989). Growth in the number of providers was particularly fast in the UK and Canada. By the mid-1980s 31 universities in the UK as well as the major polytechnics were offering one-year full-time or longer and more attractive part-time MBA programs, along with specialist master's in functional areas (Barry 1989: 64). In Canada 28 universities were doing so in the late 1980s (Blake 1989: 112). In both countries, the first degree in business also expanded, though more so in the polytechnics in the UK, while in Canada all universities had such a program at the beginning of the 1990s, which altogether accommodated 13 percent of full-time first-degree students in the country (Boothman 2000b: 295; Williams 2010: 97–98). The UK constituted a distinct case however, because of a relatively low share of students studying for the first degree, around seven percent, so that its ratio to graduate degrees – not all of which were MBAs – was even lower than the one in the US at the time (Edfelt 1988: 338; Barry 1989: 64).

The other settings where the MBA label began to have some degree of currency were the private universities or stand-alone schools in Europe. IESE in Spain had already introduced an MBA in the mid-1960s. *Bocconi*, the old private commercial school in Milan, which had been turned into a university (see Table 10.1 and Chapter 4), did the same in 1975 (Kipping, Üsdiken, and Puig 2004). In the very same year, INSEAD decided to label its one-year program MBA (see Box 10.2). In the two internationally minded schools in Switzerland, IMEDE and CEI – the latter renamed International Management Institute (IMI) in 1982 – similar programs were introduced and labelled MBA in 1975 and 1979, respectively (David and Schaufelbuehl 2015; see also Table 10.1). In 1990 IMEDE and IMI merged to form the International Institute for Management Development (IMD) – a leading provider of executive education and MBA programs today (Fragueiro and Michelini 2014).

So, this was all there was to the MBA outside the US. Nevertheless, more broadly conceived American-style business education did spread internationally during this period – transformed as it may have been in a multitude of ways. Its providers had also proliferated, some of them emulating US models more closely, others doing it more in their own ways, organizationally and with respect to content. The 1980s ended with the advent of media rankings of business schools in the US, to be followed in a decade by its appearance in Europe and the spread of accreditation from the US to other parts of the world. These institutional developments – together with the fall of the Berlin wall in 1989 – were to have an important impact not only on the business education field in the US, but elsewhere too, leading to a new wave of Americanization in the decades that followed – a story to be told in Chapter 13.

References

Adams, W. and Garraty, J. A. (1960) *Is the World Our Campus?* East Lansing, MI: Michigan State University Press.

AID (1971) *Catalogues of Third Country Training Resources in East, Near East, and South Asia*, Washington, DC: Agency for International Development.

Augier, M. and March, J. G. (2011) *The Roots, Rituals, and Rhetorics of Change: North American business schools after the Second World War*, Stanford, CA: Stanford University Press.

Bach, G. L. (1958) "Some observations on the business school of tomorrow," *Management Science*, 4(4): 351–364.

Barry, B. (1989) "Management education in Great Britain," in W. Byrt (ed.), *Management Education: An international survey*, London: Routledge, pp. 56–77.

Barsoux, J.-L. (2000) *INSEAD: From intuition to institution*, London: Macmillan.

Bátiz-Lazo, B. (2013) "The adoption of US-style business education in Mexico, 1945–2005," *América Latina en la Historia Económica*, 20(1): 158–198.

Blake, J. D. (1989) "Management education in Canada," in W. Byrt (ed.), *Management Education: An international survey*, London: Routledge, pp. 104–119.

Blanchard, M. (2012) *Socio-histoire d'une entreprise éducative: Le développement des écoles supérieures de commerce en France (fin du XIXe siècle–2010)*, Unpublished Ph.D. dissertation, Paris: École des Hautes Études en Sciences Sociales.

Boel, B. (2003) *The European Productivity Agency and Transatlantic Relations, 1953–1961*, Copenhagen: Museum Tusculanum Press.

Boothman, B. E. C. (2000a) "Culture of utility: The development of business education in Canada," in B. J. Austin (ed.), *Capitalizing Knowledge: Essays on the history of business education in Canada*, Toronto: University of Toronto Press, pp. 11–86.

Boothman, B. E. C. (2000b) "Canadian management education at the millennium," in B. J. Austin (ed.), *Capitalizing Knowledge: Essays on the history of business education in Canada*, Toronto: University of Toronto Press, pp. 295–356.

Byrt, W. (1989) "Management education in Australia," in W. Byrt (ed.), *Management Education: An international survey*, London: Routledge, pp. 78–103.

Carroll, T. H. (1959) "A foundation expresses its interest in higher education for business management," *Journal of the Academy of Management*, 2(3): 155–165.

Cheit, E. F. (1985) "Business schools and their critics," *California Management Review*, 27(3): 43–62.

Daniel, C. A. (1998) *MBA: The first century*, Lewisburg, PA: Bucknell University Press.

David, T. and Schaufelbuehl, J. M. (2015) "Transatlantic influence in the shaping of business education: the origins of IMD, 1946–1990," *Business History Review*, 89(1): 75–97.

Davila, C. (1991) "The evolution of management education and development in Latin America," *Journal of Management Development*, 10(6): 22–31.

166 Post-WWII Expansion

de Man, H. (1996) "Continuities in Dutch business education: Engineering, economics and the business school," in R. P. Amdam (ed.), *Management, Education, and Competitiveness: Europe, Japan and the United States*, London: Routledge, pp. 69–95.

Durand, T. and Dameron, S. (eds) (2008) *The Future of Business Schools: Scenarios and strategies for 2020*, Basingstoke: Palgrave Macmillan.

Edfelt, R. (1988) "U.S. management education in comparative perspective," *Comparative Education Review*, 32(3): 334–354.

Engwall, L. (2009) *Mercury Meets Minerva: Business studies and higher education – the Swedish case*, 2nd edn, Stockholm: EFI, The Economic Research Institute.

Flexner, A. (1910) *Medical Education in the United States and Canada*, New York: Carnegie Foundation for the Advancement of Teaching.

Fourcade, M. and Khurana, R. (2013) "From social control to financial economics: The linked ecologies of economics and business in twentieth century America," *Theory and Society*, 42(2): 121–159.

Fragueiro, F. and Michelini, J. (2014) "Leading breakthrough initiatives in business schools," in A. M. Pettigrew, E. Cornuel, and U. Hommel (eds), *The Institutional Development of Business Schools*, Oxford: Oxford University Press, pp. 39–68.

Gemelli, G. (1996) "American influence on European management education: The role of the Ford Foundation," in R. P. Amdam (ed.), *Management, Education, and Competitiveness: Europe, Japan and the United States*, London: Routledge, pp. 38–68.

Gemelli, G. (1998) "From imitation to competitive-cooperation: The Ford Foundation and management education in Western and Eastern Europe, 1950's–1970's," in G. Gemelli (ed.), *The Ford Foundation and Europe (1950's–1970's)*, Brussels: European Interuniversity Press, pp. 167–305.

Gleeson, R. E. (1997) "Stalemate at Stanford, 1945–1958: The long prelude to the New Look at Stanford Business School," *Selections*, 13(3): 6–23.

Gleeson, R. E. and Schlossman, S. (1995) "George Leland Bach and the rebirth of graduate management education in the United States, 1945–1975," *Selections*, 11(3): 8–37.

Gordon, R. A. and Howell, J. E. (1959) *Higher Education for Business*, New York: Columbia University Press.

Harris, R. G. (1984) "The values of economic theory in management education," *American Economic Review*, 74(2): 122–126.

Hayes, R. H. and Abernathy, W. J. (1980) "Managing our way to economic decline," *Harvard Business Review*, 58(4): 67–77.

Hill, T. M., Haynes, W. W., Baumgartel, H., and Paul, S. (1973) *Institution Building in India: A study of international collaboration in management education*, Boston, MA: Harvard University.

Ishida, H. (1997) "MBA education in Japan," *Journal of Management Development*, 16(3): 185–196.

Kettunen, K. (2013) *Management Education in a Historical Perspective: The business school question and its solution in Finland*, Ph.D. dissertation, Oulu: University of Oulu.

Khurana, R. (2007) *From Higher Aims to Hired Hands: The social transformation of American business schools and the unfulfilled promise of management as a profession*, Princeton, NJ: Princeton University Press.

Kieser, A. (2004) "The Americanization of academic management education in Germany," *Journal of Management Inquiry*, 13(2): 90–97.

Kipping, M. (1998) "The hidden business schools: Management training in Germany since 1945," in L. Engwall and V. Zamagni (eds), *Management Education in Historical Perspective*, Manchester: Manchester University Press, pp. 95–110.

Kipping, M. and Nioche, J.-P. (1998) "Much ado about nothing? The US productivity drive and management training in France, 1945-60," in T. R. Gourvish and N. Tiratsoo (eds), *Missionaries and Managers: American influences on European management education*, Manchester: Manchester University Press, pp. 50–76.

Kipping, M., Üsdiken, B., and Puig, N. (2004) "Imitation, tension, and hybridization: multiple 'Americanizations' of management education in Mediterranean Europe," *Journal of Management Inquiry*, 13(2): 98–108.

Koenig, C. and Tapie, P. (2008) "Management education in Asia," in T. Durand and S. Dameron (eds), *The Future of Business Schools: Scenarios and strategies for 2020*, Basingstoke: Palgrave Macmillan, pp. 327–335.

Leavitt, H. J. (1957) "On the export of American management education," *Journal of Business*, 30(3): 153–161.

McGlade, J. (1998) "The big push: The export of American business education to Western Europe after the Second World War," in L. Engwall and V. Zamagni (eds), *Management Education in Historical Perspective*, Manchester: Manchester University Press, pp. 50–65.

NCES (1993) *120 Years of American Education: A statistical portrait*, Washington, DC: National Center for Education Statistics.

Nishizawa, T. (1998) "The development of managerial human resources in Japan: A comparative perspective," in L. Engwall and V. Zamagni (eds), *Management Education in Historical Perspective*, Manchester: Manchester University Press, pp. 83–94.

Park, J. and Choi, M. (2011) "The Seoul National University Business School: Managing global challenge and cultural change," *Asian Case Research Journal*, 15(1): 1–36.

Pierson, F. C. (1959) *The Education of American Businessmen: A study of university-college programs in business administration*, New York: McGraw-Hill.

Porter, L. W. and McKibbin, L. E. (1988) *Management Education and Development: Drift or thrust into the 21st century*, New York: McGraw-Hill.

Puig, N. (2003) "Educating Spanish managers: The United States, modernizing networks, and business schools in Spain, 1950–1975," in R. P. Amdam, R. Kvålshaugen, and E. Larsen (eds), *Inside the Business Schools: The content of European business education*, Oslo: Abstrakt forlag, pp. 58–86.

Sass, S. A. (1982) *The Pragmatic Imagination: A history of the Wharton School, 1881–1981*, Philadelphia, PA: University of Pennsylvania Press.

Sawyer, J. A. (2000) "From commerce to management: The evolution of business education at the University of Toronto," in B. J. Austin (ed.), *Capitalizing Knowledge: Essays on the history of business education in Canada*, Toronto: University of Toronto Press, pp. 46–66.

Schmotter, J. W. (1993) "The Graduate Management Admission Council: A brief history, 1953–1992," *Selections*, 9(2): 1–11.

Taylor, D. A. (1968) *Institution Building in Business Administration: The Brazilian experience*, East Lansing, MI: Michigan State University.

Üsdiken, B. (2011) "Transferring American models for education in business and public administration to Turkey," in N. B. Criss, S. Esenbel, T. Greenwood, and L. Mazzari (eds), *American Turkish Encounters: Politics and culture, 1830–1989*, Newcastle upon Tyne: Cambridge Scholars Publishing, pp. 316–330.

Warner, M. (1987) "Industrialization, management education and training systems: A comparative analysis," *Journal of Management Studies*, 24(1): 91–112.

Whitley, R., Thomas, A., and Marceau, J. (1981) *Masters of Business? Business schools and business graduates in Britain and France*, London: Tavistock.

Williams, A. P. O. (2010) *The History of UK Business and Management Education*, Bingley: Emerald.

11

THE ASSERTION OF MANAGEMENT CONSULTING

While most efficiency engineers benefitted from World War II, their fate subsequently diverged with many of the earlier firms disappearing, while others, based on innovative methods such as Maynard's MTM system, expanded both in the US and abroad. In Europe the earlier spin-offs from the US firms, in particular Bedaux, continued to dominate their national consulting fields into the 1970s. At the same time, different kinds of firms came to prevail in the US, drawing their authority either from an association with "science" or from an image of professionalism, largely modelled after law firms and developed most comprehensively by McKinsey's Marvin Bower. These firms, their ideas as well as their professional logic also expanded to Europe and, to a lesser extent, elsewhere since the late 1950s, and gradually unified and eventually came to dominate national consulting fields there. Finally, this period also saw the emergence of a new group of challengers, when the large multinational audit and accounting firms developed their consulting activities, often based on the application or installation of IT systems.

Consulting Engineers: Mixed Fortunes

Consulting engineers or efficiency experts had dominated the early history of the management consulting field in the United States and elsewhere, initially based on an ideological or missionary logic, but turning more commercial as time went by – with Bedaux the most successful example. While World War II had provided a boost for their services, its aftermath saw many of them entering a slow decline. But there was also resilience and even revival based on innovative methods.

United States: Out With the Old, In With the New

Many of the earlier pioneers – some of them related directly to Taylor – vanished soon after World War II or even earlier. C. Bertrand Thompson, who had contributed to the establishment of a consulting field in France (Chapter 8), returned to the US in 1940, but had become disenchanted with the use of scientific management by totalitarian regimes and subsequently reinvented himself as a biochemist (Buehrens 2011). Wallace Cark, active in many European countries during the interwar period, also came back and continued his work in the US. But his firm disappeared when he died in 1948 – albeit not without engendering another well-known individual consultant, Joseph M. Juran (1904–2008), the *Architect of Quality*, so the title of his autobiography (Juran 2004). Incidentally, Juran provides a good example for the ongoing interaction between fields. A University of Minnesota engineering graduate, he worked at Western Electric before being seconded to the US Lend-Lease program during World War II, then joined Wallace Clark, and, after his death, consulted on his own. Juran was also an adjunct professor of industrial engineering at New York University and published a *Quality Control Handbook* (Juran 1951), which appeared in six editions until 2010.

Since his insistence on quality found little resonance in the US at the time, Juran subsequently exercised much of his influence in Japan. The same is true for another US pioneer of quality control systems, W. Edwards Deming (1900–1993). Their ideas helped Japanese manufacturers outclass many of their Western counterparts since the 1970s and were – interestingly and ironically – sold back to the West by other US consultants (see below). Lillian Gilbreth continued to publish and give speeches around the world (see Box 5.2). But the scientific management movement as a whole quickly waned. CIOS held another meeting in Stockholm in 1947 (Glimstedt 1998), but then, quite tellingly, renamed itself "World Council of Management," dropping the CIOS label completely in the mid-1970s – though ultimately unable to stop its descent into irrelevance (Asian Association of Management Organisations, 12 October 2015).

The fate of the pioneering, commercially oriented consulting firms in the engineering tradition was not much better. Little is known about the Emerson Engineers except for a widely publicized study at an Esso refinery in the UK in the late 1950s (Tisdall 1982: 65–71). But in the first ever survey of the largest consulting firms in the US by revenues (Higdon 1969: 309–313; see Table 11.1. for the top 20), it did not make it onto a list going up to No. 54. The firm that did make the list, ranked 44th with 80 consultants, was Albert Ramond and Associates, which was the name adopted by Bedaux's US operations after the latter's suicide in 1944 (see Chapter 8). It was still included in a 1982 directory of consulting firms with 12 named principals and offices in Chicago, New York, and Toronto (Wasserman and McLean 1982: 212), but seems to have disappeared since.

170 Post-WWII Expansion

TABLE 11.1 Top 20 Consulting Firms in the US by Billings, 1968

	Company (HQ)	Type	Founded	US dollars (million)	Consultants
1	Stanford Research Institute (Menlo Park, CA)	Science	1947	60	3,150
2	Planning Research Corporation (McLean, VA)	Engineering/ IT	1954	55	3,000
3	Booz, Allen & Hamilton Inc. (New York)	General	1914	50	1,500
4	Peat, Marwick, Mitchell & Co. (New York)	Accounting	1924	30	700
5	McKinsey & Co, Inc. (New York)	General	1926	22–25	462
6	WOFAC Company (New York)	Efficiency	1946	16	550
7	Arthur D. Little, Inc. (Cambridge, MA)	Science/ General	1886	15	230 (+150)
8	Alexander Proudfoot Company (Chicago, IL)	General	1946	15	300
9	URS Corporation (New York)	Engineering	1929	12.3	400
10	H. B. Maynard & Company (Pittsburgh, PA)	Efficiency	1934	10	450
11	Ernst & Ernst	Accounting		10	400
12	The Diebold Group (New York)	IT (Automation)	1954	8	450
13	Lybrand, Ross Bros. & Montgomery	Accounting		7.5	318
14	Management Science America, Inc. (Atlanta, GA)	IT (Programming)	1963	7.5	300
15	A. T Kearney & Company, Inc (Chicago, IL)	General	1926	7	255
16	Kurt Salmon Associates, Inc. (Atlanta, GA)	Efficiency/ General	1935	6.5	200
17	Lester B. Knight and Associates, Inc. (Chicago, IL)	Engineering	1945	6.5	225
18	Cresap, McCormick & Paget	General	1946	6	160
19	Operations Research	Science	n.a.	5.27	240
20	Stone & Webster Management Consultants (Boston, MA)	Engineering	1929	5	275

Sources: Higdon (1969: 309–311) for billings and number of consultants, based on "educated guesses" and supposedly only including consulting "chunk of the pie"; HQ, classification by type and founding year added, mainly based on Wasserman and McLean (1982).

At the same time, there was some renewal, namely by firms that had developed Taylorist work study methods further. There was in particular H. B. Maynard & Company, ranked 10th with 450 consultants and 10 million US dollars in revenues. It goes back to the Methods Engineering Council (MEC) founded by Harold B. Maynard (1902–1975) in Pittsburgh in 1934 (see further Smith 2004; Wright and Kipping 2012). Maynard had graduated in industrial engineering from Cornell University and in 1924 joined Westinghouse as a work-study engineer, developing a system to rate work effort (Lowry, Stegemerten, and Maynard 1927). In 1930 he left Westinghouse to conduct research on time and motion study, but frequently returned as a consultant. Faced with resistance from workers against direct observation and the use of the stopwatch, during the 1940s Maynard and his colleagues used micro motion filming to build up a large library of basic human motions in industrial work and developed a system labeled "Methods-Time-Measurement" (MTM) (Maynard, Stegemerten, and Schwab 1948). It allowed industrial engineers to calculate standard times for a large variety of tasks without having to observe and measure them directly, which reduced worker resistance and/or manipulation.

Reminiscent of the previous "missionary" logic, the system was put into the public domain in 1951 with the creation of the MTM Association for Standards and Research in the United States and Canada, followed by similar associations in other countries. An International MTM Directorate (IMD) was established in 1957 as an umbrella organization and still exists today (MTM International 11 October 2015). Consulting firms, including Maynard's own Methods Engineering Council (MEC), nevertheless played an important role in introducing the MTM system in the United States and elsewhere (see below). A similar consulting firm, about which little is known despite being ranked sixth with 550 consultants and revenues of 16 million US dollars in 1969 was the WOFAC Company. It went back to a partnership established shortly after the war in New York based on the proprietary Work Factor system, which was codified in a 1962 book (Quick, Duncan, and Malcolm 1962). The company still figured in the 1982 directory (Wasserman and McLean 1982: 396) with 12 offices in the US and one in Canada – albeit as a subsidiary of the Science Management Corporation, also founded in 1946, which offered a broad range of productivity related services in the private and public sectors (Wasserman and McLean 1982: 395–396; see also Kull 1978).

Maynard and WOFAC were the only "efficiency experts" left among the top 20 consulting firms in the US (see Table 11.1) – though the label was no longer used much. One could also include the firm founded by German immigrant Kurt Salmon in Atlanta, Georgia in 1935, since it focused on improving manufacturing processes in the textile industry – albeit in a more general sense rather than based on a specific system. All the other firms identified as having an engineering background were "engineering consultants," i.e., provided design and/or management of large projects or of general systems.

The variable fortunes of these efficiency-oriented consulting firms in the US were also reflected in the success they encountered in Europe after the war. Among those who left before the war and returned afterward, one can find Frank Mead and Colwell Carney, who had been managing British Bedaux, and K. B. White, who had been in charge of Wallace Clark's Paris office. Upon their return, they set up their own operations – albeit with limited success (Tisdall 1982; Kipping 1997). Bedaux's widow Fern and his brother Gaston rebuilt his operations on the European Continent from a base in Paris, apparently with some success: an advertisement by the *Groupe Bedaux* from 1969 listed additional offices in Amsterdam, Barcelona, Madrid, Milan, and Frankfurt. Most of these appear to have been small with the exception of Spain, where a subsidiary was established in 1953 and grew to about 100 consultants by 1960 (Kipping 1999, 2009).

Like in the US, it was those who had developed new systems that encountered success. This was namely the case of H. B. Maynard, which employed 330 consultants in eight European offices in the late 1960s – making it the largest US consulting firm in Europe, at least in terms of the number of professionals (Kipping 1999: 205). The Swedish car and truck manufacturer Volvo seems to have played a pioneering role here, introducing the MTM system in an engine factory in 1950, probably following the participation of Maynard at the CIOS conference in Stockholm in 1947 (Glimstedt 1998). By contrast, MTM was all but absent from Germany, namely because the dominant REFA association (see Chapter 8) decided, after a thorough examination, to endorse the Work Factor rather than the MTM system (Kipping 1997). MTM also struggled to take hold in the UK due to the domination of the Bedaux system (see Chapter 8 and below) arriving there via the Australian consulting firm W. D. Scott in the late 1950s, whose founder had also met Maynard at the CIOS conference in Stockholm in 1947. They signed an agreement, allowing Scott to help with the implementation of MTM not only in Australia, but also in Asia, the UK, and Africa (Wright and Kipping 2012).

European Consulting Engineers Dominating Europe

But apart from the success of MTM, it was the local efficiency- and production-related consulting firms that dominated the national fields in Europe into the 1970s. Many of them had emerged as spin-offs from US firms in the interwar period, but had by now become fully "nationalized" in terms of ownership and employment. This was notably the case of the UK, Europe's largest consulting field, which was dominated by the so-called "Big Four": Associated Industrial Consultants (AIC), Urwick Orr & Partners (UOP), Production Engineering (P-E), and Personnel Administration (PA) – all of them descendants of the subsidiary that Bedaux had established in London in 1926 (see Chapter 8). They were estimated to account for three-quarters of the total market in 1956, when they established the Management Consultancies Association (MCA) – originally to avoid government regulation but then used to lobby on their behalf and control access to the field (Tisdall 1982; Kipping and Saint-Martin 2005), follwed by a more traditional individually-based professional association, the Institute of Management Consultants (IMC), in 1961. In 1970, the Big Four employed a total of 2,400 consultants, far more than all US consulting firms in the whole of Europe combined. They also expanded abroad, operating in particular in Commonwealth countries – though generally without establishing a permanent presence there (Kipping 1999).

In Germany, by contrast, efficiency improvements remained almost exclusively the domain of REFA (see Chapter 8), which even became the transmitter of ideas generated elsewhere, like the Work Factor system (see above). But even Germany saw some rise in the number of independent consultants and consulting firms with 25 of them founding their own association, the *Bund Deutscher Unternehmensberater* (BDU) or Federation of German Enterprise Consultants in 1954. Among the most important with hindsight was the firm established by the engineer Gerhard Kienbaum in 1945, which moved from an initial technical and efficiency orientation to more general issues, including executive search, and already employed over 100 consultants by the mid-1960s. It also followed some of its German clients abroad, like Volkswagen to Brazil, albeit only on a temporary basis (Kipping 1997, 1999, 2009).

Countries in the rest of Europe were situated somewhere between these two extremes with the Netherlands probably coming closest to the British model (Hellema and Marsman 1997). In France, as mentioned, alongside a number of rival organizations promoting Taylor's or Fayol's ideas, consultants – many of them of US origin – had already played an important role during the interwar period. Their French spin-offs, in particular Paul Planus, together with a number of newly founded consulting firms came to dominate the French consulting field until the late 1960s (see esp. Henry 2012). Interestingly, France also became a secondary center for Spain (Kipping 1997, 2009) with offices opened by, among others, Bedaux, now based in Paris, and CEGOS, a French association that had morphed into a consulting provider after World War II (see Chapter 8). Many countries in Western Europe now had well-established national consulting fields and, in 1960, the various national associations created an umbrella organization in Paris, the European Federation of Management Consulting Associations or *Fédération européenne des associations de conseil en organisation* (FEACO).

Little is known about consulting in the rest of the world during the early part of this period, with the exception of Australia (see Wright 2000). Many countries remained closed to commercially oriented Western consultants, because they were or became state-dominated planned economies following the expansion of Soviet influence, the communist victory in China in 1949 or the strict licensing of business activities in post-independence India. Like in the case of business schools (Chapter 10), it was US public or private bodies, namely the Agency for International Development (AID) and the Ford Foundation, that exercised most influence in various developing and modernizing contexts, notably through the establishment of "productivity centers." These centers could be seen to play a consulting role and, in some

The Triumph of Science ... eh, Professionalism

The post-World War II period was marked by management consulting firms that departed significantly from the dominant engineering-based and efficiency-oriented ones that had been prevalent from the outset and throughout the inter-war period. On the one hand, there were those that derived their authority from a link with "science," which was seen as instrumental for the military and economic supremacy of the US during the war and afterward. On the other hand, there was the diverse group of "consulting management engineers," now increasingly referred to as management consultants, who were trying to build their own legitimacy on some form of "professionalism" and in opposition to a purely commercial approach. The boundaries between these two emerging "logics" are fluid and evolve at the outset frequently around "operations research" (OR). OR was a set of techniques – from simple statistics to more sophisticated modelling – developed during the war to facilitate military decision making and now widely seen as equally suitable to help managers make complex decisions – even more so following the ongoing increase in computing power (see, for an overview, Kirby 2000; also Waring 1991). It drew in new service providers from the margins of the field, and it also allowed some of the established ones to improve their standing – and enlarge their revenues.

Science on the Rise – For a While

A science-based firm, the Stanford Research Institute (SRI), was ranked first in Higdon's (1969) list. While ignored by the extant research on the history of management consulting (e.g., Kipping 1999; McKenna 2006), its contributions were important and included the dissemination of long-range planning and the multidivisional organization or M-form (see Chapter 2) as well as the development of the notion of "stakeholders" in the early 1960s (Nielson 2004: Chapter 14, p. 4). SRI was founded in 1946 as a non-profit subsidiary of Stanford University, which also provided it with over half a million US dollars in seed money. The aims, laid down in its charter were quite lofty and included "the promotion and extension of knowledge and learning", "the application of science in the development of commerce, trade and, industry," and "the improvement of the general standard of living and the peace and prosperity of mankind" (Nielson 2004: Chapter 1, p. 1). The institute was relatively self-contained, became independent from Stanford University in 1970 and changed its name to SRI International in 1977 (Nielson 2004: Chapter 1).

While initially bound by the university's policy in terms of having "to objectively research a situation [...] and not to interpret the research findings nor consult regarding their implications" (Nielson 2004: Chapter 1, p. 2), SRI's "Business Group" was very active as a consultant to both the private and public sectors – and, equally importantly, operated internationally almost from the outset. One of the crucial driving forces for spreading SRI's activities and even more so its reputation globally was Weldon B. "Hoot" Gibson (1917–2001) (see Nielson 2004 and his obituary in the *Stanford Report*, 9 May 2001). A Stanford MBA, Gibson had served in the US Army Air Corps during the war and then became Assistant Director of the US Air Force Institute of Technology, before joining SRI in 1947, retiring as a senior director in 1988. Taking a page out of the CIOS playbook – probably unknowingly – he established the International Industrial Conference (IIC), jointly with US magazine publisher Henry Luce (see, for the latter, Chapter 9). The first IIC in 1957 brought together over 600 business leaders from 63 countries for five days in San Francisco and was followed by 10 more until 1998.

Between the 1950s and the early 1980s, SRI also carried out a large number of projects for clients around the world, sustained by a network of more or less permanent offices in London, Paris, Bonn, Milan, Stockholm, Lisbon, Zurich, Tokyo, and Taiwan (for details, see Nielson 2004: Chapters 13 and 14). Among its notable activities was long-range planning, where it started a collective forecast service in 1959 with 73 corporations as subscribers, including many household names such as IBM, Ford, Shell, or Prudential Insurance, growing to over 400 by 1967. This also led to projects for specific companies regarding the strategic planning process and even the overall company organization. Among other prominent services were decision analysis and market segmentation.

Geographically, SRI became a consultant of choice in Sweden, where Gibson knew the leaders of two of the country's dominant family business groups at the time, Marcus Wallenberg and Axel Johnson. Here and in other Scandinavian countries SRI carried out hundreds of projects between the late 1950s and early 1980s, including for SAS, Volvo, ABB, and Electrolux (Nielson 2004: Chapter 14, pp. 13–16). Maybe its most lasting influence was in Japan, where in 1965 financial services group Nomura established a research institute (NRI) – with SRI providing the model and initial staff training. NRI in turn became a template for others, including the Mitsubishi Research Institute (MRI) founded in 1970. All of these continue to provide the type of collective consulting pioneered by SRI (Kipping 2002). Subsequently, SRI also conducted projects for specific clients such as Nissan, NTT, and Sumitomo Bank – often with a technology focus. But commercial consulting by the "Business Group" declined gradually and disappeared, once it was separated from economic development in the early 1980s.

Another firm that took advantage of the increased interest in and legitimacy of a science-based approach was Arthur D. Little (ADL), founded in Boston in 1886 (see Chapter 5 and, for the following, Kahn 1986). Arthur Dehon Little (1863–1935) studied chemistry at MIT but left for a lack of money and partnered

176 Post-WWII Expansion

with an experienced chemist to conduct "chemical analyses." Following the latter's accidental death, he widened the scope of activities to offer contract research in a variety of chemistry-related processes and industries, incorporated the business in 1909 with 22 employees at the time, and, in 1917 moved its headquarters to Cambridge, MA. During the interwar period ADL continued to offer analytical testing, third-party research, and product development (Kahn 1986: Chapter VII). But it also advised governments, businesses, and investors on R&D more generally and on the implications of new technologies, starting to publish in 1927 a monthly *Industrial Bulletin* addressed at "bankers, investors and industrial executives" (from the first page of the first *Bulletin* reproduced in Kahn 1986).

Its breakthrough as a management consultant, however, only came after World War II. Since several of its staff members had been involved in operations research activities during the war, the firm decided to establish a group offering OR-based consulting services (Kahn 1986: Chapter VIII; Magee 2002; Thomas 2012). The task fell to Harry Wissman, one of the few ADL consultants with a business degree – from the Harvard Business School – who in turn hired John Magee, a recent HBS graduate, as his assistant, with many of the additional OR consultants coming from the Navy's Operations Evaluation Group. The first test case in 1949 was Sears Roebuck, an extant ADL client, wanting to improve on their experientially based rules for sending out catalogs to former mail-order clients, which the group did successfully by analyzing a large set of data with the help of punch cards (Magee 2002). This was followed by work on production and inventory control for Johnson & Johnson's baby care division, where they applied linear programming.

Magee, who published various articles and books on operations research, can be considered the chief architect of ADL's transformation into a more mainstream management consulting firm – a transformation which outlasted the eventual decline of OR-related projects. Magee himself became its president and CEO from 1974 to 1988. Other factors also mattered. Thus, ADL forged a closer relationship with HBS, inviting one of its professors to the board in 1960 and endowing a professorship in 1966 (Kahn 1986: 98). Even more important was hiring former Lieutenant General James M. Gavin as a vice-president and board member in 1958 and making him president only two years later (Kahn 1986: Chapter IX). A graduate of West Point, Gavin had been the youngest commander ever of the legendary 82nd Airborne Division, the head of OR for the Joint Chiefs of Staff and the principal military advisor to Senator John F. Kennedy. According to Kahn (1986: 140), he "gave ADL a cachet, it had not before enjoyed in the status-conscious community [of business and government leaders]." He was particularly instrumental in ADL's international expansion, pushing the company into the emerging European Community with offices opened in Brussels, London, Paris, and Wiesbaden during the 1960s. Already earlier ADL had opened its first foreign office in neutral Switzerland, Zurich, to conduct studies for US multinationals.

Somewhat more uniquely, it also reached out into the decolonizing and developing world, including projects in a large number of the new African nations – many of them related to technology but also involving long-range planning in agriculture or tourism (Kahn 1986: 158–163). One of its major projects in this context demonstrates the permeability of boundaries between the fields. Thus, under the auspices of US AID, ADL organized the training of future private and public-sector managers in Nigeria, originally conducted by instructors from the US. Eventually, the firm decided to bring them to Cambridge, MA to be taught by ADL consultants and guest faculty at what was then called the Management Education Institute (MEI). In 1973, the MEI was authorized by the Massachusetts Board of Higher Education to grant an M.Sc. in Administration and became a fully accredited graduate school in 1976, with students coming from a wide range of developing countries and graduates numbering over 1,300 by the mid-1980s. The MEI was eventually renamed the ADL School of Management and became the Hult International Business School in 2003 (see below).

A Triumphant Professional Model

Another firm that drew on the interest in science and its strong government connections, was Booz Allen Hamilton, ranked second on the Higdon (1969) list, employing 1,500 consultants (see Table 11.1) – a more than tenfold increase from the less than 150 it employed in 1945 – with new offices opened across the US in quick succession (see further Kleiner 2004). An important internal factor contributing to its growth was a stronger uniformity of direction, with James L. Allen now the main decision maker, after Carl Hamilton died in 1946 and Edwin Booz increasingly withdrew, passing away in 1951. Externally, the firm offered a wide range of services to companies from many different industries. To give but a few examples, Booz decentralized operations at farm-equipment maker John Deere; moved Allstate to a full service insurer from auto only; and worked on in-flight service as a differentiator for United Airlines.

Importantly, Booz developed a special affinity for projects involving the – quickly increasing – use of computing technology, including operations research. And it continued to be deeply involved with the US federal government, mainly the Defence Department. For this purpose, in 1955 it established a subsidiary called Booz Allen Applied Research, Inc. (BAARINC), based outside Washington, DC. Its most well-known achievement during this period was the development of the computer-based Program Evaluation and Review Technique (PERT), originally designed to manage the Polaris nuclear submarine project (Kleiner 2004: 36). At one point, the BAARINC subsidiary accounted for close to 40 percent of the firm's revenues (Kleiner 2004: 41). More importantly, by design, i.e., due to the necessary security clearances, it operated separately from the rest of the firm – a separation that was already problematic at the time and eventually led to a full-fledged divorce (see Chapter 14).

178 Post-WWII Expansion

Other firms also benefitted from the post-World War II boom in government and public sector work – including those focusing on efficiency improvements (see above). Among them was a Booz spin-off, Cresap, McCormick and Paget, established in 1946 by consultants involved in the war-time Navy and Army projects (see Chapter 8). Subsequently, they focused to a significant – albeit not exclusive – extent on advising non-profit organizations such as universities, hospitals, museums, even churches, in the process contributing to their "corporatization," while at the same time transferring the notion of an organizational "mission" from these non-profits to their corporate clients (see, for details, McKenna 2006: Chapter 5; and, more critically, Guttman and Willner 1976). Another beneficiary was Robert Heller & Associates, who had done a study on the reorganization of US Congress during the war (see Chapter 8). After World War II, Heller was asked by the so-called Hoover Commission on the Organization of the Executive Branch to prepare a report on the *Management Organization and Administration of the Post Office* and then, in 1949, assisted with the organization of the newly established Department of Defense (McKenna 2006: 90−91, 97−101). Both firms are also examples of the dangers resulting from too much focus, because they suffered when government work dried up in the late 1960s and early 1970s.

McKinsey & Co. also conducted its share of government-related projects, opening an office in Washington, DC in 1951. These included a reorganization of the Eisenhower White House, the identification of possible commercial applications for nuclear power on behalf of the Atomic Energy Commission (AEC) in 1955 and, since 1958, a series of projects for NASA, whose first administrator was a former AEC member (McKenna 2006; McDonald 2013). But overall, it maintained a broad client-base and offered a wide variety of services, which according to its own promotional brochure, *Supplementing Successful Management*, even included wage incentive systems (McKinsey 1957). One of its best-selling services arose from a survey of executive compensation conducted by McKinsey partner Arch Patton on behalf of General Motors. *Fortune* and the *Harvard Business Review* published the surprising results – wages for workers had risen faster than management salaries, resulting in excellent visibility and a high demand for Patton and McKinsey in this area. Corresponding billings reached close to 10 percent of the firm's total for a number of years and Patton kept interest alive by publishing over 60 articles on the topic (McDonald 2013: 65−66).

That McKinsey came to count "just about every iconic American company" among its clients in the 1950s (McDonald 2013: 64) also had to do with a number of internal changes. These not only set the company on course for its ongoing success but also transformed the way in which the consulting field as a whole legitimized itself and acquired authority over management. First, the de facto split between its Chicago and New York offices was finally consummated officially, with the former relinquishing its rights to the McKinsey name – against an apparently substantial payment – and instead adopting the name of its lead partner, A. T. "Tom" Kearney. The latter apparently "disdained the notion of multiple offices" and it was only after he resigned in 1961 – he died in early 1962 – that the firm expanded both domestically and internationally (Anon. 2014: 14 and 21). McKinsey saw a leadership change already in 1950, when Marvin Bower (1903–2003) replaced Guy Crockett as managing partner – a position he held until 1967 followed by an even longer informal leadership role until 1992. Bower held degrees from Harvard's Law and Business Schools and had worked at a Cleveland law firm before joining James O. McKinsey in 1933 (see Chapter 8). In close association with the surging business schools, in particular HBS, he set out to transform McKinsey in the image of a law firm – moves emulated, often independently, by similar consulting firms (see Box 11.1).

All of these measures contributed to the creation of an image of professionalism (see also Kipping 2011), prompting Higdon (1969) to characterize these firms as "Big Image" consultants. In addition to building a professional image these firms also continued to develop the professional structures at the field level, starting with ACME in 1933 (see Chapter 8). Together with associations representing the growing number of smaller consulting firms, in 1968 ACME established an Institute of Management Consultants (IMC) with 143 founding members and Marvin Bower, Richard Paget and H. B. Maynard among the founding directors. Its purpose, as stated in the certificate of incorporation was "to establish management consulting as a self-regulating profession meriting the same public confidence and respect as medicine, accounting and law" (Lewin 2010: Chapter 1).

IMC, like ACME, was squarely directed against the aggressive, self-promotional behavior of firms like George S. May (see Chapter 8), who now bombarded potential clients with up to 20,000 letters per day and also organized golf tournaments to increase his visibility (Stryker 1954; Higdon 1969). His success prompted spin-offs. Thus, Alexander Proudfoot set up his own firm in Chicago in 1946 and, using similarly aggressive sales methods, came to be ranked eighth in the US in the late 1960s (Higdon 1969: 229–248). It should be noted here that firms like Booz and McKinsey also followed a commercial logic, despite their professional image. They did advertise, albeit in a much subtler way, for instance by posting job advertisements – unnecessary given the overwhelming interest by MBA graduates (McDonald 2013) or publishing articles in the *Harvard Business Review* (McKenna 2006). The latter, incidentally, served as model for the *McKinsey Quarterly* started in 1964 (see further Chapter 12).

180 Post-WWII Expansion

BOX 11.1 REMAKING MANAGEMENT CONSULTING IN THE IMAGE OF THE LEGAL PROFESSION

Hiring from élite graduate schools: While most of these firms had recruited experienced business people before World War II, Bower and others now followed the example of the leading law firms by hiring the top MBA graduates from the most reputable business schools. Given the clear structuration of the business school field (see Chapter 10), the best ones could serve as a proxy for quality in the eyes of potential clients. And MBA graduates, while having learnt the language of professional managers, were still young and impressionable enough to be moulded into the particular firm they joined – making it difficult for them to move elsewhere. Finally, hiring a significant proportion of graduates gave the management consulting firms considerable leverage. Thus, Booz Allen Hamilton's managing partner James Allen successfully pushed his alma mater, Kellogg, to abandon the undergraduate program and focus on graduate education only.

Selective access to partnership: Selection continued subsequently, modelled after what in law firms is referred to as the "Cravath system" – and as "up or out" in consulting, where only a limited number of young hires would become partners, allowing them to obtain a share of profits and participate in decision making (McKenna 2006: 206–208). This promoted internal competition and focused those wanting to succeed on cultivating relationships with potential or actual clients – in the case of the consultants, often graduates of the same business schools. Bower truly innovated by maintaining ties with those who left, treating them as "alumni," which also tended to prevent them from working for a competitor and made them into potential clients (see Chapter 14).

Importance of image: Another way to impress clients and distinguish firms from each other was based on "physical manifestations," which Bower considered "important in creating a wholly distinctive identity" (quoted by Edersheim 2004: 70). This referred to the cover of the firm's reports and the behavior and appearance of its consultants, including the prohibition of facial hair and the requirement to wear a hat – rules equally applied to "Booz men" at the time, whose wives were also expected to make an "overall contribution to the esprit de corps, harmony [...] and general welfare of the corporation" by accommodating their husbands' careers (quoted by Kleiner 2004: 35). And while his own consultants poked fun at the obligation to wear "professional grey" in a sarcastically titled Coloring Book (McKenna 2006: Chapter 6), Bower's insistence on the image and language of a profession seems to have worked: "You query a McKinsey man and he's fully aware of his membership in a profession" (a former consultant quoted by Higdon 1969: 147). It apparently worked also in Europe, where in the 1960s consultants emulated the "McKinsey look of successful young professionals" (quoted by Kipping 1999: 215).

Sources: Bhide (1995); Edersheim (2004); McKenna (2006); McDonald (2013).

Regarding the external mission of management consultants, Bower eventually codified his ideas in a book entitled *The Will to Manage* (Bower 1966) – a book McKinsey apparently handed out to some clients in order to familiarize them with the main terms and concepts of management (see, e.g., Kipping and Westerhuis 2014: 387). Possibly the most important contribution he made to the future success of the firm was to prevent his fellow partners from taking advantage of the consulting boom during the 1950s and 1960s to cash in. While McKinsey and many other firms moved away from a pure partnership model and incorporated for reasons related to taxation, liability, and pensions (Bhide 1995), some went further by outrightly selling their firms. This was the case of Booz spin-offs Fry Consultants and Cresap, McCormick and Paget, bought by, respectively, ARA Services, a predecessor of today's Aramark, in 1967 and Citibank in 1970. That same year, Booz itself went public, selling its shares on the New York Stock Exchange – a move apparently promoted by senior partner Jim Allen (Kleiner 2004: 58). Marvin Bower, by contrast combatted these trends, also within the IMC (Lewin 2010) and set an example by returning his own shares at book value when retiring in 1963 (McDonald 2013: 42–43). Hindsight proved him right, since all these firms ran into trouble when the "go-go years" ended in the early 1970s – compounded in the case of Booz by a number of unrelated acquisitions, including a chemical-testing lab and an airport-design firm. Booz eventually took itself private again in 1976 under new leadership, but to repair the reputational damage took a decade or more (Kleiner 2004: 59–77). Cresap partners also bought out Citibank in 1977 but then sold the firm to benefits consultants Towers Perrin in 1982 (for the latter's origins, see Chapter 8).

These troubles were not only due to the economic and financial turmoil following the Vietnam War and the oil crises; they were also prompted by increased competition from new entrants to the field. There was notably the Boston Consulting Group (BCG), founded by Bruce D. Henderson (1915–1992). A Vanderbilt graduate in mechanical engineering, he attended HBS, but never completed his degree and instead left to work for Westinghouse. In 1959, he entered the booming consulting field as a vice president at Arthur D. Little but, in 1963, was hired by the Boston Safe Deposit and Trust Company to create "a Management Consulting Division [...] to provide general counsel to corporate management in long-range planning and strategy" (from the official announcement at BCG 28 July 2015). To appeal to clients outside the bank, the division renamed itself Boston Consulting Group in 1968 and became fully independent during the second half of the 1970s. BCG in turn spawned other consulting firms, in particular the one established by William W. Bain (Kiechel 2010: Chapter 5). Born in 1937, Bain was also a Vanderbilt graduate, albeit in history, and in 1960 became the university's Director of Development, leading him to meet Bruce Henderson, who convinced him to join BCG in 1967. Bain rose quickly based on his ability to build strong relations with senior executives, but left in 1973 together with several other BCG consultants – apparently no longer

182 Post-WWII Expansion

prepared to wait for Henderson to make room for him at the top. Different from the predominant consulting model, Bain established long-term associations with a *single* organization in each sector rather than trying to sell similar studies to all of them.

In terms of geography, while the management consulting field's earlier center of gravity had been in the Mid-West, particularly in Chicago (see Chapter 8), during this period it moved decisively to the East with New York, Boston and, for government work, Washington as the main hubs. More importantly, these firms also expanded abroad, spreading not only their ideas, honed in the US context, but also their commercial model of knowledge dissemination as well as their professional image.

International Expansion and Replication

Compared to the scientific management consulting firms as well as those based on science, which spread their gospels quickly both at home and abroad, Booz, McKinsey and others took a while before venturing outside the United States. Thus, Booz only conducted its first foreign project – on land registration in the Philippines – in 1953, followed by others, e.g., on customs operations and the textile industry in Egypt, on the oil industry in Iran – projects that tended to be ad hoc and were often funded by US AID (Kleiner 2004). Since the 1960s, it also had a number of projects in Latin America, eventually opening an office in São Paulo, Brazil in 1969. In Europe, it first consulted state-owned Italian enterprises in the oil, chemical, and steel industries in 1956 and, in 1957, opened an office in Zurich, Switzerland, a location chosen for its centrality and neutrality – reasons that also motivated ADL to open its first foreign office there that same year.

Also in 1957 the Treaty of Rome established the European Economic Community making France, Germany, Italy, and the Benelux countries the nucleus of a growing and expanding common market. This set in motion a process whereby, simply put, the consulting firms followed their multinational clients from the US – just like Bedaux had done during the interwar period (see Chapter 8), which in turn prompted their European competitors to hire those same consultants in order to fight fire with fire (Servan-Schreiber 1967). Interestingly enough, George S. May was the first to move into the growing European markets, opening an office in Düsseldorf in 1955 after a golf tournament there. While he died in 1962 at the age of 71, his firm continued to expand and by the mid-1960s claimed to have offices in nine European countries (Higdon 1969; Kipping 1999: 205–206). But its aggressive sales methods proved unsuitable, with clients in several countries even suing the firm over unfulfilled promises (see, e.g., Tisdall 1982: 64–65). Proudfoot also expanded internationally, becoming the fourth largest consulting firm in Europe by revenues in the early 1970s and entering Africa and Australia in the subsequent decade (Wright and Kipping 2012). By the end of the 1960s though, Booz, Arthur D. Little, and McKinsey had caught up (see Table 11.2).

Assertion of Management Consulting 183

TABLE 11.2 The Expansion of US Management Consultants to Europe, 1960s

Name	Offices		Consultants		1969 revenues	
	1962	1969	1962	1969	US dollars (million)	% of total
Booz	1	2	70	111	5	9
Arthur D. Little	1	4	30	53	6	16
McKinsey	1	6	15	160	8	35
A. T. Kearney	0	5	0	60	2	15

Source: See Kipping (1999: 210).

While Booz was the first mover among these firms, it grew rather slowly in Europe – maybe because it was more diversified geographically (see above). ADL expanded faster benefiting in particular from the notoriety of its managing director Gavin (see above). US multinationals accounted for a significant part of their European business well into the 1960s. McKinsey also targeted this clientele, notably with a booklet on *International Enterprise: A New Dimension of American Business* (1962) – though its first client in Europe was the Anglo-Dutch oil company Shell, which apparently brought in the US consultants as neutral outsiders. After opening an office in London in 1959 McKinsey quickly came to work for many iconic British organizations, including the Bank of England, the BBC, as well as the National Health Service. It opened five more offices in Continental Europe, benefitting from mimetic effects, when after an initial assignment most competitors in the same sector across the continent would also contract its services (see, in general, Kipping 1999; for banking, Kipping and Westerhuis 2014). The firm was also very skilled at identifying well-connected individuals to help them gain access to the local business élites – even in Germany, where business knowledge had been exchanged cooperatively rather than being sold (see Chapter 8). Moreover, it sponsored INSEAD in the hope of replicating its MBA-based recruitment model in Europe (see Chapter 10).

The latecomers, A. T. Kearney and the Boston Consulting Group (BCG), also made quick inroads internationally, partially through acquisitions. As noted, the former had retained a national, even Mid-West focus until the departure of its founder in 1961. But its successor changed tack and, in 1964, opened a first office outside the US in Düsseldorf. To catch up in the UK, A. T. Kearney bought a small but well-known local consulting firm in 1969 (Kipping 1999). BCG, which had only been established in 1963, also used acquisitions to start its foreign activities and initially focused on more marginal markets – possibly to avoid going head to head with the established US firms. Thus, it bought Pietro Gennaro Associati in Milan in 1965 and TFM Adams in Japan in 1966, followed by a joint venture called Attwood-Boston Consultants in London in 1968. Having gained sufficient confidence and visibility, it turned the latter into its own office in 1970

184 Post-WWII Expansion

and opened two others in Paris in 1972 and Munich in 1975 (Fink and Knoblach 2003: Chapter 2.5). In hindsight, the early move to Japan proved particularly judicious, since BCG became one of the consulting firms to transfer Japanese management ideas back to the West, once they had started to prove their worth since the 1970s (see below).

BCG's early international expansion is also linked to the origins of one of the more important European management consulting firms, Roland Berger Strategy Consultants (see, for the following, Fink and Knoblach 2003: 100−102). After studying BWL in Munich, Berger joined Pietro Gennaro in Milan in 1962, but moved to the US after its acquisition by BCG and became a partner there. In 1967 he returned to Munich and set up his own consulting firm, focusing on strategy and marketing. His first highly visible project was the merger of four German tour operators into Touristik Union International, predecessor of today's TUI group. Subsequently, Berger not only grew in Germany but also abroad, opening an office in São Paulo to service German multinationals in the region and acquiring Bedaux's Spanish operations in 1985 (Kipping 2009: 72).

But while these US consultants increasingly dominated their home market and unified as well as "Americanized" European consulting fields, new challengers arose that had so far carried out their consulting activities in the hidden.

"The Accountants Are Coming!"

The above was the title − repeated for effect − of the penultimate chapter in the book by Higdon (1969). He stressed that seven out of the top 25 consulting firms by revenues were accounting and audit firms (see Table 11.1). As mentioned in Chapters 5 and 8, these firms had always provided consulting advice to their clients − albeit on an occasional and ad hoc basis and often related to bankruptcy and restructuring. Their more systematic and organized entry into consulting only occurred after World War II, when they broadened these activities and set up separate departments or divisions, usually referred to as "management advisory services" (Stevens 1981: Chapter 5). This internal specialization was facilitated by a growing consolidation within the accounting and auditing field through alliances and mergers between the major firms in the US, the UK, and Canada. During the post-World War II period, the number of large, globally operating accounting and audit firms gradually reduced to the so-called "Big Eight" (see, for the detailed "family trees" of all these firms in the UK, Boys 1989; for the US stories, Stevens 1981):

> Arthur Andersen
> Arthur Young & Co. − called Arthur Young, McLelland, Moores & Co. from 1968 to 1985

Coopers & Lybrand since 1973 – before: Cooper Brothers in the UK, Lybrand, Ross Bros. & Montgomery in the US, and McDonald Currie & Co. in Canada
Deloitte Haskins & Sells since 1978 – before: Deloitte & Co. in the UK (since 1971) and Haskin & Sells in the US
Ernst & Whinney since 1979 – before: Whinney, Murray & Co. in the UK and Ernst & Ernst in the US
Peat, Marwick, Mitchell & Co. since 1925 both in the UK and the US
Price Waterhouse since 1874 in the UK and 1890 in the US
Touche Ross since 1969; before: Touche, Ross, Bailey & Smart

As a whole, these firms were well placed to expand their consulting activities during this period – albeit with some inherent challenges. They had a head start with respect to the new computer technologies, since they were being used for accounting purposes. Faced with largely stagnant markets for audit and accounting, IT-related services offered them an opportunity to grow, but also created the potential for tensions as the consulting partners would eventually ask for more influence, even independence (McDougald and Greenwood 2012). And since they already had a close relationship with a large number of clients, both nationally and internationally, they could easily sell them these IT-based and other consulting services. However, such cross-selling set up potential conflicts of interest, which already during the 1970s prompted the Securities and Exchange Commission (SEC) to propose that clients disclose audit and consulting fees separately – a proposal that was fought by the Big Eight and, ultimately, not implemented (Stevens 1981: Chapter 8).

Among these firms, the first and foremost to take advantage was Arthur Andersen, partially driven by a leadership change following the founder's death in 1947. Under his successor Leonard P. Spacek (1907–2000), who was managing partner until 1963, then chairman until 1970, the firm grew from a largely Chicago-based operation with a few offices elsewhere in the US to the second largest accounting firm in the world with 92 offices in 26 countries, employing over 12,000 people – all the while maintaining its uniform culture (Squires et al. 2003: 44–45). Equally, if not more importantly, it also became a first mover in offering IT consulting, starting with a project helping GE to select and install its first mainframe computer in 1953. As the IT usage in US and global businesses grew, so did Arthur Andersen's related "administrative services division," reaching over 20 percent of revenues by the 1970s with a higher profitability per partner than audit. Spacek's successor therefore devised a plan to spin off the fast growing consulting activities into a separate company, but it was rejected by the still dominant audit partners in 1979, prompting him to resign. His successor offered the consulting partners more say in decision making, thus restoring internal peace – at least for the time being (Toffler and Reingold 2003: 70–78).

The other firms also saw their advisory activities grow – though not quite as decisively as Spacek at Arthur Andersen. Thus, Peat, Marwick, Mitchell & Co., which prided itself in having offered consulting since the interwar period

186 Post-WWII Expansion

(Chapter 8), also invested in its growth during the 1960s and 1970s. In 1965 it acquired the Management Systems Corporation to offer IT-related services to the federal government and, later that decade, hired partners with backgrounds in financial as well as public services, including education and health care, in order to extend its consulting services into those sectors. By 1981 it employed 1,200 consultants offering advice not only on data processing and computer systems but also on employee benefits, executive compensation, and marketing (Wise 1982: 70–71; see also Higdon 1969: 274). The other Big Eight firms saw similar developments and made similar investments in what had now become their fastest growing and most promising business (see Stevens 1981; McDougald and Greenwood 2012). As Table 11.3 shows, at the beginning of the 1980s Arthur

TABLE 11.3 Top 20 Consulting Firms in the US by Revenue, 1982

	Company (HQ)	US dollars (million)	1968 rank
1	Arthur Andersen & Co[a] (Chicago, IL)[b]	218	21
2	Booz, Allen & Hamilton, Inc[a] (New York)	210	3
3	McKinsey & Co, Inc (New York)	145	5
4	Arthur D Little, Inc[a] (Cambridge, MA)	141	7
5	William M Mercer, Inc[a] (New York)	120	n.a.
6	Towers, Perrin, Forster & Crosby[a] (New York)[c]	120	18
7	Peat, Marwick, Mitchell & Co (New York)[b]	112	4
8	Ernst & Whinney (Cleveland, OH)[b]	85	11
9	Coopers & Lybrand (New York)[b]	79	13
10	American Management Systems, Inc[a] (Arlington, VA)	65	n.a.
11	The Hay Group[a] (Philadelphia, PA)	60	n.a.
12	The Reliance Consulting Group, Inc[a] (New York)	59	n.a.
13	Price Waterhouse (New York)[b]	57	24
14	Hewitt Associates[a] (Lincolnshire, IL)	54	n.a.
15	The Boston Consulting Group, Inc (Boston, MA)	50	n.a.
16	SRI International (Menlo Park, CA)	50	1
17	Touche Ross & Co (New York)[b]	49	n.a.
18	Arthur Young & Co (New York)[b]	49	25
19	AT Kearney, Inc (Chicago, IL)	46	15
20	Science Management Corp[a] (Bridgewater, NJ)	46	n.a.

Source: Byrne (1983); 1968 rank added, based on Higdon (1969).

[a] Includes revenues from specialized, technical and/or non-management consulting services.
[b] Accounting/audit firm.
[c] Acquired Cresap, McCormick & Paget in 1982.

Assertion of Management Consulting   **187**

Andersen had become the largest consulting firm in the US – while SRI dropped to 16 – and all the Big Eight were among the top 20.

Even if Booz, McKinsey, and ADL occupied ranks 2 to 4 in the list and BCG and A. T. Kearney came 15th and 19th, the rise of the Big Eight must have worried the leading "professional" firms. Even more so, since the latter had already made efforts to increase the visibility and legitimacy of their consulting activities by joining the relevant professional associations – an effort, which as Higdon (1969: 271) had already noted earlier, made the "Big Image" firms "shudder convulsively." During the 1960s and 1970s they actually succeeded in joining the professional associations both in the UK and in the US – apparently prompting Marvin Bower to no longer attend IMC Board meetings after 1976 (Lewin 2010: Chapter 2) and McKinsey and the other "Big Image" firms to leave ACME at some point during this period.

Table 11.3 includes some of the pension and employee benefits firms established during the 1930s and 1940s (see Chapter 8): Mercer, Towers Perrin, Hay and Hewitt, ranked 5th, 6th, 11th and 14th respectively. This shows that they had not only grown but also moved sufficiently into the provision of HR-related consulting to be considered by external observers as part of the management consulting field. Even more important – with hindsight – was the appearance of IT-related firms without a basis in other professional services such as accounting or engineering: American Management Systems (AMS) and Reliance Consulting Group, ranked 10th and 12th respectively. The former had been established in 1970 by five "whiz kids" from the US Department of Defence and mainly sold software- and systems-related advice to the federal government (American Management Systems, Inc. History 10 October 2015). The latter goes back to a computer leasing company established by Saul Steinberg in 1961, which subsequently bought numerous consulting firms, including former Bedaux subsidiary AIC in the UK in 1967 (Reliance Group Holdings, Inc. History 10 October 2015).

While both of these have now disappeared, they were the forbearers of developments to come during the subsequent period, which saw massive increases in IT-related services. While not yet making the top 20 list in 1982, many of the subsequent leaders were created during this period, including, for example, the predecessor of Capgemini, founded by Serge Kampf in Grenoble in 1967, and CGI, established by Serge Godin in Québec City in 1976, which, incidentally, would purchase the bulk of AMS in 2004. Capgemini and CGI are also indicative of another future trend, which would see a certain reduction in the US hegemony of the field.

References

American Management Systems, Inc. History, 10 October 2015. www.fundinguniverse.com/company-histories/american-management-systems-inc-history.

Anon. (2014) *The A. T. Kearney Story*, Chicago, IL: A. T. Kearney.

Asian Association of Management Organisations, 12 October 2015. www.aamo.net/html/evolution.htm.

BCG, 28 July 2015. www.bcg.com/about/heritage/default.aspx.

Bhide, A. V. (1995) "Building the professional firm: McKinsey & Co.: 1939–1968," Harvard Business School Working Paper 95–10 (mimeo).

Bower, M. (1966) *The Will to Manage: Corporate success through programmed management*, New York: McGraw-Hill.

Boys, P. (1989) "What's in a name: Firms' simplified family trees on the web." www.icaew.com/en/library/historical-resources/accountancy-practices/whats-in-a-name (accessed 24 October 2015).

Buehrens, J. A. (2011) "Clarence Bertrand Thompson: 1882–1969," in M. Morrison-Reed (ed.), *Darkening the Doorways: Black trailblazers and missed opportunities in unitarian universalism*, Boston, MA: Skinner House Books, pp. 44–99.

Byrne, J. A. (1983) "Are All These Consultants Really Necessary?" *Forbes*, 10 October: 136–144.

Deloitte, 30 July 2015. http://www2.deloitte.com/us/en/pages/about-deloitte/articles/about-deloitte-history-timeline.html.

Edersheim, E. H. (2004) *McKinsey's Marvin Bower: Vision, leadership and the creation of management consulting*, New York: Wiley.

Fink, D. and Knoblach, B. (2003) *Die großen Management Consultants: ihre Geschichte, ihre Konzepte, ihre Strategien*, Munich: Vahlen.

Glimstedt, H. (1998) "Americanization and the 'Swedish model' of industrial relations: The introduction of the MTM system at Volvo in the post-war period," in M. Kipping and O. Bjarnar (eds), *The Americanization of European Business*, London: Routledge, pp. 133–148.

Guttman, D. and Willner, B. (1976) *The Shadow Government: The government's multi-billion-dollar giveaway of its decision-making powers to private management consultants, "experts", and think tanks*, New York: Pantheon Books.

Hellema, P. and Marsman, J. (1997) *De organisatie-adviseur: De opkomst en groei van een nieuw vak in Nederland 1920–1960*, Meppel: Boom.

Henry, O. (2012) *Les guérisseurs de l'économie: Ingénieurs-conseil en quête de pouvoir*, Paris: CNRS Éditions.

Higdon, H. (1969) *The Business Healers*, New York: Random House.

Juran, J. M. (ed.) (1951) *Quality Control Handbook*, New York: McGraw-Hill.

Juran, J. M. (2004) *Architect of Quality*, New York: McGraw-Hill.

Kahn, E. J. (1986) *The Problem Solvers: A history of Arthur D. Little, Inc.*, Boston, MA: Little Brown & Co.

Kiechel, W. (2010) *The Lords of Strategy: The secret intellectual history of the new corporate world*, Boston, MA: Harvard Business Press.

Kipping, M. (1997) "Consultancies, institutions and the diffusion of Taylorism in Britain, Germany and France, 1920s to 1950s," *Business History*, 39(4): 67–83.

Kipping, M. (1999) "American management consulting companies in Western Europe, 1920 to 1990: Products, reputation and relationships," *Business History Review*, 73(2): 190–220.

Kipping, M. (2002) "Why Management Consulting Developed So Late in Japan and Does It Matter?" (in Japanese), *Hitotsubashi Business Review*, 50(2): 6–21.

Kipping, M. (2009) "Management consultancies and organizational innovation in Europe," in P. Fernández Pérez and M. B. Rose (eds), *Innovation and Entrepreneurial Networks in Europe*, London: Routledge, pp. 61–80.

Kipping, M. (2011) "Hollow from the start? Image professionalism in management consulting," *Current Sociology*, 59(4): 530–550.

Kipping, M. and Saint-Martin, D. (2005) "Between regulation, promotion and consumption: Government and management consultancy in Britain," *Business History*, 47(3): 449–465.

Kipping, M. and Westerhuis, G. (2014) "The managerialization of banking: From blueprint to reality," *Management & Organizational History*, 9(4): 374–393.

Kirby, M. W. (2000) "Operations Research Trajectories: The Anglo-American experience from the 1940s to the 1990s," *Operations Research*, 48(5): 661–670.

Kleiner, A. (2004) *Booz Allen Hamilton: Helping clients envision the future*, Old Saybrook, CT: Greenwich Publishing.

Kull, D. C. (1978) "Productivity programs in the Federal Government," *Public Administration Review*, 38(1): 5–9.

Lewin, M. D. (ed.) (2010) *The History of IMC USA: A legacy of professionalism*, rev. edn, North Palm Beach, FL: Institute of Management Consultants USA.

Lowry, S. M., Stegemerten, G. J., and Maynard, H. B. (1927) *Time and Motion Study and Formulas for Wage Incentives*, New York: McGraw-Hill.

Magee, J. F. (2002) "Operations research at Arthur D. Little, Inc.: The early years," *Operations Research*, 50(1): 149–153.

Maynard, H. B., Stegemerten, G. J., and Schwab, J. L. (1948) *Methods–Time Measurement*, New York: McGraw-Hill.

McDonald, D. (2013) *The Firm: The story of McKinsey and its secret influence on American business*, New York: Simon & Schuster.

McDougald, M. G. and Greenwood, R. (2012) "Cuckoo in the nest? The rise of management consulting in large accounting firms," in M. Kipping and T. Clark (eds), *The Oxford Handbook of Management Consulting*, Oxford: Oxford University Press, pp. 93–116.

McKenna, C. D. (2006) *The World's Newest Profession: Management consulting in the twentieth century*, New York: Cambridge University Press.

McKinsey (1957) *Supplementing Successful Management*, New York: McKinsey.

McKinsey (1962) *International Enterprise: A new dimension of American business*, New York: McKinsey.

MTM International, 11 October 2015. http://mtm-international.org.

Nielson, D. L. (2004) *A Heritage of Innovation: SRI's First Half Century*, Menlo Park, CA: SRI International.

Quick, J. H., Duncan, J. H., and Malcolm, J. A. (1962) *Work-Factor Time Standards: Measurement of manual and mental work*, New York: McGraw-Hill.

Reliance Group Holdings, Inc., History, 10 October 2015. www.fundinguniverse.com/company-histories/reliance-group-holdings-inc-history.

Servan-Schreiber, J.-J. (1967) *Le défi américain*, Paris: Denoël.

Smith, K. (2004) "Living the vision seventy years later," *Maynard Exchange*, 9(4). www.hbmaynard.com/Exchange/vol9-4.pdf (accessed 28 October 2014).

Squires, S. E., Smith, C. J., McDougall, L., and Yeack, W. R. (2003) *Inside Arthur Andersen: Shifting values, unexpected consequences*, London: FT Press.

Stevens, M. (1981) *The Big Eight*, New York: Macmillan.

Stryker, P. S. (1954) "The relentless George S. May," *Fortune*, 49 (June): 140–141 and 196–208.

Thomas, W. (2012) "Operations Research vis-à-vis Management at Arthur D. Little and the Massachusetts Institute of Technology in the 1950s," *Business History Review*, 86(1): 99–122.

Tisdall, P. (1982) *Agents of Change: The development and practice of management consultancy*, London: Heinemann.

Toffler, B. L. and Reingold, J. (2003) *Final Accounting: Ambition, greed, and the fall of Arthur Andersen*, New York: Broadway Books.

Waring, S. P. (1991) *Taylorism Transformed: Scientific management theory since 1945*, Chapel Hill, NC: University of North Carolina Press.

Wasserman, P. and McLean, J. (eds) (1982) *Consultants and Consulting Organizations Directory*, 5th edn, Detroit, MI: Gale Research Company.

Wise, T. A. (1982) *Peat, Marwick, Mitchell & Co.: 85 years*, New York: Peat, Marwick, Mitchell & Co.

Wright, C. (2000) "From shopfloor to boardroom: The historical evolution of Australian management consulting, 1940s to 1980s," *Business History*, 42(1): 86–106.

Wright, C. and Kipping, M. (2012), "The engineering origins of management consulting – and their long shadow," in M. Kipping and T. Clark (eds), *The Oxford Handbook of Management Consulting*, Oxford: Oxford University Press, pp. 29–49.

12

GROWTH AND DIVERSIFICATION OF MANAGEMENT PUBLISHING

The post-World War II period saw an expansion for book publishing, the business press, and academic journals. In terms of book publishing particularly, McGraw-Hill, Prentice-Hall, and Wiley increased their lists of management publications, not least by responding to the increase in management education through textbooks. The period also involved growth for some more recent publishing houses, like Prentice-Hall, as well as the establishment of new ones. In addition, there were mergers and acquisitions, among them Pearson's purchase of Longman and Penguin. Pearson also moved into the business press by acquiring the *Financial Times* and a 50 percent stake in the *Economist*, which had benefitted from an increasing demand for business newspapers and weeklies in the US and Europe. Similarly, there was growth in scientific publishing in management. While nine of the *FT45* journals had been founded before 1946 as many as 24 were established between 1946 and 1980. In this process professional associations again played an important role.

Publishers: Expansion, New Establishments, and Restructuration

Wiley, Harper, Macmillan, and McGraw-Hill

The post-World War II period saw the beginning of a growth of publications in business and management. Thus, for the four publishers examined in Chapters 6 and 8, i.e., Wiley, Harper, Macmillan, and McGraw-Hill, Figure 12.1 shows increases in their cumulative number of books having "management" in their titles between 1946 and 1980 – rough estimates that are nevertheless likely to be indicative for the development of the four publishers.

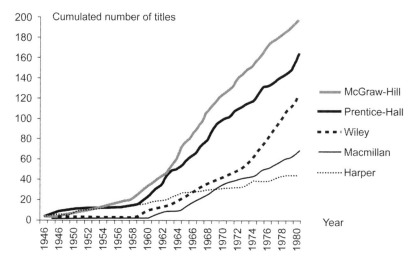

FIGURE 12.1 Estimates of the cumulated number of titles from Wiley, Harper, Macmillan and McGraw-Hill including 'management' in the period 1946–80

Figure 12.1 confirms the trend observed in the previous period, namely that McGraw-Hill developed into the most active company in management publishing (see Chapter 9). However, it also shows that Wiley is taking off, particularly in the 1970s. Macmillan expanded too, while Harper had a more limited development. As will be shown below, the four early entrants encountered increased competition in the post-World War II period.

During this period, McGraw-Hill seems to have taken the lead through a broader list of management publications than the other three: There were books in strategy (Steiner 1963; Anderson 1965; Glueck 1980), administration (Gellerman 1960; Likert 1961; Bennis 1966 and Sayles 1979), accounting (Goetz 1949; Bates 1959 and Li 1968), marketing (Mauser 1961; Boyd and Britt 1963; and Magee 1968), international business (Blough 1966; Fayerweather 1969; and Richman and Copen 1972), and production (Feigenbaum 1961; Schrieber 1965; and Levin 1972). Some of these titles included cases – demonstrating an adaptation to business school education. McGraw-Hill also took a lead in the publication of handbooks, i.e., edited volumes in which single or multiple experts in specific research areas provided overviews. Already in the 1950s it published handbooks of quality control (Juran 1951) and purchasing (Aljian 1958). They were followed in the subsequent decades by an international handbook of management (Ettinger 1965) as well as volumes on modern manufacturing management (Maynard 1970), management development (Taylor and Lippitt 1975), and management for plant engineers (Lewis 1977).

In terms of later attention, James D. Thompson's *Organizations in Action* (Thompson 1967) stands out. It has become a classic, not only for organizational scholars in the narrow sense, but also for management studies as a whole. Taking a broader business school perspective that also includes economics there can be no doubt that *Economics* (Samuelson 1948) by the later Nobel Laureate Paul Samuelson has been extremely influential, appearing in its 19th edition in 2010 (Samuelson and Nordhaus 2010). Another event during the post-war period, which would be significant for McGraw-Hill in the future, was the acquisition of the rating agency Standard & Poor's in 1966 (McGraw-Hill Financial 5 May 2015).

For Wiley with its science and engineering orientation it was quite natural − though apparently not very lucrative (see Jacobson et al. 2007: 214) − to publish titles within operations research, as this area became an important part of management studies and practice during the 1950s and 1960s (see also Chapter 11). Significant titles were *Introduction to Operations Research* (Churchman, Ackoff, and Arnoff 1957), *Management Models and Industrial Applications of Linear Programming* (Charnes and Cooper 1961), *Queues* (Cox and Smith 1961), and *Modern Production Management* (Buffa 1961). However, Wiley also published titles that paid attention to the human side of management. The most influential of these was without doubt James G. March and Herbert A. Simon's *Organizations* (March and Simon 1958), which became a classic and paved the way for future research into organizations such as *Theories of Organizations* (Hage 1980). Another early publication in the same area was *Principles of Human Relations* (Maier 1952).

These titles reflect a change in that Wiley increased the share of its publications in the social sciences, the humanities, and business in the 1968−1978 period from 22 percent to 38 percent. In this development titles in psychology were important as was Wiley's turn to the expanding textbook market. Wiley also moved into foreign markets by establishing a London office in 1960, creating Wiley Australia in 1963 and starting a Toronto office in 1968. An additional significant event was the acquisition in 1961 of Interscience, a publisher of scientific, technical, and medical titles. That same year Wiley also established a joint venture with Basic Books, a New York publisher founded in 1952 focusing on the social sciences. However, for management and business publishing the acquisition in 1977 of the Ronald Press, which had published business-oriented titles since the nineteenth century, was particularly important (see Chapters 6 and 9). Small but focused, it "would provide a platform for launching a highly successful business trade list in the 1980s" (Jacobson et al. 2007: 212–229, quote p. 232).

Macmillan joined Wiley in publishing titles on operations research, including, in the mid-1960s, *Executive Readings in Management Science* (Starr 1965), *Mathematical Studies in Management Science* (Veinott 1965), *Applied Queueing Theory* (Lee 1966), and *Mathematical Programming for Business and Industry* (Haley 1967). With this quantitative orientation it was quite natural to also publish titles in finance such as *Appraisal and Management of Securities* (Hayes 1956), *Principles of Financial Analysis* (Wessel 1961) and *Business Finance* (Archer and D'Ambrosio 1966).

Among other works were titles on top management planning and strategy (Steiner 1969; Steiner and Miner 1977) and personnel management (McFarland 1968). Within the emerging area of organization studies *Administrative Behavior* (Simon 1947) by the future Nobel Laureate Herbert A. Simon received considerable attention. In relation to these publications it is worth noting that Macmillan re-entered the US market in 1954, after having sold its American operations in 1896, and merged with the US publisher Crowell-Collier in 1960 (Jacobson et al. 2007: 218). Another circumstance to point out is that some of the mentioned books were readers that, like some of the McGraw-Hill titles, presented cases.

Harper, finally, was in 1946, according to Figure 12.1, second to McGraw-Hill in management publications, but had in 1980 been passed by both Wiley and Macmillan. Nevertheless, Harper historiographer Eugene Exman (1965: Chapter 22) labelled the period "years of expansion." An important event in that process was Harper's merger with Row, Peterson & Company in 1962, which resulted in Harper & Row. In terms of authors, Peter Drucker has already been mentioned in Chapter 9 as a significant contributor to the Harper lists (e.g., Drucker 1974). Harper also attracted Herbert A. Simon, who published two books with them: *The Science of Management Decision* (Simon 1960) and *The Shape of Automation for Men and Management* (Simon 1965). Harper publications also included a number of titles focusing on human relations: *Motivation and Personality* (Maslow 1954), *The Union Challenge to Management Control* (Chamberlain 1948), *Social Responsibility and Strikes* (Chamberlain 1953), and *Wildcat Strike* (Gouldner 1965). At the same time, Harper published titles on topics such as long-range planning (Ewing 1958) and corporate public relations (Hill 1958). In the 1970s two Harper & Row publications attracted considerable attention judging by their citations: Jeffrey Pfeffer and Gerald R. Salancik's *The External Control of Organizations* (Pfeffer and Salancik 1978) and Henry Mintzberg's *The Nature of Managerial Work* (Mintzberg 1973a).

Other Already Established Publishers

Among the other publishers Prentice-Hall appears as the significant runner-up with almost as many titles as McGraw-Hill in the post-World War II period. Moreover, Prentice-Hall not only stood out in terms of quantity; it also brought out a number of books which would attract considerable attention, with Richard M. Cyert and James G. March's *A Behavioral Theory of the Firm* (Cyert and March 1963) as the most cited and influential for later management research (see further Engwall and Danell 2002). In terms of textbooks Prentice-Hall was particularly successful through Joel Dean's *Managerial Economics* (Dean 1951), Philip Kotler's *Marketing Management* (Kotler 1967; see further, Box 12.1), and Henry Mintzberg's *The Structuring of Organizations* (Mintzberg 1979).

BOX 12.1 PHILIP KOTLER: GLOBAL MARKETING MAN

Kotler was born to Ukrainian immigrants in Chicago in 1931. After a Ph.D. in economics at MIT in 1956, he did postdoctoral work at Harvard University and at the University of Chicago in mathematics and behavioral science, respectively. In 1962 he was hired by the business school at Northwestern University – renamed J. L. Kellogg Graduate School of Management in 1979 – where he has since made his career through promotion and as the holder of various endowed chairs. By 2015 he had published 57 books and 150 articles in leading journals. Best-known among his publications is the widely used textbook *Marketing Management*, which since its first edition in 1967 has appeared in 13 editions. In addition, it has later been adapted to European markets generally (Kotler et al. 1996) as well as to German, Norwegian, and French audiences more specifically (see, Kotler and Bliemel 1995; Kotler and Blom 1992; Kotler and Dubois 1977). It has also been packaged for top managers (Kotler 1999). Kotler has not only adapted his message to other cultures but also to other contexts: non-profit organizations (Kotler and Andreasen 1975), health care organizations (Kotler 1985), congregations (Kotler 1992), hospitality and tourism (Kotler 1996), as well as whole nations (Kotler and Maesincee 1997). A basic argument in his writings is the need to consider the strategic mix of four significant marketing variables, the so-called 4P's: Product, Price, Promotion, and Place. In addition to his extensive academic authorship Kotler has over the years been a consultant to major corporations such as AT&T, Bank of America, General Electric, Honeywell, IBM, and Merck. He has also been active in a number of professional organizations, among them a foundation carrying Peter Drucker's name. Over the years he has received a large number of awards and honorary degrees. In a listing in the *Times* of London in 2005 Kotler was ranked seventh on a list of the top 50 business brains, preceded by some non-academics – Bill Gates, Jack Welch, Tom Peters, and James Collins – and only two business professors, the strategy specialists Michael Porter and C. K. Prahalad, ranked first and third respectively.

Sources: Philip Kotler 29 May 2015, Dearlove and Crainer (2005); and CKGSB Knowledge 29 May 2015.

Marketing titles were also published in this period by Richard D. Irwin, a firm that had been founded in 1933 and was acquired by Dow Jones in 1975. Prominent titles were *Theory in Marketing* (Cox and Alderson 1950), *Marketing Research* (Boyd and Westfall 1956), and *Marketing Behavior and Executive Action* (Alderson 1957). In the accounting area Irwin published *Accounting and Analytical Methods* (Mattessich 1964). Another previously founded publisher that made some contributions to the management area was Rand McNally, started in Chicago in the mid-nineteenth century and specializing in maps and travel literature. In the post-World War II

196 Post-WWII Expansion

period Rand McNally, like McGraw-Hill, embarked on the publishing of handbooks, starting with the *Handbook of Organizations* (March 1965), which summarized important topics in the emerging area of organization studies, followed by the *Handbook of Industrial and Organizational Psychology* (Dunnette 1976).

Likewise, Addison-Wesley, founded in the interwar period (see Chapter 9), published a limited number of titles in the management area in the post-World War II period. Of these, two textbooks in finance appear to have received the most attention: *Multinational Business Finance* (Eiteman and Stonehill 1973) and *Financial Theory and Corporate Policy* (Copeland and Weston 1979). During the post-war period it expanded by acquiring W. A. Benjamin in 1977 (Jacobson et al. 2007: 218).

The university presses saw a number of new foundations in the US in the 1950s (Indiana, Southern Illinois, Penn State, Ohio State, Arizona), in the 1960s (Purdue, Virginia, West Virginia, Kent State, SUNY, Alaska, Temple) and in the 1970s (Delaware, Texas A&M). The more prestigious universities thus seem to have provided role models for these followers. However, there is not much evidence of publishing in the management area by the newly established presses. Instead, it was the established ones that made such contributions. Like in the previous period Harvard was the most successful in terms of bringing out books that made an impact. The Graduate School of Business Administration at Harvard University published *Organization and Environment* (Lawrence and Lorsch 1967), Harvard University Press, *Exit, Voice and Loyalty* (Hirschman 1970), and the Belknap Press of Harvard University Press, *The Visible Hand* (Chandler 1977) – all three considered classics with many thousands of citations. Such a status has also been gained by *Strategy and Structure* (Chandler 1962) and *The Bureaucratic Phenomenon* (Crozier 1964) published by the MIT Press and the University of Chicago Press, respectively. In the United Kingdom the publication of Joan Woodward's *Industrial Organization* (Woodward 1965) was an early sign of the movement of Oxford University Press into management publishing.

Entrants and Restructuration

In the post-World War II period three additional publishers, which later on would be significant for management publications, started their operations. First was The Free Press. Founded in 1947 by Jeremiah Kaplan and Charles Liebman in Glencoe, north of Chicago, it became part of Macmillan in 1961, but was retained as an imprint (see further Kelley 2012). Their intention to publish books on civil liberties was behind the name of the company and led them to publish a number of titles in the social sciences. Among these, two in particular attracted the attention of management scholars: *Markets and Hierarchies* (Williamson 1975) by the later Nobel Laureate Oliver Williamson and *Competitive Strategy* (Porter 1980) by Michael Porter. The second foundation of interest for the management area was that of Pergamon Press. Started in 1948 by Paul Rosbaud, it was bought already in 1951 by media entrepreneur Robert Maxwell, who sold it to Dutch publisher Elsevier in 1992. As will be shown below, the latter became particularly significant in publishing scientific journals – including, by October 2015, 100 journals, classified under "business, management and accounting" (Elsevier 11 October 2015).

The third of the three publishing houses starting its activities in the post-World War II period was SAGE. It was founded in 1965 by Sara M. and George McCune, therefore the name combining the first two letters of their first names. The company was started in New York, but moved to Southern California already in 1966. Like Pergamon, SAGE has been very active in the publication of scientific journals. In October 2015, it had as many as 92 management journals on their list (SAGE 11 October 2015; see further Chapter 15). However, it has also developed a considerable list of management books. Again, similar to Pergamon, it has launched a series in management research.

Additional structural changes in management publishing were the result of a number of acquisitions. As already mentioned, Wiley bought Interscience in 1961 and the Ronald Press in 1967; Harper merged with Row, Peterson & Company in 1962; Macmillan merged with Crowell-Collier in 1960 and acquired the Free Press in 1961; Addison-Wesley bought W. A. Benjamin in 1977. Another such deal that became important for management publishing was the merger in 1971 between the two Dutch publishers Elsevier (founded in 1880; see further Box 15.1) and North-Holland (founded in 1931). Finally, Pearson further developed its presence in the field through the acquisitions of Longman in 1968, and Penguin Books in 1970 (Jacobson et al. 2007: 218).

Outside the Anglophone world *Westdeutscher Verlag* was founded in 1947 in the German town of Opladen, close to Cologne. It became the publisher for significant German scholars in business like Eugen Schmalenbach, Erich Gutenberg, and Dieter Schneider. It is today the publisher of *Schmalenbachs Zeitschrift für betriebswirtschaftliche Forschung* (see Chapter 6). And, as already mentioned above, the Dutch Elsevier started on its way toward becoming a significant publisher of scientific journals in management. In other countries as well, entries occurred of publishers taking advantage of the expanding market for academic textbooks, including, for instance, the Swedish *Studentlitteratur*, founded in 1963.

All in all, the post-World War II period saw a growth of the publication lists of the four publishers introduced in Chapter 6: Wiley, Harper, Macmillan, and McGraw-Hill. It is evident that McGraw-Hill was the most expansive with a broad list of publications in management. It also took a lead in publishing handbooks and textbooks with cases. Wiley and Macmillan both paid attention to operations research in the 1960s but also to the increasing interest in organizational issues. Although Harper had a more modest development in management publishing compared to the other three, it published a number of titles that over time received substantial attention. The period also saw considerable structural changes: both Macmillan and Harper were part of mergers and Wiley acquired another publisher. In addition, previously founded publishing houses, in particular Prentice-Hall, as well as new entrants after World War II were quite active in a

198 Post-WWII Expansion

field that was expanding due to increasing enrollments in business schools in general and the United States in particular.

The Business Press: Circulation Figures Taking Off

After the 1945 merger discussed in Chapter 9, the *Financial Times* (*FT*) was led by the editor of the former *Financial News*, Hargreaves Parkinson. During his five-year tenure, he managed to develop the paper despite newsprint restrictions after the war. His successor, Gordon Newton, who edited the paper from 1950 to 1972, was even more important in terms of moving the paper toward a broader audience, doubling the circulation to 132,000 copies between 1950 and 1961. According to the *Financial Times* historiographer David Kynaston (1988) "there has been no more important person in the history of the paper." During the Newton tenure, in 1957 Pearson acquired the *FT*. This meant greater access to financial resources and, eventually, the internationalization of the paper. In 1979 Pearson printed its first edition outside the United Kingdom in Frankfurt – with more to come after 1980 (Kynaston 1988; for Pearson, see further Box 12.2).

For the *Wall Street Journal* the post-World War II period meant a considerable expansion, too. The editorial changes in the early 1940s apparently were well received by the audience: circulation rose from 42,393 copies in 1943 to more than 145,000 copies by the end of 1949 (Wendt 1982: 313). By the time of the death in 1967 of Bernard Kilgore (managing editor between 1941 and 1965), the circulation had passed a million copies, and, 10 years later, it had reached 1.5 million. Behind this development was a geographical expansion as well as an ambition to address a broader audience. Not all of Kilgore's projects were successful though: the *National Observer*, launched in 1962 as a Sunday paper, lasted only until 1977 when it was closed down (Wendt 1982: 366−368, 417; see further Wendt 1982; Scharff 1986).

The post-World War II period also meant increasing competition for the established papers from other actors. For instance, in 1967 the *Times* of London competed directly with the *FT* by starting a pull-out section with financial news, an early sign of an increasing interest from general newspapers in financial and business news. In some European countries there was also more competition in the specialized market. Already in 1928 the French *Les Échos* had turned into a daily (see Chapter 9). And in Germany, the daily *Handelsblatt* and the monthly *Manager Magazin* were founded in 1946 and 1971, respectively. Other new titles were the Spanish *Actualidad Económica* in 1958, the Italian *Il Sole 24 Ore* in 1965, and the Swedish *Dagens industri* in 1976 (Alvarez, Mazza, and Mur 1999: 86, 170 and 129; Bringert and Torekull 1995). The last one followed the *Financial Times* model by printing on pink paper. In 1996 its owner, the Swedish Bonnier group, acquired the Danish business newspaper *Børsen*, founded already in 1896, after having been its part-owner since 1969. However, in early 2016 Bonnier sold it to a Danish media group.

BOX 12.2 PEARSON: FROM CONSTRUCTION AND ENGINEERING TOWARD A MEDIA CONGLOMERATE

Pearson, a company quoted on the London Stock Exchange since 1969, has over time become a leading actor in management publishing (see Table 15.1). The annual report for 2014 shows that the company had sales of almost five billion pounds and adjusted operating profits of 720 million pounds, corresponding to a return on invested capital of 5.6 percent. Behind these figures there is a long history starting in Yorkshire in 1844, when Samuel Pearson founded a company of construction and engineering, which his grandson Weetman Pearson, the later Viscount Cowdray, who also went into the oil industry, moved to London in 1890. The first steps into the media business came in 1921 with the acquisition of a group of provincial newspapers (see Chapter 9). Pearson diversified even further in 1932 by acquiring 80 percent of the financial advisory and asset management firm Lazard, which it owned until 2000. This stake in the financial services industry prompted Pearson, at the acquisition of the *Financial Times* in 1957, to clearly state its willingness to protect the independence of the newspaper. During the second half of the twentieth century Pearson made a number of additional moves into the media business through the acquisitions of Longman in 1968, Penguin in 1970, Addison-Wesley in 1988, the Putnam Berkley Group and HarperCollins Educational Publishing in 1996, as well as Simon & Schuster Education in 1998. Expansion continued in the twenty-first century with the acquisitions of, among others, the US educational testing and data management company NCS in 2000, the UK examination awarding body Edexcel in 2003, and the US publisher of testing material AGS in 2005. Pearson also internationalized through investments in Japan (2001), India (2004), Nigeria (2008), and Brazil (2010). Other signs of internationalization were the launch of an Asian edition of the *FT* (2003) and the start of printing in Australia (2004). All in all, the development of Pearson was characterized by a successive concentration and expansion into education as well as business publishing worldwide. However, in 2015 Pearson sold the *Financial Times* to the Japanese publisher Nihon Keizai Shimbun (see further Chapter 15).

Source: Pearson Timeline 3 June 2015.

As far as the *Economist* is concerned, in 1956, the year before Pearson became part-owner, it had more than doubled its circulation from 17,774 in 1945 to 55,175 copies. In 1970 this figure had almost doubled again and in the early 1980s, it reached 250,000 copies (Edwards 1993: 875). This expansion was not limited to the *Economist*. The new editor of *Barron's* also managed to raise circulation from 25,915 in 1941 to 62,669 in 1955 by turning it into "a magazine for

200 Post-WWII Expansion

money managers" (Wendt 1982: 316). Similarly, *Fortune* and *Forbes* benefitted from the growing demand for business news since World War II.

Academic Journals: New Titles and the Move to Publishing Firms

At the end of the interwar period nine of the titles on the *FT*45 list had been founded (see Chapter 9). As can be seen in Table 12.1 these nine journals all published papers in the post-war period that had considerable impact. This was particularly the case for the four oldest, which contained papers that in July 2014 had received close to or more than 10,000 citations.

At the very top was the *Quarterly Journal of Economics* with "A contribution to the theory of economic growth" by later Nobel Laureate Robert Solow (1956). Two other recipients of the Alfred Nobel Memorial Prize, Eugene Fama and Daniel Kahneman, authored the most cited paper in the *Journal of Political Economy* ("Agency Problems and the Theory of the Firm," Fama 1980), and *Econometrica* ("Prospect Theory: An Analysis of Decision Under Risk," Kahneman and Tversky 1979), respectively.

TABLE 12.1 The Most Cited Papers in July 2014 from the Post-war Period in the Nine *FT*45 Journals Founded before 1946

Name of journal	Most cited	Title	Cited
Quarterly Journal of Economics	Solow (1956)	A contribution to the theory of economic growth	16,102
Journal of the American Statistical Association	Dickey and Fuller (1979)	Distribution of the estimators for autoregressive time series with a unit root	14,900
Journal of Political Economy	Fama (1980)	Agency problems and the theory of the firm	9,476
American Economic Review	Alchian and Demsetz (1972)	Production, information costs, and economic organization	13,088
Journal of Applied Psychology	Hackman and Oldham (1975)	Development of the job diagnostic survey	5,061
Harvard Business Review	Greiner (1972)	Evolution and revolution as organizations grow	3,438
Accounting Review	Watts and Zimmerman (1978)	Toward a positive theory of the determination of accounting standards	2,025
Econometrica	Kahneman and Tversky (1979)	Prospect theory: an analysis of decision under risk	2,017
Journal of Marketing	Kotler and Levy (1969)	Broadening the concept of marketing	2,043

Sources: Search at Google Scholar in July 2014 on most cited papers in the nine journals published between 1946 and 1980.

While Solow (1956) is clearly a contribution to economics, the last two are both closer to management issues. The same is true for the most cited papers in the *Journal of Applied Psychology* (Hackman and Oldham 1975), the *Harvard Business Review* (Greiner 1972), the *Accounting Review* (Watts and Zimmerman 1978), and the *Journal of Marketing* (Kotler and Levy 1969). At the same time it is worth noting that also a journal like the *Quarterly Journal of Economics* published papers, which became significant for management research. A prime example is Herbert A. Simon's paper "A Behavioral Model of Rational Choice" (Simon 1955), which received almost as many citations as the above mentioned paper by Robert Solow.

New Foundations: Expansion and Specialization

The post-World War II period did not only see the publication of significant papers in the already established journals. It was also a period of expansion in the number of journals. Only within the group of journals belonging to the *FT*45 list there were 24 new titles appearing (Table 12.2). As will be shown below, there were also a number of other journal foundations.

Table 12.2 demonstrates again the significant role played by professional associations for the launching of new journals: the American Finance Association (the *Journal of Finance*), the Institute of Management Science (*Management Science*), the Operations Research Society of America (*Operations Research*), the Academy of Management (the *Academy of Management Journal* and the *Academy of Management Review*), the American Marketing Association (the *Journal of Marketing Research*), the Academy of International Business (the *Journal of International Business Studies*), etc. Like in the two previous periods there were also initiatives from individual universities and even individual scholars. It is also evident from Table 12.2 that over time the publishing of several of the journals has been taken over by the publishing houses discussed above: Wiley publishes seven of the titles, Elsevier four, and SAGE two, while five are put out by universities and five by professional associations.

Table 12.2 also reflects the development of the field in the post-World War II period in terms of specialization. Quantitative approaches were favored through the *Journal of Finance* (1946), *Management Science* (1954), and *Operations Research* (1956) – a tendency already seen above in relation to the publication lists of Wiley and Macmillan. However the decades after 1945 also saw an emerging interest in organizations, which has been demonstrated already above through titles like Simon (1947), March and Simon (1958), and Thompson (1967). The *Administrative Science Quarterly* was founded in 1956 with the just mentioned James D. Thompson as the first editor. Shortly after, in 1958, the Academy of Management, founded in 1936, started the *Academy of Management Journal*. Further signs of the increasing interest in management issues were the launching of the *California Management Review* and the *Sloan Management Review* in 1958 and 1959, respectively. There are good reasons to believe that the *Harvard Business*

202 Post-WWII Expansion

TABLE 12.2 Journals among the *FT*45 Founded in the Post-war Period

Name of journal	Founded	First publisher	Present publisher
Journal of Finance	1946	American Finance Association	Wiley-Blackwell
Management Science	1954	The Institute of Management Science (TIMS)	Informs
Administrative Science Quarterly	1956	Graduate School of Management, Cornell University	SAGE
Operations Research	1956	Operations Research Society of America (ORSA)	Informs[a]
Academy of Management Journal	1958	Academy of Management	Academy of Management
California Management Review	1958	UC Berkeley	University of California Press
Sloan Management Review	1959	MIT	MIT
Human Resource Management[b]	1961	University of Michigan	Wiley
Journal of Accounting Research	1963	University of Chicago	Wiley-Blackwell
Journal of Management Studies	1964	Society for the Advancement of Management Studies	Wiley-Blackwell
Journal of Marketing Research	1964	American Marketing Association	American Marketing Association
Journal of Financial and Quantitative Analysis	1966	University of Washington	Cambridge University Press
Organizational Behaviour and Human Decision Processes[c]	1966	James C. Naylor in collaboration with Academic Press	Elsevier
Journal of International Business Studies	1970	Academy of International Business	Palgrave Macmillan
Rand Journal of Economics[d]	1970	AT&T Bell Labs	Wiley-Blackwell
Journal of Consumer Research[e]	1974	Association of Consumer Research	University of Chicago Press
Academy of Management Review	1976	Academy of Management	Academy of Management
Accounting, Organisations and Society	1976	Anthony Hopwood in collaboration with Pergamon Press	Elsevier
Entrepreneurship Theory and Practice[f]	1976	US Association for Small Business and Entrepreneurship	Wiley-Blackwell
MIS Quarterly	1977	Association for Information Systems	University of Minnesota

Name of journal	Founded	First publisher	Present publisher
Journal of Accounting and Economics	1979	North Holland	Elsevier
Journal of Operations Management	1980	American Production and Inventory Control Society	Elsevier
Organization Studies	1980	European Group of Organization Studies with De Gruyter	SAGE
Strategic Management Journal	1980	Strategic Management Society	Wiley-Blackwell

[a] The Institute for Operations Research and the Management Sciences.
[b] 1961-72: *Management of Personnel Quarterly* (see further Huselid 2011).
[c] 1966-84: *Organizational Behavior and Human Performance*.
[d] 1970-74: *Bell Journal of Economics and Management Science*, 1975-83: *Bell Journal of Economics*.
[e] See further Kernan (1995).
[f] 1976–1988: *American Journal of Small Business*.

Review, founded in 1922, provided inspiration for these two journals. The same seems to be true for the *McKinsey Quarterly*, which first appeared in 1964 (see also Chapter 11).

The journals founded in the 1960s were to a large extent focusing on specialized areas of management: human resources (*Human Resource Management* and *Organizational Behaviour and Human Decision Processes*), accounting (the *Journal of Accounting Research* and the *Journal of Financial and Quantitative Analysis*), and marketing (the *Journal of Marketing Research*). One of the *FT*45 journals founded in the 1960s was directed toward general management, however: the *Journal of Management Studies*, published in the United Kingdom on behalf of the Society for the Advancement of Management Studies first by Blackwell and presently by Wiley-Blackwell.

The tendency to start journals directed toward particular management specializations continued in the 1970s: international business (the *Journal of International Business Studies*), marketing (the *Journal of Consumer Research*), accounting (*Accounting, Organizations and Society* and the *Journal of Accounting and Economics*), information systems (the *MIS Quarterly*), production management (the *Journal of Operations Management*), and entrepreneurship (*Entrepreneurship Theory and Practice*). In addition, another economics journal was launched as the *Bell Journal of Economics and Management Sciences*, which later on became the *Rand Journal of Economics*. Toward the end of the period the Academy of Management started a second journal, the theory-oriented *Academy of Management Review*, European organization researchers set up *Organization Studies*, and strategy scholars created the *Strategic Management Journal*.

Significant Papers Published by the Entrants

Looking at the attention attained by the articles published in the journals founded in the post-World War II period, it is for practical reasons convenient to split the population into two: the 11 journals founded between 1946 and 1965, and the 13 journals founded from 1966 to 1980. Starting with the first group (Table 12.3) it is clear that the 1952 paper in the *Journal of Finance* by later Nobel Laureate Harry Markowitz stands out as a remarkably highly cited paper, a circumstance that can be explained by its innovative approach to finance at the time. Another paper in the first group is Gilbert Churchill's "A Paradigm for Developing Better Measures of Marketing Constructs" (Churchill 1979), which demonstrates how methodology papers tend to attract attention in a scientific community. Particularly worth noting is also "A Garbage Can Model of Organizational Choice"

TABLE 12.3 The Most Cited Papers from the Post-war Period in July 2014 in the 11 FT45 Journals Founded between 1946 and 1965

Name of journal	Most cited	Title	Cited
Journal of Finance	Markowitz (1952)	Portfolio selection	18,437
Management Science	Mintzberg (1978)	Patterns in strategy formation	3,512
Administrative Science Quarterly	Cohen, March, and Olsen (1972)	A garbage can model of organizational choice	7,313
Operations Research	Little (1961)	A proof for the queuing formula: L= λ W	2,302
Academy of Management Journal	Brockhaus (1980)	Risk taking propensity of entrepreneurs	1,401
California Management Review	Mintzberg (1973b)	Strategy-making in three modes	1,450
Sloan Management Review	Schein (1967)	Organizational socialization and the profession of management	1,042
Human Resource Management	Flamholtz (1973)	Human resources accounting: Measuring positional replacement costs	103
Journal of Accounting Research	Ball and Brown (1968)	An empirical evaluation of accounting income numbers	4,979
Journal of Management Studies	Johanson and Wiedersheim-Paul (1975)	The internationalization of the firm – four Swedish cases	2,651
Journal of Marketing Research	Churchill (1979)	A paradigm for developing better measures of marketing constructs	10,274

Sources: Search at Google Scholar in July 2014 on most cited papers published between 1946 and 1980 in the 11 journals founded between 1946 and 1965.

(Cohen, March, and Olsen 1972) that can be seen as a further development of the ideas in the earlier classics in organization theory (Simon 1947; March and Simon 1958; Cyert and March 1963). Somewhat in the same tradition are two papers by Henry Mintzberg (1973b, 1978): "Strategy-making in Three Modes" and "Patterns in Strategy Formation" in the *California Management Review* and *Management Science*, respectively.

More than two thousand citations have been obtained by an accounting article (Ball and Brown 1968), an early piece by the so-called Uppsala school of international business (Johanson and Wiedersheim-Paul 1975), and an operations research paper proving a queuing formula (Little 1961). Together these three papers demonstrate the variety of academic management publishing at the time. This impression is reinforced by the remaining three papers on risk taking of entrepreneurs (Brockhaus 1980), organizational socialization (Schein 1967), and human resources accounting (Flamholtz 1973).

If a similar analysis is made of the most cited papers in the 13 journals founded between 1966 and 1980 (Table 12.4), three papers stand out. These are, first, the *Academy of Management Review* paper by Raymond Miles and his colleagues entitled "Organizational Strategy, Structure, and Process" (Miles et al. 1978), followed by a second paper representing the Uppsala approach to international business (Johanson and Vahlne 1977) in the *Journal of International Business Studies*, and Bengt Holmström's "Moral Hazard and Observability," in the *Bell Journal of Economics*, later the *Rand Journal of Economics*.

Other papers from the journals on the *FT*45 list started between 1966 and 1980 that have attracted high attention later are "Motivation Through the Design of Work: Test of a Theory" in *Organizational Behaviour and Human Decision Processes* (Hackman and Oldham 1976) and "Conjoint Analysis in Consumer Research: Issues and Outlook" in the *Journal of Consumer Research* (Green and Srinivasan 1978). For the rest of the journals in Table 12.4 top citations for papers published before 1980 are more restricted, i.e., below 1,000, and for one of them, *Entrepreneurship Theory and Practice*, very low. As will become evident in Chapter 15, these journals gained their positions in the management discipline only after 1980.

Further Additions to the Field

It is of course important to point out that the scientific journals analyzed above constitute a limited sample based on their impact today. Already in the post-World War II period a number of other management journals were started, but, as will be shown in Chapter 15, such foundations became even more common in the recent period. For the post-World War II period it is particularly worth mentioning how Robert Maxwell's Pergamon Press was active in starting new journals such as *Long Range Planning* (1968) and *Omega* (1973). Pergamon was also the original publisher of *Accounting, Organisations and Society* mentioned

206 Post-WWII Expansion

TABLE 12.4 The Most Cited Papers from the Post-war Period in July 2014 in the 13 *FT*45 Journals Founded between 1966 and 1980

Name of journal	Most cited	Title	Cited
Journal of Financial and Quantitative Analysis	Geske (1977)	The valuation of corporate liabilities as compound options	911
Organizational Behaviour and Human Decision Processes	Hackman and Oldham (1976)	Motivation through the design of work: test of a theory	4,892
Journal of International Business Studies	Johanson and Vahlne (1977)	The internationalization process of the firm-a model of knowledge development and increasing foreign market commitments	7,307
Rand Journal of Economics (formerly Bell Journal of Economics)	Holmström (1979)	Moral hazard and observability	7,145
Journal of Consumer Research	Green and Srinivasan (1978)	Conjoint analysis in consumer research: issues and outlook	2,778
Academy of Management Review	Miles et al. (1978)	Organizational strategy, structure, and process	9,093
Accounting, Organisations and Society	Otley (1980)	The contingency theory of management accounting: achievement and prognosis	999
Entrepreneurship Theory and Practice	Brophy and Shulman (1962)	A finance perspective on entrepreneurship research	56
MIS Quarterly	King (1978)	Strategic planning for management information systems	527
Journal of Accounting and Economics	Beaver and Morse (1980)	The information content of security prices	715
Journal of Operations Management	Buffa (1980)	Research in operations management	165
Organization Studies	Maurice, Sorge, and Warner (1980)	Societal differences in organizing manufacturing units: A comparison of France, West Germany, and Great Britain	450
Strategic Management Journal	Ansoff (1980)	Strategic issue management	728

Sources: Search at Google Scholar in July 2014 on most cited papers published between 1946 and 1980 in the 13 journals.

above, but not for the *British Accounting Review* (1969), which was brought out by the Academic Press. Elsevier for its part started the *Journal of Business Research* (1973) and the *Journal of Financial Economics* (1974), while its merger partner in 1971, North-Holland, had launched *Industrial Marketing Management* (1971). There were also additional journals started by professional associations such as *Business & Society* (1960) by the International Association for Business and Society, *Organizational Dynamics* (1972) by the American Management Association, and the *Journal of Management* (1975) by the Southern Management Association. A particularly interesting entrant was *Human Relations*, created in 1947 as a joint effort by the British Tavistock Institute and the US Research Center for Group Dynamics at MIT with the ambition to "establish a dialogue between scholars of different disciplinary backgrounds who seek to advance our knowledge of social relationships at and around work" (*Human Relations* 5 May 2015). It is today a SAGE journal.

All in all, during the post-World War II period the *FT*45 list of journals saw a considerable addition of titles, from nine before 1946 to 33 in 1980. Moreover, there were a number of additional journals, which are not included in the current *FT*45 list. It has again been evident how professional associations took an active role in establishing new outlets but also how various publishing houses over time have taken over their publishing. The added journals have demonstrated the increasing specialization in the field.

References

Alchian, A. A. and Demsetz, H. (1972) "Production, information costs, and economic organization," *American Economic Review*, 62(5): 777–795.
Alderson, W. (1957) *Marketing Behavior and Executive Action: A functionalist approach to marketing theory*, Homewood, IL: Irwin.
Aljian, G. W. (ed.) (1958) *Purchasing Handbook: Standard reference book on policies, practices, and procedures utilized in departments responsible for purchasing management or materials management*, New York: McGraw-Hill.
Alvarez, J. L., Mazza, C., and Mur, J. (1999) *The Management Publishing Industry in Europe*, CEMP Report No. 5, June 1999, Barcelona: IESE. www.fek.uu.se/cemp/publications/cempreports.html (accessed 6 January 2016).
Anderson, R. C. (1965) *Management Strategies*, New York: McGraw-Hill.
Ansoff, I. (1980) "Strategic issue management," *Strategic Management Journal*, 1(2): 131–148.
Archer, S. H. and D'Ambrosio, C. A. (1966) *Business Finance: Theory and management*. New York: Macmillan.
Ball, R. and Brown, P. (1968) "An empirical evaluation of accounting income numbers," *Journal of Accounting Research*, 6(2): 159–178.
Bates, G. E. (1959) *Investment Management: A casebook*, New York: McGraw-Hill.
Beaver, W. R. L. and Morse, D. (1980) "The information content of security prices," *Journal of Accounting and Economics*, 2(1): 3–28.
Bennis, W. G. (1966) *Changing Organizations: Essays on the development and evolution of human organization*, New York: McGraw-Hill.

Blough, R. (1966) *International Business: Environment and adaption*, New York: McGraw-Hill.

Boyd, H. W. and Britt, S. H. (eds) (1963) *Marketing Management and Administrative Action*, New York: McGraw-Hill.

Boyd, H. W., Jr and Westfall, R. (1956) *Marketing Research*, Homewood, IL: Irwin.

Bringert, L. and Torekull, B. (1995) *Äventyret Dagens industri: Historien om en tidnings födelse*, Stockholm: Wahlström & Widstrand.

Brockhaus, R. H. (1980) "Risk taking propensity of entrepreneurs," *Academy of Management Journal*, 23(3): 509–520.

Brophy, D, J. and Shulman, J. M. (1962) "A finance perspective on entrepreneurship research," *Entrepreneurship Theory and Practice*, 16(3): 61–71.

Buffa, E. S. (1961) *Modern Production Management*, New York: Wiley.

Buffa, E. S. (1980) "Research in operations management," *Journal of Operations Management*, 1(1): 1–7.

Chamberlain, N. W. (1948) *The Union Challenge to Management Control*, New York: Harper.

Chamberlain, N. W. (1953) *Social Responsibility and Strikes*, New York: Harper.

Chandler, A. D., Jr (1962) *Strategy and Structure: Chapters in the history of the industrial enterprise*, Cambridge, MA: MIT Press.

Chandler, A. D., Jr (1977) *The Visible Hand: The managerial revolution in American business*, Cambridge, MA: The Belknap Press.

Charnes, A. A. and Cooper, W. W. (1961) *Management Models and Industrial Applications of Linear Programming*, New York: Wiley.

Churchill, G. A. (1979) "A paradigm for developing better measures of marketing constructs," *Journal of Marketing Research*, 16(1): 64–73.

Churchman, C. W., Ackoff, R. L., and Arnoff, E. L. (1957) *Introduction to Operations Research*, New York: Wiley.

CKGSB Knowledge, 29 May 2015. http://knowledge.ckgsb.edu.cn/2013/10/08/marke ting/philip-kotler-four-ps-model-marketing-still-king.

Cohen, M. D., March, J. G., and Olsen, J. (1972) "A garbage can model of organizational choice," *Administrative Science Quarterly*, 17(1): 1–25.

Copeland, T. E. and Weston, J. F. (1979) *Financial Theory and Corporate Policy*, Reading, MA: Addison-Wesley.

Cox, D. R. and Smith, W. L. (1961) *Queues*, New York: Wiley.

Cox, R. and Alderson, W. (eds) (1950) *Theory in Marketing: Selected essays*, Homewood, IL: Irwin.

Crozier, M. (1964) *The Bureaucratic Phenomenon*, Chicago, IL: University of Chicago Press.

Cyert, R. M. and March, J. G. (1963) *A Behavioral Theory of the Firm*, Englewood Cliffs, NJ: Prentice-Hall.

Dean, J. (1951) *Managerial Economics*, Englewood Cliffs, NJ: Prentice-Hall.

Dearlove, D. and Crainer, S. (2005) "Porter thinks his way to the top," *Times*, 1 December.

Dickey, D. A. and Fuller, W. A. (1979) "Distribution of the estimators for autoregressive time series with a unit root," *Journal of the American Statistical Association*, 74(366a): 427–431.

Drucker, P. F. (1974) *Management: Tasks, responsibilities, practices*, New York: Harper & Row.

Dunnette, M. D. (ed.) (1976) *Handbook of Industrial and Organizational Psychology*, Chicago, IL: Rand McNally.

Edwards, R. D. (1993) *The Pursuit of Reason: The Economist, 1843–1993*, Boston, MA: Harvard Business School Press.

Eiteman, D. K. and Stonehill, A. I. (1973) *Multinational Business Finance*, Reading, MA: Addison-Wesley.

Elsevier, 11 October 2015. www.elsevier.com/journals/subjects/business-management-and-accounting.

Engwall, L. and Danell, R. (2002) "The behavioral theory of the firm in action," in M. Augier and J. G. March (eds), *The Economics of Choice, Change and Organization: Essays in memory of Richard M. Cyert*, Cheltenham: Edward Elgar, pp. 27–47.

Ettinger, K. E. (ed.) (1965) *International Handbook of Management*, New York: McGraw-Hill.

Ewing, D. W. (ed.) (1958) *Long-range Planning for Management*, New York: Harper.

Exman, E. (1965) *The Brothers Harper: A unique partnership and its impact upon the cultural life of America from 1817 to 1853*, New York: Harper & Row.

Fama, E. F. (1980) "Agency problems and the theory of the firm," *Journal of Political Economy*, 88(2): 288–307.

Fayerweather, J. (1969) *International Business Management: A conceptual framework*, New York: McGraw-Hill.

Feigenbaum, A. V. (1961) *Total Quality Control: Engineering and management: the technical and managerial field for improving product quality, including its reliability, and for reducing operating costs and losses*, New York: McGraw-Hill.

Flamholtz, E. (1973) "Human resources accounting: Measuring positional replacement costs," *Human Resource Management*, 12(1): 8–16.

Gellerman, S. W. (1960) *People, Problems and Profits: The uses of psychology in management*, New York: McGraw-Hill.

Geske, R. (1977) "The valuation of corporate liabilities as compound options," *Journal of Financial and Quantitative Analysis*, 12(4): 541–552.

Glueck, W. F. (ed.) (1980) *Strategic Management and Business Policy*, New York: McGraw-Hill.

Goetz, B. E. (1949) *Management Planning and Control: A managerial approach to industrial accounting*, New York: McGraw-Hill.

Gouldner, A. W. (1965) *Wildcat Strike: A study in worker-management relationships*, New York: Harper & Row.

Green, P. E. and Srinivasan, V. (1978) "Conjoint analysis in consumer research: Issues and outlook," *Journal of Consumer Research*, 5(2): 103–123.

Greiner, L. E. (1972) "Evolution and revolution as organizations grow," *Harvard Business Review*, 50(4): 37–46.

Hackman, J. R. and Oldham, G. R. (1975) "Development of the job diagnostic survey," *Journal of Applied Psychology*, 60(2): 159–170.

Hackman, J. R. and Oldham, G. R. (1976) "Motivation through the design of work: Test of a theory," *Organizational Behaviour and Human Decision Processes*, 16(2): 250–279.

Hage, J. (1980) *Theories of Organizations: Form, process and transformation*, New York: Wiley.

Haley, K. B. (1967) *Mathematical Programming for Business and Industry*, London: Macmillan.

Hayes, D. A. (1956) *Appraisal and Management of Securities*, New York: Macmillan.

Hill, J. W. (1958) *Corporate Public Relations: Arm of modern management*, New York: Harper.

Hirschman, A. O. (1970) *Exit, Voice and Loyalty: Responses to decline in firms*, Cambridge, MA: Harvard University Press.

Holmström, B. (1979) "Moral hazard and observability," *Bell Journal of Economics*, 10(1): 74–91.

Human Relations, 5 May 2015. www.tavinstitute.org/humanrelations/about_journal/aims.html.

Huselid, M. A. (2011) "Celebrating 50 years: Looking back and looking forward: 50 years of Human Resource Management," *Human Resource Management*, 50(3): 309–312.

Jacobson, T. C., Smith, G. D., Wright, R. E., Wiley, P. B., Spilka, S. B., and Heaney, B. L. (2007) *Knowledge for Generations: Wiley and the global publishing industry, 1807–2007*, New York: Wiley.

Johanson, J. and Vahlne, J.-E. (1977) "The internationalization process of the firm: A model of knowledge development and increasing foreign market commitments," *Journal of International Business Studies*, 8(1): 23–32.

Johanson, J. and Wiedersheim-Paul, F. (1975) "The internationalization of the firm: Four Swedish cases," *Journal of Management Studies*, 12(3): 305–323.

Juran, J. M. (ed.) (1951) *Quality Control Handbook*, New York: McGraw-Hill.

Kahneman, D. and Tversky, A. (1979) "Prospect theory: An analysis of decision under risk," *Econometrica*, 47(2): 263–291.

Kelley, C. (2012) "After 65 years, Free Press to be absorbed into Simon & Schuster flagship," Melville House. www.mhpbooks.com/the-complicated-history-of-free-press-takes-another-turn (accessed 28 July 2014).

Kernan, J. B. (1995) "Framing a rainbow, focusing the light: JCR's first twenty years," *Advances in Consumer Research*, 22(1): 488–496.

King, W. R. (1978) "Strategic planning for management information systems," *MIS Quarterly*, 2(1): 27–37.

Kotler, P. (1967) *Marketing Management*, Englewood Cliffs, NJ: Prentice-Hall.

Kotler, P. (1985) *Marketing for Health Care Organization*, Englewood Cliffs, NJ: Prentice-Hall.

Kotler, P. (1992) *Marketing for Congregations: Choosing to serve people more effectively*, Nashville, TN: Abingdon Press.

Kotler, P. (1996) *Marketing for Hospitality and Tourism*, Englewood Cliffs, NJ: Prentice-Hall.

Kotler, P. (1999) *Kotler on Marketing: How to create, win and dominate markets*, London: Simon & Schuster.

Kotler, P. and Andreasen, A. (1975) *Marketing for Nonprofit Organizations*, Englewood Cliffs, NJ: Prentice-Hall.

Kotler, P., Armstrong, G., Saunders, J., and Wong, V. (1996) *Principles of Marketing: The European edition*, London: Prentice-Hall.

Kotler, P. and Bliemel, F. (1995) *Marketing-Management: Analyse, Planung, Umsetzung und Steuerung*, Stuttgart: Schäffer-Poeschel.

Kotler, P. and Blom, S.-E. (1992) *Markedføringsledelse*, Oslo: Universitetsforlaget.

Kotler, P. and Dubois, B. (1977) *Marketing Management*, 3rd edn, Paris: Publi-Union.

Kotler, P. and Levy, S. J. (1969) "Broadening the concept of marketing," *Journal of Marketing*, 33(1): 10–15.

Kotler, P. and Maesincee, S. (1997) *The Marketing of Nations: A strategic approach to building national wealth*, New York: The Free Press.

Kynaston, D. (1988) *The Financial Times: A centenary history*, London: Viking.

Lawrence, P. R. and Lorsch, J. W. (1967) *Organization and Environment*, Boston, MA: Graduate School of Business Administration, Harvard University.

Lee, A. M. (1966) *Applied Queueing Theory*, London: Macmillan.

Levin, R. I. (ed.) (1972) *Production Operations Management: Contemporary policy for managing operating systems*, New York: McGraw-Hill.

Lewis, B. T. (ed.) (1977) *Management Handbook for Plant Engineers*, New York: McGraw-Hill.

Li, D. H. (1968) *Accounting, Computers, Management Information Systems*, New York: McGraw-Hill.

Likert, R. (1961) *New Patterns of Management*, New York: McGraw-Hill.

Little, J. D. C. (1961) "A proof for the queuing formula: L= λ W," *Operations Research*, 9(3): 383–387.

Magee, J. F. (1968) *Industrial Logistics: Analysis and management of physical supply and distribution systems*, New York: McGraw-Hill.

Maier, N. R. F. (1952) *Principles of Human Relations: Applications to management*, New York: Wiley.

March, J. G. (ed.) (1965) *Handbook of Organizations*, Chicago, IL: Rand McNally.

March, J. G. and Simon, H. A. (1958) *Organizations*, New York: Wiley.

Markowitz, H. (1952) "Portfolio selection," *Journal of Finance*, 7(1): 77–91.

Maslow, A. H. (1954) *Motivation and Personality*, New York: Harper.

Mattessich, R. (1964) *Accounting and Analytical Methods*, Homewood, IL: Irwin.

Maurice, M., Sorge, A., and Warner, M. (1980) "Societal differences in organizing manufacturing units: A comparison of France, West Germany, and Great Britain," *Organization Studies*, 1(1): 59–86.

Mauser, F. F. (1961) *Modern Marketing Management: An integrated approach*, New York: McGraw-Hill.

Maynard, H. B. (ed.) (1970) *Handbook of Modern Manufacturing Management*, New York: McGraw-Hill.

McFarland, D. E. (1968) *Personnel Management: Theory and practice*, New York: Macmillan.

McGraw-Hill Financial, 5 May 2015. www.mhfi.com/about/our-history#sthash.xvCtgbw 2.dpbs.

Miles, R. E., Snow, C., Meyer, A. and Coleman Jr (1978) "Organizational strategy, structure, and process," *Academy of Management Review*, 3(3): 546–562.

Mintzberg, H. (1973a) *The Nature of Managerial Work*, New York: Harper & Row.

Mintzberg, H. (1973b) "Strategy-making in three modes," *California Management Review*, 16(2): 44–53.

Mintzberg, H. (1978) "Patterns in strategy formation," *Management Science*, 24(9): 934–948.

Mintzberg, H. (1979) *The Structuring of Organizations*, Englewood Cliffs, NJ: Prentice-Hall.

Otley, D. T. (1980) "The contingency theory of management accounting: Achievement and prognosis," *Accounting, Organisations and Society*, 5(4): 413–428.

Pearson Timeline, 3 June 2015. http://timeline.pearson.com.

Pfeffer, J. and Salancik, G. R. (1978) *The External Control of Organizations: A resource dependence perspective*, New York: Harper & Row.

Philip Kotler, 29 May 2015. www.kellogg.northwestern.edu/faculty/directory/kotler_p hilip.aspx#biography.

Porter, M. E. (1980) *Competitive Strategy: Techniques for analyzing industries and competitors*, New York: The Free Press.

Richman, B. M. and Copen, M. (1972) *International Management and Economic Development: With particular reference to India and other developing countries*, New York: McGraw-Hill.

Samuelson, P. A. (1948) *Economics: An introductory analysis*, New York: McGraw-Hill.

SAGE, 11 October 2015. www.sagepub.in/journals.nav.

Samuelson, P. A. and Nordhaus, W. D. (2010) *Economics*, 19th edn, Boston, MA: McGraw-Hill Irwin.

Sayles, L. R. (1979) *Leadership: What effective managers really do − and how they do it*, New York: McGraw-Hill.

Scharff, E. E. (1986) *Worldly Power: The making of the Wall Street Journal*, New York: Beaufort Books.

Schein, E. (1967) "Organizational socialization and the profession of management," *Sloan Management Review*, 30(1): 53–65.

Schrieber, A. N. (1965) *Cases in Manufacturing Management*, New York: McGraw-Hill.

Simon, H. A. (1947) *Administrative Behavior: A study of decision-making processes in administrative organization*, New York: Macmillan.

Simon, H. A. (1955) "A behavioral model of rational choice," *Quarterly Journal of Economics*, 69(1): 99–118.

Simon, H. A. (1960) *The New Science of Management Decision*, New York: Harper.

Simon, H. A. (1965) *The Shape of Automation for Men and Management*, New York: Harper & Row.

Solow, R. M. (1956) "A contribution to the theory of economic growth," *Quarterly Journal of Economics*, 70(1): 65–94.

Starr, M. K. (ed.) (1965) *Executive Readings in Management Science*, New York: Macmillan.

Steiner, G. A. (1969) *Top Management Planning*, New York: Macmillan.

Steiner, G. A. (ed.) (1963) *Managerial Long-range Planning*, New York: McGraw-Hill.

Steiner, G. A. and Miner, J. B. (1977) *Management Policy and Strategy: Text, readings, and cases*, New York: Macmillan.

Taylor, B. and Lippitt, G. L. (eds) (1975) *Management Development and Training Handbook*, London: McGraw-Hill.

Thompson, J. D. (1967) *Organizations in Action*, New York: McGraw-Hill.

Veinott, A. F. (ed.) (1965) *Mathematical Studies in Management Science*, New York: Collier-Macmillan.

Watts, R. L. and Zimmerman, J. L. (1978) "Towards a positive theory of the determination of accounting standards," *Accounting Review*, 53(1): 112–114.

Wendt, L. (1982) *The Wall Street Journal: The story of Dow Jones & the nation's business newspaper*, Chicago, IL: Rand McNally.

Wessel, R. H. (1961) *Principles of Financial Analysis: A study of financial management: Text with cases*, New York: Macmillan.

Williamson, O. E. (1975) *Markets and Hierarchies: Analysis and antitrust implications: A study in the economics of internal organization*, New York: Free Press.

Woodward, J. (1965) *Industrial Organization: Theory and practice*, London: Oxford University Press.

PART IV

Markets Reign

The period covered in the fourth part of this book ranges from the early 1980s to the present day with a focus on the late twentieth and early twenty-first century.

Economically, this period was characterized by the opening of the globe to a capitalist market system. It started with economic reforms in China in the late 1970s, followed by the fall of the Berlin Wall in 1989 with a subsequent transformation of Central and Eastern European economies and then the abolishing of the strict licensing regime in India. Emerging markets − namely the BRIC countries, Brazil, Russia, India, and China − experienced fast growth and multinationals have recomposed and extended their value chains across borders helped by further development of information and communication technologies as well as more liberalization of finance, trade, and investment. The twenty-first century saw a recurrence of crises − the burst of the dot.com bubble, many corporate scandals, notably Enron, and the Great Recession following the financial meltdown of 2008, ultimately halting or slowing growth in many parts of the world and leading to a questioning of capitalism and its consequences, including climate change.

Socially, the world appears as interconnected as never before, namely due to communication technologies and social media, resulting in a convergence of consumption patterns and tastes but also resistance and − at times violent − rejection of what some refer to as Globalization 2.0. Middle classes grew in many parts of the world, driving consumption, while elites based on increasingly ostentatious wealth became more visible everywhere − prompting some backlash against the so-called "one percent." Remaining income differentials, demographic pressures and many localized conflicts prompted significant migratory movements, which created additional insecurity among working and middle classes in the developed world − already feeling threatened by the consequences of technological change and globalization, seen to be leading to growing income inequality and the erosion of the welfare state.

Politically, the triumph of markets was not always followed by the introduction of democratic government – and the little progress made was often rolled back by increasingly authoritarian regimes. There have also been growing sectarian divides in many parts of the world, often erupting in violence. Even democratic countries experienced internal divisions and stalemates, including in the United States. Its hegemonic role is being questioned and challenged in an increasingly multi-polar world with countries like Russia and China becoming more assertive. Efforts at global governance are being made – based on not always transparent motives and driven increasingly by private interests as well as non-governmental organizations.

13

THE BUSINESS SCHOOL AND THE MBA BECOME "GLOBAL"

The period from the late 1980s to the present day brought about many significant changes in business education. In the US, the university-based business schools and the MBA continued in much the same way, as did the strong research orientation and the position of the US as the world center in the production of academic business knowledge. Nevertheless, financial pressures due to diminishing state funding, rising costs, more intense competition, and the arrival of media rankings, meant that US business schools increasingly operated in "market-driven" ways. Outside the US, the scope and scale of changes were much more marked, driven by growth and international expansion at an unprecedented scale. In parallel, schools or faculties, and higher education fields as a whole became subject to a new round of Americanization, through institutional mechanisms such as accreditation and rankings, leading to a convergence toward the use of the "business school" and "MBA" labels also outside Anglophone countries – albeit with persistent variation in the actual content.

US Business Schools: A Transforming and Spreading Model

Becoming More Market-driven at Home

Despite temporary setbacks, business education in the US continued to grow after the late 1980s. Estimates were that at the beginning of the twenty-first century close to 1,300 schools – more than 90 percent of accredited colleges and universities – had an undergraduate degree in business and around 900 universities were offering graduate degrees (Pfeffer and Fong 2002: 78). Throughout the 1990s and the 2000s business constituted around 20 percent of all the undergraduate degrees awarded in the US, a share reached by the early 1980s. Likewise, the proportion of the master's in business continued to increase, levelling at around 25 percent of graduate degrees in the 2000s (NCES 2012: 453).

In the meantime, the ratio of the bachelor's to the master's degree continued to fall, so that by 2010 it had gone down to about two to one, with 365,093 undergraduate and 187,213 master's – though not exclusively MBAs – granted that year (NCES 2012: 453). Meanwhile, there was a proliferation in the types of master's degrees on offer with a shift toward part-time, weekend, and executive versions as well as specialized programs, a recent study by the AACSB (2014: 24) showing that only a quarter of enrollment at the graduate level was in the traditional two-year full-time MBA. An accompanying expansion has been in executive education, which not only serves as a major source of revenue for US business schools but has turned into an industry in itself where private providers such as corporate universities and consulting firms also partake (Zell 2001).

While continuing growth has often been hailed as an indicator of success, there has also been a revival of business school criticism, leading Augier and March (2011: 310), for example, to suggest that a "counterreformation" has been underway since the 1980s, basically in opposition to the route taken after the Carnegie and Ford Foundation reports (see Chapter 10). Most of these critical assessments have essentially repeated what has been said earlier on, indicating that not much had changed in US business schools. There have again been complaints, for example, that there is little diversity and that business schools are continuing with what they have been doing since the 1950s (e.g., Friga, Bettis, and Sullivan 2003). Again, the claim has been that they were not really educating managers but rather analysts, mainly for consulting firms and investment banks (Mintzberg 2004). Likewise, the age-old criticism that business school research is irrelevant to practitioners has been repeated over and over (e.g., Bennis and O'Toole 2005).

There have also been some swings in this renewed wave of business school criticism. US business schools have now been blamed for moving away from their "professionalization" logic. This aftereffect has been attributed, on the one hand, to the neoliberal turn and the concomitant shift of attention to shareholder value as well as the accompanying ascendance of economic approaches in business school research and teaching (Khurana 2007). Insufficient attention to ethics and social responsibility has also been highlighted, more than previously, as business schools received part of the blame for corporate wrongdoings that came to be revealed in the early 2000s, such as the infamous Enron case (e.g., Trank and Rynes 2003). Fingers were also pointed at business schools after the 2008 financial crisis (Pettigrew, Cornuel, and Hommel 2014). On the other hand, the argument has been that the distancing from a professional logic has come about due to changes in resource and institutional environments. Most notable, it is argued, have been reductions in public funding for higher education, which has led to greater dependence on student tuitions, donations, and executive education (Trank and Rynes 2003). These conditions have increased competition not only among US business schools but also with for-profit providers and consulting firms (Friga, Bettis, and Sullivan 2003).

Rivalry has also been fuelled by the significance that media rankings have gained since the 1990s, which has disrupted to some degree the academically based status order that had previously been established within the organizational field of business education in the US (Elsbach and Kramer 1996). US business schools have, therefore, tended to become more and more driven by a commercial logic (Trank and Rynes 2003). Indicative of this tendency have been increases in tuitions, a proliferation of non-traditional master's programs, an upsurge in higher-margin executive education, and much greater attention to marketing and public relations activities. MBA students and corporate recruiters have increasingly come to be seen as "customers," leading to an overwhelming career and salary focus and a watering down of course content and grading. This has been coupled with a weakening emphasis on the creation of new academic knowledge as well as a lessening of support for doctoral education (Zell 2001). It should be noted though that the US still seems to maintain its attractiveness internationally as the world's center for doctoral study. As the latest AACSB (2014) data show, the ratio of non-US doctoral graduates in US business schools remains at the order of about 44 percent as opposed to 14 percent in master's and eight percent in undergraduate degrees.

What clearly distinguishes the last decades from the previous period are the expansion of business school accreditation and the appearance of media rankings – both spreading from the US elsewhere.

Accreditation: A US Institution Expanding – and Replicated – Internationally

Until the late 1990s, business school accreditation was an American institution – absent elsewhere, mainly due to the more significant role that the state occupied in governing higher education in most other countries. Beginning in 1997 however, accreditation entered into and then rapidly spread in Europe as well as in Latin America and Asia. The first move in promoting accreditation outside the US came from the AACSB, which had been in existence since 1916 as an association of US business schools and as an accrediting agency from the 1960s onwards (see Box 13.1). AACSB's initial step toward internationalization dated back to 1964 but had remained very limited, only three university business schools in Canada obtaining accreditation over a period of 30 years (Flesher 2007). The initiative in the mid-1990s was a much more deliberate attempt to expand internationally in view of a narrowing home "market" and the emergence of domestic competitors as well as the growth of business education in other regions of the world (Zammuto 2008; see also Box 13.1).

BOX 13.1 AACSB: FROM AMERICAN ASSOCIATION TO GLOBAL ACCREDITATION

The Association of Collegiate Schools of Business was formed in the US in 1916. It became the AACSB in 1925 with the addition of American to its name. The declared purpose of the association was "to promote and improve higher business education in North America." In essence, its main aim was to increase the recognition and prestige of business schools within the academic community. Initial growth was modest with membership reaching a total of 56 by 1946. From its beginnings until well after World War II, the AACSB was not an accrediting agency but served as a platform for the exchange of views mainly among deans. The modest standards that were set concerned qualification for membership. Neither were there any standards for graduate education until 1961. The shift toward becoming an accrediting agency was prompted by the influx of students after the GI Bill (see Chapter 10). There was also the threat that other groups such as the American Accounting Association could begin accrediting accounting programs. The AACSB was fully recognized as an accrediting agency by the National Commission on Accrediting for undergraduate programs in 1961 and for the master's degrees in 1964. Membership was equated with accreditation in 1965. In 1968 a distinction was introduced between the two, and the label "association" was replaced by "assembly." Thereafter AACSB accreditation began to be viewed in the US as a mark of distinction for better and more research-oriented business schools. However, accreditation was made easier after 1991 as the AACSB moved from "universal" to more flexible, so-called "mission-based" standards as well as a peer review process. These changes enabled an extension of its US market, as teaching-oriented schools could now seek accreditation too, and the number of accredited US business schools went up from 323 in 1996 to 509 in 2014 (Table 13.1). AACSB's international expansion was even more marked. In line with its new strategy it had changed its name in 1997 to "AACSB – the International Association for Management Education" and then in 2001 dropped the words "American Assembly" and became the "Association to Advance Collegiate Schools of Business" (in short "AACSB International"). The standards were revised yet again in 2003, introducing even greater flexibility, mainly to expand its capacity to deal with the higher diversity among schools outside the US. And from only three in 1996, non-US accreditations of AACSB passed the 200 mark less than 20 years later, strengthening the claim that it had become a "global association" (see Table 13.1). Yet, as an AACSB historian has remarked "no one would argue that all vestiges of an 'American Association' have disappeared" (Flesher 2007: 17).

Sources: Dirksen and Kroeger (1966); Durand and McGuire (2005); Flesher (2007); Khurana (2007); MacKenzie (1966); Porter and McKibbin (1988); Zammuto (2008).

AACSB's intentions to extend its accreditation service outside the US prompted a countermove in Europe. In 1997, the year that the AACSB accredited the first non–North American business school, the European Foundation for Management Development (EFMD) introduced its own accreditation scheme: EQUIS – the European Quality Improvement System (Durand and McGuire 2005). In the very same year, the UK-based Association of MBAs (AMBA) also turned to accreditation – though somewhat differently in that it only accredited MBA programs (of all types) and not business schools as a whole. A number of leading schools in Europe were involved in the development and promotion of EQUIS. Although the AACSB served as the model, purportedly the aim of EQUIS was to bring a "European dimension" into accreditation. The European element essentially meant a greater emphasis on the international nature of the school and on the strength of the relations with the business world (Zammuto 2008). Yet, in view of AACSB's expansionist policies, soon EQUIS – and AMBA too – began to extend beyond Europe.

The international spread of accreditation through the three main accrediting agencies has been fast. In fact, various non-US schools have gone for double or even triple accreditations (Zammuto 2008). As shown in Table 13.1, by 2006, i.e., in less than 10 years, AACSB had accredited 86 schools in 29 countries other than the US. In the same period, its major competitor EQUIS had accredited 92 schools and AMBA 117 MBAs, in roughly the same number of countries. Figures reported in Table 13.1 suggest that the pace of growth for AACSB outside the US – and similarly that for AMBA – have since been faster than for EQUIS. Notably, the same table also indicates that while AACSB continues to expand internationally, the penetration of EQUIS and AMBA into the US has been negligible. As the center–periphery model discussed in Chapter 3 attests, in the case of accreditation too, the US, as the world's center of education for business, remains nationally focused and closed to influence from the outside.

The literature has provided various accounts for the fast diffusion of accreditation internationally. Some have suggested that it is due to obtaining status advantages, more so perhaps nationally, in view of increased competition for domestic and foreign students (e.g., Durand and McGuire 2005; Zammuto 2008). Others have taken an institutional perspective and argued that accreditation has become a "rationalized myth" and, since it is adopted by the more prestigious schools, has tended to spread through mimetic and normative processes (e.g., Bell and Taylor 2005).

The burgeoning of accreditation in the last couple of decades has not escaped criticism either. From a US perspective, there have been claims that accreditation is not a major concern either for students or recruiters (Trank and Rynes 2003). Allegedly its value has been reduced especially for leading business schools not only because of their own status but also due to the increasing power of media rankings in defining reputational differences. This has been more so as the AACSB has taken a more comprehensive orientation and moved away from

220 Markets Reign

TABLE 13.1 Universities, Faculties and Schools of Business Accredited by the End of 2006 and 2014

	AACSB		EQUIS		AMBA	
	2006	2014	2006	2014	2006	2014
AFRICA						
Egypt	1	1	–	1	–	1
Morocco	–	–	–	–	–	1
South Africa	–	2	2	2	2	5
Tunisia	–	–	–	–	–	1
ASIA						
China (including Hong Kong)	3	16	3	17	1	23
Chinese Taipei	2	11	–	1	–	–
India	–	3	–	2	1	7
Indonesia	–	1	–	–	–	–
Israel	1	1	–	–	–	–
Japan	2	2	–	1	–	1
Kazakhstan	–	–	–	–	–	1
Kuwait	1	2	–	–	–	–
Lebanon	–	1	–	–	–	1
Malaysia	–	1	–	–	–	–
Philippines	1	1	1	–	–	1
Qatar	–	1	–	–	–	–
Saudi Arabia	1	1	–	–	–	1
Singapore	2	3	1	3	–	1
South Korea	3	14	–	3	–	–
Thailand	–	2	–	2	–	–
United Arab Emirates	1	4	–	–	–	–
EUROPE						
Austria	–	–	–	1	–	1
Belgium	2	2	3	4	2	2
Croatia	–	1	–	–	–	1
Cyprus	–	–	–	–	1	1
Denmark	–	2	2	2	–	4
Finland	–	2	2	2	1	3
France	11	22	15	17	12	20
Germany	3	9	2	5	–	4
Greece	–	–	–	–	3	3
Hungary	–	–	–	–	–	1
Iceland	–	–	–	–	–	2
Ireland	1	1	1	1	3	5

	AACSB		EQUIS		AMBA	
	2006	*2014*	*2006*	*2014*	*2006*	*2014*
Italy	–	1	1	2	2	3
Monaco	–	–	–	–	1	1
Netherlands	3	4	3	5	5	6
Norway	–	1	2	2	–	1
Poland	–	1	1	1	1	3
Portugal	–	2	1	2	2	6
Russia	–	–	–	1	5	11
Slovenia	–	1	–	1	1	1
Spain	2	4	4	4	5	5
Sweden	–	–	3	3	–	1
Switzerland	2	3	3	4	2	5
Turkey	1	3	–	1	–	–
Ukraine	–	–	–	–	–	1
United Kingdom	10	25	18	25	39	43
LATIN AMERICA and the CARRIBEAN						
Argentina	1	1	1	1	3	6
Brazil	1	2	2	4	3	5
Chile	2	2	–	1	3	5
Colombia	–	1	1	1	1	5
Costa Rica	1	1	1	1	–	–
Ecuador	–	1	–	–	–	–
Jamaica	–	–	–	–	–	1
Mexico	3	4	1	2	2	3
Trinidad and Tobago	–	–	–	–	1	1
Peru	–	3	–	1	3	3
Uruguay	–	–	–	–	–	2
Venezuela	1	1	–	1	1	1
NORTH AMERICA						
Canada	17	20	4	10	3	4
United States	442	509	2	3	1	1
OCEANIA						
Australia	4	12	9	8	3	2
Fiji	–	–	–	–	–	1
New Zealand	3	7	3	4	4	5
TOTAL Accredited	528	715	92	152	117	223
TOTAL Countries	30	48	28	41	31	52

Sources: The 2006 data are from Urgel (2007) and show accreditations as of the end of September of that year. Data for 2014 are based on listings on the websites of AACSB (www.aacsb.edu), EQUIS (www.efmd. org), and AMBA (www.mbaworld.com) at the end of the year (accessed 31 December 2014).

"universal" standards to a "mission-based" approach. Thus, in the US the significance of the AACSB has become confined to business schools that enjoy neither high status nor a reputation arising from inclusion in the rankings (Trank and Washington 2009). AACSB's recent mission-based approach has also been viewed as yet another factor in leading business schools to succumb to market pressures rather than uphold their professionalization logic (Trank and Rynes 2003).

Concerns expressed from a non-US perspective have been somewhat different. Despite the status distinction that accreditation, mainly the AACSB label, is often taken to confer by many outside the US, it has been criticized by some due to the homogenizing pressures that it creates for schools or departments of business. The AACSB, in particular, has been viewed as a major mechanism of Americanization (e.g., Kieser 2004). Nevertheless, the international interest in getting AACSB accreditation continues. Whereas there were, by the end of 2014, AACSB accredited business schools in 47 countries other than the US, in the same year the association had "educational members" in 86 countries (AACSB 2014: 8). As membership likely indicates the intention to obtain AACSB certification, it is yet another indicator that, despite criticisms, accreditation has become, like the rankings, an important fixture in the institutional environment of many non-US business schools.

Media Rankings: Defining and Measuring Reputation

It was in 1988 that *Business Week* published the first biennial ranking of US business schools, based on a survey gauging the "satisfaction" of MBA graduates and recruiters (Elsbach and Kramer 1996). Others, such as *Forbes* and the *Wall Street Journal*, followed suit (see Collet and Vives 2013 for criteria employed by various rankings). The emergence and rise of media rankings in the US have been variously attributed to an increasing interest in the MBA given its pervasiveness and the strengthening concerns with accountability (Morgeson and Nahrgang 2008). Others, however, have also associated them with the long-standing discourse critical of US business school research and teaching, as rankings have served to re-affirm a "market" or "customer" focus (Augier and March 2011).

It took an additional 10 years for rankings to reach Europe. The *Financial Times* (*FT*) published a ranking of European MBA programs for the first time in 1998, followed the next year by one that also included North American business schools. In 2002 the weekly *Economist* also started such a ranking (Collet and Vives 2013). Unlike in the US where rankings have been initiated by the media and typically viewed as an external "coercive" force (e.g., Trank and Rynes 2003: 197), Wedlin (2011) has characterized the development of the *FT* rankings as a "co-construction" in which some of the leading European business schools were involved. As such, the *FT* rankings emerged as a reaction to the US-based ones, which until then had not included schools outside the US. *FT*'s combined listing implied that European – and later other non-US – business schools were being considered similar to and assessed together with US-based ones.

Changes in the ranks of individual business schools and their significant repercussions for constituencies have been documented for the US context (e.g., Zell 2001). However, studies based on *Business Week* data have shown that over the years rankings have tended to be rather stable at the top, while volatility has been greater at the lower levels (e.g., Morgeson and Nahrgang 2008). Such stability in the higher ranks has been associated with strong reputation effects as well as disparities in business school resources. In a more recent study on *FT* MBA rankings, Collet and Vives (2013) have also found that the overall distribution of schools across the regions of the world has not varied in the last decade. Yet, although US business schools have remained dominant, schools from Europe and Asia have risen markedly in the ranks at the expense of the US ones, even at the very top. Collet and Vives (2013) have attributed these changes to the faster rate of salary increases for MBA graduates from European and Asian business schools in the last decade relative to their American counterparts – which, they argue, has been due to the increasing legitimacy of MBA education outside the US.

Rankings have expanded in range over time. The *Financial Times*, for example, has been publishing since 2005 additional lists for executive MBAs, online MBAs, master's programs, and executive education (Wedlin 2011: 204). Following the *FT*, regional rankings have also appeared in Asia and Latin America (Collet and Vives 2013). Despite widespread questioning of their validity both from within and outside academia, rankings have now become a well-established and highly influential element in the institutional environment not only for US business schools but also for many outside the US.

Globalizing the "Business School" and the "MBA"

The accredited schools and those which can get into the rankings, constitute only a small part of the expansion that has taken place outside the US. Current estimates suggest that there are over 15,000 providers of business education, spread literally across every country in the world (AACSB 2014: 14–16). This explosive growth has been attributed, typically, to changes in the economic and political context in the last two or three decades. There have been references to increased pressures resulting from globalization or the liberalization of financial markets and privatization. As Collet and Vives (2013: 557) have put it succinctly, "the global rise of financial capitalism might have achieved what could not be achieved in postwar Europe by the Ford Foundation, U.S. federal agencies in charge of administrating the Marshall Plan, European agencies, and national governments" (see Chapter 10). In addition, neoliberal economic policies have meant reduced funding for public universities, as a result of which business education – particularly graduate and executive versions – have come to be viewed as lucrative avenues for revenue generation. Inspired by US models, governments have also intervened and altered regulatory frameworks in higher education resulting in the expansion of graduate degrees. In Europe this has been in the form of a standardization initiative by the European Union (EU) known as the Bologna Accord (see below) and in various other countries as reforms at the national level, often together with the liberalization of higher education.

The outcome has been a growth of the MBA – or some version of the graduate business degree, much more so than before the 1990s (see Chapter 10). The undergraduate or first degree in business has also continued to increase, as it had done in the three or so decades after World War II. Yet, a recent AACSB (2014: 17) survey shows, for example, that the proportion of the undergraduate degree to the graduate is now lower in all regions of the world relative to the US. Although based only on data obtained from AACSB members, these figures are indicative of the recent proliferation, outside the US, of the master's in business and, particularly, the MBA. This is not to suggest, however, that the expansion has always or even mostly occurred in the form of the conventional US-type two-year full-time MBA format. Often shorter, typically 12-month, versions have been developed. Moreover, even more than in the US, there has been a proliferation of part-time, executive, or customized MBAs as well as of various types of specialized master's programs. In fact, a recent AACSB (2014: 24) survey suggests that among its non-US members, enrollment in the conventional two-year full-time MBA is proportionately lower and in the non-traditional formats much higher than in the US business schools.

The present panorama of the burgeoning MBA as well as business education at large has had to do with expansion both in countries where it had already infiltrated prior to the 1990s and in those where it literally did not exist before. Nevertheless, in both cases the pace and the organizational form within which the growth of the MBA took place and how it evolved vis-à-vis the first or undergraduate degree has varied across countries.

Expansion in Europe: Still in Different Ways and to Varying Degrees

The UK has been one country in Europe where there has literally been an explosion of business schools and the MBA and its variants (Collet and Vives 2013). As discussed in Chapter 10, growth had already started in the UK in the 1980s – not least due to cuts in public funding of universities (Tiratsoo 2004). Symbolic for the increasing trend after the 1990s was the founding of separate schools in the two ancient universities, Cambridge and Oxford, in 1990 and 1991 respectively (Williams 2010). There are currently more than a hundred MBA programs offered by a similar number of university-based business schools in the UK (Thomas 2008). Typically, the full-time MBA has been transformed into a 12-month format and has been accompanied by a wide range of specialist and part-time versions as well as executive education and distance learning. Notably, those studying business constituted around 20 percent of all graduate students in the country (Pettigrew, Cornuel, and Hommel 2014). This had to do with the attractiveness of the UK graduate business programs, especially the full-time ones, for foreign students. However, these semblances with the US have also made the organizational field of business education in the UK highly competitive and forced business schools to become, like their US counterparts, increasingly market-driven — charging high fees for MBAs, specialist master's, and executive education (Starkey and Tiratsoo 2007).

The MBA and its variants have increased, though variably, across other parts of Europe too. As mentioned above, this has been facilitated by the signing of the Bologna Accord in 1999 among the member states of the EU. A major element of this EU-wide agreement — endorsed later by some non-member countries — was the adoption of the US-like three-cycle system, i.e., the bachelor, the master, and the doctorate, with the aim of harmonizing higher education in Europe. In some countries, the development of the MBA as well as executive education found a much more fertile ground in private stand-alone schools or those attached to private universities, which had already made a head start prior to the 1990s. But, despite a varying pace of implementation across countries, the Bologna Accord also opened up the possibility of introducing and expanding the range of separate master's degrees, including the MBA, in public universities.

France constitutes a paramount case of the MBA and executive education flourishing mainly among private actors. The switch toward the graduate degree came when the private stand-alone schools, now referred to as the *grandes écoles de commerce* either re-labelled their existing first-degree programs as an MBA or introduced the *mastère* or the MBA as separate degrees. Some of the public universities did the same, though their locus continued to be the first degree and doctoral education (Dameron and Durand 2008). It was instead the *grandes écoles de commerce* that began to dominate graduate and executive education. They are now considered as *the* business schools of France, most of which actually adopted the label itself or its variant "school of management." Here too, increases in the number of schools since the 1980s have resulted in a more competitive organizational field not unlike the US or the UK. The leading, more selective *grandes écoles de commerce* have also been adept at developing an international orientation — making France second only to the UK in the number of AACSB (other than the US), EQUIS, and AMBA accreditations (see Table 13.1).

A division similar to the one in France, incubating already before the 1990s, has also become established in Spain and, to a more limited degree, in Italy. In Spain, the main force behind the growth of graduate and executive education have been the private, mostly Catholic university-based or stand-alone schools such as IESE, IE, and ESADE (see Chapter 10 for their backgrounds). The first-degree and doctoral education, on the other hand, has remained largely within the purview of the public universities, though the latter too have begun to offer university master's after the 1990s (Gutiérrez and Ortega 2008). The picture has been very much the same

226 Markets Reign

in Italy, though the private sector remains confined mainly to *Bocconi* and a few others such as the LUISS Business School in Rome and the public *Politecnico di Milano*'s quasi-private school of management (Kipping, Üsdiken, and Puig 2004).

Similar changes have also been taking place in Germany, a country where, as shown in Chapters 7 and 10, business education had come to be dominated almost entirely by the first degree in BWL or business economics at public universities. Following the Bologna Accord, universities have begun introducing master's degrees, though they were not likely to be called the MBA. However, in the last decade some public universities, such as Mannheim and Goethe Frankfurt, have set up business schools in the form of non-profit companies and have been offering various MBA and executive training programs (Möslein and Huff 2008). Also, akin to the early days of commercial education in Germany (see Chapter 4), private stand-alone schools sponsored by business associations or corporations have begun to appear such as the WHU Otto Beisheim School of Management near Koblenz and the European School of Management and Technology (ESMT) in Berlin. Although a few of the public universities have also ventured to obtain AACSB, EQUIS, or AMBA accreditations, it is the quasi-private organizational forms like the one in Mannheim and the non-university private schools that have been at the forefront – a few of them also managing to get into the European rankings.

In other parts of Europe, private actors have so far had almost no role to play in the spread of the MBA and its variants. In the Nordic countries, for instance, it was the publicly sponsored stand-alone schools that took the lead in adopting the MBA. With the advent of Bologna, master's programs proliferated in these schools, as they did at the universities (Engwall 2004). In all these countries, the MBA has typically been introduced in its part-time executive version and, when offered full-time like at the Copenhagen Business School for example, it has been in the 12-month format similar to the UK.

Expansion in Asia and Latin America: Governments Intervene

Government interventions have had an important part to play in the promulgation of the business school and the MBA in various countries in Asia. In India for example, following economic liberalization measures initiated in 1991 business education was liberalized, resulting in an explosive growth, mainly, of private providers. According to a recent AACSB (2014: 14–16) report, India currently has the highest number of schools in the world, both stand-alone and university-based, offering tertiary business education. However, the public Indian institutes of management or IIMs, which pioneered graduate education in business with US aid after World War II, have retained their elite position. Although still not granting a legally recognized degree, one that is called Post Graduate Programme (PGP) rather than MBA, two of the early IIMs, Ahmedabad and Bangalore, as well as the private Indian School of Business (ISB) have begun to appear in the *FT* rankings (see Koenig and Tapie 2008).

Intervention by government took a different form in Japan. With support from industry, a few American-style university-based graduate schools and the MBA had already begun to emerge in the late 1980s to provide less costly alternatives to an MBA in the US for self-financing students or sponsoring companies (Okazaki-Ward 2001). The number of MBA programs and its variants increased in the 2000s following successive government-initiated reforms to relax regulations pertaining to graduate studies and to encourage universities to establish "professional graduate schools" like in the US. By 2010 the MBA was offered in more than 30 business schools, typically part-time, with an enrollment second only to the graduate law schools (Shimizu and Higuchi 2009–2010), though still remaining low relative to comparable countries. Moreover, as Table 13.1 demonstrates, very few Japanese schools appear to have shown an interest in obtaining American or European accreditations.

As another example, the appearance of the MBA in South Korea occurred after the official recognition of the degree by governmental authorities in the early 2000s. This was again part of an attempt to restructure the higher education field along US lines. By the end of the decade, 13 business schools had been permitted to offer the degree (Park and Choi 2011). High-priced MBAs, typically of 12-month duration as well as weekend executive versions were now on offer. Following in the footsteps of the US, accreditations increased quickly, making South Korea the country with the second highest number of AACSB-certified schools in Asia after China (Table 13.1).

The business education boom in Latin America has also come about following the market-oriented reforms during the 1990s – though continuing largely at the first-degree level (see Chapter 10). Alcadipani and Caldas (2012: 37), for example, have provided striking figures for Brazil, suggesting that currently one million students are enrolled annually in 2,000 first-degree programs in business. The MBA as well as executive education have also flourished, mainly through private universities and newly created stand-alone schools. Yet, even in the more prominent among the latter in Brazil as well as in Latin America more generally the MBA and its variants have been and still are of the part-time or the executive kind (see, e.g., Gomez-Samper 2009).

New Areas of Expansion

An important complement to the international expansion of the business school and the MBA has come from countries where neither existed prior to the 1990s. The organizational fields of business education that emerged literally in all Central and Eastern European countries as well as the post-Soviet republics was driven by the quest to adjust to a market-based economy and the accompanying rise in demand for business studies. These emergent fields were shaped both by transformation in public higher education and legislative changes licensing the creation of private providers. An additional source of influence was foreign assistance. Reminiscent of the aftermath of World War II, US and, at this occasion, also European aid programs were activated for linking business schools in Western countries with the prospective ones in Central and Eastern Europe (Larçon and Hmimda 2008). Private providers mushroomed in parallel, though often having to contend with legitimacy problems and, in some cases, suffering from a lack of official recognition (Bandelj and Purg 2006). Nevertheless, a few of them have been able to establish a stronger profile. Both these latter schools and the more prominent public ones have also begun developing an international orientation by getting US and European accreditations (see Table 13.1).

Clearly one country where the business school and the MBA have appeared late but grown very fast has been the People's Republic of China. The initial steps in the formation of a field of business education were in fact taken earlier than in Central and Eastern Europe. Both the US and the European Union (EU) were involved at this early stage. The EU initiative led to the creation of the China Europe International Business School (CEIBS) in 1994, though its MBA was officially recognized only in 2002 (AACSB 2011). In 1991 the government had endorsed the founding of nine Chinese business schools (Goodall, Warner, and Lang 2004). Since then the organizational field has developed in a manner that mostly comprised business – or management – schools based in comprehensive or more specialized public universities (see, e.g., Choi and Lu 2013: 569). Altogether, more than 180 schools were offering the MBA by 2010 – with an estimated total enrollment of around 30,000 students. Unlike many of the late-developing countries referred to above, the MBA programs in China have also included the two-year full-time format in addition to part-time and executive versions, though the former appear to be decreasing more recently (Chen and Yang 2010). There are also the so-called international MBA programs run jointly with foreign partners and taught in English (Li and van Baalen 2007). Notably, as Table 13.1 shows, there has been a marked jump in the number of schools that have received one or more of the American and European accreditations. Moreover, not only those based in Hong Kong but also those in mainland China have begun to appear in, for example, the *FT* rankings.

Internationalization

A distinguishing feature of the most recent period for management education has been an increasing reference to internationalization and expanding educational-cum-organizational arrangements purportedly to that end. Greater internationalization of business has served as the backdrop for such claims and practices. It has also been spurred on by competitive as well as revenue generation motives on the part of business schools.

Concerns with internationalization were expressed first within the US, epitomized by Porter and McKibbin's (1988) book, where it was explicitly raised as a shortcoming of American business schools. Internationalization in this instance was understood as incorporating into curricula material from outside the US and topics such as international business – concerns that still persist within this context (see, e.g., AACSB 2011). However, more recently, internationalization has gained other connotations. It has come to be understood as an organizational attribute, as a part of the educational experience or as extending activities across national borders – what Engwall and Kipping (2013) have referred to as insourcing, outsourcing, and foreign direct investment (see Chapter 3).

In the first sense, internationalization is seen as related to the composition of faculty members and students. As pointed out above, internationalization has been stressed, for example, as one of the distinctive aspects of EQUIS accreditation not only to distinguish it from its competitor, the AACSB, but also as a characteristic predominantly attributed to European business schools. It has also been made a part of the *Financial Times* ranking criteria – though still not finding its way into US-based rankings (see Collet and Vives 2013). Second, internationalization has referred to various arrangements geared toward providing students with learning opportunities in other national contexts. Quite often these initiatives have involved various forms of alliances among leading business schools from core or semi-peripheral countries, in some cases extending to the periphery as well. Such partnerships have been built around Executive MBA programs often including a US business school and a few others from Europe and elsewhere like the Trium Executive MBA (NYU Stern, LSE, HEC Paris) or the EMBA-Global (Columbia, LBS, HKU). Another case in point is the pre-experience full-time Master in Management (MIM) program run within the framework of the Community of European Management Schools and International Companies (CEMS), created at the end of the 1980s and nowadays, having extended outside Europe, comprising 29 countries.

The third form of internationalization involves the opening of branch campuses abroad. The prime motive in these kinds of initiatives has been generating additional revenue, building on the reputation that either the country, such as the US, or the particular school possesses. They have therefore mainly involved EMBA programs and non-degree executive education, typically operated in relatively wealthy countries but where business education has been late-developing such as INSEAD and ESSEC in Singapore or Chicago Booth in Hong Kong. Not all of these initiatives have been success stories however, as Alajoutsijärvi, Juusola, and Lamberg (2014) have shown for the investments into Dubai.

A variant of this direct mode of entry, again for business schools in core and semi-peripheral countries, has been expanding internationally through local partnerships often targeted at countries where business education has been almost non-existent. As pointed out above, these initiatives can be considered foreign assistance for cross-national transfers, very much akin to the aftermath of World War II (see Chapters 3 and 10). This has been, as also mentioned above, the primary route in the post-1990 development of business schools in much of Central and Eastern Europe (CEE) as well as China (Bandelj and Purg 2006).

Finally, there have been claims that the creation of *FT* rankings can be viewed as a step in the making of what has been variously referred to as the "international" or "global" field of "business schools" or "management education"

(Wedlin 2011; Collet and Vives 2013). However, this purported expansion or internationalization of field boundaries has essentially been a construction from a European or, more broadly, a non-US perspective. Admittedly, there has been some increasing awareness of non-US schools as one of the new competitors for US business schools (see, e.g., Friga, Bettis, and Sullivan 2003). And, as mentioned above, after the introduction of the *FT* rankings, US media have started publishing international, meaning non-US lists too – though typically separate from the US schools. Given its position as the world's center, the national focus has persisted in the US not only in the media but also within academia, where only rankings by *Business Week* are typically considered (e.g., Morgeson and Nahrgang 2008: 27).

These different conceptions indicate that, while leading business schools in Europe and a few elsewhere may now be claiming a new "international business school" identity (Wedlin 2011), US business schools are still very much focused on their own national field. This is also demonstrated by criticisms – mentioned above and in Chapter 10 – that have been voiced in the US concerning business schools in that particular context. The questioning of business schools and management education in more fundamental ways by critical management scholars has also been directed at the archetypal forms typical in the US – and to some degree the UK (see, e.g., Grey 2004). There has been very little in the way of criticism from within the semi-periphery or the periphery. In the latter case, critical views have largely been targeting the extensive American influence and not business education per se – and this despite the lack of evidence that business education is related to economic development.

So, given also the growth figures, there seems to be little indication that business education is under strong challenge either in the US or in other parts of the world. Setbacks such as a decline in demand here and there or some movement away from the full-time MBA may indeed be real. It could be that in the US this might work particularly against business schools other than the elite. Yet, as this book has shown, business schools in the US – and elsewhere – have been very adept at adapting to the material and institutional contexts that they have had to confront. Whether the same will be the case in the years to come remains to be seen but as yet there are no credible signs that they will disappear from higher education fields or that their authority will wane in the foreseeable future.

References

AACSB (2011) *Globalization of Management Education: Changing international structures, adaptive strategies, and the impact on institutions*, Tampa, FL: AACSB International.

AACSB (2014) *2014 Business School Data Guide*, Tampa, FL: AACSB International.

Alajoutsijärvi, K., Juusola, K., and Lamberg, J.-A. (2014) "Institutional logics of business bubbles: Lessons from the Dubai business school mania," *Academy of Management Learning & Education*, 13(1): 5–25.

Alcadipani, R. and Caldas, M. P. (2012) "Americanizing Brazilian management," *Critical Perspectives on International Business*, 8(1): 37–55.

Augier, M., and March, J. G. (2011) *The Roots, Rituals, and Rhetorics of Change: North American business schools after the Second World War*, Stanford, CA: Stanford University Press.

Bandelj, N., and Purg, D. (2006) "Networks as resources, organizational logic, and change mechanism: The case of private business schools in post-socialism," *Sociological Forum*, 21(4): 587–622.

Bell, E. and Taylor, S. (2005) "Joining the club: The ideology of quality and business school badging," *Studies in Higher Education*, 30(3): 239–255.

Bennis, W. G. and O'Toole, J. (2005) "How business schools lost their way," *Harvard Business Review*, 83(5): 96–104.

Chen, X. and Yang, B. (2010) "Copying from others or developing locally? Successes and challenges of MBA education in China (1990–2010)," *Journal of Chinese Human Resource Management*, 1(2): 128–145.

Choi, S.-J. and Lu, J. (2013) "Returnee faculty members, network position and diversification strategy: An analysis of business schools in China," *Asia Pacific Business Review*, 19(4): 559–577.

Collet, F. and Vives, L. (2013) "From preeminence to prominence: The fall of U.S. business schools and the rise of European and Asian business schools in the Financial Times global MBA rankings," *Academy of Management Learning & Education*, 12(4): 540–563.

Dameron, S. and Durand, T. (2008) "Management education and research in France," in T. Durand and S. Dameron (eds), *The Future of Business Schools: Scenarios and strategies for 2020*, Basingstoke: Palgrave Macmillan, pp. 162–185.

Dirksen, C. J. and Kroeger, A. (1966) "Summary of the major events of the association from 1916–1966," in *The American Association of Collegiate Schools of Business, 1916–1966* Homewood, IL: Richard D. Irwin, pp. 181–252.

Durand, R. and McGuire, J. (2005) "Legitimating agencies in the face of selection: The case of AACSB," *Organization Studies*, 26(2): 165–196.

Elsbach, K. D. and Kramer, R. M. (1996) "Members' responses to organizational identity threats: Encountering and countering the Business Week rankings," *Administrative Science Quarterly*, 41(3): 442–476.

Engwall, L. (2004) "The Americanization of Nordic management education," *Journal of Management Inquiry*, 13(2): 109–117.

Engwall, L. and Kipping, M. (2013) "The internationalization of international management education and its limitations," in D. Tsang, H. Kazeroony, and G. Ellis (eds), *The Routledge Companion to International Management Education*, London: Routledge, pp. 319–343.

Flesher, D. L. (2007) *The History of the AACSB International, Volume 2, 1966–2006*, Tampa, FL: AACSB.

Friga, P. N., Bettis, R. A., and Sullivan, R. S. (2003) "Changes in graduate management education and new business school strategies for the 21st century," *Academy of Management Learning & Education*, 2(3): 233–249.

Gomez-Samper, H. (2009) "Business schools in Latin America: Global players at last?" in A. Davila and M. M. Elivira (eds), *Best Human Resource Management Practices in Latin America*, London: Routledge, pp. 170–179.

Goodall, K., Warner, M., and Lang, V. (2004) "HRD in the People's Republic: The MBA with 'Chinese characteristics'?" *Journal of World Business*, 39(4): 311–323.

Grey, C. (2004) "Reinventing business schools: The contribution of critical management education," *Academy of Management Learning & Education*, 3(2): 178–186.

Gutiérrez, I. and Ortega, J. (2008) "Higher education in business: The case of Spain," in T. Durand and S. Dameron (eds), *The Future of Business Schools: Scenarios and strategies for 2020*, Basingstoke: Palgrave Macmillan, pp. 186–214.

Khurana, R. (2007) *From Higher Aims to Hired Hands: The social transformation of American business schools and the unfulfilled promise of management as a profession*, Princeton, NJ: Princeton University Press.

Kieser, A. (2004) "The Americanization of academic management education in Germany," *Journal of Management Inquiry*, 13(2): 90–97.

Kipping, M., Üsdiken, B., and Puig, N. (2004) "Imitation, tension, and hybridization: Multiple 'Americanization's' of management education in Mediterranean Europe," *Journal of Management Inquiry*, 13(2): 98–108.

Koenig, C. and Tapie, P. (2008) "Management education in Asia," in T. Durand and S. Dameron (eds), *The Future of Business Schools: Scenarios and strategies for 2020*, Basingstoke: Palgrave Macmillan, pp. 327–335.

Larçon, J. P. and Hmimda, N. (2008) "Business education in Central and Eastern Europe," in T. Durand and S. Dameron (eds), *The Future of Business Schools: Scenarios and strategies for 2020*, Basingstoke: Palgrave Macmillan, pp. 302–308.

Li, L. and van Baalen, P. (2007) "Indigenization of management education in China," *Higher Education Policy*, 20(2): 169–193.

MacKenzie, O. (1966) "The development of AACSB standards," in *The American Association of Collegiate Schools of Business, 1916–1966*, Homewood, IL: Richard D. Irwin, pp. 84–145.

Mintzberg, H. (2004) *Managers, Not MBAs: A hard look at the soft practice of managing and management development*, San Francisco, CA: Berrett-Koehler.

Morgeson, F. P. and Nahrgang, J. D. (2008) "Same as ever it was: Recognizing stability in Business Week rankings," *Academy of Management Learning and Education*, 7(1): 26–41.

Möslein, K. M. and Huff, A. S. (2008) "Management education and research in Germany," in T. Durand and S. Dameron (eds), *The Future of Business Schools: Scenarios and strategies for 2020*, Basingstoke: Palgrave Macmillan, pp. 133–161.

NCES (2012) *Digest of Education Statistics*, Washington, DC: National Center for Education Statistics.

Okazaki-Ward, L. I. (2001) "MBA education in Japan: Its current state and future direction," *Journal of Management Development*, 20(3): 197–235.

Park, J. and Choi, M. (2011) "The Seoul National University Business School: Managing global challenge and cultural change," *Asian Case Research Journal*, 15(1): 1–36.

Pettigrew, A. M., Cornuel, E., and Hommel, U. (2014) "Introduction," in A. M. Pettigrew, E. Cornuel, and U. Hommel (eds), *The Institutional Development of Business Schools*, Oxford: Oxford University Press, pp. 1–5.

Pfeffer, J. and Fong, C. T. (2002) "The end of business schools? Less success than meets the eye," *Academy of Management Learning and Education*, 1(1): 78–95.

Porter, L. W. and McKibbin, L. E. (1988) *Management Education and Development: Drift or thrust into the 21st century*, New York: McGraw-Hill.

Shimizu, R. and Higuchi, Y. (2009–10) "The value of MBA education in the Japanese labor market," *The Japanese Economy*, 36(4): 61–104.

Starkey, K. and Tiratsoo, N. (2007) *The Business School and the Bottom Line*, Cambridge: Cambridge University Press.

Thomas, H. (2008) "U.K. business schools," in T. Durand and S. Dameron (eds), *The Future of Business Schools: Scenarios and strategies for 2020*, Basingstoke: Palgrave Macmillan, pp. 117–132.

Tiratsoo, N. (2004) "The 'Americanization' of management education in Britain," *Journal of Management Inquiry*, 13(2): 118–126.

Trank, C. Q. and Rynes, S. L. (2003) "Who moved our cheese? Reclaiming professionalism in business education," *Academy of Management Learning & Education*, 2(2): 189–205.

Trank, C. Q. and Washington, M. (2009) "Maintaining an institution in a contested organizational field: The work of the AACSB and its constituents," in T. B. Lawrence, R. Suddaby, and B. Leca (eds), *Institutional Work: Actors and agency in institutional studies of organizations*, Cambridge: Cambridge University Press, pp. 236–261.

Urgel, J. (2007) "EQUIS accreditation: Value and benefits for international business schools," *Journal of Management Development*, 26(1): 73–83.

Wedlin, L. (2011) "Going global: Rankings as rhetorical devices to construct an international field of management education," *Management Learning*, 42(2): 199–218.

Williams, A. P. O. (2010) *The History of UK Business and Management Education*, Bingley: Emerald.

Zammuto, R. F. (2008) "Accreditation and the globalization of business," *Academy of Management Learning & Education*, 7(2): 256–268.

Zell, D. (2001) "The market-driven business school: Has the pendulum swung too far?" *Journal of Management Inquiry*, 10(4): 324–338.

14

CONSULTING AS GLOBAL BIG BUSINESS

What marked this period was an overall expansion and the rise of information and communication-related consulting, which evolved from a largely technical issue into a core concern of top management. First was the so-called Y2K "bug," then a need to adapt ever more sophisticated IT systems to ever more complex and geographically widespread organizations. While many IT firms seized this opportunity, the accounting-related firms ultimately retained their dominant position, based on their first mover advantages – despite a brief hiatus caused by the Enron scandal and Sarbanes-Oxley. Engineering-based firms all but vanished during this period, while the strategy ones experienced mixed fortunes with McKinsey, the Boston Consulting Group (BCG), and Bain cementing their position as the "Elite Three." Geographically, consultants now covered much of the globe with their operations, albeit in a more dispersed way, with the development and emergence of semi-peripheries, while the US remained the clear center – certainly in terms of demand.

The End of Engineering? Kind of…

As seen in Chapter 5, the engineering-based consultants were at the origin of management consulting in the nineteenth century and thrived during the first half of the twentieth century extending their reach beyond the factory into offices and beyond the private sector into public administration. They operated against the backdrop of a broader, global movement promoting what has widely come to be referred to as "scientific management." These consulting firms received important boosts during both world wars, driven by the need for productivity enhancements. This also ensured them a prominent role in the post-World War II period – at least outside the US, when some of them remained among the largest consulting firms.

But from the 1960s onwards, their influence and public visibility gradually waned as top managers shifted their concerns toward questions of corporate organization and strategy – a sub-field occupied by other firms with diverse origins (see Chapter 11 and below).

In the UK the so-called "Big Four," AIC, UOP, P-E, and PA (see Chapters 8 and 11), maintained their leading role through the 1970s, but quickly declined in the subsequent decades – and have now mostly disappeared. The first to go was Urwick Orr and Partners (UOP), despite having moved toward the new types of services in strategy and organization, contributing for instance to the dissemination of the decentralized multidivisional organization among large British companies – second only to McKinsey (Channon 1973). This forward-looking approach might have actually precipitated its end, because it made the consultant firm more attractive for potential acquirers – in this case the surging accounting firm Price Waterhouse. The latter bought UOP in 1984 partially to reduce its dependence on projects generated by its own audit partners, which did drop to around 35 percent as a result of both the acquisition and the Management Consulting Services (MCS) department's increasing reputation (Jones 1995: 314–315).

Next to go were AIC and P-E, which merged in 1987 eventually adopting the P-E International name. In 1993 the latter was acquired by Cray Electronics – no relation to the US supercomputer manufacturer – then sold three years later to UK-based IT recruitment company Lorien. After a complex series of further sell-offs and acquisitions P-E's remnants – though no longer identifiable by their own name – in 2013 ended up in the US-based Development Alternatives, Inc. (DAI), an economic development company founded in 1970 (DAI 18 August 2015). How P-E eventually vanished sheds some light on the openness of management consulting to other surrounding field(s) of specialist advisory services – with rather fluid boundaries between them.

One of the British "Big Four" did get away by moving itself to the margins of the management consulting field: PA, which had been founded as a spin-off from AIC by Ernest Button in 1943. It quickly surpassed the other three, but started struggling during the 1970s, when "new competitors were replacing the old competitors," with the former including the accountants, the strategy firms, and "numerous IT consultancies [that] were growing rapidly" (Jackson and Smalley 2011: 114). Ups and downs continued during the subsequent decade with the firm eventually making two fundamental changes in the late 1980s: to focus on its technology- and innovation-related consulting services, which had gradually been increasing since the 1960s, and to sell equity to its own consultants, with the proceeds used in part for acquisitions to increase PA's global footprint, which had largely been confined to the UK and Australia (Jackson and Smalley 2011: Chapter 8). The firm recovered, albeit now operating on the margins of the field, and, according to its annual report, in 2014 employed around 2,500 people in over 20 offices around the world.

One could argue that a kind of closing line under the engineering-based chapter of the management consulting field's history was drawn in October 2007, when Accenture, formerly Andersen Consulting, acquired H. B. Maynard and integrated the remaining 90 employees into its own organization with the declared objective to "help our clients achieve both operational and workforce efficiency more quickly than ever" (Accenture 18 August 2015). But while Maynard and most similar firms disappeared, the services they provided actually live on. One could consider business process reengineering (BPR), which was the craze during the 1990s and aimed at improving organizational efficiency and customer focus by removing layers of middle management, as an extension of the earlier efforts focusing on worker productivity (Fincham and Evans 1999). Moreover, at the beginning of the twenty-first century many of the top management consulting firms, including those with a focus on strategy, still obtained a non-negligible part of their fees from operational efficiency projects (Wright and Kipping 2012: Table 2.2).

And there are others with an even more significant focus on efficiency improvements. One of them was George S. May (see Chapters 8 and 11), which seems to have survived into the twenty-first century (see Wright and Kipping 2012: 40), but has now vanished except for a LinkedIn page (George S. May International 25 October 2015). Alexander Proudfoot, established in 1946 to emulate May's hard sales model, has been more successful. After a significant decline in the 1990s, it went public in the UK in 2001, adopting the name Management Consulting Group (MCG) as an umbrella for a number of acquired firms – some of which were sold again or wound down. In 2007, it bought Kurt Salmon Associates, founded in 1935, which had provided efficiency-based services to manufacturers of soft goods such as textiles (see Chapter 8), but declined as its clients off-shored these activities – a decline that a diversification into health care and financial services consulting was unable to stop. Today, MCG continues to focus predominantly on productivity improvements with Alexander Proudfoot and Kurt Salmon as its brands and a combined turnover of around 400 million US dollars in 2014 (MCG 2014).

IT and its Beneficiaries: Established Actors and Newcomers

The Accountants: Forward to the Past?

As seen in previous chapters, the accounting and audit firms were among the first to provide consulting-type services since the nineteenth century. These activities were often related to bankruptcy cases but remained marginal despite some increase during the Great Depression. They became more central after World War II, when many of the larger firms that were emerging from a series of alliances and mergers set up specific management advisory departments – and even joined the professional associations in management consulting. The increasing use of information and communication technologies within business provided an opportunity for them to expand, but also created internal tensions within the firms and growing concerns among regulators about the cross-selling of services (see Chapter 11).

The 1980s and early 1990s saw two parallel developments: On the one hand, there was further consolidation among the "Big Eight" accounting and audit firms reducing their number to six (Stevens 1991). The first important merger occurred in 1987, when Peat Marwick combined with Klynveld Main Goerdeler (KMG), which itself had only been formed in 1979 as an association between Klynveld Kraayenhof from the Netherlands; Main Lafrentz & Co from the US and Dr. Reinhard Goerdeler's *Treuhandgesellschaft* from Germany – partially as a reaction to the international dominance of the Anglo-American firms. KPMG, as it was called eventually, brought together two firms with rather distinct geographical coverage and was hence not seen as reducing the number of "big" firms. It nevertheless prompted further consolidation in 1989, when Ernst & Whinney and Arthur Young merged into Ernst & Young and Deloitte Haskins & Sells combined with Touche & Ross into Deloitte & Touche – the latter a rather long-winded and complex process, since some national partnerships initially opted for different combinations. In 1998 the resulting "Big Six," which also included Arthur Andersen, became the "Big Five" with the merger between Price Waterhouse and Coopers & Lybrand to PwC.

On the other hand, the growth of consulting activities in all of these firms continued unabated throughout the 1980s. At the beginning of the decade management advisory services (MAS) accounted on average for 15 percent of revenues and employed 1,500 professionals worldwide for each of the "Big Eight" but were already seen as "the most promising market" according to one of their managing directors (Stevens 1981: 118–119). That promise did come true within a decade, since at the beginning of the 1990s consulting, as it was now increasingly called, reached 40 percent or more of revenues and, apparently, accounted for "the lion's share of profits" (Stevens 1991: 19). This development renewed tensions that had earlier been resolved in favor of the audit partners (see Chapter 11). At the same time, growth in auditing slowed and competition increased, especially after the American Institute of Certified Public Accountants (AICPA) had allowed its members to advertise, following a 1978 Supreme Court decision overturning a ban on advertising by lawyers.

The conflict between audit and consulting partners first came to a head at Arthur Andersen – an earlier truce proving to be temporary (see Chapter 11). The latter kept asking for more autonomy based on their growing contribution to the firm (see Table 14.1). And the argument that audit partners brought in most of the consulting clients was no longer valid either. That share had dropped to 20 percent at the time and even at KPMG was only around 40 percent (Anon. 1988).

Arthur Andersen's "Management Information Consulting Division," as it was officially called at the time, would have actually become larger than auditing had

TABLE 14.1 Arthur Andersen, Revenue Shares and Growth, 1984–1987

	Auditing			Consulting			Tax			Total
	US dollars (million)	Share (%)	Year-on-Year Growth	US dollars (million)	Share (%)	Year-on-Year Growth	US dollars (million)	Share (%)	Year-on-Year Growth	US dollars (million)
1984	702.9	51		391.8	28		293.2	21		1,387.9
1985	767.1	49	9.1	477.3	30	21.8	329.5	21	12.4	1,573.9
1986	903.7	47	17.8	635.9	33	33.2	384.4	20	16.7	1,924.0
1987	997.9	43	10.4	838.4	36	31.8	479.5	21	24.7	2,315.8

Sources: Squires et al. (2003: 84); own calculations.

the latter not been combined with tax in 1988. This reeked of desperation and only delayed the inevitable, as did the earlier proposal of a non-compete clause for those leaving the firm, possibly prompted by the departure of the head of the consulting division to advertising giant Saatchi & Saatchi the previous year and his new employer's offer to purchase the division – duly rejected by Andersen. Things got worse when his successor was dismissed for asking an acquaintance at Morgan Stanley for a valuation of a consulting firm of Andersen's size. A year later, to prevent a full scission, the audit partners turned the division into a separate business unit, renamed Andersen Consulting (AC) – with a significant degree of autonomy, including its own profit pool, pay scales, recruitment, and branding (see, for this and the following, Squires et al. 2003: Chapters 5 and 6; Toffler and Reingold 2003: 78–86).

But the agreement already contained the seeds for further infighting, since it had provisions for ongoing transfer payments, based on revenues, which quickly came to benefit the auditors. Moreover, Arthur Andersen retained the right to offer its own business consulting services to clients – initially limited to those with revenues of 175 million US dollars or less. This meant that both increasingly went after the same projects. A full "divorce" was the only option and finally happened in 2000, brokered by the International Chamber of Commerce. AC became an independent entity against a final payment of 1.2 billion US dollars and, as part of the agreement, changed its name to Accenture on January 1, 2001, conducting an IPO later that year.

With hindsight Accenture was lucky, because Andersen got caught up in the accounting fraud and eventual demise of US energy company Enron, where it had been the auditor and also provided consulting services. Found to have failed at the former and to have shredded documents to obscure its role, the firm was barred from auditing any publicly quoted companies in the US in 2002 – which prompted its partners to join other auditing and consulting firms here and elsewhere around the world, reducing the "Big Five" to the "Big Four." The original sentence was overturned by the US Supreme Court in 2005 – too late though to repair the damage caused to Andersen's reputation and rebuild the lost relationships. More importantly, the Enron case once again exposed the conflicts of interest between acting as a legally mandated auditor and the purely commercially motivated sale of ever more consulting services (Boyd 2004; Coffee 2006; McDougald and Greenwood 2012) – an issue addressed by the Sarbanes-Oxley Act of 2002, which also attempted to close many of the loopholes exploited by Enron.

The other "Big Five" experienced similar tensions and, during the 1990s, also created relatively independent consulting units. These tension, as well as concerns about conflicts of interest by the Securities and Exchange Commission (SEC) in the US prompted all of them to rethink the value of combining audit and consulting services. Already before Enron and Sarbanes-Oxley most decided to separate the two. Thus, Ernst & Young sold its consulting arm to French IT-service provider and consultant Cap Gemini (see below) in May 2000. KPMG formally

240 Markets Reign

demerged its consulting unit and spun it off in an IPO in 2001. Headquartered in McLean, Virginia and renamed BearingPoint in 2002, it grew quickly by incorporating many of the business consulting units and partners of the defunct Andersen, reaching over 15,000 employees worldwide, and mainly provided technology-based services to the US federal government, including the Marine Corps. But the firm ran into accounting trouble [sic], was investigated by the SEC, and took on significant debt, which eventually forced it into bankruptcy protection in 2009 (Lazo 2009). It was largely sold off to competitors, with PwC for instance buying parts of the US and the Japanese operations. The remaining country units, most of them European, regrouped and are now part of a much smaller firm with around 3,000 employees (BearingPoint 25 October 2015). This story shows that being in a growing area of consulting did not suffice, but that well managed operations were equally important, given the increasing scale and duration of projects.

Back in 2002, PwC also readied itself for a spin-off renaming its consulting division "Monday" – a choice inviting quite some ridicule, but later that year sold it to IBM Global Services (see below). Deloitte & Touche made similar plans, preparing to rebrand and sell-off Deloitte Consulting, created in 1995. But both the renaming and the IPO were abruptly shelved in 2003, the firm invoking "external factors including the tight credit market and the uncertain state of the economy" as the main reasons (cited by Haines 2003). However, a few years after the "aborted breakup" a *Business Week* article highlighted that, in hindsight, Deloitte has been lucky, since consulting revenue had grown again reaching 8.9 billion US dollars, equivalent to 45 percent of its overall global revenue (Byrnes 2007). The other "Big Four" firms also benefitted from this "comeback of consulting," with corresponding global revenues of 5.3 billion US dollars at KPMG, 3.7 billion at PwC, and 2.4 billion at EY. They continued to expand, also in terms of the scope of their consulting activities, by gobbling up parts of failing competitors (see above) and troubled strategy consultants (see below). Today, at least according to some estimates, the "Big Four" are back on top of the management consulting field in terms of revenues (see Table 14.2).

As should already be apparent from the variation between the two sources, these numbers have to be taken with caution, since what should be included in consulting is up for debate and difficult to measure – also given the "dissolving" boundaries of the field (Hill 2014). Be that as it may, consulting provided by the Big Four audit and accounting firms is clearly back – and apparently back on top. But so are some of the issues that caused the earlier troubles, posing the question, as one industry expert already did in 2007: "Have you learned your lesson, or is this going to turn out badly again?" (quoted by Byrnes 2007). In terms of conflicts of interest, firms seem to provide their consulting services mainly to companies they do not audit, but some cross-selling still occurs. More importantly, consulting revenues continue to grow faster – and are once again poised to overtake audit revenues. Whether the various measures taken, such as pooling all profits independent of activity and distributing them to individual partners

Consulting as Global Big Business 241

TABLE 14.2 Two Estimates of the Largest Global Consulting Firms in 2013

	Gartner			*Kennedy*		
	Firm	Revenue (billion US dollars)	Growth (%)	Firm	Revenue (billion US dollars)	Growth (%)
1	Deloitte	14.7	6.0	Deloitte	18.3	7.0
2	PwC	12.7	10.0	PwC	16.1	10.5
3	EY	12.1	12.7	EY	13.7	10.1
4	KPMG	10.7	5.2	KPMG	11.3	6.5
5	Accenture	4.1	4.4	Accenture	7.3	−2.5
6	IBM	4.0	2.1	IBM	4.0	−0.4
7	McKinsey	2.3	5.5	McKinsey	5.9	4.5
8	Booz Allen Hamilton	2.1	−2.9	BCG	3.6	7.0
9	CGI	1.5	3.4	Booz Allen Hamilton	3.4	−5.5
10	CSC	1.4	−3.6	Mercer	3.3	1.6

Sources: Consultancy.uk (2015) for Gartner; estimates for Kennedy Consulting Research drawn from graph in Hill (2014).

according to their personal performance (Byrnes 2007), can prevent future internal conflicts, remains to be seen.

From the Margins to the Center of the Field: IT Firms

While the accountants clearly had a head start in IT-related consulting, IT-service companies also entered the field on a larger scale since the 1990s and quickly managed to build strong positions (see Table 14.2). Many of these firms had origins going back to the 1960s or 1970s (see Chapter 11) – even to the nineteenth century for IBM. Originally, most of them helped their clients buy and install the most appropriate hard- and software; many also came to provide outsourcing, i.e., data processing for others, on a permanent basis. Some of these firms eventually moved to offer advice on adapting IT systems to organizations and vice versa and/or deciding which parts of the organization to outsource. These activities can clearly be considered management consulting, because they led to important strategic decisions about the boundaries of client organizations and their internal structures and processes. The IT-based firms also asserted their position in the field by joining the relevant professional bodies (see Chapter 11; also Kipping and Kirkpatrick 2013).

When did that transition from IT service to consulting occur? Difficult to say in most cases. Some never quite made it. One of the earliest firms to offer outsourcing was Electronic Data Services (EDS) founded by Ross Perot in 1962, originally leasing time on mainframe computers before buying their own and also managing data processing facilities for clients. The company went public in 1968 and in 1984 was acquired by GM. Its business continued to evolve around facilities management, outsourcing, and data processing systems design until the mid-1990s, when it also moved into consulting. Thus, in 1993 EDS bought a small financial services consulting firm and in 1995 it acquired one of the most venerable of the "Big Image" firms, A. T. Kearney, with the intention to create "a new competitive force in the global management consulting arena" (EDS History Timeline 2008: 12). While EDS was spun-off by GM the following year, the two cultures never really meshed and A. T. Kearney became independent again following a management buyout in 2006, albeit now much smaller than most of its erstwhile rivals (see below). In 2008 EDS itself was purchased by Hewlett-Packard (HP), intent on breaking into the lucrative service business, and began operating as HP Enterprise Services the following year, but even under the new ownership never quite moved beyond outsourcing (Hardy 2012).

The most dominant IT company for much of the twentieth century, IBM, seems to have kind of stumbled into the consulting business. Some (viz., McKenna 2006: 22–23) have argued that its entry into consulting was delayed by the consent decree the company had signed in 1956 with the US Department of Justice, intent on limiting, among others, the cross-selling between hardware, software, and services. However, when the company decided to formally establish the IBM Consulting Group in 1992 following an outsourcing agreement with Eastman Kodak in 1989 and a surge in the demand for consulting from its clients in the early 1990s, the consent decree had yet to be revoked; its restrictions were only phased out from 1996 onwards (Wiener 2002). But with the stroke of a pen, the company became a formidable force in the management consulting field, since the Group comprised from the outset "1,500 consultants worldwide to provide management and information technology-related consulting services to companies and organizations in 30 countries," as the company's own website remarks rather laconically (IBM 7 January 2016; for more details, see IBM Corporate Archives 2002). Over the subsequent decade the consulting business grew exponentially reaching 30,000 professionals by the time it acquired the consulting arm of PwC in 2002, which doubled its size.

This meteoric rise coincided with the tenure of Lou Gerstner as CEO of IBM between 1993 and 2002. He is widely credited for the turnaround of the company's fortunes. After receiving an MBA from HBS, Gerstner had actually joined McKinsey, where he became a partner, before leaving for an executive position at American Express in 1978, then moving to RJR Nabisco as CEO in 1989 before being lured to the top job at IBM. While his vision and leadership might have played some role, there were also other factors at play, namely: (i) the decision, made before Gerstner's tenure, to hire a senior partner from Booz Allen Hamilton to head the group (Anon. 1995); (ii) some luck resulting from the widespread panic among companies about the so-called "Y2K bug," which was supposed to wreak havoc in all computers on January 1, 2000 and created strong demand for IT-consulting; and (iii) probably most important, the fact that the group could draw on the relationships IBM had created over many decades with leading corporations in all sectors of the economy around the world. Due to its long history and overall size, IBM also had specific expertise in most sectors.

Other companies could not rely on their previous relationships, sector-specific know-how and established global presence, but had to build all of these gradually. This was for example the case of the Canadian firm CGI, originally meaning *Conseillers en gestion et informatique*, i.e., management and IT consultants (see further Lofty 2015). CGI was founded in 1976 by two 26-year-old entrepreneurs, Serge Godin and André Imbeau, in the former's basement in Québec City, and then moved to Montréal as the company grew. Despite its original aim to provide management consulting, the company adapted to the evolving market in IT services and started offering systems integration, outsourcing, and business process improvement. It very judiciously used acquisitions – 75 in total until 2014 – to enlarge its know-how, industry expertise, and geographic reach, first in North America, then, more recently, in Europe. Its latest target, in 2012, was the UK-based IT-consultant Logica, which had originally been founded in 1967 as a systems integrator and, in 2002, merged with the Computer Management Group (CMG), itself set up in 1964. Through this acquisition CGI basically doubled its size, now counting 68,000 employees, and established a more global – mainly North American and European – footprint.

The story of CGI is indicative of the broader developments in IT-service based consulting, namely: (i) the crucial role of large-scale outsourcing contracts, often with governments, as a starting point; (ii) the importance of acquisitions in the expansion of these companies, which made them very adaptable and allowed them to act strategically, but also obliged them to access capital markets through a partial or full floatation and required a different form of governance, even if their founders continued to play an important role during the initial decades; and (iii) the more global origins of several service providers, even if most of them eventually converged on the United States to take advantage of lucrative federal government contracts there.

A firm that originally was even more peripheral than the Canadian CGI was Sogeti or *Société pour la gestion et le traitement de l'information*, i.e., information management and processing company (see further Gaston-Breton 1999). It was founded in Grenoble in the French Alps in 1967 by Serge Kampf, who after graduating in law and economics initially worked at Bull, the French equivalent of IBM. In the mid-1970s, the company moved its headquarters to Paris and renamed itself Cap Gemini Sogeti, adopting the names of two companies acquired earlier: the French CAP (*Centre d'analyse et programmation*) and the US-based Gemini Computer Systems. The company moved more decisively into the consulting field during the 1990s on both sides of the Atlantic with the acquisition of United Research and the MAC Group in the US in 1990, marketing consultants Gruber, Titze und Partner in Germany in 1993, and strategy consultants Bossard in France in 1997. To finance these acquisitions it partially floated on the stock exchange in 1985 and, in 1991, sold another part to a strategic investor, the systems integrator Debis, owned by Germany's Daimler Benz. Struggles over control ensued, until Cap Gemini regained its independence in 1998. As noted above, in 2000 it acquired the consulting arm of Ernst & Young, propelling it into the ranks of the largest global IT-services firms, but causing "indigestion" problems as one observer put it (Phillips 2001). Despite all these efforts and expenses, Capgemini Consulting remains a rather minor actor today, with only about 4,000 out of the group's 180,000 employees.

How much the field has changed due to the rise of IT services and IT-related consulting can be seen from the decision by Booz Allen Hamilton (BAH) to split itself into two. The company had been driven by both strategy and technology at least since the establishment of BAARInc in the 1950s, with an ebb and flow in the resulting tensions (see Chapter 11). In 2008 the increasingly successful and powerful IT- and technology-based business, which earned most of its revenues from the federal government in the US, finally decided to spin off "commercial management consulting" and international activities into what was called Booz & Co. BAH itself joined the likes of Accenture, CGI, and IBM, with a private equity firm taking an important stake followed by a floatation on the New York Stock Exchange in 2014. When a temporary non-compete agreement expired, it also entered into the strategy sub-field, launching a "Strategic Innovation Group" with 1,800 staff (see BAH 2014: 22). That same year Booz & Co. was acquired by PwC and renamed Strategy& (see also below).

The Marginal and Ephemeral: Inside Out and "Fast Five"

The Capgemini–Debis story above points to another group of entrants into an increasingly crowded field – those that originated as internal IT divisions of specific companies, then started to provide services to third parties, and eventually became independent. A case in point is Cognizant. It goes back to a majority-owned joint venture initially called DBSS that Dun & Bradstreet (D&B) formed in 1994 with India's Satyam at the behest of Wijeyaraj (Kumar) Mahadeva, an HBS graduate from Sri Lanka, who had previously worked at McKinsey and AT&T and recognized the potential to outsource software maintenance and services to India. In 1996, it was spun off as part of a larger unit by D&B, bought out Satyam in 1997 and became fully independent in 2003 (Cognizant 25 October 2015). Initially benefitting from work related to Y2K, Cognizant soon started to provide business process outsourcing and also grew by purchasing internal IT units from other companies. More recently, it has made acquisitions targeting technology-oriented consulting firms, mainly in Europe, but remains largely focused on IT outsourcing with two-thirds of its workforce of around 220,000 located in India.

India with its well-educated, relatively low-cost engineers remains the hub of the global outsourcing industry, where Cognizant as well as many others like

IBM or Accenture have most of their related operations. It is also home to a number of Indian firms that took advantage of the same conditions: Tata Consultancy Services (TCS) – which was established in 1968 to provide in-house services to Tata Group companies, but soon offered systems and software design to third parties – is publicly traded since 2004 and, growing in part through acquisitions, had revenues of over 15 billion US dollars in 2014 (TCS 25 October 2015); Infosys, which was founded in 1981, conducted an IPO in 1993, grew and globalized in part through acquisitions of other IT-service providers and today has revenues of close to 10 billion US dollars, mainly based on software and systems design, maintenance as well as outsourcing services (Infosys 25 October 2015); and Wipro (Hamm 2006), which goes back to the Western India Vegetable Products company founded in Mumbai in 1945, changed its focus to IT and outsourcing during the 1970s and 1980s under the founder's son, and had revenues of 8 billion US dollars in 2014. So far, these companies have tended to remain focused on providing outsourcing services though and have yet to start competing with any significance in the management consulting field.

Another group of firms that had an ephemeral presence but left some traces, which might become more influential in the future, were the so-called "Fast Five" (Hammonds 2001): VIANT, Scient, Razorfish, iXL, and MarchFIRST. They were founded during the mid-1990s offering companies help with their web design and Internet presences – novelties at the time. As their moniker suggests, they grew very fast and took advantage of the dot.com boom of the late twentieth century for IPOs. But when the boom turned out to be a bubble, bursting in 2001, and as web design quickly became child's play, they declined as fast as they had risen, with Viant acquired by another start-up, which then went bankrupt, while Scient folded into iXL and, together with MarchFIRST, was acquired by Razorfish. The latter was taken private and eventually bought by Microsoft in 2007, which in turn sold it to the leading global advertising agency, Paris-based Publicis, in 2009 (Creamer and Klaasen 2009). With 2,000 employees worldwide, Razorfish is today a global leader in interactive advertising.

This story and the involvement of Publicis point to another actor on the margins of the management consulting field, namely the global advertising agencies, which had already shown some interest, when Saatchi & Saatchi poached the head of Andersen's consulting division in the late 1980s and offered to purchase the division (see above). Given the increasing need for managers to communicate with various stakeholders, this might become a more strategic issue prompting the development of communication consulting as an important sub-field, where such agencies might be well placed (see further Engwall and Kipping 2013).

While there has been significant movement in the IT-related part of the consulting field, including a massive number of acquisitions, most of the firms, which entered since the 1970s seem to have focused on IT services, including outsourcing, rather than on advice to top management – even if the two tend to be difficult to distinguish given the strategic nature of the associated changes in

246 Markets Reign

business processes. But there is no doubt that these developments are driving the commercialization of the field to new heights. Thus, while some of these firms sought the mantle of professional recognition at the outset by joining the relevant bodies (see above), they no longer seem so interested after having established their own image and reputation through massive advertising – and many have left the associations again (see Kipping 2011). There is also no doubt that these firms became very global with more integrated structures than the federations of national accounting firms in the previous period. And while there continue to be differences between national management consulting fields, namely in terms of their level of development, these are likely to be less pronounced going forward. As for the origins of these firms, the US remains important, namely as a market for their services. But an increasing number of firms are based in semi-peripheral countries, like Canada or France, and an erstwhile periphery, India, is now providing most of the back office and outsourcing services.

Strategy and Organization Consulting: Melting Ice Cubes?

After living through – and barely surviving – the turmoil of the 1970s, in the subsequent decades the strategy and organization firms were faced with the seemingly inexorable rise of IT-related management consulting – probably somewhat masked by the overall growth in the field. And while the strategy firms appear to have held on to the notion that only they represented "true" management consulting, the accounting and IT firms were no longer afraid of invading their sub-field in the process of enlarging and mainstreaming their services – mainly through acquisitions (see above and below).

In addition, the strategy consultants came to confront a possibly even more dangerous challenge: increased public scrutiny and criticisms. This went to the core of their business, i.e., their professional image, which took them so much care to build and which provided them with legitimacy and definitional power and authority toward their clients and within the management arena more broadly. While earlier observers had characterized them as "doctors of management" and "business healers" (see Chapter 11), a 1983 article in *Forbes* now asked "Are All These Consultants Really Necessary?"– with an implied "No" answer (Byrne 1983). The article provided many examples where consulting assignments failed and even had negative results for the client companies – failures that indiscriminately involved all the "Big Image" firms, including Booz, McKinsey, BCG, and ADL. It also highlighted, albeit indirectly, the addictive nature of consulting services and the way consultants promoted them using fear – a theme later picked up in the academic literature (see esp. Ernst and Kieser 2002): "Consultants have become the shamans of U.S. business – and they don't hesitate to sell themselves as such. A shaman will threaten the tribe: Unless I do my dance, the rains won't come" (Byrne 1983).

Subsequent book-length treatments, written by journalists or former consultants, took even more critical views of consulting, already visible in their titles:

The Witch Doctors (Micklethwait and Wooldridge 1996), which still used the medical imagery, now turned negative, and looked at consulting firms and individual management gurus (see also Chapter 2); *Dangerous Company* (O'Shea and Madigan 1997), based on court cases against consulting malpractice; *Con Tricks* (Ashford 1998) and *Rip-Off* (Craig 2005), both by former consultants from unidentified firms; *Consulting Demons* (Pinault 2000) as well as *House of Lies* (Kihn 2005). The latter was written by a former Booz consultant, and came to form the basis for a successful TV series, entering its fifth season in 2016. These firms were also subject to internal humor if not scorn, as was already evident from the "Consultants' Coloring Book" at McKinsey in the 1960s (reproduced partially by McKenna 2006: Chapter 6). Thus, in the 1990s Andersen Consulting (AC) employee James Sanchez, whose identity remained hidden despite an internal manhunt, until he left the firm, created a web-based comic called "Bigtime Consulting" – renamed "Indenture," when AC turned into Accenture (Bigtime Consulting 25 October 2015).

Consulting bashing became a fashion in itself. And it did pose a serious threat to firms that relied on people to believe in what they said and did – both those working within the firm and those buying their services. So, how did these firms deal with these challenges, both market pressures from the newcomers and the questioning of the value of their services? In 2002, the *Economist* ran an article entitled "Consultant, Heal Thyself" (Anon. 2002), all but predicting the demise of strategy consulting: "Strategy has now become a commodity. […] The advice of a management consultant has lost its mystery. […] [M]anagement consultants may no longer have a profitable business model." But while this turned out to be correct for some firms, which shrank beyond recognition or even disappeared, others coped well, some even strengthening their image and position.

As mentioned, one of the first to go had been Urwick Orr, acquired by Price-Waterhouse in 1985. Next came A. T. Kearney (ATK), bought by EDS in 1995 (see above). Things went well originally, with EDS investing into ATK's "infrastructure, marketing and intellectual capital development" (Anon. 2014: Chapter 4). But after the burst of the dot.com bubble, revenues shrank and hidden tensions and cultural differences quickly came to the fore, prompting considerations of a sale with Monitor as a possible acquirer (see below). But in 2005 management bought out the firm, which was now only half its peak size and quite tellingly described by one of its partners as "a melting ice cube in a room with a rising ambient temperature" (Anon. 2014: 56). Not surprisingly therefore, it has been mentioned as a target for an acquisition or merger. The same is true for other mid-size strategy consultants, including Germany's Roland Berger & Partners (see Chapter 11), where Deutsche Bank had been a majority owner since the late 1980s before being required to disinvest by US regulators a decade later. Since 2010, Berger has apparently rejected offers from both Deloitte and EY trying to grow on its own instead (Gapper 2013).

While ATK and Berger have survived – so far, other ice cubes have melted. This is the case of Arthur D. Little (ADL), which applied for bankruptcy protection in 2002 and was bought by Paris-based Altran Technologies, founded in 1982 by two former Peat Marwick consultants with a focus on technology and innovation consulting. While the nonprofit Arthur D. Little School of Management was spun off and became Hult International Business School, Altran rebuilt ADL focusing on technological expertise in different industries, such as energy, automotive, or health care. In 2011 Altran funded a management buyout, with the "new" ADL much smaller – employing approximately 1,000 consultants worldwide with a minor presence in the US – but more similar to its erstwhile origins.

Monitor was not so lucky. Founded by famous Harvard Business School professor and strategy author Michael Porter (see Chapter 15) and several others with ties to HBS in 1985, the firm once rivalled the likes of McKinsey and BCG. But it was hard hit by the meltdown of 2008, when "pure" strategy took a back seat to operational improvements. Monitor also suffered from bad publicity surrounding the extensive work it had done since 2005 for Gaddafi and his regime in Libya, involving famous academics, such as former Kennedy School Dean Joseph Nye, Stanford's Francis Fukuyama, and the LSE's Anthony Giddens, and including the plan for a book to extol the Colonel and his ideas. Monitor eventually filed for bankruptcy protection in 2012 (Stockman 2011; Denning 2012) and was bought by Deloitte the following year. It now operates as Monitor Deloitte – a mere drop in an organization with over 200,000 employees worldwide.

But there are others, which did not melt, namely the now so-called "Big Three" or "Elite Three" strategy consultants: McKinsey, BCG, and Bain (see further e.g., Chin 2013). This is not to say that they were not challenged by the rise of IT or consulting bashing – a fact also recognized in academic research (Armbrüster and Kipping 2002; Christensen, Wang, and Bever 2013). But they coped and found various ways to continue to define management – possibly even more so than before. One important feature was their investment in visible knowledge development and dissemination – trying to demonstrate "thought leadership." Their consultants continue to publish management books, following the model of the bestselling *In Search of Excellence* written by McKinsey consultants Tom Peters and Robert Waterman in 1982 (see Chapters 2 and 15) – with the former later admitting that some of the underlying data had actually been invented (Byrne 2001). They also (co)author articles in practitioner-oriented academic journals, in particular the *Harvard Business Review* (see also Chapters 12 and 15), issue their own periodical publications mimicking the latter, i.e., the *McKinsey Quarterly*, *BCG Perspectives*, and *Bain Insights*, and publish regular reports on a variety of "hot" topics.

In 1990, McKinsey even established a Global Institute with a research-like profile in terms of addressing broader questions. A recent ranking of global think tanks confirmed the success of these efforts with the Global Institute coming second among the private sector ones after the Economist Intelligence Unit and consulting firms occupying 12 of the top 35 spots (McGann 2015). The ranking, incidentally, also shows similar efforts being made by the accounting- and IT-based firms, with EY, Accenture, IBM, and Deloitte ranked 4th, 11th, 16th, and 17th respectively.

In terms of specific consulting firms, Bain probably benefitted from being smaller, hence less visible, and also from its unique business model, where it largely provided "shadow management" for a single client per sector and, at times, engaged in what it called "tied economics" arrangements, linking their remuneration to client results. It has also been successful at capturing certain trends quite early, for instance with several of its partners in 1984 establishing Bain Capital, led by Mitt Romney until 1999, which created a model applied by many private equity firms today in terms of not only taking stakes in companies but also providing advice. This allowed retaining talent during the dot.com boom as many consultants left other firms to establish their own ventures. And in 2000, it created a non-profit organization, called "The Bridgespan Group," providing strategy advice to other non-profits – anticipating the quest of many millennials to make social contributions.

While thought leadership had been a defining feature of BCG from the outset with the BCG matrix and the experience curve, it also drew an advantage from having been one of the first Western consulting firms to establish a stronghold in Asia since the 1960s (see Chapter 11). They benefitted in particular from the interest in Japanese manufacturing during the 1980s and early 1990s, introducing what they called time-based competition in quite a number of Western firms. Somewhat unluckily, they published the corresponding book just before the burst of the Japanese bubble economy (Stalk and Hout 1990). Subsequently, BCG grew its presence in the region by opening additional offices, starting with Kuala Lumpur in 1992.

Given its size, visibility, and ambitions, McKinsey was probably the most challenged of the "Elite Three." Initially, it tried to enter the surging IT-related sub-field itself, first by acquiring the small Information Consulting Group in 1989 – with little success since more than half of its partners had left a few years later; then, in 1997, by setting up a global Business Technology Office (BTO), which did become the third largest McKinsey "office" in revenue terms after the US and Germany by 2011 (McDonald 2013: 200–203) – but still pales in scale compared to the huge IT-based consulting firms discussed above.

More importantly, McKinsey and its image were challenged again early in the twenty-first century (see, for the following, McDonald 2013: Chapter 9). First due to its very close association with the scandal surrounding Enron in 2001 – most visibly through HBS graduate and former McKinsey partner Jeff Skilling, who joined Enron and became its CEO after having consulted them and is currently serving a long-term prison sentence. But McKinsey not only provided advice and personnel to Enron, it also celebrated the company in many of its publications (see Chapter 2). And, while less visible, McKinsey had also provided

250   Markets Reign

strategic direction to other companies that subsequently went bankrupt, including Swissair and K-Mart (Byrne 2002). And then, less than a decade later, came the cases of its director Anil Kumar and its former long-time managing director Rajat Gupta, who were both found guilty of trading insider information to the Galleon hedge fund (McDonald 2013: 307–320).

McKinsey quickly dissociated itself from what they considered rotten apples, and, like after Enron, launched a publicity offensive, which also involved a strong engagement toward the reform of capitalism from the inside (e.g., Barton 2011; FCLT 25 October 2015) – in itself certainly a very laudable objective. What probably helped most to limit the damage to its reputation and its business was a rather unique asset: its substantial global alumni network, which makes the firm largely immune from outside critiques and provides a relatively stable client base. This network resulted from a combination of its long history, its systematic up-or-out policy, and its strong corporate culture – all legacies of the firm that Marvin Bower built in the 1950s and 1960s (see Chapter 11). Subsequently, McKinsey and, to a lesser extent, other elite firms had come to be considered as a way to "leap straight into the chief executive chair of some company" (Mintzberg 1996: 66), which attracted not only some of the best MBAs to the firm but also helped place its alumni in leading positions. Largely confined to business and the Anglo-American countries at the outset (Byrne 1993), this network now spans the globe and most sectors of the economy, polity, and society – even reaching into academia (see Box 14.1).

However, while the "Elite Three" and in particular McKinsey have carved out strong positions, the strategy sub-field within management consulting remains highly contested (see also Chin 2015). As seen above, in 2013 Deloitte bought the bankrupt Monitor, now operating as Monitor Deloitte; in 2014 PwC acquired Booz & Co, renaming it Strategy; and that same year Accenture took 8,000 consultants out of its over 300,000 employees to create Accenture Strategy (Hill 2014). In general, boundaries within and around the overall management consulting field appear to be "dissolving" (Hill 2014) or at least are becoming ever more permeable – probably making for further challenges and changes in the years and decades to come.

Consulting as Global Big Business 251

BOX 14.1 MCKINSEY IS EVERYWHERE

The McKinsey alumni network is unique in its extent, the high-level positions at which many of them can be found, and its reach, both in terms of geography and areas of activity. Cases of former McKinsey consultants joining other companies have been mentioned throughout this volume, including IBM's Lou Gerstner (see above). Current examples include Best Buy CEO Hubert Joly, Google CEO Sandar Pichai, Facebook COO Sheryl Sandberg, and the Management Board Chairman of German Commerzbank, Martin Blessing. McKinsey is now widely seen as a good training ground for future leaders. Thus, the daughter of Renault and Nissan CEO Carlos Ghosn, Caroline, worked at McKinsey, before setting up the early career website Levo – with Sandberg as an angel investor (Abrams 2014); and Delphine Arnault, daughter and heir apparent of LVMH Chairman and CEO Bernard also passed through the firm (Bagley 2014). The network increasingly reaches into politics and government. Former Conservative party leader and UK Foreign Secretary William Hague is a McKinsey alum and so is Obama's National Security Advisor Susan E. Rice. Chelsea Clinton also worked at the firm between 2003 and 2006. More recently, McKinsey alumni are entering academia, including as professors, with Pankaj Ghemawat a prominent example (see Chapter 2), but even more so as senior academic administrators – part of a broader movement to introduce business and management principles into university governance and the public sector as a whole (Engwall 2015). Thus, the current pro-vice-chancellor and executive dean of the Aston Business School in the UK, George Feiger, was a partner at McKinsey and also worked in financial services; and in 2015 Scott C. Beardsley was appointed dean of the University of Virginia Darden School of Business after 26 years at McKinsey. But the firm does not have a total monopoly on these positions. The current dean of the Kellogg School of Management, Sally Blount, had actually worked at BCG before embarking on an academic career. She nevertheless appointed a former McKinsey partner as one of her associate deans (Byrne 2012).

References

Abrams, R. (2014) "Online Career Site Receives $7 Million Angel Investment," *New York Times*, 11 February.

Accenture, 18 August 2015. https://newsroom.accenture.com/industries/retail/accenture-completes-acquisition-hb-maynard-and-co-inc-expanding-workforce-performance-capabilities.htm.

Anon. (1988) "Accountant, consult thyself," *The Economist*, 10 September.

Anon. (1995) "IBM as consultant: A transformation history," *Chain Store Age*, 71(9): 2C.

Anon. (2002) "Consultant, heal thyself," *The Economist*, 31 October.

Anon. (2014) *The A.T. Kearney Story*, Chicago, IL: A. T. Kearney.

Armbrüster, T. and Kipping, M. (2002) "Strategy consulting at the crossroads: Technical change and shifting market conditions for top-level advice," *International Studies in Management & Organization*, 32(4): 19–42.

Ashford, M. (1998) *Con Tricks: The world of management consultancy and how to make it work for you*, London: Simon & Schuster.

Bagley, C. (2014) "Fashion's First Daughter," *W magazine*, 22 August. www.wmagazine. com/fashion/2014/08/delphine-arnault-lvmh/photos.

BAH (2014) *Defining Moments: A century of character, service, and vision*, McLean, VA: Booz Allen Hamilton Inc.

Barton, D. (2011) "Capitalism for the long term," *Harvard Business Review*, 89(3): 84–91.

BearingPoint, 25 October 2015. www.bearingpoint.com.

Bigtime Consulting, 25 October 2015. www.bigtimeconsulting.org.

Boyd, C. (2004) "The structural origins of conflicts of interest in the accounting profession," *Business Ethics Quarterly*, 14(3): 377–398.

Byrne, J. A. (1983) "Are all these consultants really necessary?" *Forbes*, 10 October: 136–144.

Byrne, J. A. (1993) "The McKinsey mystique," *Businessweek*, 19 September.

Byrne, J. A. (2001) "The real confessions of Tom Peters," *Bloomberg Businessweek*, 2 December.

Byrne, J. A. (2002) "Inside McKinsey," *Businessweek*, 8 July: 54–62.

Byrne, J. A. (2012) "A Harvard MBA gives Kellogg the McKinsey treatment," *Poets & Quants*, 23 September.

Byrnes, N. (2007) "The comeback of consulting," *Bloomberg Businessweek*, 2 September.

Channon, D. F. (1973) *The Strategy and Structure of British Enterprise*, London: Macmillan.

Chin, E. (2013) "The MBB trio in strategy consulting: A tale of three kingdoms." www. beatoncapital.com/2013/08/the-mbb-trio-in-strategy-consulting-a-tale-of-three-kingdoms (accessed 26 October 2015).

Chin, E. (2015) "State of the MBB, Next Four and Big Four strategy consulting empires." www.beatoncapital.com/2015/06/state-of-thembb-next-four-and-big-four-strategy-consult ing-empires (accessed 26 October 2015).

Christensen, C. M., Wang, D., and Bever, D. van (2013) "Consulting on the cusp of disruption," *Harvard Business Review*, 91(10): 106–114.

Coffee, J. C. (2006) *Gatekeepers: The professions and corporate governance*, Oxford: Oxford University Press.

Cognizant, 25 October 2015. www.fundinguniverse.com/company-histories/cogniza nt-technology-solutions-corporation-history.

Consultancy.uk (2015) "10 largest management consulting firms of the globe," 15 June. www. consultancy.uk/news/2149/10-largest-management-consulting-firms-of-the-globe (accessed 28 August 2015).

Craig, D. (2005) *Rip-off! The scandalous inside story of the management consulting money machine*, London: The Original Book Company.

Creamer, M. and Klaasen, A. (2009) "Publicis Groupe buys Razorfish from Microsoft for $530 million," *AdvertisingAge*, 9 August.

DAI, 18 August 2015. http://dai.com/who-we-are/history.

Denning, S. (2012) "What killed Michael Porter's monitor group?" *Forbes*, 20 November.

EDS History Timeline (2008) https://web.archive.org/web/20090331200616/http:// www.eds.com/about/history/timeline.aspx (accessed 27 August 2015).

Engwall, L. (2015) "Corporations and universities," *European Review*, 23(4): 501–510.

Engwall, L. and Kipping, M. (2013) "Management consulting: Dynamics, debates and directions," *International Journal of Strategic Communication*, 7(2): 84–98.

Ernst, B. and Kieser, A. (2002) "In search of explanations for the consulting explosion," in K. Sahlin-Andersson and L. Engwall (eds), *The Expansion of Management Knowledge*, Stanford, CA: Stanford University Press, pp. 47–73.

Fincham, R. and Evans, M. (1999) "The consultants' offensive: Reengineering: from fad to technique," *New Technology, Work and Employment*, 14(1): 32–44.

FCLT, 25 October 2015. *Focusing Capital on the Long Term*. www.fclt.org/en/home.html.

Gapper, J. (2013) "The strategy consultants in search of a strategy," *Financial Times*, 28 August.

Gaston-Breton, T. (1999) *La saga Cap Gemini*, Paris: Éditions Point de mire.

George S. May International, 25 October 2015. www.linkedin.com/company/george-s. -may-international.

Haines, L. (2003) "Rebranding kiss of death strikes Deloitte Consulting." www.theregister. co.uk/2003/04/07/rebranding_kiss_of_death_strikes (accessed 29 August 2015).

Hamm, S. (2006) *Bangalore Tiger: How Indian tech upstart Wipro is rewriting the rules of global competition*, New York: McGraw-Hill.

Hammonds, K. H. (2001) "Scient's near-death experience," *Fast Company*, 43 (February): 98–109.

Hardy, Q. (2012) "H.P. takes $8 billion charge on E.D.S. acquisition," *New York Times*, 8 August.

Hill, A. (2014) "Dissolving of boundaries lets in more consultancy competitors," *Financial Times*, 10 November.

IBM, 7 January 2016. http://www-03.ibm.com/ibm/history/history/year_1992.html.

IBM Corporate Archives (2002) "IBM Global Services: A brief history." http://www-03. ibm.com/ibm/history/documents/pdf/gservices.pdf (accessed 20 August 2015).

Infosys, 25 October 2015. www.fundinguniverse.com/company-histories/infosys-technolo gies-ltd-history.

Jackson, C. and Smalley, M. (2011) *The Story of the PA Consulting Group: 1943–1992*, Northampton: RA Retirers Association.

Jones, E. (1995) *True and Fair: A history of Price Waterhouse*, London: Hamish Hamilton.

Kihn, M. (2005) *House of Lies: How management consultants steal your watch and then tell you the time*, New York: Warner Business Books.

Kipping, M. (2011) "Hollow from the start? Image professionalism in management consulting," *Current Sociology*, 59(4): 530–50.

Kipping, M. and Kirkpatrick, I. (2013) "Alternative pathways of change in professional service firms: The case of management consulting,' *Journal of Management Studies*, 50(5): 777–807.

Lazo, A. (2009) "BearingPoint seeks bankruptcy protection," *Washington Post*, 19 February.

Lofty, S. (2015) "M & A as a competitive advantage: The case of CGI," MBA Independent Study, Schulich School of Business, Toronto.

McDonald, D. (2013) *The Firm: The story of McKinsey and its secret influence on American business*, New York: Simon & Schuster.

McDougald, M. G. and Greenwood, R. (2012) "Cuckoo in the nest? The rise of management consulting in large accounting firms," in M. Kipping and T. Clark (eds), *The Oxford Handbook of Management Consulting*, Oxford: Oxford University Press, pp. 93–116.

MCG (2014) *Annual report and accounts*, Management Consulting Group PLC. www.mcgp lc.com/pdf/mcgplc-full-year-report-2014-v2.pdf (accessed 7 January 2016).

McGann, J. G. (2015) "Global Go To Think Tank Index," University of Pennsylvania, Think Tanks and Civil Societies Program.

McKenna, C. D. (2006) *The World's Newest Profession: Management consulting in the twentieth century*, New York: Cambridge University Press.

Micklethwait, J. and Wooldridge, A. (1996) *The Witch Doctors: What management gurus are saying, why it matters and how to make sense of it*, London: Heinemann.

Mintzberg, H. (1996) "Musings on management," *Harvard Business Review*, 74(4): 61–67.

O'Shea, J. and Madigan, C. (1997) *Dangerous Company: The consulting powerhouses and the businesses they save and ruin*, New York: Times Business.

Phillips, T. (2001) "Indigestion: Cap Gemini's merger struggles," *New York Times*, 23 November.

Pinault, L. (2000) *Consulting Demons: Inside the unscrupulous world of global corporate consulting*, New York: Harper Business.

Squires, S. E., Smith, C. J., McDougall, L., and Yeack, W. R. (2003) *Inside Arthur Andersen: Shifting values, unexpected consequences*, London: FT Press.

Stalk, G. and Hout, T. M. (1990) *Competing Against Time: How time-based competition is reshaping global markets*, New York: The Free Press.

Stevens, M. (1981) *The Big Eight*, New York: Macmillan.

Stevens, M. (1991) *The Big Six: The selling out of America's top accounting firms*, New York: Simon & Schuster.

Stockman, F. (2011) "Local consultants aided Khadafy," *Boston Globe*, 4 March.

TCS, 25 October 2015. www.tcs.com/about/heritage_values/Pages/default.aspx.

Toffler, B. L. and Reingold, J. (2003) *Final Accounting: Ambition, greed, and the fall of Arthur Andersen*, New York: Broadway Books.

Wiener, H. (2002) "TFH Flashback: After 40 years, the consent decree is lifted," *The Four Hundred*, 11(11), 18 March. www.itjungle.com/tfh/tfh031802-story10.html (accessed 19 August 2015).

Wright, C. and Kipping, M. (2012) "The engineering origins of management consulting – and their long shadow," in M. Kipping and T. Clark (eds), *The Oxford Handbook of Management Consulting*, Oxford: Oxford University Press, pp. 29–49.

15

MERGERS AND MASS MARKETS IN MEDIA

The most recent period has seen considerable authority building for business media, which have been part of a concentration process with successive mergers and acquisitions leading to a limited number of large multinational multi-media houses. These have taken advantage of a growing demand for textbooks as well as increasing pressures on management scholars to publish or perish, namely in journals. At the same time there has been a movement from traditional publishing towards a wider media field. Various kinds of economic information have become significant features of broadcasting media as well as new IT-related media. Nevertheless, old imprints are maintained within the larger organizations and some of the old textbook titles are coming back in edition after edition. All in all, the most recent period is characterized by increased commercialization and internationalization. Actors have become larger and more profit-oriented and the symbiosis with business schools (through textbooks, academic publishing, and rankings), consulting (through popular publishing), and practice (also through popular publishing) has intensified.

Publishers: Concentration among Multinational Multimedia Companies

Wiley, Harper, Macmillan, and McGraw-Hill: Considerable Changes

The four publishers established early — Wiley, Harper, Macmillan, and McGraw-Hill — have been part of major structural changes during the most recent period, including mergers, acquisitions, and the loosening of field boundaries. Among the four, Wiley is still an independent company with a continuing family interest but also quoted on the New York Stock Exchange. It has expanded not only through organic growth but also through a number of acquisitions. In 1989 it

256 Markets Reign

acquired Liss, a publisher of journals in the natural and life sciences, and in 1996 VCH, a publisher of scientific titles based in Germany. And in 1997 it took over Van Nostrand Reinhold, an old competitor in scientific publishing, from Thomson. Two years later, Wiley acquired 55 higher education titles and the publishing house Jossey-Bass from Pearson, the British multinational publishing and educational company. In this way Jossey-Bass got a more stable ownership after periods with Maxwell Communications from 1989 to 1994, the media conglomerate CBS (as Viacom) from 1994 to 1998, and Pearson from 1998 to 1999 (Jacobson et al. 2007: 272, 373–380, 392, and 427).

Later acquisitions included Hungry Minds in 2001, which meant that Wiley brought into its publication lists the widely read *For Dummies* series as well as the study guides *CliffNotes*, the *Webster's New World* dictionaries, *Frommer's* travel guides, the *Betty Crocker* and *Weight Watchers* cookbooks, the *Burpee* gardening titles, and the *Howell Book House* pet series. The resulting broader revenue base (Jacobson et al. 2007: 393–397) made it possible for Wiley to acquire the German GIT Verlag in 2002, founded in 1969 and specializing in science, industry, technology, and medicine. Even more significant for its journal portfolio was the acquisition of UK-based Blackwell in 2007, which at the time of the merger had "partnerships with 665 academic, medical, and professional societies, […] published 825 journals and had more than 6,000 books in print" (Jacobson et al. 2007: 432; see further on Blackwell, pp. 434–437).

More recent acquisitions include, in 2012, Deltak, a provider of platforms and services to support online higher education, and, in 2013, FIZ Chemie Berlin, "a provider of online database products for organic and industrial chemists" (Wiley 5 May 2015). Taken together these acquisitions meant that Wiley experienced a considerable global growth with a significant expansion in scientific publishing in a large number of disciplines. It also meant the exploitation of modern information technology through electronic publishing and online databases. For the management area the acquisition of Blackwell had the effect that a number of titles, among them *FT*45 journals (see Table 15.2), now are published by Wiley-Blackwell. Wiley has also an extensive list of monographs in various aspects of management such as leadership (e.g., Schein 1985; Lawrence 2010), organization design (Galbraith 2005), marketing (e.g., Normann 1984; Grönroos 2007), finance (e.g. Fabozzi and Markowitz 2011), and information technology (e.g., Cortada 2009).

While Wiley has remained an independent company, this is not the case for Harper. As mentioned in Chapter 12, in 1962 it acquired Row, Peterson & Company, becoming Harper & Row. In 1987 this company, in turn, was bought by Rupert Murdoch's News Corporation and in 1989 was renamed HarperCollins after mergers and acquisitions with Collins & Sons as well as Scott Foresman and Little Brown. However, in 1996 HarperCollins sold its Educational Publishing to Pearson, and three years later acquired the Hearst Book Group including William Morrow & Company and Avon Books. As a result, in 2015 HarperCollins describes itself as "a broad-based publisher with strengths in literary and commercial fiction, business books, children's books, cookbooks, narrative nonfiction, mystery, romance, reference, pop culture, design, health, wellness, and religious and spiritual books" (HarperCollins 5 May 2015).

As far as business books are concerned, its titles have been mainly popular management books. Among their authors is Kenneth Blanchard, co-author of *The One Minute Manager* (Blanchard and Johnson 1981) with several other titles (e.g., Blanchard, Zigarmi, and Zigarmi 1985; Blanchard and Peale 1988; Blanchard and Shula 2002). Other well-known management books from Harper & Row and HarperCollins are *In Search of Excellence* by the two McKinsey consultants Thomas J. Peters and Robert H. Waterman (1982), *Reengineering the Corporation* by Michael Hammer and James Champy (1993), and several books by management guru Peter Drucker (1981, 1985 and 1989), including the 34th printing of his 1954 book *The Practice of Management* in 1980 (see Box 9.2).

The third of the four early entrants, Macmillan, sold out its US operations in 1896, but re-entered in 1952 as St. Martin's Press (James 2002: xxvii, 187; see also Chapters 6 and 12). In 1994 Macmillan Publishing USA, including the above mentioned Jossey-Bass, was acquired by the media conglomerate Paramount (previously Gulf+Western). However, in 1998 Pearson acquired Macmillan as well as Simon & Schuster Educational, Professional and Reference, Jossey-Bass, Allyn & Bacon, and Prentice-Hall. But one year later it sold Macmillan to the German Verlagsgruppe Georg von Holtzbrinck, which created the Macmillan group, where Palgrave Macmillan deals with the academic publishing (Jacobson et al. 2007: 271–273 and 427). It has over the years published a large number of titles in management, for example, books by Karen Legge on human resource management (Legge 1995), Dimitris Chorafas on transaction management (Chorafas 1998), Robert Cooper on corporate treasury (Cooper 2003), Neil Hood on the multinational subsidiary (Hood 2003), James Abegglen on Japanese management (Abegglen 2006), and Peter Buckley on multinationals (Buckley 2006). Palgrave Macmillan also publishes a dozen journals in management, with the *Journal of International Business Studies* as the most prestigious due to its inclusion in the *FT*45 list (see Table 12.2). In May 2015 Palgrave Macmillan was merged with Springer Science+Business Media into Springer Nature (Springer 18 February 2016).

The last of the four, McGraw-Hill, strengthened its position in the field of higher education through the acquisition, in 1988, of the school and college division of Random House and, in 1996, of the Times Mirror Higher Education, including Irwin, Mosby College, and Wm. C. Brown. Further additions to the company were made in 1999 and 2000 through the acquisitions of Appleton-Lange and Tribune Education, respectively (Jacobson et al. 2007: 272 and 427). Thereafter McGraw-Hill took a number of steps into digital education: online assessment (2006), a device for "all-digital teaching and learning exchange for higher education" (2009), an "automated service that captures class lectures for college students" (2010), a system "to provide universal access to its digital content and tools directly from any learning management system at any college or

258 Markets Reign

university" (2011), and the adoption of an "industry-leading adaptive learning technology, directly to students" (2012). At the same time the company was quite successful with new editions of old books from acquired companies, particularly Irwin. *Principles of Corporate Finance* (Brealey and Myers 1980) was thus in 2014 published in its 11th edition, *Management Control Systems* (Anthony, Dearden, and Vancil 1965) in its 18th edition (Anthony and Govindarajan 2014) as well as in a first European edition (Anthony et al. 2014), and *Transnational Management* (Bartlett and Ghoshal 1992) in its seventh edition (Bartlett and Beamish 2014). In addition, McGraw-Hill published a number of other titles, among them *Management Education and Development: Drift or Thrust into the 21st Century?* (Porter and McKibbin 1988) which has particular relevance for the present book by questioning features of management education in the US (see Chapters 10 and 13).

In 2011 the McGraw-Hill Company was split into two: McGraw-Hill Education and McGraw-Hill Financial. While the basis for the first of these was traditional publishing, the second had started with the acquisition in 1966 of the rating firm Standard & Poor's (see Chapter 12). In 2013 McGraw-Hill Education was sold to the private-equity firm Apollo Global Management LLC (McGraw-Hill Education May 5 2015). The case of McGraw-Hill thus provides further evidence for the restructuring of the field as well as for the move towards modern information technology. It also demonstrates an interest in publishing houses by private equity as a rather clear indication for their commercial potential. Needless to say, McGraw-Hill Financial today plays a significant role in the business world as a whole.

Further Restructuration of the Field

Thus, mergers and acquisitions have been numerous in the publishing field. Regarding the additional publishers mentioned in Chapter 12, i.e., Irwin, Prentice-Hall, Rand McNally, Addison-Wesley, The Free Press, Pergamon Press, and SAGE, Irwin was, as mentioned, acquired by McGraw-Hill. Similarly, Prentice-Hall, which ended up with Pearson in 1998, brought the new owner a number of well-cited monographs, such as Richard Scott's *Organizations: Rational, Natural and Open Systems* (Scott 1981), Gary Yukl's *Leadership in Organizations* (Yukl 1981), Henry Mintzberg's *Power in and Around Organizations* (Mintzberg 1983), and *Positive Accounting Theory* by Watts and Zimmerman (1986). Rand McNally is still a going concern but with limited publishing in the management area. Addison-Wesley, which had published the bestseller *Corporate Cultures* (Deal and Kennedy 1982), was in 1988 acquired by Pearson and in 1998 merged with Simon & Schuster into Pearson Education. In this way Pearson also got The Free Press, the publisher, among others, of Oliver Williamson's *The Economic Institutions of Capitalism* (Williamson 1985), which since 1994 was part of Simon & Schuster. Pergamon Press was acquired by Elsevier in 1992. SAGE, however, remained independent and considerably expanded its publication of books as well as journals (see further below).

Another important event in the publishing industry related to the management publishing field was that Random House – after a period with Advance Publications from 1980 to 1998, which divested Random House Higher Education to McGraw-Hill in 1988 – became a part of the German publishing group Bertelsmann, which in 1986 had already acquired Doubleday. Bertelsmann also bought Springer-Verlag in 1999 but then sold BertelsmannSpringer in 2003 to British investment groups, which merged it in 2004 with the Dutch Kluwer Academic Publishers into Springer Science+Business Media. Earlier mergers had occurred between Wolters and Kluwer in 1987 as well as between Reed and Elsevier in 1992 (on Elsevier, see Box 15.1).

BOX 15.1 ELSEVIER: SCIENCE, PRESTIGE – AND PROFITS

Elsevier, part of the RELX Group – previously Reed Elsevier after a merger with Reed in 1992 – was in 2015 one of the world's major journal publishers with over 2,500 journals, among them the prestigious *The Lancet* and *Cell*. In addition it offers 33,000 book titles, and various web-based digital solutions such as *ScienceDirect, Scopus, Elsevier Research Intelligence* and *ClinicalKey*. Among its titles are also a number of publications in the management area. It is a highly profitable business that has prompted protests from the scientific community against very high prices, the bundling of journals into packages to libraries and the restriction of the free exchange of information. The present profitability contrasts with the first half of the twentieth century when Elsevier had economic problems. Founded in 1880 in Amsterdam, the company was in the 1930s struggling with considerable debts and large stocks of unsold books. In response to these problems a new management turned abroad by selling encyclopaedias on the Belgian market and starting to publish German scientific texts, first in German and later on in English. This led, among other things, to the creation of Elsevier's *Encyclopedia of Organic Chemistry*, which was officially announced after the end of World War II in 1946. The first volumes were well received but did not attract enough subscribers to make the project economically successful and it was therefore sold to Springer in 1953. It had given Elsevier scientific prestige however, which made established scientists approach the company for the publication of their journals. One of them was *Biochemica et Biophysica Acta*, which became the platform for Elsevier's expansion into the market of scientific journal publication. Over time Elsevier increased the number of journals considerably by launching new ones but also through the acquisitions of other companies such as North-Holland in 1971 and Pergamon Press in 1992 – ultimately going from deficits to high profits. In 2004 Elsevier also took up the competition with Thomson Reuters' Web of Science by launching its own data base Scopus.

Sources: Andriesse (2008); Elsevier 4 June 2015; and the *Guardian* 4 June 2015.

In the 1980s, Thomson divested the *Times*, the *Sunday Times*, and some other parts of the group, and then, in 1998 acquired the Reuters group, turning Thomson Reuters into a leading supplier of economic information (for further information on Thomson, see Box 15.2). It also became a significant provider of systems for peer reviews of scientific papers and bibliometrics through the Web of Science. At the same time Thomson sold Routledge, a social sciences publisher founded in 1851, which it had acquired in 1987, to Taylor & Francis, which in turn was merged into the multinational media company Informa in 2004. Nevertheless, Routledge remains a separate imprint, describing itself as "the world's leading academic publisher in the Humanities and Social Sciences" (Routledge 5 May 2015). It publishes more than a thousand journals, of which about one-fifth are in the area of "Economics, Finance, Business & Industry."

While generally marked by concentration, the field also saw a new entrant in 1986: Edward Elgar. This is a family-owned international company that considers itself "a leading international publisher of academic books and journals in economics, finance, business and management, law, environment, public and social policy" (Edward Elgar 5 May 2015). It publishes both monographs and journals in the management area.

These changes among the commercial publishers put considerable pressure on the university presses. While the 1960s were good years for the university presses as a result of the expansion of the academic system, in the following decades they faced economic cutbacks as library costs, particularly for the commercially published journals, went up. Iowa University Press for instance was sold to Blackwell in 2000 and University of Idaho Press was closed down in 2004. In addition, university presses tended to collaborate more. Thus, some large university presses, like the University of Chicago Press, the Michigan University Press, and the Johns Hopkins University Press, came to serve as distributors for a number of smaller presses (Jagodzinski 2008: 12). In the management area, Harvard particularly received considerable visibility through the publication of titles like *Relevance Lost* (Johnson and Kaplan 1987), *Organizational Ecology* (Hannan and Freeman 1989), and *The Transformation of Corporate Control* (Fligstein 1990). With respect to business education the establishment of Harvard Business Publishing in 1994 for the selling of cases and articles was a significant step.

On the other side of the Atlantic the period saw increasing attention to the management area from both Oxford University Press and Cambridge University Press. As far as Oxford University Press is concerned, its expansion in the management publishing field was preceded by a careful analysis of the market (Musson 1991) based on *Competitive Strategy* (Porter 1980) and the classical marketing article "Marketing Myopia" (Levitt 1960). Consequently, Oxford University Press added a line of titles to its already large publication list: as of 2000–2001 it was the largest of the university presses with an annual revenue of 600 million US dollars, twice as much as Cambridge University Press and way beyond the American university presses (Thompson 2005: 87–89 and Box 6.1).

Mergers and Mass Markets in Media **261**

BOX 15.2 THOMSON REUTERS: FROM FLEET STREET TO WEB OF SCIENCE

The history of Thomson Reuters is closely related to the late Roy Thomson, the first Baron of Fleet, born in Toronto in 1894. His engagement in the media business started in 1934 with the acquisition of the Timmins Press in Northern Ontario and continued with further acquisitions in Canada, before he started his move into the United Kingdom by acquiring *The Scotsman* in 1953. Later in the 1950s he went into television through a commercial television franchise for Central Scotland. He also acquired the Kemsley Group, which included a number of national and regional UK newspapers, among them the *Sunday Times*. In 1967 Thomson also bought the *Times* of London from the Aston family as well as a number of other newspapers in North America and the United Kingdom. In addition he created a travel company in 1965, and in the early 1970s joined a consortium to exploit oil in the North Sea. At Roy Thomson's death in 1976 the company was thus a veritable conglomerate. His son Kenneth successively changed the company by divesting the interests in Scottish television in 1977, the *Times* of London in 1981, the interests in North Sea oil in 1989, all remaining UK newspapers in 1995, the Thomson travel agency in 1998 and North American newspapers in 2000. Instead he concentrated the business on textbook publishing and the handling of financial, healthcare, legal, and bibliometric information through a number of new investments. Among the acquisitions, that of the Institute of Scientific Information (ISI) in 1992 is particularly relevant here, since it meant a step into the measurement of academic output with a focus on citations, impact factors, and rankings. Highly significant is of course also the merger between Thomson and Reuters, which occurred after the death of Roy Thomson's son Kenneth in 2006 and further developed the orientation toward information processing. Although a significant part of the activities of Thomson Reuters focuses on business information, another important part concerns the handling of bibliometric information through the Web of Science and through its platforms for the handling of manuscripts for academic journals.

Source: Thomson Reuters Company History 4 June 2015.

As a result of the changes summarized above, the management publishing field in 2013 was to a large extent controlled by a limited number of multinational media companies with Pearson, Reed Elsevier, Thomson Reuters, Wolters Kluwer, and Random House at the top (Table 15.1). Further down the list are Holzbrinck, ranked 9, Wiley, ranked 12, Springer Science+Business Media, ranked 16, and HarperCollins, ranked 19. The two British university presses in Oxford and Cambridge are also among the 50 largest book publishers in the world, ranked 21 and 43 respectively. Between them is Simon & Schuster, ranked 29. Although there is a dominance of Anglo-American companies in the

262 Markets Reign

TABLE 15.1 The Largest Publishers Involved in Management Publishing in 2013

Rank	Publishing company (group or division)	Revenue (million US dollars)	Country	Owner	Country of ownership
1	Pearson	9,158	UK	Pearson (Corp.)	UK
2	Reed Elsevier	5,934	UK/NL/US	Reed Elsevier (Corp.)	UK/NL/US
3	Thomson Reuters	5,386	US	Woodbridge Company	Canada
4	Wolters Kluwer	4,766	NL	Wolters Kluwer	NL
5	Random House	3,328	Germany	Bertelsmann AG	Germany
8	McGraw-Hill Education	2,292	US	McGraw-Hill Companies	US
9	Holtzbrinck	2,220	Germany	Verlagsgruppe Georg von Holtzbrinck	Germany
12	Wiley	1,783	US	Wiley	US
16	Springer Science + Business Media	1,298	Germany	BC Partners, EQT and GIC Investors	UK, Sweden, Singapore
19	HarperCollins	1,189	US	News Corporation	US
21	Oxford University Press	1,125	UK	Oxford University	UK
29	Simon & Schuster	790	US	CBS	US
43	Cambridge University Press	396	UK	Cambridge University	UK

Sources: Publishers Weekly 5 May 2015. For similar evidence, see Thompson (2005: 58–59).

list, there is also Dutch, German, and Swedish ownership in the field – especially when it comes to publishing in languages other than English. In that context the publishing of management textbooks has become very attractive and profitable due to the growing enrollment in business education (see Chapter 13). By contrast, the research monograph has been pushed back by an increasing emphasis on journal article publications (see, for a general discussion of this phenomenon, Thompson 2005: 82–110, and regarding the textbook market, 195–306).

Based on the above evidence there can be no doubt that the management publishing field has undergone a strong restructuration since the preceding period with mergers and acquisitions of previously independent companies into large multinational multimedia companies. In the words of Hemmungs-Wirtén (2007: 404), "the growth of an increasingly transnational and global media market, conglomeratization, content, and convergence proved a combination that dramatically, and permanently, changed the face of publishing between 1970 and 2000." Similar conclusions are drawn by a number of others such as Thompson (2005: 47–77, and 2010: 100–145), Schiffrin (2000) and De Bellaigue (2004).

The Business Press: Changing Ownerships in Booming Markets

The most recent period has also been a boom period for the business press. Deregulation of financial markets and a general market orientation meant that business news expanded in all types of media worldwide. Thus, the *Financial Times* had, according to Kynaston (2009) "become one of the very few genuinely international papers as it completed its first century [in 1988]." Already two years earlier it had passed 250,000 copies in circulation, of which one-fourth came from overseas. A worldwide expansion followed: The *FT* started printing in New York in 1985, followed by Paris in 1988, Tokyo in 1990, Madrid, Stockholm, and Los Angeles, all in 1995, then Hong Kong in 1996. It also launched and sometimes closed down regional editions – as was the case with the German-language *FT Deutschland*. As a result, the *FT* reached a total circulation of 500,000 copies in 2001. Even more readers were attracted when the platform FT.com was introduced in 1995 with a paid-for model launched in 2002. According to Kynaston (2009) "[b]y the end of that year, unique monthly users had reached over 3.2 million and page views over 50 million." In the first quarter of 2014 the *FT* had, according to a Deloitte assured survey, 665,000 subscribers to its print and digital publication. But in July 2015 Pearson sold the *FT* to the Japanese business media group Nikkei (Pearson 28 July 2015). The deal did not include Pearson's 50 percent ownership in the *Economist*, which, in 2002, had followed the *Financial Times'* 1998 initiative to publish ranking lists of business schools (see Chapter 13) – lists that have meant a special relationship and authority in relation to management education (see further Wedlin 2006: 6–7). In August 2015, the stake in the *Economist* was instead sold to the Agnelli family (Yeomans 2015).

The *Wall Street Journal*, the US counterpart to the *Financial Times'* had been published by Dow Jones & Co. since its early years and was owned by the Bancroft family from the 1920s onwards (Wendt 1982). However, in 2007 Dow Jones & Co. was acquired by Rupert Murdoch's News Corporation, which since 1987–1989 owned HarperCollins (see above) and now added the Dow Jones index, the *Wall Street Journal*, and the business weekly *Barron's* (Pérez-Peña 2007). This provided a strong relationship to the business community for Murdoch's media empire, particularly since the *Wall Street Journal* in 2010 was the largest US newspaper with a circulation of 2.1 million including 414,000 subscribers of the electronic edition (Plambeck 2010). Moreover, through ranking lists of business schools since 2001 it provides links to management education.

Business Week, founded in 1929 by McGraw-Hill, also changed ownership in the most recent period. It was sold in 2009 to Bloomberg LP, a company providing electronic services to the financial markets, founded in 1981 by Michael Bloomberg, the Mayor of New York between 2001 and 2013 – services now supplemented with a recognized magazine. After the acquisition it was renamed *Bloomberg Businessweek*. Again, a special relationship to business schools can be noted through rankings, starting with the ranking of MBA programs in 1988 (see

264 Markets Reign

Chapter 13). Similar rankings had been launched five years earlier by another of the established business magazines, *Forbes*. Like *Business Week* it found a new owner in the twenty-first century as the Hong Kong–based investor group Integrated Whale Media Investments bought *Forbes* in 2014 (Trachtenberg 2014). *Fortune*, finally, has remained a title published by Time Inc. and is best known for its listings of the largest corporations.

Business newspapers and magazines were also successfully published outside the Anglo-American countries. Among those titles mentioned in Chapter 9, the French *Les Échos* as well as the German *Wirtschaftswoche* and *Manager Magazin* continued publication into the twenty-first century. *Les Échos* also experienced an ownership change, when Pearson, which had bought the newspaper in 1988, sold it to luxury goods conglomerate LVMH in 2007. *Wirtschaftswoche* was part of Verlagsgruppe Georg von Holtzbrinck (see above) but, together with a number of other titles like *Handelsblatt*, was sold to another member of the von Holtzbrinck family in 2009 (Von Hülsen 2009), while the Spiegel group remained the majority owner of *Manager Magazin*. *Wirtschaftswoche* has, like its Anglo-American counterparts, provided ranking lists of educational institutions. Some new titles appeared during this period, such as the Spanish *Expansión* and the Chinese *Economic Observer* founded in 1986 and 2001, respectively.

In addition to the rankings of business schools and programs, bestseller lists of management books also became a significant feature of the business press in the most recent period. These helped to diffuse what Gibson Burrell (1989: 307) has referred to as the "Heathrow Organization Theory". Well-known examples from the 1980s and 1990s on these bestseller lists were: *Competitive Strategy* (Porter 1980), *Corporate Cultures* (Deal and Kennedy 1982), *In Search of Excellence* (Peters and Waterman 1982), *Change Masters* (Kanter 1983), *Competitive Advantage* (Porter 1985), *When Giants Learn to Dance* (Kanter 1989), *Strategic Flexibility* (Hamel and Prahalad 1994), and *Reengineering the Corporation* (Hammer and Champy 1993). These lists constituted a link between the media and business schools as well as consulting firms, since the authors were generally business school faculty members or consultants. At the same time ideas and practices taught in business schools or used in consulting projects came from such popular books (Engwall 2012). They also became very important for the creation of corporate images, i.e., the branding of corporations, business schools, and consulting firms. Thus the business press was important in promoting books by successful leaders such as Lee Iacocca (Iacocca 1984) as well as their biographies (e.g., Crainer 1999 on Jack Welch of General Electric and Maynard 1995 on Jack Smith of General Motors) – books, which served to popularize and further legitimize management through the omnipotent, indeed heroic imagery that they have typically contained (see further Guthey, Clark, and Jackson 2009).

In conclusion, the restructuring of the publishing field discussed above also had an effect on the business press. The major titles have become part of larger media conglomerates, where online publishing and information retrieval are growing in

Mergers and Mass Markets in Media **265**

importance. At the same time the business press has been important for the establishment of business school rankings and the promotion of management books.

Academic Journals: Scholars and Publishers in Interaction

Another Dozen FT*45 Journals*

In the previous three periods *FT*45 titles were added by five, four and twenty-four titles, respectively. The additional 12 titles were started in the most recent period (Table 15.2). Again, there were initiatives of professional associations: Informs (The Institute for Operations Research and the Management Sciences), the Canadian Academic Accounting Association, the Academy of Management, the Society for Financial Studies, and the Production and Operations Management Society. Some journals were also started by publishers, including Elsevier, Kluwer, and North-Holland. Together the new journals demonstrate the

TABLE 15.2 Journals among the *FT*45 Founded since 1980

Name	Founded	First publisher	Present publisher
Journal of Business Ethics	1982	D. Riedel Publishing	Springer Science+Business Media
Marketing Science	1982	Informs	Informs
Contemporary Accounting Research	1984	Canadian Academic Accounting Association	Wiley-Blackwell
Journal of Business Venturing	1986	Elsevier	Elsevier
Academy of Management Perspectives	1987	Academy of Management	Academy of Management
Review of Financial Studies	1988	Society for Financial Studies with Oxford University Press	Oxford University Press
Journal of Financial Economics	1989	North-Holland	Elsevier
Information Systems Research	1990	Informs	Informs
Organization Science	1990	Informs	Informs
Journal of Consumer Psychology	1992	Lawrence Erlbaum Associates	Elsevier
Production and Operations Management	1992	Production and Operations Management Society	Wiley
Review of Accounting Studies	1996	Kluwer	Springer Science+Business Media

increasing specialization that management research is undergoing. It should also be noted that some of the titles have changed hands since their foundation. This is again a reflection of the structural changes in the management publishing field discussed above. Moreover, as pointed out by Thompson (2005: 100–101), the transition of journal publication from professional societies to commercial publishers often implies increases in subscription prices.

An interesting feature is that the two professional associations Informs and Academy of Management both are adding to their earlier publications. Informs, which has its roots in operations research, broadened its publication efforts to include marketing (*Marketing Science*), informatics (*Information Systems Research*), as well as organization research (*Organization Science*), and in 2015 launched yet another journal, this time in the strategy area: *Strategy Science* (Strategy Science 1 August 2015). As for the Academy of Management it started a more practitioner-oriented journal in 1987, first called the *Academy of Management Executive*, then renamed the *Executive* in 1990, changed back to the *Academy of Management Executive* in 1993, and finally received its present name, the *Academy of Management Perspectives*, in 2006 (ResearchGate 5 May 2015). This development clearly demonstrates a perceived need – and the difficulty – to address the business community at a time when academic research was moving away from practical issues (see also Chapter 13). It could also be seen as an effort to match the *Harvard Business Review*, the *Sloan Management Review*, and the *California Management Review* as well as publications by consulting firms such as the *McKinsey Quarterly*.

In terms of topics, the new journals and their inclusion in the *FT*45 list illustrate the development of the management discipline. Among the new titles are thus one on business ethics, another on business venturing, and two directed toward finance. All three topics were receiving more interest from the 1980s onward. It can also be noted that some of the new journals have been able to obtain impact factors above the 2013 average of 2.962 (Table 15.3): *Organization Science* (3.807), the *Journal of Financial Economics* (3.769), the *Review of Financial Studies* (3.532), and the *Journal of Business Venturing* (3.265).

Among the journals at the top are both flagships of the Academy of Management: the *Academy of Management Review* (7.827) and the *Academy of Management Journal* (4.974) as well as the *Journal of Finance* (6.033), the *Quarterly Journal of Economics* (5.966), and the *MIS Quarterly* (5.405). At the other end, below the average, are eight of the twelve new titles but also some of the longer established titles such as *Management Science*, founded in 1954 (2.524), the *Administrative Science Quarterly* (1956/2.394), the *Accounting Review* (1926/2.234), the *Journal of the American Statistical Association* (1888/2.114), the *California Management Review* (1958/1.994), the *Harvard Business Review* (1922/1.831), *Operations Research* (1956/1.500), and the *Sloan Management Review* (1959/0.970). It therefore seems that first mover advantages have been limited within the population of *FT*45 journals.

Mergers and Mass Markets in Media **267**

TABLE 15.3 Two-year Impact Factors, 2013, and Years of Foundation for the *FT*45 Journals

Name of journal	Two-year impact factor 2013	Founded
Academy of Management Review	7.817	1976
Journal of Finance	6.033	1946
Quarterly Journal of Economics	5.966	1886
MIS Quarterly	5.405	1977
Academy of Management Journal	4.974	1958
Journal of Operations Management	4.478	1980
Journal of Applied Psychology	4.367	1917
Journal of Marketing	3.819	1936
Organization Science	3.807	1990
Journal of Financial Economics	3.769	1989
Journal of Political Economy	3.617	1892
Journal of International Business Studies	3.594	1970
Review of Financial Studies	3.532	1988
Econometrica	3.504	1933
American Economic Review	3.305	1911
Journal of Management Studies	3.277	1964
Journal of Business Venturing	3.265	1986
Strategic Management Journal	2.993	1980
Organizational Behavior and Human Decision Processes	2.897	1966
Journal of Accounting and Economics	2.833	1979
Academy of Management Perspectives	2.826	1987
Journal of Consumer Research	2.783	1974
Journal of Marketing Research	2.660	1964
Management Science	2.524	1954
Organization Studies	2.504	1980
Journal of Accounting Research	2.449	1963
Entrepreneurship Theory and Practice	2.447	1976
Administrative Science Quarterly	2.394	1956
Information Systems Research	2.322	1990
Accounting Review	2.234	1926
Marketing Science	2.208	1982
Journal of the American Statistical Association	2.114	1888
Accounting, Organisations and Society	2.109	1976
California Management Review	1.944	1958
Journal of Financial and Quantitative Analysis	1.877	1966
Harvard Business Review	1.831	1922
Production and Operations Management	1.759	1992

Name of journal	Two-year impact factor 2013	Founded
Journal of Consumer Psychology	1.708	1992
Journal of Business Ethics	1.552	1982
Contemporary Accounting Research	1.533	1984
Operations Research	1.500	1956
Human Resource Management	1.395	1961
Rand Journal of Economics	1.219	1970
Review of Accounting Studies	1.167	1996
Sloan Management Review	0.970	1959
Median	2.722	1970

Significant Papers and Author Origins

An analysis of the most cited papers in each of the *FT*45 journals in the recent period (Table 15.4) reveals that some of them have received considerable attention. At the very top is the *Journal of Marketing* paper "Reinventing Marketing to Manage the Environmental Imperative" from 2011 by Philip Kotler, a guru among marketing scholars (see Box 12.1). The following five papers were published in *Organizational Behavior and Human Decision Processes* (Ajzen 1991), *Academy of Management Review* (Eisenhardt 1989), *Administrative Science Quarterly* (Cohen and Levinthal 1990), the *Journal of Marketing Research* (Fornell and Larcker 1981), and the *Journal of Political Economy* (Romer 1990).

As shown in Table 15.4 all the mentioned articles were published in journals founded before the most recent period. The first paper to break this tendency is "A Dynamic Theory of Organizational Knowledge Creation" (Nonaka 1994) in *Organization Science*, which explicitly was founded in 1990 as a challenger to existing organization journals. Another successful new entrant is the *Journal of Financial Economics* with the paper "Common Risk Factors in the Returns on Stocks and Bonds" (Fama and French 1993) with a later Nobel Laureate as one of the co-authors. It is also worth noting that the Japanese management scholar Ikujiro Nonaka managed to publish two papers on the top list: the above mentioned "A Dynamic Theory of Organizational Knowledge Creation" (Nonaka 1994) and "The Knowledge-creating Company" (Nonaka 1991) in the *Harvard Business Review*.

Further information on publication behavior in the most recent period can be obtained through a comparison with the results from studies of a sample of 15 management journals covering all major areas of research (Engwall and Danell 2011). This sample included six general management journals (the *Academy of Management Journal*, the *Academy of Management Review*, the *Journal of Management*, the *Journal of Management Studies, Management Science*, and the *Strategic Management*

TABLE 15.4 The 15 Top Papers in the *FT*45 Journals in the Recent Period According to Google Scholar in December 2014

Journal name	Founded	Reference	Title	Citations
Journal of Marketing	1936	Kotler (2011)	Reinventing marketing to manage the environmental imperative	37,093
Organizational Behavior and Human Decision Processes	1966	Ajzen (1991)	The theory of planned behavior	29,189
Academy of Management Review	1976	Eisenhardt (1989)	Building theories from case study research	27,836
Administrative Science Quarterly	1956	Cohen and Levinthal (1990)	Absorptive capacity: a new perspective on learning and innovation	23,919
Journal of Marketing Research	1964	Fornell and Larcker (1981)	Evaluating structural equation models with unobservable variables and measurement error	22,760
Journal of Political Economy	1892	Romer (1990)	Endogenous technological change	18,643
Organization Science	1990	Nonaka (1994)	A dynamic theory of organizational knowledge creation	15,007
Journal of Applied Psychology	1917	Podsakoff et al. (2003)	Common method biases in behavioral research: a critical review of the literature and recommended remedies	13,690
Journal of Financial Economics	1989	Fama and French (1993)	Common risk factors in the returns on stocks and bonds	13,627
Management Science	1954	Davis, Bagozzi and Warshaw (1989)	User acceptance of computer technology: a comparison of two theoretical models	11,601
MIS Quarterly	1977	Venkatesh et al. (2003)	User acceptance of information technology: Toward a unified view	9,810
Strategic Management Journal	1980	Peteraf (1993)	The cornerstones of competitive advantage: A resource-based view	8,945
Harvard Business Review	1922	Nonaka (1991)	The knowledge-creating company	8,160

Journal name	Founded	Reference	Title	Citations
Econometrica	1933	Melitz (2003)	The impact of trade on intra-industry reallocations and aggregate industry productivity	7,158
Information Systems Research	1990	DeLone and McLean (1992)	Information systems success: the quest for the dependent variable	7,072

Sources: Search on Google Scholar in December 2014.

Journal), two organization journals (the *Administrative Science Quarterly* and *Organization Studies*), four accounting journals (the *Accounting Review, Accounting, Organizations and Society*, the *Journal of Accounting and Economics*, and the *Journal of Accounting Research*) and three marketing journals (the *Journal of Consumer Research*, the *Journal of Marketing*, and the *Journal of Marketing Research*). For this sample it was found that during the 1981–1992 period 83 percent of the authors came from North America (the United States and Canada), 11 percent from Europe and 6 percent from the rest of the world.

In the 2005–2009 period, however, the North American dominance had been reduced to 64 percent, while the share of European authors had increased to 24 percent and the rest of the world accounted for 12 percent. Among the top 50 institutions there was only one outside North America in 1981–1992, the University of Manchester, but six in 2005–2009: the Hong Kong University of Science and Technology (HKUST), Erasmus University, INSEAD, Tilburg University, London Business School, and the National University of Singapore. This suggests a relatively strong dominance of a limited number of North American business schools in management journal publications. Similar results are also reported by Heck and Jensen (2007: 114) in their analysis of the papers in the *Accounting Review* between 1926 and 2005: "16 [US] universities are consistently in the top 30 and 12 [US] universities are consistently in the top 20." They also demonstrate the scientization of the discipline: non-academic papers have disappeared almost completely and been replaced by papers dealing with "accountics," i.e., "the mathematical science of values" (p. 117).

In terms of the North American dominance in management journals, Üsdiken (2014) has also shown in a comparison of five US journals (the *Academy of Management Journal*, the *Academy of Management Review*, the *Administrative Science Quarterly*, *Organization Science*, and the *Strategic Management Journal*) and five European journals (the *Journal of Management Studies*, the *British Journal of Management*, *Organization Studies*, *Human Relations*, and the *International Journal of Management Reviews*) that over the 1960–2010 period the decline of US authors has been much lower in the US-based journals than in the European ones. In addition, he shows that the convergence between US and European research styles, as exhibited in the 10 journals, is still limited (see also Üsdiken 2010; Üsdiken and Wasti 2009; Vogel 2012).

Further Growth in Journals

It should be stressed that the journals analyzed above are just a part of the total population of management journals. The expansion of the academic system and the pressure to publish in order to show performance has led to the launching of a large number of new journals over the years. More recently this expansion has come to include online journals. SAGE, for instance, has started SAGE Open, which presents itself as follows: "SAGE Open is an open access publication from

SAGE. It publishes peer-reviewed, original research and review articles in an interactive, open access format. Articles may span the full spectrum of the social and behavioral sciences and the humanities" (SAGE Open 5 May 2015). For this type of publications the publishers earn their revenues through fees. In the case of SAGE Open the acceptance fee in early 2016 was 395 US dollars.

Another open access initiative are the journals published by the non-profit organization Public Library of Science, which emerged in 2000 with the circulation of an open letter by a number of distinguished researchers to promote Open Access. This eventually led to the launching of seven electronic journals under a pay-to-publish model, primarily within science and medicine (PLOS 13 October 2015).

However, the development of information technology has also brought predatory actors into the system. One of them is Scientific Research Publishing, which according to Beall (2012: 9) exists for two reasons: "First, it exists to exploit the author-pays Open Access model to generate revenue, and second, it serves as an easy place for foreign (chiefly Chinese) authors to publish overseas and increase their academic status." Among its more than 200 titles there are a number of recently launched management journals (Scientific Research 5 May 2015): *IBusiness* (2009), the *Journal of Service Science and Management* (2010), the *American Journal of Industrial and Business Management* (2011), the *Journal in Financial Risk Management* (2012), the *Open Journal of Accounting* (2012), and the *Open Journal of Business and Management* (2013). An additional example is Comprehensive Research Journals, which among its titles has the *Comprehensive Research Journal of Management and Business Studies* (CRJMBS 5 May 2015), started in 2013. Like Scientific Research Publishing, Comprehensive Research Journals is considered to belong to a list of questionable publishers. In early 2014 such publishers were estimated to be 477, a number that had increased dramatically from about 20 in 2012 (Beall 2014).

It should also be mentioned that publishing online was adopted already in the 1990s by the established journals. Wiley, for instance, in 1999 launched Wiley InterScience for online access to its journals and other publishers have followed suit. This in turn facilitates the access of articles through databases, namely via subscriptions by university libraries. For individuals, publishers also offer copies of single articles at a cost. Some offer authors the option of open access at a fee, which of course may be positive for citations. Many governments nowadays require that research they have funded be available through open access (Anon. 2013).

The introduction of electronic databases has also facilitated a strong development and use of bibliometrics, i.e., the quantitative analysis of citations of individual articles and the impact of journals. This field has experienced a spectacular growth since the seminal paper "Citation Indexes for Science" by Eugene Garfield (1955), not least through the classification of journals according to impact factors and the evaluation of institutions and individuals on the basis of bibliometrics. In the management area the use of bibliometrics has become particularly strong through the rankings of business schools based on metrics such as the *FT*45 and the

Mergers and Mass Markets in Media **273**

list established by the UK-based Association of Business Schools (ABS). Needless to say, the use of bibliometrics has not only advantages as pointed out in the contributions to Blockmans, Engwall, and Weaire (2014). One effect is that book publishing has become less popular among European management scholars, who instead go for the – not always successful – submission of papers to top journals.

The expansion of the field in terms of both authors and outlets has led to difficulties in following the stream of publications. In response to this, publishers have created various services for researchers. Elsevier, for instance, has launched a Research Highlights App (Elsevier 5 May 2015). In addition, various kinds of search engines, such as Google Scholar, have become significant tools for researchers. This in turn has meant that the words used in the titles of papers have become increasingly vital.

In conclusion, among the journals on the *FT*45 list an additional dozen have been founded in the recent period by professional associations as well as by publishers. Their foundations – as well as that of many other new journals – can be seen as a reflection of an increasing specialization but also of the opportunities seen by publishers. The latter have both launched new journals and taken over journals from professional associations on the basis of their electronic systems for handling manuscripts and their superior marketing capacities. This in turn has had the effect that a few publishers now hold a dominant position in management journal publishing, like in social science in general where the top five publishers – Reed-Elsevier, Wiley-Blackwell, Springer, Taylor & Francis, and SAGE – accounted for 70 percent of publications in 2014 (Larivière, Haustein, and Mongeon 2015: 8). Some of the new journals have become rather successful in terms of impact, which makes it reasonable to assume that the advantages of early movers are limited. It is also evident that some of the papers in the *FT*45 journals have attained considerable attention. In addition, it is apparent that the development of information and communication technologies has changed the conditions for academic publishing.

Looking Ahead

The media has undergone considerable changes during the four periods covered by this book, with a major restructuration of the field, particularly in the last period. In view of what has happened in other industries (Gaughan 2015), it is quite natural to believe that these changes will continue. In line with the reasoning of Levitt (1960) we can anticipate publishers to try and find new solutions in order to avoid myopic behavior. This means that publishing can be expected to increasingly occur electronically and through print-on-demand, which, in turn, will facilitate tailor-made solutions for textbooks and other educational material. In this way adaptations to cultural differences as well as student background can easily be accomplished, which will further stimulate internationalization. The development of information technology is also likely to stimulate interactive solutions through online courses, which would mean a still further blurring of boundaries between business schools and the media.

A significant issue in online courses will be the way educational providers are able to charge for their courses. Similarly, the electronic publishing of business news requires feasible solutions to revenue creation from advertisers and readers. In terms of academic journals, the problem appears to be the opposite, i.e., to break the strong position of publishers. This will not be easy, since the academic community is very eager, and increasingly so, to publish their research results in order to promote their careers. In addition, they demand to have electronic access to the growing number of publications, something their academic institutions have to pay for. This in turn will put strong pressure on university budgets and increase calls for priorities among the numerous titles. In the management area an even more intensive debate can be expected regarding rigor and relevance, i.e., regarding the apparently decreasing practical relevance of the research published (e.g., Davis 2015). Nevertheless, there are reasons to believe that the significance of the media is here to stay, and might even become stronger (see further Thompson 2005: 309−437; Thompson 2010: 312−368; Fitzpatrick 2011; Bhaskar 2013).

References

Abegglen, J. C. (2006) *21st-century Japanese Management: New systems, lasting values.* Basingstoke: Palgrave Macmillan.

Ajzen, I. (1991) "The theory of planned behavior," *Organizational Behavior and Human Decision Processes*, 50(2), 179–211.

Andriesse, C. D. (2008) *Dutch Messengers: A history of science publishing, 1930–1980*, Leiden: Brill.

Anon. (2013) "Free-for-all: Open-access scientific publishing is gaining ground," *Economist*, 168: 4 May.

Anthony, R. N. and Govindarajan, V. (2014) *Management Control Systems*, 18th edn, Boston, MA: McGraw-Hill.

Anthony, R. N., Dearden, J., and Vancil, R. F. (1965) *Management Control Systems: Cases and readings*, Homewood, IL: Irwin.

Anthony, R. N., Govindarajan, V., Hartmann, F. G., Kraus, K., and Nilsson, G. (2014) *Management Control Systems*, European edn, Maidenhead: McGraw-Hill Education.

Bartlett, C. A. and Beamish, P. W. (2014) *Transnational Management: Text, cases and readings in cross-border management*, 7th edn, New York: McGraw-Hill Education.

Bartlett, C. A. and Ghoshal, S. (1992) *Transnational Management: Text, cases and readings in cross-border management*, Homewood, IL: Irwin.

Beall, J. (2012) "Five scholarly open access publishers," *The Charleston Advisor*, 13(4): 5–10.

Beall, J. (2014) "List of predatory publishers 2014," *Scholarly Open Access*, 2 January. http://scholarlyoa.com/2014/01/02/list-of-predatory-publishers-2014 (accessed 5 May 2015).

Bhaskar, M. (2013) *The Content Machine: Towards a theory of publishing from the printing press to the digital networks*, London: Anthem Press.

Blanchard, K. H. and Johnson, S. (1981) *The One Minute Manager*, New York: Morrow.

Blanchard, K. H. and Peale, N. V. (1988) *The Power of Ethical Management*, New York: W. Morrow.

Blanchard, K. H. and Shula, D. (2002) *The Little Book of Coaching: Motivating people to be winners*. London: HarperCollinsBusiness.

Blanchard, K. H., Zigarmi, P., and Zigarmi, D. (1985) *Leadership and the One Minute Manager: Increasing effectiveness through situational leadership*, New York: William Morrow and Co.

Blockmans, W., Engwall, L., and Weaire, D. (eds) (2014) *Bibliometrics: Use and abuse in the Review of Research Performance*, London: Portland Press.

Brealey, R. and Myers, S. (1980) *Principles of Corporate Finance*, New York: McGraw-Hill.

Brealey, R. and Myers, S. (2014) *Principles of Corporate Finance*, 11th edn, New York: McGraw-Hill.

Buckley, P. J. (2006) *The Multinational Enterprise and the Globalization of Knowledge*, Basingstoke: Palgrave Macmillan.

Burrell, G. (1989) "The absent centre: The neglect of philosophy in Anglo-American management theory," *Human Systems Management*, 8(4): 307–312.

Chorafas, D. N. (1998) *Transaction Management: Managing complex transactions and sharing distributed databases*, Basingstoke: Macmillan.

Cohen, W. M. and Levinthal, D. A. (1990) "Absorptive capacity: A new perspective on learning and innovation," *Administrative Science Quarterly*, 35(1): 128–152.

Cooper, R. (2003) *Corporate Treasury and Cash Management*, Basingstoke: Palgrave Macmillan.

Cortada, J. W. (2009) *How Societies Embrace Information Technology: Lessons for management and the rest of us*, Hoboken, NJ: Wiley.

Crainer, S. (1999) *Business the Jack Welch Way: 10 secrets of the world's greatest turnaround king*, New York: Amacom.

CRJMBS, 5 May 2015. www.crjournals.org/CRJMBS/About.htm.

Davis, F. D., Bagozzi, R. P., and Warshaw, P. R. (1989) "User acceptance of computer technology: A comparison of two theoretical models," *Management Science*, 35(8): 982–1003.

Davis, G. F. (2015) "Editorial essay: What is organizational research for?" *Administrative Science Quarterly*, 60(2): 179–188.

Deal, T. E. and Kennedy, A. A. (1982) *Corporate Cultures*, Reading, MA: Addison-Wesley.

De Bellaigue, E. (2004) *British Book Publishing as a Business since the 1960s: Selected essays*, London: British Library.

DeLone, W. H. and McLean, E. R. (1992) "Information systems success: The quest for the dependent variable," *Information Systems Research*, 3(1): 60–95.

Drucker, P. F. (1980 [1954]) *The Practice of Management*, 34th printing, New York: Harper & Row.

Drucker, P. F. (1981) *Toward the Next Economics and Other Essays*, New York: Harper & Row.

Drucker, P. F. (1985) *Management: Tasks, responsibilities, practices*, New York: Harper & Row.

Drucker, P. F. (1989) *The New Realities: In government and politics, in economics and business, in society and world view*, New York: Harper & Row.

Edward Elgar, 5 May 2015. www.e-elgar.co.uk.

Eisenhardt, K. M. (1989) "Building theories from case study research," *Academy of Management Review*, 14(4): 532–550.

Elsevier, 5 May 2015. www.elsevier.com/journal-authors/highlights.

Elsevier, 4 June 2015. www.elsevier.com/about/company-information.

Engwall, L. (2012) "Business schools and consultancies: The blurring of boundaries," in M. Kipping and T. Clark (eds), *The Oxford Handbook of Management Consulting*, Oxford: Oxford University Press, pp. 365–385.

Engwall, L. and Danell, R. (2011) "Britannia and her Business Schools," *British Journal of Management*, 22(3): 432–442.

Fabozzi, F. J. and Markowitz, H. M. (2011) *Equity Valuation and Portfolio Management*, Hoboken, NJ: Wiley.

Fama, E. F. and French, K. R. (1993) "Common risk factors in the returns on stocks and bonds," *Journal of Financial Economics*, 33(1): 3–56.

Fitzpatrick, K. (2011) *Planned Obsolescence: Publishing, technology, and the future of the academy*, New York: New York University Press.

Fligstein, N. (1990) *The Transformation of Corporate Control*, Cambridge, MA: Harvard University Press.

Fornell, C. and Larcker, D. F. (1981) "Evaluating structural equation models with unobservable variables and measurement error," *Journal of Marketing Research*, 18(1): 39–50.

Galbraith, J. R. (2005) *Designing the Customer-centric Organization: A guide to strategy, structure, and process*, San Francisco, CA: Jossey-Bass.

Garfield, E. (1955) "Citation indexes for science: A new dimension in documentation through association of ideas," *Science*, 122(3159): 108–111.

Gaughan, P. A. (2015) *Mergers, Acquisitions and Corporate Restructurings*, 6th edn, Hoboken, NJ: Wiley.

Grönroos, C. (2007) *In Search of a New Logic for Marketing: Foundations of contemporary theory*, Chichester: Wiley.

Guardian, 4 June 2015. www.theguardian.com/science/2012/feb/02/academics-boycott-p ublisher-elsevier.

Guthey, E., Clark, T., and Jackson, B. (2009) *Demystifying Celebrity*, London: Routledge.

Hamel, G. and Prahalad, C. K. (1994) *Competing for the Future*, Boston, MA: Harvard Business School Press.

Hammer, M. and Champy, J. (1993) *Reengineering the Corporation: A manifesto for business revolution*, New York: Harper Business.

Hannan, M. T. and Freeman, J. (1989) *Organizational Ecology*, Cambridge, MA: Harvard University Press.

HarperCollins, 5 May 2015. http://corporate.harpercollins.com/about-us/company-profile.

Heck, J. L. and Jensen, R. E. (2007) "An analysis of the evolution of research contributions by the *Accounting Review*, 1926–2005," *Accounting Historians Journal*, 34(2): 109–141.

Hemmungs-Wirtén, E. (2007) "The global market 1970–2000: Producers," in S. Eliot and J. Rose (eds), *A Companion to the History of the Book*, Oxford: Blackwell, pp. 395–405.

Hood, N. (2003) *The Multinational Subsidiary: Management, economic development and public policy*, Basingstoke: Palgrave Macmillan.

Iacocca, L. (1984) *Iacocca: An autobiography*, New York: Bantam Books.

Jacobson, T. C., Smith, G. D., Wright, R. E., Wiley, P. B., Spilka, S. B., and Heaney, B. L. (2007) *Knowledge for Generations: Wiley and the global publishing industry, 1807–2007*, New York: Wiley.

Jagodzinski, C. M. (2008) "The university press in North America: A brief history," *Journal of Scholarly Publishing*, 40(1): 1–20.

James, E. (ed.) (2002) *Macmillan: A publishing tradition*, Basingstoke: Palgrave.

Johnson, H. T. and Kaplan, R. S. (1987) *Relevance Lost: The rise and fall of management accounting*, Boston, MA: Harvard Business School Press.

Kanter, R. M. (1983) *The Change Masters: Innovation for productivity in the American corporation*, New York: Simon & Schuster.

Kanter, R. M. (1989) *When Giants Learn to Dance: Mastering the challenge of strategy, management in careers in the 1990s*, New York: Simon & Schuster.

Kotler, P. (2011) "Reinventing marketing to manage the environmental imperative," *Journal of Marketing*, 75(4): 132–135.

Kynaston, D. (2009) "A brief history of the Financial Times," mimeo. http://gale.cengage.co.uk/images/FT%20Brief%20History%20by%20David%20Kynaston.pdf (accessed 12 October 2015).

Larivière, V., Haustein, S., and Mongeon, P. (2015) "The oligopoly of academic publishers in the digital era," *PLoS ONE*, 10(6): e0127502. doi:10.1371/journal.pone.0127502 (accessed 13 October 2015).

Lawrence, P. R. (2010) *Driven to Lead: Using the four drive theory to cultivate better leaders*, New York: Wiley.

Legge, K. (1995) *Human Resource Management: Rhetorics and realities*, Basingstoke: Macmillan.

Levitt, T. (1960) "Marketing myopia," *Harvard Business Review*, 38 (July–August): 45–56.

Maynard, M. (1995) *Collision Course: Inside the battle of General Motors*, New York: Birchlane Press.

McGraw-Hill Education, 5 May 2015. www.mheducation.com/about/about-us.

Melitz, M. J. (2003) "The impact of trade on intra-industry reallocations and aggregate industry productivity," *Econometrica*, 71(6): 1695–1725.

Mintzberg, H. (1983) *Power in and Around Organizations*, Englewood Cliffs, NJ: Prentice-Hall.

Musson, D. (1991) *Management Education and Publishing Opportunities in the 1990s: Market entry strategy for Oxford University Press*, MBA thesis, The Management School, Imperial College of Science, Technology and Medicine, London.

Nonaka, I. (1991) "The knowledge-creating company," *Harvard Business Review*, 69(6): 96–104.

Nonaka, I. (1994) "A dynamic theory of organizational knowledge creation," *Organization Science*, 5(1): 14–37.

Normann, R. (1984) *Service Management: Strategy and leadership in service business*, Chichester: Wiley.

Pearson, 28 July 2015. https://www.pearson.com/news/announcements/2015/july/pearson-to-sell-ft-group-to-nikkei–inc-.html.

Pérez-Peña, R. (2007) "News Corp. completes takeover of Dow Jones," *New York Times*, 14 December.

Peteraf, M. A. (1993) "The cornerstones of competitive advantage: A resource-based view," *Strategic Management Journal*, 14(3): 179–191.

Peters, T. J. and Waterman, R. H., Jr (1982) *In Search of Excellence: Lessons from America's best-run companies*, New York: Harper & Row.

Plambeck, J. (2010) "Newspaper circulation falls nearly 9%," *New York Times*, 26 April.

PLOS, 13 October 2015. https://www.plos.org/about.

Podsakoff, P. M., MacKenzie, S. B., Lee, J. Y., and Podsakoff, N. P. (2003) "Common method biases in behavioral research: A critical review of the literature and recommended remedies," *Journal of Applied Psychology*, 88(5): 879–903.

Porter, L. W. and McKibbin, L. E. (1988) *Management Education and Development: Drift or thrust into the 21st century?* New York: McGraw-Hill.

Porter, M. E. (1980) *Competitive Strategy*, New York: Free Press.

Porter, M. E. (1985) *Competitive Advantage*, New York: Free Press.

Publishers Weekly, 5 May 2015. www.publishersweekly.com/pw/by-topic/industry-news/fina ncial-reporting/article/58211-the-global-60-the-world-s-largest-book-publishers-2013.html.

ResearchGate, 5 May 2015. https://www.researchgate.net/journal/1558-9080_Academy_ of_Management_Perspectives_The.

Romer, P. M. (1990) "Endogenous technological change," *Journal of Political Economy*, 98(5, part 2): S71–S102.

Routledge, 5 May 2015. www.routledge.com.

SAGE Open, 5 May 2015. http://sgo.sagepub.com/about-us.

Schein, E. H. (1985) *Organizational Culture and Leadership*, Chichester: Wiley.

Schiffrin, A. (2000) *The Business of Books: How international conglomerates took over publishing and changed the way we read*, London: Verso.

Scientific Research, 5 May 2015. www.scirp.org.

Scott, W. R. (1981) *Organizations: Rational, natural and open systems*, Englewood Cliffs, NJ: Prentice-Hall.

Springer, 18 February 2016. www.springer.com/gp/about-springer/media/press-releases/ corporate/springer-nature-created-following-merger-completion/256626.

Strategy Science, 1 August 2015. http://pubsonline.informs.org/journal/stsc.

Thomson Reuters Company History, 4 June 2015. http://thomsonreuters.com/en/a bout-us/company-history.html.

Thompson, J. B. (2005) *Books in the Digital Age: The transformation of academic and higher education publishing in Britain and the United States*, Cambridge: Polity Press.

Thompson, J. B. (2010) *Merchants of Culture: The publishing business in the twenty-first century*, Cambridge: Polity Press.

Trachtenberg, J. A. (2014) "Forbes sold to Asian investors," *The Wall Street Journal*, 19 July. www.marketwatch.com/story/forbes-sold-to-asian-investors-2014-07-19 (accessed 5 May 2015).

Üsdiken, B. (2010) "Between contending perspectives and logics: Organizational studies in Europe," *Organization Studies*, 31(6): 715–735.

Üsdiken, B. (2014) "Centres and peripheries: Research styles and publication patterns in 'top' US journals and their European alternatives, 1960–2010," *Journal of Management Studies*, 51(5): 764–789.

Üsdiken, B. and Wasti, S. A. (2009) "Preaching, teaching and researching at the periphery: Academic management literature in Turkey, 1970–1999," *Organization Studies*, 30(10): 1063–1082.

Venkatesh, V., Morris, M. G., Davis, G. B., and Davis, F. D. (2003) "User acceptance of information technology: Toward a unified view," *MIS Quarterly*, 27(3): 425–478.

Vogel, R. (2012) "The visible colleges of management and organization studies: A bibliometric analysis of academic journals," *Organization Studies*, 33(8): 1015–1043.

Von Hülsen, I. (2009) "Millionendeal: Dieter von Holtzbrinck kauft Halbbruder Zeitungen und Zeitschriften ab," *Spiegel Online*, 26 March. www.spiegel.de/kultur/gesellscha ft/millionendeal-dieter-von-holtzbrinck-kauft-halbbruder-zeitungen-und-zeitschriften-a b-a-615662.html (accessed 5 May 2015).

Watts, R. L. and Zimmerman, J. L. (1986) *Positive Accounting Theory*, Englewood Cliffs, NJ: Prentice-Hall.

Wedlin, L. (2006) *Ranking Business Schools: Forming fields, identities and boundaries in international management education*, Cheltenham: Edward Elgar.

Wendt, L. (1982) *The Wall Street Journal: The story of Dow Jones & the nation's business newspaper*, Chicago, IL: Rand McNally.

Wiley, 5 May 2015. http://exchanges.wiley.com/blog/2013/02/13/recent-wiley-acquisitions.

Williamson, O. E. (1985) *The Economic Institutions of Capitalism*, New York: Free Press.

Yeomans, J. (2015) "Pearson to sell stake in The Economist for £469m", *Telegraph*, 12 August. www.telegraph.co.uk/finance/newsbysector/mediatechnologyandtelecoms/11797 837/Pearson-to-sell-stake-in-The-Economist-for-469m.html (accessed 16 February 2016).

Yukl, G. A. (1981) *Leadership in Organizations*, Englewood Cliffs, NJ: Prentice-Hall.

16

CONCLUSIONS

Commoditizing Management?

This book has aimed to address three interrelated questions regarding business schools, management consultants, and business media, asking when and how these three sets of actors (i) became institutionalized, i.e., taken-for-granted within economically developed or developing countries; (ii) started to be seen as "authorities," i.e., having their views on management being widely accepted, including by practicing managers themselves; and (iii) contributed to the expansion of management and the belief that everything can be managed. Conceptualizing these sets of actors as "organizational fields," the core of the book used a historical, comparative, and integrative approach to provide an in-depth overview of the emergence, development, and changes for each of these fields over four externally defined periods from the mid/late-nineteenth century through World War I, then through World War II, next to the early 1980s and finally into the twenty-first century. This chapter summarizes the processes of institutionalization and authority-building identified for business schools, management consultants, and business media over the whole century and a half, discusses their contribution to the expansion of management over the same period and its current outcome, and offers some very tentative considerations for their possible role in the future.

Processes: The Trajectories of the Three Fields

From Survival to Legitimacy and Authority

As noted at the beginning of the book, none of the three sets of actors could expect to be taken for granted from the outset. All of them faced various degrees of difficulty in asserting their right to exist, let alone become an accepted, integral part of the relevant *extant* organizational fields, i.e., higher education for business schools, accounting as well as engineering for consulting, and publishing for business media – fields that themselves continued to evolve. It was even more difficult to take the next steps from mere acceptance to gaining their own legitimacy as clearly identifiable and respected organizational fields and, ultimately, the ability to exercise authority over management practice by (i) turning *business school* degrees into a near-obligatory passage to managerial positions, (ii) having the advice of *management consultants* accepted voluntarily and on a regular basis by powerful executives, and (iii) being considered *business publications* with relevant and reliable information and guidance for managerial decision makers or high-quality research for management scholars.

To be sure, having such authority does not necessarily mean that these sets of actors provide the "best" education, advice, or guidance, leading to superior decisions and better practices. It only means that they have become taken-for-granted, even indispensable in these roles. To give more specific illustrations: an MBA degree, particularly from a prominent business school, is often considered as a ticket for senior management positions – regardless of the particular person's actual skills. Similarly, managers will at times hire consultants to justify already planned changes or even enhance their own position within the organization – which only works if consulting advice in general and the particular consulting firm are widely seen as legitimate "authorities" in these matters. Likewise, an endorsement or a critique from a well-known management author or a business paper might influence a company's reputation and even its stock price – independent of the underlying fundamentals, with Enron as a case in point.

So, how did they do it? The way these three sets of actors succeeded in becoming accepted originally was, in a nutshell, by drawing on – and largely imitating – extant templates or forms of organizing in their respective institutional and national contexts. This was not dissimilar, for instance, to the way in which Edison replicated extant systems and practices of gas lighting to make his electric lighting acceptable – leading to not necessarily the most effective, but still enduring outcomes, like the use of lamp shades (Hargadon and Douglas 2001). Once accepted, these fields then associated themselves with broader societal logics and their related discourses to cement their definitional power, with the – once again, evolving – notions of "science" and "profession" playing particularly prominent roles. Based on these broader notions they created and, if necessary, changed vocabularies and images that developed their own dynamics in terms of shaping behavior but also lingered even as practices moved on. This explains for instance the continuing use of the MBA label, even if the subject of study is no longer accurately captured by "business *administration*" – originally chosen as a parallel to the then well-respected "public administration"; or why consultants continue to refer to themselves as "professionals" and their senior managers as "partners" – labels drawn from the practice of the earlier established law firms.

282 Conclusions

More specifically, what today are widely and globally referred to as *business schools* faced a double challenge at their inception: In the national contexts in which they emerged, on the one hand, they had to distinguish themselves from the large number of for-profit or secondary schools that had been founded to supply the growing number of businesses with vocationally trained personnel. On the other hand, their claim to provide "higher" education was met with skepticism if not rejection within the higher education field, where they sought their place. The solution – which varied according to their contexts – came by latching on to extant exemplars. In the US, this meant claiming to be a "professional school," following the model set by law and medicine, which had already become part of universities. Among the early movers in Europe, in France the aspiration was to become like the engineering *grandes écoles*, which were already occupying a central position within the higher education field in training the country's elite in public and private realms. In Germany, by contrast, the way to gain acceptance and legitimacy was to emulate the university with the accompanying attempt to develop a science – though one that would purportedly help to solve practical problems.

To go beyond sheer survival, which was not assured as some earlier failures and the initially low student numbers attested, in the US they turned to claiming "higher aims" such as a sense of public responsibility and service to society to be inculcated in business people. The school of business at Harvard that was moving to the center of an expanding and increasingly structured field was most vocal in this respect – its "professional" model, despite allusions to science, was inspired by the school of law. In Germany, the *Handelshochschulen* were initially established as stand-alone schools, but never gave up on their scientific aspirations and, within less than three decades, became incorporated into universities as faculties of *Betriebswirtschaftslehre* (BWL). After World War II, a similar – albeit not consciously copied – association with "science" became the main foundation of claims to authority by business schools in the US, accompanied by the increasing prevalence of the view of management as a "science-based profession." Subsequently, the salience of science and the science-based view of management gradually spread from the US to most other parts of the world, helping business schools and business graduates to gain a similar aura and legitimated authority. It is important to note that the "science" notion was never exclusive or universal. The law-inspired model promulgated by the Harvard Business School since the interwar period also persisted – with HBS and its various "clones" still commanding wide recognition and prestige, and the associated case method having become the most popular way of teaching business.

The early *management consultants* were both in a more fortunate and, at the same time, less enviable position. Those giving advice to the growing number of ever larger businesses emanating from the industrial revolutions tended to have a background in either accounting or engineering – similar to those directing them. As these were established professions, legitimacy was not really an issue. But at the same time their advice remained marginal and largely "hidden," mainly confined, for the accountants, to specific situations such as restructuring after bankruptcy or, for the engineers, to more technical questions – illustrated quite tellingly by Taylor's international fame originally being based on his development of "high speed steel." A breakthrough came for the latter with the claim to make management "systematic" and, even better, "scientific," combined with promises to resolve the tensions between managers and workers and the ills of the capitalist system more generally. Scientific management and the associated methods eventually faded but the association with "science" was revived on a regular basis: First, after World War II operations research propelled firms such as the Stanford Research Institute and Arthur D. Little to the forefront; then, since the 1980s IT-based and data-driven management helped the accounting-based first movers and a variety of IT-based firms become such large actors within the field.

But, like in the business school field, "science" was not the only way to legitimacy and authority. To distinguish themselves from scientific management and some overly aggressive commercial providers, a group of other, more broadly oriented often so-called business survey firms sought recognition by building a "professional" image since the interwar period – initially still in association with the extant professions as apparent in James O. McKinsey's description of his firm as "accountants and management engineers." They succeeded, also commercially, during and after World War II by mimicking the structures, practices, and behaviors of the legal profession – similar to and in partial symbiosis with the surging Harvard Business School. McKinsey and others also took this model with them when expanding abroad since the 1960s, spreading a "professional" terminology and imagery that is now used globally even by the recently dominant firms with a "science," i.e. IT orientation – cementing their own position at the top of the field's structure. Another interesting and revealing parallel between HBS and McKinsey is their growing network of alumni – many of them actually "graduates" of both. This, in addition to their image, helped them weather recent scandals and, more importantly, extended their authority beyond business into all walks of the economy, polity, and society at an ever more global scale.

In terms of *business media*, the early movers could also rely on already established fields and organizational forms and practices. Thus, it was mainly the book publishers with a focus on science or literature, such as Wiley, Harper, Macmillan, and McGraw-Hill, that added a limited number of business-related titles to their lists – initially with a focus on engineering and then scientific management, while those which focused almost exclusively on business, such as the Ronald Press, published predominantly on accounting. The same is true for academic outlets, where those wanting to publish on business-related issues had to rely on journals in established academic disciplines, namely in economics, psychology, and statistics. An exception was the German *Zeitschrift für handelswissenschaftliche Forschung* founded in 1906, which struggled however to find both contributors and subscribers. Additional journals specifically oriented toward business had to

284 Conclusions

wait, in the US for example, until the interwar period, when in 1922 those schools based at highly reputable universities, respectively Harvard and Chicago, launched the *Harvard Business Review* and the *University Journal of Business*, mainly to provide publication outlets for their own faculty members.

In contrast to academic journals, the business press developed much earlier on both sides of the Atlantic with the foundations of two dailies, the *Financial Times* and the *Wall Street Journal* in the 1880s, and two periodicals, the *Economist* and *Forbes* in 1843 and 1917, respectively. Their challenge was a different one. Capitalizing on a growing interest in economic information, particularly about the stock market, they tried to distinguish themselves from the extant general press – most visibly the *Financial Times* by printing on pink paper. Their circulation numbers originally remained low though, only picking up during the stock market boom of the 1920s and, even more so, following the Great Crash of 1929, when a number of additional titles were launched – possibly driven by a sensationalist interest in the fortunes of the stock market, the health of the economy as well as struggling or bankrupt companies. These interests – and their readership – increased further after World War II and the popularization of stock ownership since the 1980s – making the *Wall Street Journal*, for instance, the newspaper with the highest circulation in the US.

The authority of business schools, management consultants, and business media has not remained unquestioned though. Thus, there have always been doubts about the quality of education provided by these schools and the strong association with science did not quell them, but raised the issue of how rigor could be combined with relevance, or not – an issue also directed at the majority of the growing number of academic journals. And as soon as management consultants became more visible, the question was raised why they were needed at all. Since the 1990s, "consulting bashing" even became a kind of management fashion of its own. In that respect, both the business press and popular management authors have also been chastised for too easily embracing ideas or celebrating companies that eventually proved a failure or a fraud.

Toward a Single US-dominated Global Model?

Today, the three fields have become increasingly international rather than national in scope; their terminology is almost exclusively in English and derived from the US model. The best examples are probably the labels "business school" and "MBA," which nowadays have replaced or are used as addenda to names or acronyms of schools in native languages. Most of the dominant actors among business schools, management consultants, and business media are also of US origins. This is very evident in the rankings of business schools and their programs: those by US journals or magazines tend to either only rank US schools, ignoring the rest of the world or listing the ones from outside the US separately – with only the UK-based *Financial Times* providing an integrated global ranking. The same is true for accreditations, where the US-based AACSB has many foreign accredited schools and members, while its European counterpart EQUIS is all but absent from the United States. Likewise for management consulting, where the overwhelming majority of the largest and most visible firms today are of US origin and where even ideas generated elsewhere were disseminated by these firms – as was the case for Japanese management techniques reaching the West via US consulting firms. In the business media field, today the majority of books are in English, despite a few major publishers being based in the Netherlands and Germany. The same is true for the business press and for the highest ranked academic journals – with all of the latter in English and 31 out of the 45 journals on the *Financial Times* list as well as 17 out of 20 on the *Business Week* one based in the US.

Such US dominance was not a given. At the outset, alternative models existed and they influenced others, in some areas more so than the US model. This was clearly the case for the origins of today's business schools, where the US "professional school" model was rather unique, while the German model in particular – both for the stand-alone *Handelshochschulen* and for the university-based BWL faculties – was copied widely, namely in the Nordic countries, the Southern and Eastern European peripheries as well as in Japan. Similarly, in the early twentieth century Taylor's ideas were widely and often enthusiastically received elsewhere, but their application remained very limited and there were also local alternatives like Henri Fayol's broader conception of a manager's role in France and alternative ways of disseminating "rationalization," like the German RKW and REFA associations. Business publishing was also nationally based for much of the nineteenth and part of the twentieth centuries – not least for linguistic reasons. And in terms of international projection, Germany was again an early leader, the first to launch business-related academic journals and Eugen Schmalenbach's books being quickly translated into many languages.

So, how did business schools, management consultants, and business media become so international and US-dominated? The answer, once again, has to do with what could be called "piggy-backing." The increasing economic, military, and political superiority of the United States, especially since World War II, clearly brushed off on all three authorities. There is also the sheer size and attractiveness of the US market, which helped local actors and drew in foreign entrants, who then often became "Americanized." In addition, since the interwar period there was direct support for the US-based actors – through individual initiatives, networks, and private foundations as well as the US government and its various agencies, in particular during the 1950s and 1960s and then again following the fall of the Berlin Wall in 1989. And there were US multinationals, which served as a "bridge." The leading US actors within the three fields also expanded or, in the case of business schools and notably Harvard Business School, created "clones" around the world after World War II. Following organic growth as well as a succession of mergers and acquisitions, the major management

286 Conclusions

consulting and business media firms are today large multinationals, many of them headquartered in the US but competing with each other globally. While business schools remain predominantly nationally based, rankings and accreditations as well as the flow of students and graduates have also created a single, international field, where the large US actors naturally dominate.

In terms of origins of today's *business schools*, during the first half of the twentieth century European stand-alone commercial schools – and BWL faculties in Germany or commerce ones in the UK – co-existed with the university-based "professional schools" in the US. But following World War II and with US economic, military, and political supremacy behind them, US business schools were readily behaving like and becoming accepted as authorities internationally. They were prodded and funded by US aid agencies and philanthropic organizations, such as the Ford Foundation, to go to other parts of the "free world" to teach business and to demonstrate how business education needed to be carried out. The "New Look," science-based business school, created in the US during the 1950s, further reinforced that dynamic and accentuated the position of the United States as the world's center in educating for and researching business – even if its actual influence remained constrained in various ways during the subsequent decades. Diffusion accelerated again since the 1990s largely due to the concomitant spread of US-based institutions such as accreditations and rankings. It was also associated with the increasing international influence of US higher education models more broadly, including the increasing recognition of the master's as a distinct degree or the pressure on universities to generate their own income.

From the outset, *management consulting* was an American invention, even if the establishment of a recognizable field took quite some time even in the United States with Harrington Emerson establishing the first multi-office firm before World War I. Similar firms set up by other Taylor followers and competitors and, even more so, the one founded by Charles E. Bedaux in 1916 eventually created the field in the US and also kick-started national fields elsewhere in the world through the offices they established there – and the local spin-offs they engendered, which remained and grew as most of the former returned to the US at the outset of World War II. But it was the "management engineers" of the interwar period and the "professional" model they created and exported to Western Europe and other parts of the world since the 1960s that cemented US hegemony not only in terms of the consulting services they offered but also in terms of the predominant *image* of a management consultant, including their look and behavior – and in the process gradually unified distinct national markets. This image prevailed even as some of these firms faltered and became marginalized by the consulting giants descending from accounting or IT-service firms, most of which tend to have their main origins in the US and/or UK and today operate in a globally distributed way – with their outsourcing services and many back office functions located in India.

Business media, by contrast, have early roots in many of the developed countries with publications mainly in native languages. Some international diffusion of business-related publications occurred at the outset in English, French, and German, mainly due to the lack of publications in the national language at the time the new schools of commerce were founded. For instance, when the Stockholm School of Economics started in 1909 almost all the literature was in German. At the same time some publications from the US were already translated into national languages – with Frederick W. Taylor the prime example. Later on, English as a working language has become more or less taken for granted and translations have become less frequent. However, to reach broad audiences around the globe, some publishers bring out international or European editions in order to somewhat play down the increasingly US-dominated contents of their books. The Anglo-American dominance is also noticeable in terms of the majority of the large multinational business media companies having their origins and/or headquarters in the United States and even more so, when it comes to the leading academic journals, which, as already mentioned, are all published in English and have their editorial base mostly in the US. As business elites are becoming more global, especially those working within large multinationals, they are increasingly reading popular management books and the international business press in the English original – also due to the increasing need for immediacy satisfied by online editions, hence reinforcing the Anglo-American dominance of the field.

Again, a word of caution is necessary here. Business schools, management consultants, and business media are not entirely global and some of their dominant actors are not based in the US or even the UK. Suffice to point to INSEAD or IMD among the highly respected business schools, even if their language of instruction is also English; to the Canadian CGI, the French Capgemini and even the German Roland Berger among the leading consulting firms; and Elsevier, Wolters Kluwer, or Bertelsmann among the globally active media conglomerates. And there are, for all three fields, a myriad of smaller actors, most of which have never appeared and will never appear on any business school rankings or lists of the largest firms in management consulting and business media. They continue to play highly salient roles in providing localized business education and management consulting services or nationally specific textbooks (Engwall 2000) or business news (Grafström 2006) – albeit often copied from the major global models and providers (e.g., for consulting Crucini and Kipping 2001).

From Missionary Zeal to Market-orientation

Not only are these three fields increasingly global and dominated by US models and actors, these actors are also largely – or at least increasingly – driven by a commercial logic: many business schools supplement tuitions and external donations as well as, in many cases, government funding with income from executive

288 Conclusions

education; consulting firms charge exorbitant fees, even for their most junior staff members, while exploiting global salary differentials, for example, between India and the West; and publishers monetize the quest for ever more journal publications with expensive subscription rates for bundles of these journals. At the same time many actors today are involved in more than one field: business schools not only offer undergraduate or graduate programs but also provide tailor-made executive programs, and allow, or sometimes encourage, professors to do consulting – with some even publishing journals and books; many consulting firms not only provide advice but also publish books and (online) journals and have become involved in running business schools through their alumni; and business media multinationals not only supply textbooks or have to a considerable extent taken over the academic journals from professional associations, they also measure research output through proprietary systems like the Web of Science or Scopus and rank business schools in their newspapers and magazines.

Money was not always the goal – or at least not the primary one. Many of the schools of commerce also espoused a civilizing mission – especially but not only in contrast with the private, for-profit schools. And, they aimed at elevating the status and the societal consciousness of businessmen. Many of the early consultants were driven by a missionary zeal for betterment seeing consulting only as one way to disseminate their ideas. And similar ideas were disseminated very successfully in Germany through inter-firm cooperation mediated by associations – with associative channels also present, albeit less predominant, in many other countries, including the US. Publishers certainly looked for commercial viability but, as mentioned, many of the early business journals and newspapers struggled and were kept alive out of interest. Academic journals in general were originally launched by professional associations or universities for intellectual rather than profit motives. And while individuals, such as Frederick Taylor or Lillian Gilbreth, continuously crossed boundaries between fields, this was mainly to spread their ideas – not to "colonize" other fields, like many multinational actors do today.

Again, how did this happen? When did the dissemination of management knowledge become an "industry," dominated by big business? Part of the explanation can be found in the broader context, which has become increasingly market driven, in particular following the global triumph of capitalism since the 1980s. Part of it is linked to the process of Americanization discussed above – since the context there has always been more commercial or market-oriented, also due to the less important role of the state. This did clearly affect the business schools, many of which had to raise their own funds. It also affected the consultants in a rather interesting way with the federal government in the US becoming a user of consulting services from the early days, consequently providing an important additional market for these consultants and implicitly furthering their commercialization. As for the business media, the global conglomerates developed efficient systems for manuscript handling, bibliometrics, and marketing,

Conclusions **289**

which many professional associations found attractive and therefore left the handling of their journals to these companies. In addition, the latter, often after being approached by specialized researchers, started a number of new journals. Consequently, the media giants got a rather firm grip over scientific publishing and were rewarded by high profit margins. The internationalization of the fields and their increasing colonization by actors from other fields during the most recent period also seems to have played a role. It increased competition and hence forced a greater market-orientation onto the various actors.

Almost everywhere many of the predecessors of today's *business schools* had to contend with questions of demand and revenue generation from the outset, as they were entering either a tuition-based field as in the US or were private initiatives like in Germany and France. Such concerns persisted throughout most of the twentieth century to the extent that these conditions prevailed. The rise of a commercial logic has been most notable from the 1990s onwards, starting in the US. The increase in market-orientation was driven, on the one hand, by cuts in public funding and, on the other, the advent of the rankings. As a result, US business schools were becoming more dependent on student tuitions, donations, and executive education as well as having to operate in an environment that was now more competitive – not only nationally but internationally as well, due to the increase in the prominence of some foreign business schools. A greater commercial orientation also spread to countries where similar conditions prevailed such as the UK or where schools were predominantly in private hands, like in France. And among these, a commercial logic pervaded in particular the business schools that were associating themselves with an international identity, aiming to compete not only amongst themselves but also with the ones in the US – prompting these schools as well as many in the US to turn toward entering into alliances or opening branch campuses in other countries.

During the early twentieth century, commercially driven, market-oriented *consulting* was the exception as a vehicle or carrier for the dissemination of scientific management, not the rule. Most of the pioneers saw it as *one* of many ways to spread their gospel. But a growing number of actors did identify it as a business opportunity, among them first and foremost Charles E. Bedaux and, in a much more aggressive manner, George S. May. The former also took this logic abroad with new offices often leading to local spin-offs, hence more competition and a further spread of the commercial logic. But even Bedaux's success was limited and in a number of countries consultants played a minor role – with Germany probably the most extreme case, since associations such as REFA largely monopolized dissemination, namely by training vast numbers of work study engineers. Other countries, including Soviet Russia, China, and Japan, had comparable arrangements – at least for some time, and similar associations could also be found elsewhere, namely in France and at the international level. The commercial logic prevailed though and expanded more significantly since World War II – initially hidden behind the mantle of professionalism with spin-offs once again playing an

290 Conclusions

important role. It came fully to the fore since the 1980s and 1990s, when consulting projects – and the firms providing them – became much larger and a part of numerous external services contracted by their clients. At the same time, the dangers of an excessive focus on commercial success also became apparent – in particular through the Enron case, but ultimately did little to question, let alone roll back the now clearly dominant market orientation.

The *business media* too has long since had a commercial logic. However, publishing companies also have traditions as cultural institutions, i.e., aiming to contribute to culture through the publication of fiction authors or, depending on the context, for the church. The university presses in Cambridge and Oxford, for instance, which nowadays are quite active in management publishing, were once standing on the publication of bibles. Or take The Free Press; founded to publish books on civil liberties, it eventually took on Michael Porter's (1980) *Corporate Strategy*. Publishing management titles – i.e., business textbooks, business periodicals, and, more recently, academic journals – can therefore be considered as a turn toward a more commercial logic. Some successful textbooks, like those by Philip Kotler on marketing, have become veritable money machines with edition after edition, year after year. An additional sign of this stronger commercial logic is the fact that successful smaller publishers became attractive for the growing media conglomerates leading to the numerous acquisitions in the field. Reports on profit margins also demonstrate that the business model of the global media conglomerates is quite successful, apparently in particular for the academic journals. Their relative standing is continuously manifested through impact factors, which provide a power base both in relation to the research community and their libraries that are urged by faculty members to subscribe.

Again, despite the obvious triumph of markets and commercial logics in all three fields, some words of caution are in order. Like so often, there are still other logics in play. Thus, while hiding a commercial orientation, ongoing appeals to "science" and to "professionalism" do act as a kind of brake on the former's excesses in both business schools and management consulting firms. And there are still some collective arrangements within consulting, for instance with the various research institutes in Japan – originally established based on the template of the Stanford Research Institute. Similarly, there continue to be academic journals in business and management that are run not by commercial publishers but by professional associations – with some of the latter even launching new titles recently.

Outcomes: Turning "Management" into a Global Commodity

What this book has also tried to do – in addition to tracing the trajectories of business schools, management consultants, and business media toward their current position as highly visible and relevant "authorities" on management – is to gauge their respective contributions to the expansion of management itself – leading to a situation, where management today is everywhere, and has become what could be called a "commodity." Tentatively, the developments of the three fields presented in this book do suggest that they have indeed contributed to this process of commoditization.

Part of this process was a linguistic one, and it is here where their role in the expansion of management and their definitional power is probably most apparent. Thus, US *business schools* again had an important part to play in popularizing the idea of "management" – though they were rather late in fully embracing the term. That this did happen was associated partly with "management" gaining an identity as a separate discipline in the US, like finance and marketing. This was perhaps best indicated by the founding of the Academy of Management in 1936. Concomitantly, authors from US business schools associating themselves with this developing speciality began to publish books in the 1950s where management was framed as a top level activity engaged with the task of running the entire enterprise, which subsumed all functional activities such as finance, marketing, and personnel. With this approach the idea of the general manager began to spread, i.e., that there is some general management knowledge that can be practiced in any type of organization irrespective of its environment, technology, or history. Consequently, management began to be used in ways that were detached from its traditional association with business and, by the 1970s, there was a broader acceptance of the view that what business schools were doing was "management education" – and a few of them even changed their name to "School of Management." This interpretation of management as a more encompassing task relevant for and applicable in all kinds of organized activity, paved the way for the expansion of management into almost all realms of life, particularly from the 1990s onwards.

Consultants embraced the term "management" much earlier than business schools. As discussed in detail, the first visible and conscious development of consulting activities was related to "scientific management" – even if its remit was originally limited to the management of the shop floor, trying to improve the productivity of individual workers. But its proponents quickly extended their ambitions and activities from the shop floor to the office and to public administrations and even society as a whole. They nevertheless kept calling themselves efficiency or consulting engineers rather than management consultants. It was another group, offering more comprehensive business surveys, that used the term management for self-description since the interwar period – originally in the combination "management engineer." Occasionally since the 1930s and consistently after World War II they started to refer to themselves as management consultants and to their activity as management consulting or management consultancy in the UK – also to shed any association with the earlier focus on the shop floor and efficiency improvements. Consultants, it should be noted, were also involved in spreading management terminology to their clients – obviously in conjunction with the organizational changes they suggested to these clients, but also, and less well known, in spreading the language and the underlying concepts through their publications, with McKinsey, for instance, handing out *The Will to Manage* by

292 Conclusions

Marvin Bower (1966) to their clients or promoting the need for bankers to become managers in the pages of its *Quarterly* (for both, see Kipping and Westerhuis 2014).

The *business media*, by contrast, espoused the "management" term much later – not all that surprising since most of their publications would reactively reflect reality, not necessarily shape it proactively. An interesting and visible turning point in this respect are the English translations of Henri Fayol's 1916 treatise on *Administration industrielle et générale*, which by many is seen as an expression for the self-perception of modern "managers" with its insistence on planning and control. It was first translated in 1930 under the title *Industrial and General Administration* published by Pitman in London and received little attention. It was published again in a different translation by the same publisher in 1949, this time entitled *General and Industrial Management* – note not only the use of the "management" term but also the inversion in the order of the attributes! This time it did receive considerable attention, partially because of the foreword written by well-known British management thinker and consultant Lyndall Urwick. Probably more importantly, the later edition and its title seem to have fit the *Zeitgeist* portraying the notion of management, in both wording and content, as a general skill – which forms the basis for its subsequent expansion and commoditization.

The growing focus on management since World War II is also manifest in the increasing number of newly established academic journals carrying the word "management" in their title. The early ones, such as *Management Science*, founded in 1954, the *Academy of Management Journal*, founded in 1958, and the *Journal of Management Studies* (1964) had a number of followers in the 1970s and 1980s such as the *Journal of Management* (1975), the *Strategic Management Journal* (1980), the *European Management Journal* (1982) and the *Scandinavian Journal of Management* (1984). These journals were established in the 1950s and 1960s, after management became a separate, identifiable discipline (see above). As for the business press, they have maintained their original titles from a time when "management" was still associated with running a household and cooking. But the few more recently founded periodicals, like the German *Manager Magazin* established in 1971, confirm that management had become a more widely used and encompassing notion – and also advantageous for selling copy. Incidentally the German edition of the *Harvard Business Review*, published since 1979 is called *Harvard Business Manager*.

In addition to their relatively clear – but somewhat uneven – contribution in spreading the "management" terminology, the three sets of actors can also be seen to have played a role in expanding management as a practice and as a social group. Thus, in terms of the *business schools*, there has been an explosive growth of the MBA, purportedly the ultimate degree for "knowing" about management, beginning in the US after World War II and then since the 1980s in many other parts of the world. And, as was mentioned in Chapter 1, their graduates now appear to have penetrated even the Vatican. Today, given the scale that under-graduate programs and the MBA have reached with an expanding range of part-time and executive versions, "knowledge" about management has clearly been turned into a commodity – not only in the US but in many other places too. As a result, even the MBA is by itself no longer a ticket for senior management positions, which nowadays appears to be confined potentially only to the graduates of the most prominent business schools – or those who have spent some time at one of the elite consulting firms.

For *consultants*, they appear instrumental in spreading management as a practice from early on. Thus, with respect to scientific management, they developed and deployed systems that clearly had separate and identifiable roles for those supervising and those executing – systems they, together with the separation between managers and workers, spread from factories to offices and to all kinds of private and public organizations. The subsequent type of consultants, initially called "management engineers," went even further in terms of spreading organizational templates, and in particular the multi-divisional or M-form, that required an increasing number of managers with different levels of decision-making authority, for which the consultants also created systems for the organization to incentivize and control them. Driven by their own – veiled or open – commercial interests, consultants pushed hard to introduce these templates in many sectors and many countries, in particular during the post-World War II period, thus helping to expand the number of managers within organizations and as a social group. Their role in expanding management is somewhat more complex in the most recent period, when the large accounting- and IT-based consulting firms now dominating the field clearly commoditized their own services – namely through the creation of elaborate knowledge management systems (e.g., Hansen, Nohria, and Tierney 1999). But these services were often designed to sort of automate tasks formerly carried out by middle managers – or outsource them, with outsourcing actually spreading management even further afield.

The *business media* have clearly played a significant role in turning management into a global commodity. Before World War II the publishing of business books was relatively limited, circulation of business media was at rather low levels and the academic journals in the area were few. In contrast, after World War II publishing of books, circulation figures, and the foundation of academic journals took off in an expanding market for business education, business news, and academic publishing. In this process, as pointed out above, US actors came to play a particularly significant role by stimulating a demand for textbooks, popular books, newspapers, periodicals, and academic publishing. An important part of this process was an increasing spread of the idea of the general manager, i.e., that any organization – such as a bank, a hospital, or a university – can be run according to the same principles as a car manufacturing company. In this way business media have penetrated into wider and wider circles. This process has also been reinforced by an increasing interest in financial news in media of all kinds, not only the traditional newspapers and periodicals, but also on the radio, television, and more recently all sorts of information technology solutions. Among the latter

294 Conclusions

it is particularly worth noting the links between business media and markets for economic information. The link between the *Wall Street Journal* and the Dow Jones index has a long history, and very recently the Japanese stock market index Nikkei has created a similar link by acquiring the *Financial Times*. And for management research, the information systems for scientific publications developed by Thomson Reuters and Elsevier are contributing to its commoditization.

Final Considerations: Better Ways?

This book has shown how business schools, management consultants, and business media succeeded in gaining not only legitimacy as actors but also significant authority to define what "good" management is or should be. As organizational fields they are today marked by US dominance and a strong commercial logic. It is also apparent that through this process of authority building and with their current definitional power these sets of actors have contributed to the expansion and, ultimately, commoditization of management – most clearly in spreading the term and a whole language of management but apparently also in terms of an extension of the various realms to which these ideas are thought to be applicable and, the related growth of managers as a social group. The remaining question is whether this is a good thing or put more specifically: should these actors be so ubiquitous and powerful?

There are actually many voices that would answer no, with sometimes quite stinging criticisms levelled in particular at the business schools and consultants almost from the get go. Critiques of the former have tended to revolve around striking a balance between the practical applicability required by their target audience and their own quest for recognition in the research-driven superordinate field of higher education. The resulting goal conflict seems difficult to resolve – a difficulty attested to by the longstanding debates about rigor vs. relevance. What could be done is to rethink the ultimate objective of managers in general and the education necessary to achieve it. Its historical trajectory, as recounted in this book, offers possible ways forward in this respect. On the one hand, this might mean relinquishing the long held claim of being a professional school and the underlying idea of management as a profession and revert back to the earlier days of seeing it as a preparation for specialist careers in business, where some general management knowledge and skills are combined with more specialist instruction to prepare for or complement extant professions. This exists already in joint MBA/Law degrees or business school courses that are also counted toward professional exams but could easily be extended to other areas such as health care or project management and grown more generally – ultimately dispensing with the MBA as a general management degree. On the other hand, one could also revive the idea of the liberalizing mission of the original schools with the aim to educate "better" people and hence lead to managers making more socially responsible decisions. Going into this direction would restore some of the moral authority that managers have lost as a result of the recurrent and most recent crises and – if taken seriously – might lead to better outcomes for business and society as a whole.

Critiques of consultants suggest, among other things, that they take advantage of managers' insecurities, sell expensive recommendations based on standardized templates, i.e., prêt-à-porter at the price of haute couture, and take no responsibility for their ultimate outcomes. Improvements might take three possible directions: one is using the growing availability of relevant metrics to actually measure outcomes and adjust remuneration accordingly – a practice already being adopted by some consulting firms, but which also carries the risk of encouraging "gaming" to improve these metrics. Another suggestion would be linked to changes discussed above for business schools. Since the latter supply the majority of consultants, more broadly educated and socially sensitized graduates would quickly change the dynamics for consulting firms as well. This would actually respond to a trend observable among millennials, who seem to care as much or even more about the social impact of what they do than about the money they make – a trend apparently already recognized by some consulting firms, which try to attract graduates by offering them to work on pro bono projects or by setting up not-for-profit consulting to not-for-profit clients. A third option would be to develop alternatives based on the exchange rather than sale of knowledge – a model that dominated knowledge dissemination during the first half of the twentieth century – and might just come back based on IT-based social networks.

As for *business media* there are a number of concerns to be addressed. They are to a large extent related to the strong concentration of the field with a few dominant actors controlling the publishing of books, newspapers, periodicals, and academic journals, all driven by a commercial logic, as discussed above. Critics have therefore questioned to what extent alternative perspectives are presented in the management literature, critical articles are printed in the newspapers and the periodicals, and non-Anglo-American research can find its way into the most prestigious journals. Obviously, the success of such alternatives depends to a significant extent on those who control both the contents and its dissemination. For instance, when selecting textbooks, it would be important for faculty members, and their students, to consider alternatives. It is also crucial that both authors and readers consider alternatives in terms of newspapers and periodicals as well as academic journals. For the latter, it appears particularly crucial that evaluations of faculty members return to a practice of assessing the contents of scientific production rather than just counting publications and citations in a select group of journals.

To be clear, the objective here is not to turn the clock back. Business schools, management consultants, and business media will continue to define management. The change should be in the kind of management that they are backing with their authority.

References

Bower, M. (1966) *The Will to Manage: Corporate success through programmed management*, New York: McGraw-Hill.

Crucini, C. and Kipping, M. (2001) "Management consultancies as global change agents? Evidence from Italy," *Journal of Organizational Change Management*, 14(6): 570–589.

Engwall, L. (2000) "Foreign role models and standardisation in Nordic business education," *Scandinavian Journal of Management*, 15(1): 1–24.

Grafström, M. (2006) *The Development of Swedish Business Journalism: Historical roots of an organisational field*, Doctoral dissertation, Uppsala: Uppsala University.

Hansen, M. T., Nohria, N., and Tierney, T. (1999) "What's your strategy for managing knowledge?" *Harvard Business Review*, 77(2): 106–116.

Hargadon, A. B. and Douglas, Y. (2001) "When innovations meet institutions: Edison and the design of the electric light," *Administrative Science Quarterly*, 46(3): 476–501.

Kipping, M. and Westerhuis, G. (2014) "The managerialization of banking: From blueprint to reality," *Management & Organizational History*, 9(4): 374–393.

Porter, M. E. (1980) *Competitive Strategy: Techniques for analyzing industries and competitors*, New York: The Free Press.

INDEX

AACSB (American Association of
  Collegiate Schools of Business) 25, 93–4,
  96, 99, 154, 155, 216, 217, 218–9, 220–1,
  222, 223, 224, 225–9
Aalto University School of Business 54
ABB (Asea Brown Boveri) 175
Abbott, J. 76
Abegglen, J. 257
Abernathy, W. J. 155
Abrahamson, E. 18
Abrams, R. 251
Academic Press 202, 207
Academy of International Business 201, 202
Academy of Management 34, 201, 202,
  203, 265, 266, 291
Academy of Management Executive 266
Academy of Management Journal 201, 202,
  204, 266, 267, 268, 271, 292
Academy of Management Perspectives 265, 266,
  267
Academy of Management Review 201, 202,
  203, 205, 206, 266, 267, 268, 269, 271
academic journals 82–6, 137–42, 200–206,
  265–73
Accenture 4, 236, 239, 241, 244, 245, 247,
  249, 250 *see also* Andersen Consulting
Accounting, Organisations and Society 202,
  205–6, 267
Accounting Review 124, 137, 138, 140, 141,
  200, 201, 266, 267, 271
accreditation of business schools 217–22
Ackoff, R. L 193

Actualidad Económica 198
Adams, W. 160
Addison-Wesley 133, 196, 197, 199, 258
*Administration: The Journal of Business
  Analysis and Control* 132
Administrative Science Quarterly 201, 202,
  204, 266, 267, 268, 269, 271
Administrative Staff College (Henley) 161
Admission Test for Graduate Study in
  Business (ATGSB) 153–4 *see also*
  Graduate Management Admission Test
  (GMAT)
Advanced Management Programme,
  Harvard Business School 100
Agency for International Development
  (AID) 155, 157–8, 160, 161, 173, 177,
  182 see also Economic Cooperation
  Administration (ECA); International
  Cooperation Administration
Agnelli, G. 120
Agnew, H. E. 140
Ahmedabad Institute of Management 158,
  160, 226
Aitken, H. 65
Ajzen, I. 268, 269
*Akademie für Handel, Verkehr und
  Verwaltung,* St. Gallen 50
Alajoutsijärvi, K. 32, 229
Albert Ramond and Associates 121, 169
Alcadipani, R. 227
Alchian, A. A. 200
Alchon, G. 111

298 Index

Alderson, W. 195
Alexander Proudfoot 170, 179, 236
Alford, R. R. 27
Aljian, G. W. 192
Allen, D. G. 43, 47, 48, 61, 97, 99
Allen, J. L. 123, 177, 180
Allstate 177
Allyn & Bacon 257
Altran Technologies 248
Aluminum Company of America (Alcoa) 70
Alvarez, J. L. 198
Amatori, F. 2
Amdam, R. P. 105
American Association of Public
    Accountants 63
American Association of University
    Instructors in Accounting 124
American Bankers' Association 53
American Economic Association 65, 83, 124
American Economic Review 83, 84, 140, 141,
    200, 267
American Express 242
American Finance Association 201, 202
American Institute of Certified Public
    Accountants (AICPA) 63, 237
*American Journal of Industrial and Business
    Management* 272
American Journal of Railway Appliances 77
American Journal of Small Business 203
American Machinist 65
American Management Association 207
American Management Systems 186, 187
American Marketing Association 138, 201,
    202
American Marketing Journal 140
American Society for Public Administration
    142
American Society of Mechanical Engineers
    (ASME) 64–7
Americanization 32, 134, 165, 215, 222,
    288
Amos Tuck School of Administration and
    Finance 47, see also Dartmouth College
Andersen, A. E. 19, 121–2, 132
Andersen Consulting (AC) 4, 236, 239, 247
    see also Accenture, Arthur Andersen & Co.
Andreasen, A. 195
Andrews, K. R. 100
Andriesse, C. D. 259
Ansoff, I. 206
Anthony, R. N. 258
Apple, M. W. 34
Appleton 78–9

Appleton-Lange 257
ARA Services 181
Archer, S. H. 193
Armbrüster, T. 248
Arnault, D. 251
Arnoff, E .L. 193
Arthur Andersen & Co. 184, 185, 186,
    237–8, 239
Arthur D. Little 60, 170, 175, 181, 182,
    183, 186, 248, 283 *see also* Little, A. D.
Arthur D. Little School of Management
    248
Arthur Young & Co. 61, 62, 63, 184, 186,
    237
Ashford, M. 247
Ashley, W. J. 53
Ashridge Management College 161
Asian Association of Management
    Organisations 169
Asian Institute of Management (AIM) 158,
    160
Associated Industrial Consultants (AIC)
    120, 172, 187, 235 *see also* Bedaux, C. E.
Association of Business Schools (ABS) 273
Association of Consulting Management
    Engineers (ACME) 125, 179, 187
Association of MBAs (AMBA) 219, 220,
    221, 225, 226
A. T. Kearney & Company 60, 124, 170,
    183, 186, 187, 242, 247
Atomic Energy Commission (AEC) 178
AT&T 195, 202, 244
Attwood-Boston Consultants, London 183
Augier, M. 14, 16, 26, 35, 96, 99, 150,
    151, 152, 216, 222
Ausschuß für wirtschaftliche Fertigung (AWF)
    114, 115
Axelrod, B. 19
auditing and accounting firms: Big Eight
    184–7, 237; Big Five 27, 237, 239; Bix
    Six 237; Big Four 61, 120, 172–3, 235,
    239, 240
Avon Books 256

Babbage, C. 15
Bach, G. L. 151
Bagley, C. 251
Bagozzi, R. P. 269
Bailes, K. 114
Bain, W. W. 181–2
Bain Consultants 182, 234, 248, 249
Bain Insights 248
Baird, J.W. 84

Balch, W. 2
Ball, R. 204, 205
Bandelj, N. 228, 229
Barber, L. 81
Barley, S. R. 18
Barnard, C. 16, 129, 133, 134
Barnes, R. M. 130
Barron, C. W. 81, 136
Barron's National Financial Weekly 136, 137, 199, 263
Barry, B. 164
Barsoux, J.-L. 159
Bartlett, C. A. 258
Barton, D. 250
Bates, G. E. 192
Bátiz-Lazo, B. 158, 160, 161
Baughman, J. L. 135
BCG Perspectives 248
Beall, J. 272
Beamish, P. W. 258
Beardsley, S. C. 251
BearingPoint 240 *see also* KPMG
Beatty, J. 135
Beaver, W. R. L. 206
Bedaux, C. E. 15, 72, 110, 117–20, 125, 172, 182, 286, 289
Bedeian, A. G. 4, 17, 18
Bedriftsøkonomisk Institutt (BI) 105
Bell, E. 219
Bell Journal of Economics and Management Science 202, 203, 205, 206
Benders, J. 4
Benjamin, W. A. 196, 197
Bennis, W. G. 36, 192, 216
Bergenstresser, C. 81
Berle, A. A. 10–11
Berlin Wall 213
Berry, G. 136
Berry, W. 136
Bertelsmann AG 133, 259, 262, 287
Bethel, L. L. 130, 131
Bethlehem Steel 66, 70
Die Betriebswirtschaft 85
Betriebswirtschaftslehre (BWL) 52, 86, 101, 102, 282 *see also* Schmalenbach, E.
Bettis, R. A. 35, 216–7, 230
Bever, D. van 248
Bhaskar, M. 274
Bhide, A. V. 180, 181
bibliometric 272–3
Bigtime Consulting 247 *see also* Indenture
Binda, V. 13
Biochemica et Biophysica Acta 259

Birmingham University Faculty of Commerce 52–3
Blackford, M. G. 2
Blackwell 78, 256, 260
Blake, J. D. 164
Blanchard, K. H. 257
Blanchard, M. 50, 51, 54, 103–4, 163
Blessing, M. 251
Bliemel, F. 195
Blockmans, W. 273
Bloemen, E. 112–3
Blom, S.-E. 195
Bloomberg, M. 263
Bloomberg Businessweek 263–4 *see also* *Business Week*
Blough, R. 192
Blount, S. 251
Blumberg, S. K. 111
Boel, B. 156
Boffey, L. F. 130, 131
Bologna Accord 224, 225, 226
Boothman, B. E. C. 55, 106, 162, 164
Booz, Allen & Hamilton 60, 123, 125, 170, 177, 180, 181, 182, 183, 186, 187, 241, 242, 244, 246, 247
Booz, E. G. 123, 125
Booz Allen Applied Research, Inc. (BAARINC) 177
Booz Eminent Scholar Award 34
Born, M. 134
Børsen 198
Bossard Consultants 243–4
Bossard, J. H. S. 47, 94, 96, 98, 99, 100, 101
Boston Consulting Group (BCG) 34, 181, 183–4, 186, 187, 234, 241, 246, 248, 249 *see also* Attwood-Boston Consultants; TFM Adams
Boston Globe 81
Boston Safe Deposit and Trust Company 181
Bottomley, H. 80
Bower, M. 124, 168, 179, 180, 181, 187, 250, 292
Boyd, C. 239
Boyd, H. W. 192, 195
Boyns, T. 113
Brandeis, L. 65, 68, 84
Braverman, H. 16
Brealey, R. 258
Brech, E. F. L. 14, 15, 16, 66, 67, 68, 70, 111, 112
Bretton Woods financial system 147

BRIC (Brazil, Russia, India, and China) markets 213
Briggs, A. 111
Bringert, L. 198
British Accounting Review 207
British American Tobacco 113
British Columbia, University of 162
British Journal of Management 271
Britt, S. H. 192
Brockhaus, R. H. 204
Broehl, W. G., Jr. 43, 47
Brophy, D. J. 206
Brown, P. 205
Brownlow, L. 15
Brownlow Committee 142
Bruce, K. 16
Buckley, P. 257
Buehrens, J. A. 169
Buffa, E. S. 193, 206
Bull France 243
Bulletin de la Société de l'Industrie minérale 85
Bund Deutscher Unternehmensberater (BDU) 173
Burnham, J. 11
Burpee, gardening titles 256
Burrell, G. 264
Business & Society 207
business media: academic disciplines in 283–4; adaptability in 273–4; alternative perspectives in 295; Anglo-American dominance of 287; authority of 281, 284; booming market for 263–5; business-related issues 283–4; circulation figures for business press 198–200; commercial logic and market-orientation of 287–90; commoditization of management 290–4; cross-national comparisons and linkages 30–3; cultural institutions, traditions as 290; dailies and periodicals, development of 284; development trajectory of 29–30, 280–4; early roots of 287; emergence of 280–4; expansion, circulation increases and new titles 136–7; expansion and globalization of management 290–4; expansion of publishing houses 191–8; focus on management, growth of 292; global commoditization of management through 293–4; global conglomerates, developments of 288–9; growth in interwar period for 127–34; growth and diversification of management publishing 191, 200–203, 204, 205–7; growth in journal publication 271–3; information

technology (IT), development of 273–4; innovative ways forward for 294–5; interactions with business schools and management consultants 33–6; international progression of 284–7; internationalization of 32–3; interwar period management publications 130–1; logics of 27–8; management, espousal of 292; management and business publishing frontrunners 74–81; management knowledge, "industry" of dissemination of 287; mergers and mass markets in 255–74; multinational multimedia publishers 255–62; new academic journals 200–7; online solutions 274; as organizational fields 24–9; ownership changes 263–5; "piggybacking" in development of 285–6; publishing entrants to 196–8; relations with business schools and management consultants 28–9; restructuration in 258–62; restructuring among publishing houses 196–8; scientific disciplines, organization of 82–3; specialized challengers to established newspapers 78–81; structural changes 27; US domination in sphere of 284–5
business schools: American-style business education, foreign progress for 155–64; Americanization of 32; Asia, expansion in 226–7, 228; Australia, developments in 104; authority of 281, 284; Canada, developments in 104; Central and Eastern Europe, expansion in 227–8; commercial logic and market-orientation of 287–90; commoditization of management 290–94; criticisms of, beginnings of 97; cross-national comparisons and linkages 30–33; curricular and administrative structuring, continuing developments of 92–3; development trajectory of 29–30, 280–4; developments within university education 160–1; diversity in, continuing developments 91–3; early expansions 45–53; emergence of 280–84; Europe, expansion in (differences in) 224–6; expansion and stratification 96–9; foreign expansion from US, divergence of developments in 99–104; foundations (failed and successful) in US 45–8; France, developments in 101–2; Germany,

Index **301**

developments in 99–101; growth of business education outside US (and limitations of) 162–5; higher commercial education, organization of 41–5; innovative ways forward for 294–5; interactions with management consultants and media 33–6; international circulation of US and European models 53–5; internationalization 32–3, 228–30, 284–7; Italy, developments in 103; Japan, developments in 103; Latin America, expansion in 227; logics of 27–8; market-driven US schools 215–17; MBA degree programs 28, 30, 33, 97, 98; explosive growth of 292–3; globalization of 223–30; Harvard introduction of 47; in US, 'new look' and 151–5; media rankings, definition and measurement of reputation with 217, 222–3; multiple moves and influences in Europe 48–53; Netherlands, developments in 103; nomenclature, changes in 93–5; Nordic countries, developments in 105; as organizational fields 24–9; origins of 286; "piggy-backing" in development of 285–6; pioneering initiatives 45–53; post-war transformation in US 149–52; post-war US offensive 155–6; professional recognition, struggle for 91–9; professionalism 93–6, 282, 291; relations with management consultants and media 28–9; schools (and faculties) of commerce established in Europe (1819–1919) 49–50; schools and institutes established overseas post-war based on US models 157–8; science thrust in (1950s) 154; societal consciousness of businessmen, aim of development of 288; stand-alone schools 156–60; state involvement in Europe 44–5; status of 98; structural changes 27; Turkey, developments in 103; United Kingdom, developments in 102; university-based graduate schools, MBA degree programs and 161–2; university focus in US 42–4; US domination in sphere of 284–5; US model in Europe 104
Business Week 137, 153, 222, 223, 230, 240, 263–4, 285 *see also Bloomberg Businessweek*

Button, E. 120, 235
Byrne, J. A. 35, 186, 246, 248, 250, 251
Byrnes, N. 240, 241
Byrt, W. 106, 162, 164

Caldas, M. P. 227
California Management Review 201, 202, 204, 205, 266, 267
Cambridge University 27, 44, 53, 104, 161, 224
Cambridge University Press 27, 76, 77–8, 79, 128, 131, 141, 202, 224, 260, 261, 262
Canadian Academic Accounting Association 265
Cantor, N. F. 131
Cap Gemini/Capgemini 4, 187, 239, 243, 244, 287
Carey, E. G. 68
Carnegie Corporation Report (1959) 150–1, 154, 216
Carnegie Institute of Technology 150, 151
Carney, C. 172
Carroll, L. 77
Carroll, T. H. 150
Cassis, Y. 11
CBS 256, 262
Cell 259
Central and Eastern European economies 213
Central Institute of Labour (CIT), Soviet Russia 114
Centre de Préparation aux Affaires (CPA) 106, 124, 159
Centre d'Études Industrielles (CEI), Switzerland 157, 162, 164
Cerf, B. 133
CGI 187, 241, 243, 244, 287
Chamberlain, N. W. 194
Chamberlin, E. 132
Champy, J. 4, 257, 264
Chandler, A. D., Jr. 2, 11, 12–3, 17, 115, 134, 196
Channon, D. F. 13, 235
Charnes, A. A. 193
Cheit, E. F. 155
Chen, X. 228
Chicago University School of Commerce and Administration 124
Chin, E. 248, 250
China Europe International Business School (CEIBS) 228
Chinese Institute of Scientific Management 114

302 Index

Choi, M. 158, 227
Choi, S.-J. 228
Chorafas, D. N. 257
Christensen, C. M. 139, 248
Christy, J. 72, 118, 120
Church, A. H. 130
Churchill, G. 204
Churchman, C. W. 193
Citibank 181
Clark, B. R. 25, 42, 43, 44
Clark, C. 140, 141
Clark, E. 66
Clark, J. M. 129
Clark, T. 19, 264
Clark, W. 114, 123, 129, 139, 169, 172
Clarkson, E. R. C. 63
Clarkson Gordon 63
CliffNotes 256
ClinicalKey 259
Clinton, C. 251
Clothier, R. 130, 131
Coffee, J. C. 61, 239
Cognizant 244–5
Cohen, M. D. 204, 205
Cohen, W. M. 268, 269
Cole, W. M. 84
College of Business Administration, Seoul
    National University 158
Collet, F. 222, 223, 224, 229, 230
Colli, A. 2
Collins 78
Collins, J. 195
Collins & Sons 256
Columbia Business School 150, 229
*Comité Internationale de l'Organisation
    Scientifique du Travail* (CIOS) 113, 169,
    172, 175
Comité national de l'organisation française
    (CNOF) 117
Commercial Press, Shanghai 141
*Commission générale de l'organisation
    scientifique du travail* (CGOST) 117
*Commission Générale d'Organisation
    Scientifique* (CEGOS) 117, 173
Commons, J. R. 84
Community of European Management
    Schools and International Companies
    (CEMS) 229
Comprehensive Research Journals 272
*Comprehensive Research Journal of Management
    and Business Studies* 272
Computer Management Group (CMG)
    243

Computer Sciences Corporation (CSC)
    241
Contemporary Accounting Research 265, 268
Continental 120
Converse, P. D. 140, 141
Conyngton, H. R. 79
Cook, W. F. 84
Cooper, R. 257
Cooper, W. W. 151, 193
Cooperative League 111
Coopers & Lybrand 185, 186, 237
Copeland, M. 138, 140, 141
Copeland, T. E. 196
Copen, M. 192
Copenhagen Business School 54, 226
Copley, F. B. 130, 131
Cornuel, E. 216, 225
corporate scandals 213
Cortada, J. W. 256
Coulter, M. 17
Coutant, F. R. 140
Cox, D. R. 193
Cox, G. V. 132
Cox, R. 195
Craig, D. 247
Crainer, S. 195, 264
Crampton, J. 121
Cray Electronics 235
Creamer, M. 245
Cresap, McCormick & Paget 123, 170,
    178, 181, 186
Crockett, H. G. 125, 179
Crowell-Collier 194, 197
Crozier, M. 196
Crucini, C. 287
Cullen, P. G. 32
Cummings, L. L. 34
Cyert, R. M. 151, 194, 205

Daft, R. L. 17
Dagens industri 198
Daily Telegraph 81
Daimler Benz 244
Dale, E. 14, 17
D'Ambrosio, C. A. 193
Dameron, S. 162, 225
Danell, R. 194, 268
Daniel, C. A. 153
Dartmouth College 47, 53, 95
Darwin, C. 79
Datar, S. M. 32
Dauphine University, Paris 163
David, D. K. 98

David, R. J. 60
David, T. 162, 164
Davila, C. 158, 160, 163
Davis, F. D. 269
Davis, G. F. 274
Davis, R. C. 130, 131
De Bellaigue, E. 262
de Man, H. 163
Deal, T. E. 258, 264
Dean, J. 132, 194
Dearden, J. 258
Dearlove, D. 195
Debis Systems Integration 244
decartelization of German and Japanese
    industries 147
Delhi Commercial College 54
Deloitte Haskins & Sells 185, 237
Deloitte & Co. 5, 63, 185, 240, 241, 247,
    248, 249, 250, 263
Deloitte & Touche 237
DeLone, W. H. 270
Deming, W. E. 169
Denning, S. 248
Dennison, H. S. 111
Demsetz, H. 200
Deutsche Bank 247
Development Alternatives, Inc. (DAI) 235
Dewhurst, J. F. 47, 94, 95, 96, 98, 99, 100,
    101
Dickey, D. A. 200
Dickinson, Z. C. 96
Dickson, W. J. 132
Diebold Group 170
Diemer, H. 76, 77
DiMaggio, P. J. 25–6, 33
Dirksen, C. J. 96, 218
Dockery-Cockrell Commission 63
Donham, W. B. 95, 96–7, 98, 99, 100,
    106, 138, 139
Doriot, G. 106, 159
Doubleday 259
Douglas, Y. 281
Dow Jones 81, 82, 136, 195, 263, 294
Drucker, P. F. 12, 16, 17, 129, 134–6, 139,
    194, 195, 257
Dubois, B. 195
Dun & Bradstreet (D&B) 244
Dunbar, C. F. 84
Duncan, J. C. 79, 84
Duncan, J. H. 171
Dunn, M. B. 28
Dunnette, M. D. 196
Dunod et Pinat 134

DuPont 12, 119
Durand, R. 218, 219
Durand, T. 162, 225
Dyas, G. P. 13

Eastman Kodak 119, 242
Les Échos 137, 198, 264
École des Hautes Études Commerciales
    deMontréal 54
École des Hautes Etudes Commerciales (HEC),
    Paris 49, 51, 54, 103–4, 163, 229
École Spéciale de Commerce et d'Industrie 48–9
    see alsoÉcole Supérieure de Commerce de
    Paris (ESCP)
Écoles supérieures de commerce 54; Algiers 54;
    Bordeaux 49; Dijon 50; Le Havre 49;
    Lille 49; Lyon 49; Marseille 49;
    Montpellier 49; Mulhouse 49; Nancy
    49; Rouen 49
École Supérieure de Commerce de Paris (ESCP)
    48, 49, 103, 163; see also École Spéciale
    de Commerce et d'Industrie
École Supérieure des Sciences Économiques et
    Commerciales (ESSEC) 49, 51, 163, 229
Econometrica 135, 136, 138, 139, 141, 200,
    267, 270
Economic Cooperation Administration
    (ECA) 155 see also Agency for
    International Development (AID);
    International Cooperation
    Administration (ICA)
Economic Observer 264
Economist 80, 82, 136, 137, 191, 199, 222,
    247, 263, 284
Edersheim, E. H. 180
Edfelt, R. 153, 154, 161, 162, 164
Educational Testing Service (ETS) 153 see
    also Admission Test for Graduate Study
    in Business (ATGSB)
Edward, Duke of Windsor 118, 120
Edward Elgar 260
Edwards, R. D. 80, 136, 199
Eisenhardt, K. M. 268, 269
electronic databases 272–3
Eiteman, D. K. 196
Electric Storage Battery Company 70
Electrolux 175
Electronic Data Services (EDS) 241–2, 247
Elkind, P. 19
Elsbach, K. D. 217, 222
Elsevier 78, 197, 201, 202, 203, 207, 258,
    259, 261, 262, 265, 273, 287, 294
Elsevier Research Intelligence 259

304 Index

Emerson, H. 15, 59, 69, 70, 72, 113–4, 116, 118, 286
Emerson, S. 70, 116
Emerson Efficiency Engineers 70, 72 115–6
Engwall, L. 12, 13, 14, 18, 28, 32–3, 36, 42, 49–50, 52, 53, 54, 82, 105, 122, 161, 163, 194, 226, 229, 245, 251, 264, 268, 273, 287
Enron 19, 213, 216, 234, 239, 249–50, 281, 290
Enteman, W. F. 1
Entrepreneurship Theory and Practice 202, 203, 205, 206, 267
Erasmus University 54, 271
Ernst, B. 19, 246
Ernst & Ernst 170, 185
Ernst & Whinney 61, 185, 186, 237
Ernst & Young 5, 237, 239, 244 *see also* EY
Escola de Administração, Universidade Federal da Bahia 158
Escola de Administração de Empresas de São Paulo (FGV-EAESP) 157, 160, 161
Escuela de Administración de Empresas (EAE), Spain 157
Escuela de Administración de Negocios para Graduados (ESAN), Peru 158, 160
Escuela de Administración y Finanzas (EAFIT), Colombia 158
Escuela de Graduados en Administración, ITESM, Mexico 158, 161
Escuela de Organización Industrial (EOI), Spain 157, 161
Escuela Nacional de Contabilidad y Administración, Universidad Nacional Autónoma de México (UNAM) 157
Escuela Superior de Administración de Empresas (ESADE), Spain 157, 161, 163, 225
Escuela Superior de Contabilidad y Administración, Instituto Politécnico Nacional (IPN), Mexico 158
Esquerre, P.-J. 79
Ettinger, K. E. 192
Ettinger, R. P. 133
European Economic Community (EEC) 147, 182 *see also* European Union (EU)
European Foundation for Management Development (EFMD) 219
European Institute for Advanced Studies in Management (EIASM) 162
European Management Journal 292
European Productivity Agency (EPA) 155, 159

European Quality Improvement System (EQUIS) 219, 220, 221, 225, 226, 229, 285
European School of Management and Technology (ESMT), Berlin 226
European Union (EU) 224, 225, 228 *see also* European Economic Community (EEC)
Ewing, D. W. 194
Executive 266
Exman, E. 76, 131, 194
Expansión 264
Exportakademie, Vienna 50
Evans, M. 236
EY (formerly Ernst & Young) 5, 61, 240, 241, 247, 249

Fabozzi, F. J. 256
Fairchild, G. 18
Fama, E. F. 142, 200, 268, 269
Fast Five internet consulting firms 244–5
Fauri, F. 50, 52, 105, 106
Faust, M. 4, 18
Fayerweather, J. 192
Fayol, H. 16, 17, 19, 71, 85, 112, 117, 129, 134, 173, 285, 292
FCLT (Focusing Capital on the Long Term) 250
Fear, J. R. 13
Fédération européenne des associations de conseil en organisation (FEACO) 173
Fehling, A. W. 45, 50, 51, 52, 55, 101, 103
Feigenbaum, A.V. 192
Feiger, G. 251
Feldenkirchen, W. 13
Ferraro, F. 34
Fesler, J. W. 111
Fiat 120
Le Figaro 81
Financial News 80, 136, 198
Financial Times 35, 81, 82, 83, 136,191, 198, 199, 222, 223, 229, 263, 284–5, 294; beginnings of business publishing 80, 81; *FT Deutschland* 263; building audiences 136, 138, 139–40; early developments in business publishing 82, 83
Fincham, R. 19, 236
Fink, D. 60, 184
Fisher, I. 77
Fitzpatrick, K. 274
Fitzsimons, P. 1
FIZ Chemie Berlin 256
Flaherty, J. E. 135

Index 305

Flamholtz, E. 204, 205
Flanner, J. 118
Flesher, D. L. 99, 217, 218
Flexner, A. 95, 151
Fligstein, N. 13, 14, 25, 26, 28–9, 140, 260
Follett, M. P. 112
Fong, C. T. 33, 35, 215
For Dummies series 256
Forbes 80, 81, 82 136, 137, 200, 222, 246, 264, 284
Forbes, B. C. 81, 136
Ford, Bacon & Davis 125
Ford, H. 15, 134
Ford Foundation 26, 150, 151, 152, 154, 155, 156, 159–60, 162, 173–4, 216, 223, 285
Ford Motor Company 175
Fornell, C. 268, 269
Forrester, D. A. R. 86
Fortune 125, 137, 178, 200, 264
Foster, R. 19
Fourcade, M. 151, 153
Fowler, F. G. 1
Fowler, H. W. 1
Fragueiro, F. 159, 164
Francis (Pope) 5
Franko, L. G. 13
Fraser, C. 97
Free Press 196, 197, 258, 290
Freeland, R. F. 12
Freeman, J. 260
French, K. R. 268, 269
Friedland, R. 27
Friedman, M. 140, 141
Friga, P. N. 35, 216–7, 230
Frisch, R. 138
Frost, P. J. 34
Fruin, W. M. 11
Fry, G. S. 123
Fry Consultants 181
Fukuyama, F. 248
Fuller, W. A. 200
Furusten, S. 34, 122

Gaddafi, M. 248
Galbraith, J. R. 134, 256
Galileo, G. 10
Gantt, H. L. 15, 67, 68, 84, 116
Gantt chart 116
Gapper, J. 247
Gardiner, G. 131
Garfield, E. 272
Garraty, J. A. 160

Garvin, D. A. 32
Gastev, A. 114
Gates, B. 195
Gaughan, P. A. 273
Gavin, J. M. 176, 183
Gay, E. F. 48, 95, 99
Geissler, L. R. 84
Gellerman, S. W. 192
Gemelli, G. 156, 158, 159
General Electric 119, 195, 264
General Motors 12, 70, 135, 178
George, C. S., Jr. 14, 15, 16
George S. May Company 60, 125, 179, 182, 236, 289, see also May, G. S.
Gerstenberg, C. W. 133
Gerstner, L. 242, 251
Geske, R. 206
Ghemawat, P. 34, 251
Ghoshal, S. 258
Ghosn, Carlos 251
Ghosn, Caroline 251
Gibson, W. B. 175
Giddens, A. 248
Giddings, F. H. 83
Gilbreth, F. B., Jr. 68
Gilbreth, F. B. 15, 68, 69, 71, 113, 134
Gilbreth, L. M. 68, 69, 71, 77, 113, 169, 288
Gilman, S. W. 84
GIT Verlag 256
Gleeson, R. E. 43, 47, 48, 97, 99, 150, 151, 152, 153
Glimstedt, H. 169, 172
Gloeckner, G. A. 85
Glueck, W. F. 192
Godin, S. 187, 243
Goerdeler, R. 237
Goethe University Frankfurt 226
Goetz, B. E. 192
Going, C. B. 76, 77
Gomez-Samper, H. 227
Goodall, K. 25, 228
Google Books 1–2
Google Scholar 141, 200, 204, 206, 270, 273
Gordon, R. A. 47. 94, 99, 100, 150, 151–2
see also Ford Foundation Report
Götze, H. 78
Gouldner, A. W. 194
Govindarajan, V. 258
Gowin, E. B. 132
Graduate Business Admission Council (GBAC) 154
Graduate Management Admission Council (GMAC) 154

306 Index

Graduate School of Business
    Administration, Korea University 158
Graduate School of Business
    Administration, Yonsei University 158
Graduate School of Industrial
    Administration (GSIA), Carnegie
    Institute of Technology 53, 150, 151
Grafström, M. 287
Graham, P. 69
grandes écoles 13, 26, 44–5, 51, 54, 104, 119,
    225, 282
Greatbatch, D. 19
Great Depression 91, 92, 110, 122, 124,
    136, 236
Green, P. E. 205, 206
Greenwood, R. 25, 27, 28, 63, 185, 186,
    239
Greenwood, R. G. 14, 16
Greiner, L. E. 200, 201
Grey, C. 230
Gronke, H. 60
Grönroos, C. 256
Gruber, Titze und Partner, Germany 243
Guillén, M. F. 17, 18, 71, 134
Gulick, L. H. 15, 16, 111, 112
Gunnarsson, E. 13
Gupta, R. 250
Gushée, E. T. 130, 131
Gutenberg, E. 197
Guthey, E. 264
Gutiérrez, I. 225
Guttman, D. 178

H. B. Maynard & Company 170, 171, 172,
    179, 236, see also Maynard, H. B.
Hackman, J. R. 200, 201, 205, 206
Hadden, B. 137
Hage, J. 193
Hague, W. 251
Haines, L. 240
Haley, K. B. 193
Hall, G. S. 84
Hall, M. 133
Halsey, F. A. 65, 118
Hamel, G. 264
Hamidiye Ticaret Mektebi, Istanbul 49
Hamilton, C. L. 123, 177
Hamm, S. 245
Hammer, M. 4, 257, 264
Hammonds, K. H. 245
Handelsblatt 198, 264
Handelshochschulen in Germany 51–2, 93,
    101–3, 282, 285; Aachen 50–51; Berlin

49, 52, 53, 54, 55; Cologne 49, 51, 52,
    53, 85; Königsberg 49, 101; Leipzig 49,
    51, 52, 55, 86; Mannheim 49, 101, 103;
    Nuremberg 101
Handfield-Jones, H. 19
Hannah, L. 11
Hannan, M. T. 260
Hansen, M. T. 293
Hardy, C. 26
Hardy, Q. 242
Hargadon, A. B. 281
Harper 134, 255–7; establishment of (1817)
    75, 76; growth in interwar period for
    129–31; postwar expansion for 191, 194,
    197–8
Harper, James and John 76
Harper & Row 194, 256, 257
HarperCollins 199, 256–7, 261, 262, 263
Harper magazines 76, 135
Harris, R. G. 154
Harvard Business Manager 292
Harvard Business Publishing 260
Harvard Business Review 34, 135, 140, 141,
    178, 179, 200, 201, 248, 284, 292;
    audiences for business publishing,
    widening of 137, 138, 139; mergers and
    mass markets in media 266, 267, 268,
    269
Harvard Business School (HBS) 19, 27, 66,
    68, 111, 113 ,122, 137–8, 163, 176,
    178–9, 181, 242, 244, 248, 249, 282,
    283; business education, establishment of
    92, 98–9, 111; Dean Donham and the
    case method at 97; making business
    education scientific 150, 153, 154, 159,
    160; Harvard Graduate School of
    Business Administration 47–8
Harvard University Press 79, 133, 196
Harvey, P. 55
Haskins & Sells 185
Haskins, C. W. 63
Häußner, J. 60
Haustein, S. 273
Haveman, H. A. 60
Hawley, F. B. 84
Hawthorne studies 15, 98, 129, 132
Hay, E. N. 122
Hay Group 186–7
Hayek, F. A. von 140, 141
Hayes, D. A. 193
Hayes, R. H. 155
Haynes, B. R. 43, 45, 46, 94
Hearst Book Group 256

Heck, J. L. 136, 271
Hedmo, T. 82
Heilman, R. E. 95, 98, 99
Heinemann 134
Hellema, P. 120, 173
Helsinki School of Economics 54
Hemmungs-Wirtén, E. 262
Hempel, E. H. 130
Henderson, B. D. 181–2
Hevesi, D. 4
Hewitt, E. 122
Hewitt Associates 186–7
Hewlett-Packard (HP) 242
Higdon, H. 121, 123, 124, 125, 169, 170, 174, 177, 179, 180, 182, 184, 186, 187
Higuchi, Y. 227
Hijmans, E. 120
Hill, A. 240, 241, 250
Hill, J. 75–6
Hill, J. W. 194
Hill, L. H. 131,
Hill, T. M. 54, 158, 160
Hinings, C. R. 28
Hirschman, A. O. 196
Hitotsubashi University 55
Hitt, M. A. 18
Hmimda, N. 228
Hoffman, A. J. 26, 27
Hogate, K. C. 136
Holmström, B. 205, 206
Holtzbrinck 257, 262, 264
Hommel, U. 216, 225
Hong Kong University of Science and Technology (HKUST) 271
Hood, N. 257
Hook, C. R. 131
Hoover, S. R. 76–7, 85
Hoover Commission on the Organization of the Executive Branch 178
Hotchkiss, W. E. 47, 95–6
Hotelling, H. 140, 141
Hout, T. M. 249
Howell, J. E. 47. 94, 99, 100, 150, 151–2 see also Ford Foundation Report
Howell Book House 256
Hoxie, R. F. 79
Huczynski, A. A. 19
Huff, A. S. 226
Hult International Business School 177, 248 see also Arthur D. Little School of Management
Human Relations 207, 271

Human Resource Management 202, 203, 204, 268
Hungry Minds 256
Huselid, M. A. 203
Huxley, T. 79

Iacocca, L. 35, 264
IBM Consulting Group 175, 241, 242–3, 244, 249
IBM Global Services 240
IBusiness 272
Idaho University Press 261
Illinois University Commerce Program 45–6
Imbeau, A. 243
Indenture 247
Indian Institute of Management, Calcutta 158, 160
Industrial Bulletin 176
Industrial Engineering Magazine 68
Industrial Marketing Management 207
Industrial Organization 196
Information Systems Research 265, 266, 267, 270
Informs (Institute for Operations Research and the Management Sciences) 202, 203, 265, 266
Infosys 245
INSEAD (L'Institut européen d'administration des affaires) 157, 159, 161, 164, 271, 287
Institut d'Administration des Entreprises (IAE), France 157, 160, 161, 162
Institut pour l'Étude des Méthodes de Direction de l'Entreprise (IMEDE), Switzerland 157, 164
Institut Supérieur de Commerce Saint Ignace, Antwerp 49
Institut Supérieur de Commerce de l'Etat, Antwerp 49
Institute for Operations Research 265
Institute of Administrative Sciences, University of Tehran 157
Institute of Business Administration, University of Karachi 157
Institute of Chartered Accountants in England and Wales (ICAEW) 61
Institute of Management Consultants (IMC), UK and USA 173, 179, 181, 187
Institute of Management Science 201
Instituto Católico de Administración y Dirección de Empresas (ICADE), Spain 157, 161, 163

308 Index

Instituto Centroamericano de Administración de Empresas (INCAE) 158, 160
Instituto de Administração, Universidade Federal do Rio Grande do Sul 158
Instituto de Estudios Superiores de Administración (IESA), Venezuela 158, 160
Instituto Panamericano de Alta Dirección de Empresa (IPADE) 158, 160
Instituto Superior de Estudios de la Empresa (IESE), Universidad de Navarra 34, 157, 160, 164, 225
Insull, A. 122
Integrated Whale Media Investments 264
International Association for Business and Society 207
International Chamber of Commerce (ICC) 239
International Cooperation Administration (ICA) 155 see also Agency for International Development (AID); Economic Cooperation Administration (ECA)
International Industrial Conference (IIC) 175
International Institute for Management Development (IMD) 164, 287
International Journal of Management Reviews 271
International Labour Organization (ILO) 113
International Management Institute (IMI) 121, 113, 164
International MTM Directorate (IMD) 171
Iowa University Press 260
Irwin (Richard D. Irwin Publications) 195, 257, 258
Ishida, H. 164
Isletme Iktisadi Enstitüsü (IIE), Istanbul Üniversitesi 157, 161
Istituto Post-universitario per lo Studio dell'Organizzazione Aziendale (IPSOA) 157, 161
Istituto Superiore per Imprenditori e Dirigenti d'Azienda (ISIDA), Italy 157
iXL 245

Jackson, B. 264
Jackson, C. 235
Jackson, H. P. 43, 45, 46, 94
Jacobson, T. C. 75, 76, 78, 79, 131, 193, 194, 196, 197, 256, 257
Jagodzinski, C. M. 77, 79, 260

James, E. 76, 77, 131
James, E. J. 43–4, 46, 47, 53–4
James O. McKinsey and Company, Accountants and Management Engineers 124–5
Japanese efficiency movement 113
Jastrow, I. 54
Jeacle, I. 111
Jensen, M. 11
Jensen, R. E 138, 271
Jitsugyo Senmon Gakko, Japan 55
Johanson, J. 204, 205, 206
John, R. R. 11
John Day & Co. 134
John Deere 177
Johns Hopkins University Press 77, 79, 260
Johnson, A. 175
Johnson, H. T. 260
Johnson, S. 257
Johnson & Johnson 176
Joint Stock Companies Act (1844) 61
Joly, Hervé 13
Joly, Hubert 251
Jones, C. 28
Jones, E. 61, 235
Jones, E. D. 81, 84, 94, 95
Jones Day law firm 124
Jonson, B. 69
Jossey-Bass 256, 257
Journal in Financial Risk Management 272
Journal of Accounting and Economics 203, 206, 267, 271
Journal of Accounting Research 202, 203, 204, 267, 271
Journal of Applied Psychology 83–4, 140, 141, 200, 201, 267, 269
Journal of Business 131, 141, 142, 284
Journal of Business Ethics 265, 268
Journal of Business Research 207
Journal of Business Venturing 265, 266, 267
Journal of Consumer Psychology 265, 268
Journal of Consumer Research 202, 203, 205, 206, 267
Journal of Finance 201, 202, 204, 266, 267
Journal of Financial and Quantitative Analysis 202, 203, 206, 267
Journal of Financial Economics 207, 265, 266, 267, 268, 269
Journal of International Business Studies 201, 202, 203, 205, 206, 257, 267
Journal of Management 207, 268, 292
Journal of Management Studies 202, 203, 204, 267, 268, 271, 292

Journal of Marketing 132, 137, 138, 140, 141, 200, 201, 267, 268, 269, 271
Journal of Marketing Research 201, 202, 203, 204, 267, 268, 269, 271
Journal of Operations Management 203, 206, 267
Journal of Political Economy 83, 84, 140, 141, 200, 267, 268, 269
Journal of Service Science and Management 272
Journal of the American Statistical Association 83, 84, 140, 141, 200, 266, 267
Juusola, K. 32, 229
JSTOR 141
Juran, J. M. 116, 130, 131, 169, 192

Kahn, E. J., Jr. 60, 175–7
Kahneman, D. 142, 200
Kajima Trust Bank 70
Kampf, S. 187, 243
Kanigel, R. 15, 65, 66, 67
Kanter, R. M. 139, 264
Kaplan, J. 196
Kaplan, R. S. 260
Kaplan, S. 19
Karsten, L. 105
Kearney, A. T. 124, 178–9
Keio University 164
Keir, D. 78
Kelley, C. 196
Kennedy, A. A. 258, 264
Kennedy, J. F. 176
Kennedy Consulting Research 241
Kereskedelmi Akadémia, Budapest 50
Kernan, J. B. 203
Kester, R. 132
Kettunen, K. 54, 105, 161, 163
Keynes, J. M. 132, 140, 141
Khurana, R. 14, 25, 47, 48, 95–7, 100, 101, 150, 151, 153, 154, 216, 218
Kiechel, W. 181
Kieser, A. 19, 101, 102, 103, 105, 163, 222, 246
Kihn, M. 247
Kilgore, B. 136, 198
Kim, P. S. 2, 10, 60
King, W. R. 206
Kingsley, C. 77
Kipling, R. 77, 79
Kipping, M. 5, 13, 15, 26, 28, 32–3, 42, 49–50, 54, 61, 69, 71, 104–6, 114, 115, 117–9, 120, 156–8, 163–4, 171–5, 179, 180, 181–3, 226, 229, 236, 241, 245, 246, 248, 287, 292

Kirby, M. 174
Kirkpatrick, I. 241
Kjaer, P. 101, 102, 103, 105
Klaasen, A. 245
Klein, H. J. 60
Kleiner, A. 123, 177, 180, 181, 182
Klopfer, D. 133
Kluwer Academic Publishers 259
Klynveld Main Goerdeler (KMG) 237 *see also* KPMG
K-Mart 250
Knoblach, B. 60, 184
Knowles, A. S. 130, 131
Kobe University 161
Koenig, C. 164, 226
Kohler, E. 138
Koontz, H. 16
Kotler, P. 194, 195, 200, 201, 268, 269, 290
KPMG 237, 239–40, 241 *see also* Klynveld Main Goerdeler
Kraines, O. 63
Kramer, R. M. 217, 222
Kreis, S. 5, 119
Kroeger, A. 96, 218
Kruk, M. 86
Kull, D. C. 171
Kumar, A. 250
Kunda, G. 18
Kurt Salmon Associates 170, 171, 236 *see also* Salmon, K.
Kurtz, H. 81, 137
Kynaston, D. 80, 136, 198, 263

Lamberg, J.-A. 32, 229
Lang, V. 25, 228
Lancaster, J. 69
Lancet 259
Lansburgh, R. H. 130, 131
Larcker, D. F. 268, 269
Larçon, J.-P. 228
Larivière, V. 273
Lasser, J. K. 130
Laughlin, J. L. 84
Lawrence, P. R. 196, 256
Lawrence, T. B. 26
Lawrenson, J. 81
Lazo, A. 240
Le Châtelier, H. 15, 71, 116
Leavitt, H. J. 156
Lee, A. M. 193
Lee, R. R. 46
Leffingwell, W. H. 130, 131

310 Index

Legge, K. 257
Lester B. Knight and Associates 170
Levin, R. I. 192
Levinthal, D. A. 268, 269
Levitt, T. 139, 260, 273
Levy, S. J. 200, 201
Lewin, M. D. 179, 181, 187
Lewis, B. T. 192
Li, D. H. 192
Li, L. 228
Liebman, C. 196
Likert. R. 192
Lindblom, C. E. 142
Lindenfeld, D. F. 51, 52, 102
LinkedIn 236
Lippitt, G. L. 192
Liss 256
Little, A. D. 175–6 see also Arthur D. Little
Little Brown 256
Locke, R. R. 1, 44, 45, 52, 99, 102, 103, 104
Lockwood, J. 45
Locomotive Engineer 77
Lofty, S. 243
Logica 243
Lombard, F. 118
London Business School (LBS) 271;
  London Graduate School of Business
  Studies, University of London 158
London Financial Guide 80
London School of Economics and Political
  Science (LSE) 49, 53
Long Range Planning 205
Longmans 78, 191, 197, 199
Longobardi, E. C. 48, 49–50, 53
Lorien 235
Lorsch, J. W. 196
Lounsbury, M. 27
Lowry, S. M., 130, 131, 171
Lu, J. 228
Luce, H. R. 137, 175
Luigi Bocconi, Milan 49, 50; Business School
  164, 226
LUISS Business School, Rome 226
LVMH (Louis Vuitton Moët Hennessy)
  251, 264
Lybrand, Ross Bros. & Montgomery 170, 185
Lyon, L. S. 43, 46, 94, 95

McAdam, D. 25, 26, 28–9
McCrea, R. 46
McCraw, T. K. 2

McCune, G.197
McCune, S. M. 197
McDonald, D. 124, 178, 179, 180, 181, 249, 250
McDougald, M. S. 61, 185, 186, 239
McFadden, D. 142
McFarland, D. E. 194
McGann, J. G. 249
McGlade, J. 155
McGraw, J. H. 76
McGraw-Hill 257–8, 259, 263;
  establishment of (1889) 74, 75–6;
  growth in interwar period for
  129–31; postwar expansion for 191–3,
  197–8
McGraw-Hill Education 258, 262
McGraw-Hill Financial 76, 193, 258
McGuire, J. 218, 219
McKenna, C. D. 13, 60, 123, 124, 174, 178, 179, 180, 242, 247
MacKenzie, O. 218
McKibbin, L. E. 154, 155, 218, 228, 258
McKinsey, J. O. 124–5, 132, 138, 179, 283
McKinsey & Co. 5, 13, 19, 59, 122–3, 235, 241, 242, 244; alumni network, extent
  of 251; assertion of management
  consulting 170, 178–9, 181, 182, 186,
  187; globalization of consulting business
  246, 247, 248, 249–50
McKinsey Award 34
McKinsey Quarterly 34, 179, 203, 248, 266, 292
McLean, B. 19
McLean, E. R. 270
McLean, J. 169, 170, 171
Maciariello, J. A. 135
Machiavelli, N. 15, 60
Macmillan 196, 197, 257; establishment of
  (1843) 74, 75, 76; growth in interwar
  period for 127–8; postwar expansion for
  191, 193–4, 197–8
Macmillan, A. 76–7
Macmillan, D. 76–7
Macmillan's Magazine 77
McNair, M. P. 97, 98, 132
Madigan, C. 36, 247
Magee, J. 176
Maguire, S. 26
Mahadeva, W. K. 244
Maier, C. S. 111
Maier, N. R. F. 193
Main Lafrentz & Co. 237
Malcolm, J. A. 171

Index **311**

management: authorities on 4–5; business media 4; business schools 5; defining management 5–6; development of, perspectives on 9–20; expansion and transformation of practice 12–13; as fashion 18–20; historical perspective on 5–6; human relations and scientific management 15–17; ideas in, early origins of 14–16; as innovation 14–18; management consultants 4–5; management thought, Wren's history of 17–18; manager backgrounds, change in 13–14; managerialism 1; multi-divisional (M-form) organizations 12–13, 174, 293; origins of managers and 10–12; origins of word 1–2; as practice 9–10; scientific management, human relations and 16–17; spread of usage 2–4; term and practice, application as 1

management books 129–34, 134–6, 197, 248, 257, 264–5, 287

Management Consultancies Association (MCA), UK 172–3

management consultants: accountancy and auditing, consolidation of 184–7; accountants and beginnings of 61–64; accounting, ongoing trends in 121–22; American invention 286; Americanization of 32; authority of 281, 284; business process reengineering (BPR) 236; Charles E. Bedaux (and firm of) 117–19; expansion overseas by 119–21; China, waning of efforts in 113–4; collective arrangements within 290; commercial logic and market-orientation of 287–90; commoditization of management 290–4; consulting engineers 168–74; consulting firms by billings, top 20 (1968) 170; consulting firms by revenue, top 20 (1982) 186; cooperative logic in Germany 114–5; critiques of, suggestions from 295; cross-national comparisons and linkages 30–3; development trajectory for 29–30, 280–4; dissemination of ideas of scientific management 70–2; efficiency, growth of business in 115–20; élite graduate schools, hiring from 180; Elite Three 235, 248, 249, 250; emergence of 67–70, 280–4; European consulting engineers 172–4; European expansion of US consultants 182–3; expansion and globalization of management 290–4;

external mission for 181; Frederick W. Taylor and beginnings of 59, 60, 64, 65–66, 67, 68, 70; human resources consulting 121; image, importance for 180; information technology (IT) 236–46; innovative ways forward for 294–5; interactions with business schools and media 33–6; international expansion, replication and 182–4; international progression of 284–7; internationalization of 32–3; Japan, waning of efforts in 113; legal precedent in remaking of consulting 180; Lillian Gilbreth, first lady of management 69–70; logics of 27–8; Lyndall F. Urwick, management propagator 111–3, 117; management advisory services (MAS) 237; management engineering 283; management knowledge, 'industry' of dissemination of 287; operations research 174, 176, 177, 193, 197, 205, 266, 283; as organizational fields 24–9; origins of consulting, perspectives on 59–61; "piggy-backing" in development of 285–6; professional views on prospects for (interwar perspective) 121–4; professionalism 289–90; authority in 177–82; science and 174–84; quality in US consulting firms, focus on 169–72; relations with business schools and media 28–9; Russia, waning of efforts in 114; science, emphasis on 174–7; scientific management 234–6; development of 283, 291–2; efficiency experts and 64–72; selective access to partnership 180; strategy and organization consulting 246–51; structural changes 27; Taylorist ideology and practice, expansion of 110–3; US and beginnings of scientific management and 64–6; US consulting engineers 115–7; US domination in sphere of 284–5

Management Consulting Group (MCG) 236

Management Consulting Services (MCS) 235

Management Education Institute (MEI) 177 *see also* Arthur D. Little School of Management, Hult International Business School

Management Research Groups (MRGs) 111, 112, 117

Management Science 201, 202, 204, 205, 266, 267, 268, 269, 292

312 Index

Management Science America 170
Management Systems Corporation 186
Manager Magazin 1, 4, 198, 264, 292
Manchester Business School, Manchester University 158
Manchester Guardian 80–1, 259
Mannheim University 226
Manufacturers' Research Association (MRA) 111
Marceau, J. 157–8, 159, 162
March, J. G. 14, 16, 26, 35, 96, 97, 99, 150, 151, 152, 153, 193, 194, 196, 201, 204, 205, 216, 222
MarchFIRST 245
Marketing Science 265, 266, 267
Markowitz, H. 204, 256
Marsh, C. S. 46
Marsh, S. 60
Marsh & McLennan 122
Marshall, L. C. 25, 41, 44, 94–6, 98, 99, 132
Marshall Fields 124
Marshall Plan 155, 161, 223
Marsman, J. 120, 173
Maruzen Co., Tokyo 141
Marwick, J. 121
Maslow, A. H. 194
Massachusetts Board of Higher Education 177
Massachusetts Institute of Technology (MIT) 68, 100, 119, 160, 175, 195, 202, 207; Sloan School of Management 160
Master in Management (MIM) program 229
Mattessich, R. 195
Maurice, M. 206
Mauser, F. F. 192
Maxwell, R. 196–7, 205
Maxwell Communications 256
May, G. S. 60, 125, 179, 182, 236, 289
Mayer, M. 13
Maynard, H. B. 130, 131, 168, 171, 172, 179, 192, 236
Maynard, M. 264
Mayo, E. 15–6, 98, 122, 130, 131
Mazza, C. 198
MBA 28, 30, 33, 47, 97, 98–100, 115; Executive MBA 223, 229; explosive growth of 292–3; globalization of 223–30; Harvard introduction of 47–8; in US, "new look" and 152–5
McDermott, K. 61
McDonald Currie & Co 185

Mead, F. 172
Means, G. C. 10–11
Meckling, W. H. 11
Meiji University 161
Melitz, M. J. 270
Mellon, W. L. 151
Merkle, J. E. 65, 70, 71, 114
Merriam, C. 15
Methods-Time-Measurement (MTM) 171, 172
Meyer, H.-D. 49–50, 51, 52, 99, 101
Meyer, J. W. 33
Michaels, E. 19
Michelini, J. 159, 164
Michigan State University (MSU) 160
Michigan University Press 260
Micklethwait, J. 4, 18, 247
Microsoft 245
Midvale Steel 66
Miles, R. E. 205, 206
Miner, J. B. 194
Mintzberg, H. 194, 204, 205, 216, 250, 258
MIS Quarterly 202, 203, 206, 266, 267, 269
MIT Press 134
Mitchell, R. 121
Mitsubishi Research Institute (MRI) 175
Mitsui Company 81
Mixter, C. W. 84
Mogensen, A. H. 130, 131
Moggridge, D. E. 131
Mongeon, P. 273
Monitor 247, 248, 250
Montgomery, R. H. 79
Montgomery Ward 121
Mooney, B. 81
Mooney, J. D. 16, 17
Moore, J. H. 75, 76
Moore, M. V. 121
Morgan Stanley 239
Morgenstern, O. 132
Morgeson, F. P. 222, 223, 230
Morrini, A. M. 72
Morse, D. 206
Möslein, K. M. 226
Moutet, A. 71, 72, 116, 117, 120
MTM International 171 *see also* Methods-Time Measurement
Mumbai Commercial College 54
Mur, J. 198
Murdoch, R. 256, 263
Murphy, M. E. 104
Musson, D. 260
Myers, S. 258

Nahrgang, J. D. 222, 223, 230
NASA (National Aeronautics and Space Administration) 178
National Association of Accredited Commercial Schools (US) 43
National Center for Education Statistics (NCES) 153, 215–6
National Industrial Conference Board (NICB), USA 118
National Marketing Review 140
National Observer 198
National University of Singapore 271
Nature 77
Naylor, J. C. 202
Nederlandsche Handels-Hoogeschool (Rotterdam) 49, 54
Nelson, D. 11, 15, 65, 66, 67, 69
Neue Zürcher Zeitung 81
Neumann, J. von 132
New Deal 91, 122
New York American 4, 81
New York Stock Exchange (NYSE) 181, 244, 255
New York Times 81
New York University's Stern School of Business 34
News Corporation 256, 262, 263
Newton, G. 198
Nicholson, J. L. 79
Nicolai, A. T. 139
Nielson, D. L. 174–5
Nihon Kezai Shimbun 81
Nikkei 81
Nioche, J.-P. 104, 106, 158
Nippon Electric 71
Nishizawa, T. 55, 105, 161
Nissan 175
Noble, D. F. 64, 65
Nohria, N. 293
Nomura Research Institute (NRI) 175
Nonaka, I. 268, 269
Nordhaus, W. D. 193
Nordisk tidskrift i organisation 137
Norges Handelshøyskole (Bergen) 105
Normann, R. 256
North-Holland 197, 207, 259, 265
Northwestern University School of Commerce 121
NTT Communications 175
Nye, J. 248
Nyland, C. 16
Nystrom, P. H. 132, 140

Obama, B. 251
Ocasio, W. 27, 28
Okazaki-Ward, L. I. 227
Oldham, G. R. 200, 201, 205, 206
Olsen, J. 204, 205
Omega 205
Open Access model 272
Open Journal of Accounting 272
Open Journal of Business and Management 272
Operations Research 201, 202, 204, 266, 268
Operations Research Society of America 201, 202
Organization Science 265, 266, 267, 268, 269, 271
Organization Studies 203, 206, 267, 271
Organizational Behavior and Human Decision Processes 202, 203, 205, 206, 267, 268, 269
Organizational Dynamics 207
Orr, L. 120
Ortega, J. 225
O'Shea, J. 36, 247
O'Toole, J. 36, 216
Otley, D. T. 206
Owen, R. 15
Oxford University 27, 44, 53, 104, 112, 162, 224, 261
Oxford University Press 77, 78, 79, 83, 196, 260, 262, 265

Pacioli, L. 15
Paget, R. 123, 179
Palgrave, F. T. 77
Palgrave Macmillan 202, 257
Paramount 257
Paris Chamber of Commerce 48, 51, 159
Park, J. 157–8, 227
Parker, L. D. 112
Parkhurst, F. A. 130, 131
Parkinson, H. 198
Parsons, W. 81, 137
Peale, N. V. 257
Pearson 133, 191, 197, 199–200, 256, 257, 258, 261, 262, 263
Pearson, S. 199
Pearson, W. (Viscount Cowdray) 199
Peat, Marwick, Mitchell & Co. 121, 170, 185–6, 237, 248 *see also* KPMG
Penguin Books 197
Penrose, E. T. 12
Pérez-Peña, R. 263
Pergamon Press 196–7, 202, 205–7, 258, 259

314 Index

Perot, R. 241–2
Personnel Administration (PA) 120, 172, 235
Peteraf, M. A. 269
Pettigrew, A. M. 216, 225
Pfeffer, J. 33, 34, 35, 194, 215
Phelps, O. W. 94, 98–100
Phillips, T. 244
Pichai, S. 251
Pierson, F. C. 46, 47, 97–100, 149, 151 *see also* Carnegie Corporation Report
Pietro Gennaro Associati, Milan 183, 184
Pinault, L. 247
Pindur, W. 2, 10, 60
Pirelli, P. 120
Pitman 134
Plambeck, J. 263
Planning Research Corporation 170
Planus, P. 116, 173
Plato 60
PLOS 272
Podolny, J. M. 34
Podsakoff, P. M. 269
Podsakoff, N. P. 269
Poffenberger, A. T. 140, 141
Politecnico di Milano 226
politics: capitalism, opposition with totalitarianism 91; China and Russia, assertiveness of 214; Cold War politics 148; colonialism, imperialism and 40; commerce and investment, opening up of 40; decolonization 148; global governance efforts 214; internal divisions 214; internationalism 91; isolationism 91; markets, triumph of 214; Nazi regime in Germany 103; October Revolution (1917) 91, 114; sectarian divides 214; trade union influence, waning of 148
Pollard, S. 10
Porter, L. W. 154, 155, 218, 228, 258
Porter, M. 139, 195, 196, 248, 260, 264, 290
Potthoff, E. 86
Powell, W. W. 25–6, 33
Prahalad, C. K. 195, 264
Preinreich, G. A. D. 140, 141
Prentice-Hall 133, 191, 194, 197, 257, 258
Price, B. 68
Price Waterhouse 61, 63, 121, 185, 186, 235, 237, 247
PriceWaterhouseCoopers (PwC) 237, 240, 241, 242, 244, 250
Procter & Gamble 124

Production and Operations Management 265, 267
Production and Operations Management Society 265
Production Engineering (P-E) 119–20, 172, 235
Program Evaluation and Review Technique (PERT) 177
Proudfoot, A. 170, 179, 182, 236
Prudential Insurance 175
Public Administration Quarterly 142
Publicis 245
Publishers Weekly 262
Puig, N. 26, 50, 54, 105, 156,158, 163, 164, 226
Purg, D. 228, 229

Quarterly Journal of Accountics 138
Quarterly Journal of Economics 67, 68, 83, 140, 141, 200, 201, 266, 267
Quick, J. H. 171
Quigel, J. P., Jr. 69, 70, 116

Raffety, F. W. 2
Ramond, A. 118
Rand Journal of Economics 202, 203, 205, 206, 268
Rand McNally 195–6, 258
Random House 133, 257, 259, 261, 262
Rathenau, W. 15
Razorfish 245
Read, D. 80
Reay, T. 28
Redlich, F. 41, 45, 46, 48, 52, 53, 54, 102
Reed-Elsevier 273
Regia Istituto Superiore di Scienze Economiche e Commerciali, Bari 49
Regia Scuola Superiore di Applicazione per gli Studi Commerciali, Genoa 49
Regia Scuola Superiore di Commercio, Venice 49
Reichsausschuß für Arbeitszeitermittlung (REFA) 115, 120, 172, 173, 285, 289
Reichskuratorium für Wirtschaftlichkeit (RKW) 114–5, 117
Reiley, A. C. 16, 17
Reingold, J. 185, 239
Reliance Consulting Group 186, 187
Reliance Group Holdings 187
Remington Typewriter Company 116
Renault 116
Retail Research Association 111
Reuter, P. 81

Reuters 81, 82, 133, 260–62, 294
Reuter's Telegram Company 81
Review of Accounting Studies 265, 268
Review of Financial Studies 265, 266, 267
Revue de métallurgie 71
Rice, S. E. 251
Richman, B. M. 192
Ritson, P. 112
RJR Nabisco 242
Robbins, S. P. 17
Robert Heller & Associates 125, 178
Robinson, E. M. 130, 131
Robinson, J. 132
Rockefeller Foundation 113
Roethlisberger, F. J. 132
Rogers, S. E. 2, 10, 60
Roland Berger Strategy Consultants 184, 247, 287
Romer, P. M. 268, 269
Romney, M. 249
Ronald Press 78, 79, 132, 193, 197
Roosevelt, F. D. 15, 91, 111
Rosbaud, P. 196
Rose, D. C. 130
Rosenberg, J. M. 81, 136
Routledge 78, 261
Row, Peterson & Company 194, 197, 256
Rowland, F. H. 130
Rowntree, S. 111–2
Rüegg, W. 44
Rumelt, R. P. 13
Ruml, F. 42, 43, 46, 47, 94, 95, 98, 99
Russell, P. 2
Rynes, S. L. 216, 217, 219, 222

Saatchi & Saatchi 239
SAGE 197, 201, 202, 203, 207, 258, 271–2, 273
Sahlin (-Andersson), K. 18, 25 28, 36
Saint-Martin, D. 173
Saitō, T. 103
Salancik, G. R. 194
Salmon, K. 171 *see also* Kurt Salmon Associates
Samuelson, P. A. 193
Sanchez, J. 247
Sandberg, S. 251
Sanders, T. H. 119
Santa Fe Railroad 70
Sarbanes-Oxley Act 234, 239
SAS (Scandinavian Airlines System) 175
Sass, S. A. 43, 46, 96, 158, 160
Sawyer, J. A. 106, 162

Sayles, L. R. 192
Scandinavian Journal of Management 292
Scarbrough, H. 19
Schär, J. F. 85
Scharff, E. E. 81, 136, 198
Schaufelbuehl, J. M. 162, 164
Schein, E. H. 204, 205, 256
Schiffrin, A. 262
Schlitz 121
Schlossman, S. 43, 47, 48, 97, 99, 150, 151, 153
Schmalenbach, E. 85, 86, 99, 197, 285 *see also Betriebswirtschaftslehre*
Schmalenbachs Zeitschrift für betriebswirtschaftliche Forschung 85, 197
Schmidt, F. 85
Schmotter, J. W. 153
Schneider, D. 197
Schoenfeld, H. M. 85, 86
Schrieber, A. N. 192
Schulz, A.-C. 139
Schumpeter, J. 135, 138
Schwab, J. L. 171
Science Management Corporation 171, 186
ScienceDirect 259
Scient 245
Scientific Research Publishing 272
Scopus 259
Scotsman 261
Scott Foresman 256
Scott, R. 258
Scott, W. D. 79, 123, 130, 131
Scott, W. G. 16–7
Scott, W. R. 24, 25, 27, 28
Sears Roebuck 12, 176
Securities Act (1933) 63
Securities and Exchange Commission (SEC) 185, 239, 240
Sells, E. W. 63
Servan-Schreiber, É. 137
Servan-Schreiber, J.-J. 182
Sharpe, W. 142
Shell (Royal Dutch Shell) 175
Shenhav, Y. 11
Sheridan, J. 80
Shils, E. 27, 31
Shimizu, R. 227
Shula, D. 257
Shulman, J. M. 206
Sieben, G. 86
Sillén, O. 122

316 Index

Simon, H. 112, 142, 151, 193, 194, 201, 205
Simon & Schuster 199, 257, 258, 261, 262
Simpson, B. 81
Sine, W. D. 60
Skilling, J. 19, 249
Sloan, A. P. 35
Sloan Management Review 201, 202, 204, 266, 268
Small, A. W. 84
Smalley, M. 235
Smith, A. 11
Smith, J. 264
Smith, J. G. 44, 49–50, 52, 53, 104
Smith, K. 171
Smith, K. G. 18
Smith, W. L 193
social conditions: Americanization 147–8; consumerism 213; income differentials 213–4; interconnectability 213; managerial class, establishment of 91; migratory movements 213–4; professional associations, formation of 39; totalitarianism, rise of 91–2; US management systems, dissemination of 147–8; welfare states, erosion of 214; workforce, opening to women of 91; working class, emergence of 39
Society for Financial Studies 265
Society of Incorporated Accountants 61
Socrates 60
Il Sole 24 Ore 198
Solow, R. M. 200, 201
Sorensen, C. E. 35
Sorge, A. 206
Spacek, L. P. 185
Spencer, H. 79
Spender, J.-C. 1
Sports Illustrated 137
Spriegel, W. R. 130, 131
Springer 78, 134, 257, 259
Springer-Verlag 259
Squires, S. E. 121, 185, 238, 239
Srinivasan, V. 205, 206
St. Martin's Press 257
Stachanovism 114
Stalin, J. (and Stalinism) 91, 114
Stalk, G. 249
Standard Oil of New Jersey 12
Stanford Report 175
Stanford Research Institute (SRI) 170, 174–5, 283, 290
Stark, M. 2

Starkey, K. 225
Starr, M. K. 193
Stegemerten, G. J. 130, 131, 171
Steinberg, S. 187
Steiner, G. A. 192, 194
Stevens, A. C. 84
Stevens, M. 184, 185, 186, 237
Stevens Institute of Technology 66, 67
Stille, A. 5
Stillman, Y. 111
Stockholm School of Economics 54, 122, 287
Stockman, F. 248
Stone & Webster Management Consultants 170
Stonehill, A. I. 196
Storey, G. 81
Strategic Management Journal 203, 206, 267, 268–71, 292
Strategy& 244
Strategy Science 266
Stryker, P. S. 179
Studentlitteratur 197
Sturdy, A. 19
Suchman, M. C. 26
Suddaby, R. 27
Sullivan, R. S. 35, 216–7, 230
Sumitomo Bank 175
Sunday Times 136, 260
Sutcliffe, P. 78, 79
Sutton, R. I. 34
Swedish Industries Federation 122
Swissair 250

Tapie, P. 164, 226
Tarrant, J. J. 135
Tata Consultancy Services (TCS) 245
Taussig, F. W. 84
Tavistock Institute 207
Taylor, B. 192
Taylor, D. A. 157–8, 160, 161
Taylor, F. W. (and Taylorism) 15, 16, 19, 34, 59, 74, 75, 82–3, 128, 132, 169, 173, 283, 286, 287, 288; early consultants 59, 63, 64, 66, 67, 69–70; grandfather of management consulting 60, 66; new directions in consulting 110, 111, 112, 115, 120
Taylor & Francis 83, 260, 273
Taylor, S. 219
Taylor Society 67, 112–3
Taylor-Thompson System 116
Technische Hochschulen 45, 52, 103

Technology Press 134
Tedlow, R. S. 2
TFM Adams 183
Thanheiser, H. T. 13
Thelin, J. R. 42
Thomas, Alan 157–8, 159, 162
Thomas, Albert 113
Thomas, H. 224
Thomas, R. M., Jr. 133
Thomas, W. 176
Thompson, C. B. 67, 68, 116, 169
Thompson, D. 1
Thompson, J. D. 192–3, 201
Thompson, J. B. 27, 260, 262, 266, 274
Thompson, S. E. 76
Thomson, A. 111, 112
Thomson, K. 261
Thomson, R. 261
Thomson, R. D. 130, 131
Thomson Reuters 259, 260, 261, 262
Thornton, P. H. 27, 28
Tidskrift för affärsekonomi 137
Tierney, T. 293
Tilburg University 105, 271
Time Inc. 264
Time 4, 137
Times 81, 195, 198, 260
Times Mirror Higher Education Group 257
Timmins Press 133
Tinbergen, J. 139
Tiratsoo, N. 224, 225
Tisdall, P. 60, 68, 119, 169, 172, 173, 182
Toffler, B. L. 185, 239
Tokyo Stock Exchange 81
Tosdal, H. R. 130
Touche Ross & Co. 185, 186, 237
Touristik Union International (TUI) 184
Towers, Perrin, Forster & Crosby 122, 181, 186, 187
Towers Watson 122
Towne, H. R. 65
Trachtenberg, J. A. 264
Trank, C. Q. 216, 217, 219, 222
Treaty of Rome (1957) 159, 182
Treuhandgesellschaft 237
Tribe, K. 51, 52, 53, 54, 55, 101, 102, 103
Tribune Education 257
Tsinghua University, Beijing 113
Tsutsui, W. M. 71, 113
Tulane University School of Commerce 45
Torekull, B. 198
Tversky, A. 142, 200

Twain, M. 76
Twentieth Century Fund (TCF) 111, 113
Tyndall, J. 79

Ueno, Y. 113
United Airlines 177
Universidad Comercial de Deusto, Bilbao 50, 163
University Journal of Business 141 *see also Journal of Business*
University of Chicago Press 77, 79
University of Toronto 55; Institute of Business Administration 162
University of Western Ontario 162
university presses 27, 75, 77, 79, 132, 134, 135, 196, 260, 261, 290
Urgel, J. 220–1
URS Corporation 170
Urwick, L. F. 14, 15,16, 66, 67, 68, 70, 104, 111, 120, 134, 292
Urwick Orr & Partners (UOP) 112, 120, 172, 235, 247
US Research Center for Group Dynamics 207
US Steel 124
US Supreme Court 239
Üsdiken, B. 26, 28, 32, 42, 50, 54, 101, 102, 103, 105, 156–8, 160, 163, 164, 226, 271

Vahlne, J.-E. 205, 206
Valleriani, M. 10
van Baalen, P. 105, 228
van Bijsterveld, M. 4
van den Berg, R.-J. 4
Van Nostrand Reinhold 256
Vancil, R. F. 258
VCH 256
Veblen, T. 5
Veinott, A. F. 193
Venice Arsenal 10
Venkatesh, V. 269
Verlagsgruppe Georg von Holtzbrinck 257, 262, 264
Viacom 256
VIANT 245
Vives, L. 222, 223, 224, 229, 230
Vogel, R. 271
Volkswagen 173
Volvo 172, 175
Von Hülsen, I. 264

Walker, F. A. 83
Wall Street Journal 80, 81, 135, 136, 198, 222, 263, 284, 294

318 Index

Wallace, C. H. 114, 123, 129, 139, 169, 172
Wallenberg, M. 175
Wallerstedt, E. 13, 122
Wallerstein, I. M. 31
Walter de Gruyter 78
Wang, D. 248
Waring, S. P. 174
Warner, M. 17, 25, 161, 206, 228
Warren, J. R. 132
Warshaw, P. R. 269
Washington College Commercial School 46
Washington, M. 222
Washington Post 81
Wasserman, P. 169, 170, 171
Wasti, S. A. 271
Waterman, M. H. 132
Waterman, R. H., Jr 34, 248, 257, 264
Watertown Arsenal 65, 66
Watts, R. L. 200, 201, 258
Weaire, D. 273
Weber, M. 17
Wedgewood, J. 60
Wedlin, L. 28, 34, 35, 222, 223, 230, 263
Welch, J. 35, 195, 264
Wellington, O. 124
Wellington & Company 124
Wendt, L. 81, 136, 198, 200, 263
Wessel, R. H. 193
Westdeutscher Verlag 197
Westerhuis, G. 13, 181, 183, 292
Weston, J. F. 196
Western Electric, Hawthorne plant 15
Westfall, R. 195
Westinghouse 171, 181
Westminster Press 133
Wharton School of Finance and Economy 45–6
Whinney, Murray & Co 185
White, K. B. 172
Whitley, R. 158, 159, 162
Whittington, R. 13
WHU Otto Beisheim School of Management 226
Wiedersheim-Paul, F. 204, 205
Wiener, H. 242
Wiener Handelsakademie 49
Wildair, H. 2
Wiley 256; establishment (1807) 75, 76; growth in interwar period 129–31; postwar expansion 191–193, 197–8

Wiley, C. 76, 256
Wiley-Blackwell 203, 255–6, 265, 273
Wiley InterScience 272
William Barclay Peat & Co. 121
William M. Mercer 122, 186
William Morrow & Company 256
Williams, A. P. O. 161, 162, 164, 224
Williamson, O. E. 12, 196, 258
Willner, B. 178
Wilson, J. 80
Wilson, J. F. 111, 112
Wingate, J. W. 133
Wipro 245
Wirtschaftswoche 137, 264
Wise, T. A. 186
Wissman, H. 176
Witzel, M. 2, 4, 15, 17–18, 70, 135
WOFAC Company 170, 171
Wolf, W. B. 124
Wolters Kluwer 261, 262, 287
Woodward, J. 196
Wooldridge, A. 4, 18, 247
Wooten, M. 26, 27
Work Factor system 171
Wrege, C. D. 113
Wren, D. A. 4, 14, 15, 16, 17, 18, 68, 116
Wright, C. 15, 61, 69, 171, 172, 173, 182, 236
Wright, C. D. 84

Yang, B. 228
Yeomans, J. 263
Y2K "bug" 234, 242–4
Yoder, D. 131
Yukinori, H. 70
Yukl, G. 258
Yunxiang, C. 113

Zamagni, V. 12, 49–50, 52, 53, 54
Zammuto, R. F. 99, 217, 218, 219
Zan, L. 10
Zeitschrift für Handelswissenschaft und Handelspraxis 85
Zeitschrift für handelswissenschaftliche Forschung 85, 283
Zell, D. 34, 35, 216, 217, 223
zfbf Schmalenbachs Business Review 85
Zigarmi, D. 257
Zigarmi, P. 257
Zimmerman, J. L 200, 201, 258
Zunz, O. 12